Divorce is hard enough by itself without you having to struggle through a legal system that tends to make things worse instead of better. If you follow my advice, you will have a much better chance for getting through this in one piece.

My life's work has been developing ways to help people take control and make wise choices when going through a divorce. After producing self-help materials (since 1971) and introducing paralegal services for the public (1973), the next step was to reinvent the practice of law to create something affordable and effective—a legal service that solves problems instead of causing them. So, in 1989, Sherman, Williams and Lober was formed and Divorce Helpline was born. Doing your own divorce with the help of an experienced Divorce Helpline attorney is possibly the most effective and affordable way a person can get through a divorce, in or out of court.

If you have questions to ask or problems to solve—if you want a friendly, reliable attorney to act as your coach—call Divorce Helpline. Tell them Ed Sherman sent you.

How to Solve Divorce Problems in California

...in or out of court!

2nd Edition

A GUIDE FOR PETITIONERS AND RESPONDENTS

By **Ed Sherman**
Divorce Specialist Attorney

For the divorce that is not going smoothly
Do Your Own Contested Divorce

Nolo Press
occidental
501 Mission Street, Suite 2
Santa Cruz, CA 95060
(831) 466-9922

DATED MATERIAL

THIS BOOK WAS PRINTED IN

FEBRUARY 2004

Do not use an old edition of this book!
Out-of-date information can cause trouble.

Laws and forms change fairly often, usually in January and July. Using an old edition of this book can be dangerous if the information or forms in it are wrong! **Make sure you are using the most current edition.** If the date above is over one year old, you are taking chances.

FREE UPDATE NOTICES

look for new laws, forms & fixes
at www.nolodivorce.com/alerts

30% off on updates

If you have an older copy of this book and want to update, tear off the cover and mail it to us with $20.97 plus tax and shipping = $27.49 total. You can also get the essential companion, *How to Do Your Own Divorce*, for 30% off, too—that's only $49.98 including tax and shipping for *both* books!

ISBN: 0-944508-50-2
Library of Congress Card Number: 2004100991

TABLE OF CONTENTS

Dedicated to the millions of Californians who must carry one of life's heaviest burdens through a treacherous, dysfunctional legal system.

It could easily be better, but it isn't. So, as with so many things in life, you're better off doing it yourself.

Acknowledgments

Many outstanding lawyers and a family court judge drew from their professional experience, rolled up their sleeves and dug in, working hard on our first draft to help make this book better than it otherwise would have been. Our heartfelt thanks to:

Hon. Roderic Duncan, judge (ret.), Oakland
Stephen G. Stanton, attorney, Napa

Family Law Facilitators:
Judith Beck, San Rafael
James F. Dawson, Lakeport
Chris Doehle, Crescent City
David J. Golde, Redding
Marilyn W. Mirano, Orange
Larry Maloney, Riverside

Divorce Helpline staff attorneys:
Peggy Williams
Anne Lober
Charma Pipersky
Janet Thompson

Design and Graphics: Ed Sherman
Cover Design: Ed Sherman, Thompson & Thompson Creative Services
Photo credits: Pages 1 and 3: Tod Tsukushi. Page 2: David Weintraub

START IN THE RIGHT PLACE
with the right material

1. If you have **AN EMERGENCY**

or have been **served with papers**
that require **immediate attention,**
read chapters 10–14 **right now,**
then start from the beginning.

Served with a Petition? Respond now!
See chapter 2 and Book 1.

2. If your case is **JUST STARTING** or **UNCONTESTED**

*Use Book 1, **How To Do Your Own Divorce***

This is where you start and where you will remain if no one goes to court to solve problems.

Your case is uncontested if

- Petition filed, possibly a Response too, *and*
- Your spouse doesn't enter the case, *or*
- You can reach agreement without legal action

3. If your case has **PROBLEMS** and is not going smoothly or if it just *might* become **CONTESTED**

*Also use Book 2, **How To Solve Divorce Problems***

How to solve problems out of court, talk to your spouse, negotiate and settle, defend against legal action, and use legal action to help solve problems. If you need to take legal action, you will also need Book 1.

Your case has problems if

- You are not safe and financially stable for at least a few months, *or*
- Your parenting arrangements are not acceptable right now, *or*
- You think your ex might try to pull a fast one, *or*
- You can't get information needed to decide what's yours, *or*
- Too much upset on one side or the other to work anything out, *or*
- Things are dragging on and going nowhere and that's not okay

Your case is contested if

- Petition *and* Response filed; *and*
- Your spouse starts legal activity; *or*
- You need court orders for custody or support; *or*
- A preemptive strike is needed to beat the other side to the punch; *or*
- Legal action is required to get information or documents; *or*
- Agreement can't be reached through negotiation

Relationship between How to Do Your Own Divorce and How to Solve Divorce Problems

In the text, we refer to these as "Book 1" and "Book 2"

Book 1
HOW TO DO YOUR OWN DIVORCE
—The Out of Court Divorce

This is the book you use to start your case. It is the only book you will need if you can resolve divorce issues and your spouse does not go to court to oppose the divorce. Covers the laws and includes all forms necessary to complete your divorce.

Book 2
HOW TO SOLVE DIVORCE PROBLEMS
—In California, In or Out of Court

If your case is not going smoothly, Book 2 shows you how to solve problems, talk to your spouse, negotiate and settle, defend against legal action, use legal action to help solve problems. If you have to go to court, you will need forms and instructions in this book, plus some found in Book 1.

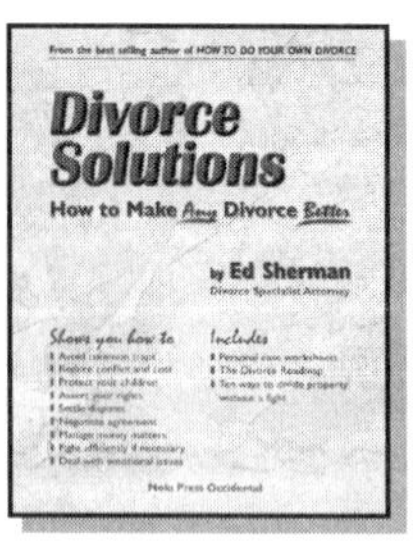

More depth on problem solving . . .

DIVORCE SOLUTIONS ***—How to Make Any Divorce Better***

This book deals at length with solutions for practical, emotional and financial problems. Portions of this book that discuss emotional upset and how to negotiate are condensed into two chapters in ***How to Solve Divorce Problems,*** which is specifically for California and focuses more on legal action. It could be very helpful to have all three books.

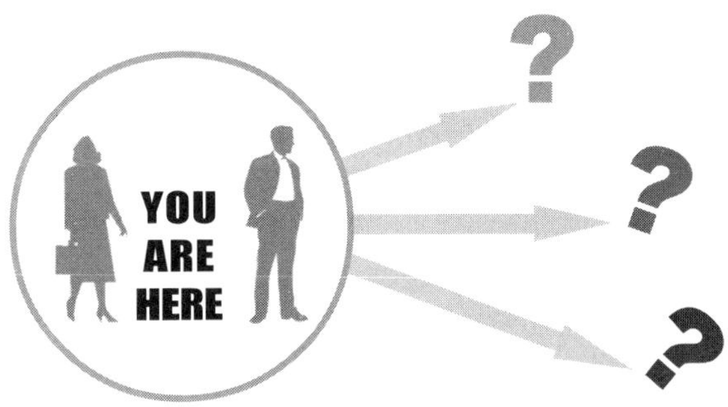

CHAPTER 1
YOU ARE HERE –which way to go, what it takes

A. Deal with emergencies first
B. Three ways you can go in your case
C. What it takes to get where you want to go

A Deal with emergencies first

In the legal system, an emergency is something that requires court orders and can't wait the several or many weeks that it takes to get a hearing on a motion. You have an emergency if you have good reason to believe that, unless you get immediate court orders, something bad will happen very soon. For example:

- You or your children are in imminent danger; *or*
- Property will be taken, transferred, wasted, or hidden; *or*
- Your children will be physically removed or hidden away from you.
- Legal papers have been served on you that require you to show up in court very soon.

If you have an emergency, go immediately to chapters 10–14 and deal with it. Come back here later and pick up where you left off.

B Three ways you can go in your case

At any given point in any case, there are only three things you can do:

1. Take legal action
2. Negotiate
3. Do nothing

As a general rule, you should always encourage and work toward a negotiated settlement unless there is a good reason *not* to. In many situations, you can take legal action *and* negotiate at the same time.

1. Reasons to choose legal action

a. Emergency .... (chapters 10-13)
b. Respond to action from the other side .... (chapter 14)
c. Get needed information .... (chapter 17)
d. Strategic need for action .... (see below)
e. Put pressure on negotiations, move case forward ...... (see below)
f. "I don't know, we just always do it that way" .... (for lawyers only)

2. Reasons you would choose NOT to negotiate

You should *always* encourage negotiation and work toward a settlement *unless* there is a good reason not to. Using techniques in chapters 3 and 4, people who might otherwise fall easily into conflict can now find new opportunities to make negotiation work. However . . .

- Sometimes legal action is required to get negotiation to work and you end up doing both at the same time. For example, your spouse has been dragging feet or avoiding you, so you file a motion and the pressure of a court date coming up gets things moving.
- There are times and situations where you should *not* negotiate, or at least not yet:
  a. You are dealing with an abusive or controlling spouse
  b. You have a strategic need for legal action first
  c. Your spouse refuses to give you copies of essential documents
  d. There are uncontrollable levels of upset, fear, or anger on either side

a) **Abusive or controlling spouse.** Abuse is fundamentally a matter of domination and control, and includes everything from psychological manipulation to physical attack. To the abusive spouse the court looks like a new weapon to use against you. Almost any degree of effort to dominate and control you qualifies your spouse as an abuser and serves as an indication that you have better things to do before you start negotiating. First, you need to take some legal action to get into a position of strength and to establish structure for your negotiations—*then* you can try to negotiate. Read Part Two and choose a legal action that promises to be useful in your particular situation.

b) **Strategic need for action.** In certain situations, orders may be needed immediately, *before* you start negotiating. In other cases, you will use legal action to improve the effectiveness of negotiation. It is often possible to take legal action and negotiate at the same time.

- **Emergencies.** If you have an immediate need for protection for you, your children, or your property, you need a restraining order right away and there's no time to stop and talk. If your spouse is going to take the kids and go over the border, you need an order to try to stop that instantly. If you have *no* money to live on and your spouse has some but won't give you any, you need to file a support order immediately. If you have an emergency situation, read chapters 10–13, take care of it, then come back here later.

- **Under attack.** If the other side it throwing legal action at you, you need to stand up and assert yourself, take some legal actions of your own, and sort things out before you can settle into talks. You don't want to negotiate from weakness while under siege.

- **Child custody orders.** Here is an unfortunate feature of our legal system: when it comes to custody and visitation, status quo (the way things have been for a while) is *everything*. If the children are doing okay, then the way parenting has been working at the time you get to court is the way things will probably stay unless you have a truly powerful case or can get a voluntary agreement to change things. So, if your spouse is unwilling to cooperate in a stable and reliable parenting arrangement that is agreeable to you, you might be better off going straight to court rather than continuing to negotiate to change a situation that you don't want, thereby giving it time to become "status quo." Sometimes, getting the right parenting arrangement immediately is very important if it looks like you are eventually going to end up in a custody battle anyway. Take legal action but keep negotiating too, if possible, trying to get an agreement for a reasonable status quo you can live with.

- **First to accuse.** Another terrible feature of our system is that there *could* be an advantage to being the first one to accuse the other through an OSC. If the first to accuse gets an immediate custody order, the court process could drag on for months before the parties finally get to a hearing when, if the child is doing okay, the judge is not likely to change the status quo that the "temporary" order created. This is bad, because it means that in a doubtful situation, you can't wait for the other parent to accuse you of something. We don't want you to jump at the other parent's throat, but you must be aware of the problem if your spouse's attorney might decide to jump at yours. If you fear this possibility and want to avoid it, you have two choices: (1) get into good communication with your spouse so that he/she won't accuse you, or (2) file your OSC/TRO first (chapters 11–16). Of course, if the accusation is true, it should be made. When there is no valid basis for an accusation, it might help to go with your spouse to a counselor or mediator. However, if your spouse is an abuser/controller, it isn't likely to work and you need to realize that you are subject to attack.

- **Support order.** The obligation for support doesn't start until there is an agreement or an order. This means that you can't go back for support that wasn't paid to you before you file a motion for support. Therefore, if you are not getting adequate support right now relative to the amount your spouse earns, you might decide that it is worth it to file a motion at once for support orders. If you do, keep negotiating, if possible. This action could increase the level of conflict, so think carefully and be sure it's worth it before you take this step. On the other hand, if your spouse is a controlling abuser, you may not have much to lose. Keep negotiating, if possible, while legal action proceeds.

- **Strategic orders.** In some cases, for strategic reasons you will want orders *before* you negotiate. For example, you are at a disadvantage and want to bargain from strength, so you use a strategic legal action to improve your position. If your case lacks structure and clarity, a motion to advance some small part of your case can give your entire situation some structure. A court hearing can be like a reality check—it strips away illusions. Or, let's say your case is stalled because your spouse won't pay attention, cooperate, and take care of business, so you make a motion to get your spouse's attention focused on the negotiation. If a hearing is fast approaching, the pressure is on to work things out.

c) **Spouse refuses to give you essential information.** You can certainly *start* to negotiate and make getting information and copies of documents a top priority, but at some point it becomes a requirement for further negotiation. First, try to get whatever you need yourself, using the methods in chapter 8. For items you can't get that way, make polite, then firm, requests for what you need, then finally a demand by a certain date. If your spouse still won't give you what you need, you *must* stop negotiating and start discovery. Don't waste time; go to chapter 17 and start right away. When you have the information and documents you need, you might be ready to negotiate again.

d) **Uncontrollable levels of upset, fear, or anger on either side.** You can't negotiate business issues when either side is in a highly emotional state and unable to control it. You should not make important decisions if your own judgment is not reliable. Chapters 3 and 4 tell you how to deal with emotional issues so you can get down to business.

3. Reasons to choose to do nothing

Very often, doing nothing, especially in the legal system, is the best thing you can do. Assuming your living situation is reasonably safe and stable for at least the next few weeks or months, and assuming that you don't need court action for any of the reasons discussed above, doing nothing for awhile allows emotions to cool and gives your spouse time to get used to the idea that the divorce is happening, or get used to what the law requires, or to new ideas that you have proposed in settlement talks.

C What it takes to get where you want to go

What it takes

Effort. You have a lot to learn and the deeper you get into conflict, the more complicated it gets. Representing someone is work, whether a lawyer does it or you do it for yourself. This might be the most important job you ever undertake, and, like any new job, you have to work extra hard to learn it. Work hard, get help if you need it, do a good job, and you will be well paid for your effort.

Organization. You need to be very meticulous and detailed on this job. We show you how to keep good notes, records, and files. Don't take this lightly! A confused file will cause *you* to become confused.

Objectivity. It is widely said that a lawyer who represents himself has a fool for a client. This is because a lawyer must be objective. If you are going to be your own attorney, you must struggle to be objective. This is one reason we recommend that, if you can afford it, you get a Divorce Helpline attorney to act as your coach and guide. The neutral lawyer brings experience and objectivity to your case. The more emotional you are, the more you need assistance.

Confidence. It takes confidence to represent yourself. You can't be afraid of face-to-face negotiations with the other side or going to court, otherwise you can be bullied into accepting less than you are entitled to. Having reliable information can help you gain confidence, but if you read this book and still feel insecure, get help. Find a reliable attorney to act as your coach and guide—you need someone in your corner. The more you lack confidence, the more you need help.

Who can help

Paralegals. Independent paralegals—by law they are now called Legal Document Assistants—can help you do paperwork, but they cannot give you legal advice or counseling because they don't have the training or background for it.

Family Law Facilitators. Every county has a Family Law Facilitator's office where you can get free assistance. Some offices only work on child support matters, while others will help with almost any aspect of doing your own divorce. We hear the quality of service ranges from poor to very good. Certainly, the facilitators who helped us review this book were mostly excellent. Demand far exceeds supply, so it takes a lot of time and persistence to get help. Contacting facilitators by phone might be difficult, in which case you should go in. If you have time—or no other choice—find out what help you can get. Read this book before you go in and don't forget to take all your notes and paperwork with you.

Divorce Helpline was created to change the way attorneys practice divorce and to provide expert support for people who are doing their own divorces. Operated by Sherman, Williams Lober & Thompson, a law corporation, our experienced family law attorneys serve as your coach, guide, and assistant. In many cases, if requested, we can work with both sides. We can help anyone, anywhere, by phone, or in person at our offices in San Jose, Sacramento, Walnut Creek and Santa Cruz. We also do mediation at those locations. Learn more about Divorce Helpline, including rates and services, in the CD that comes with this book, at our web site at **www.divorcehelp.com**, or call 800-359-7004.

What to do next

If you need to take immediate legal action, or respond immediately to legal action against you, go to Parts Two and Three. Otherwise, go on to chapter 2 and learn how the legal system works and how to make talking with your spouse effective and productive.

Part One
Solving Problems Out of Court

CHAPTER 2

WHEN A CASE BECOMES CONTESTED

A divorce case starts when one spouse files a Petition and serves it on the other spouse. If the other spouse does nothing, Petitioner goes through some red tape and it's finished. Unless there was a written agreement, the other spouse had no say in the process. If the other spouse *does* want to participate, he or she must file a Response. The Response gives the other spouse equal standing with Petitioner, so from this point forward neither party has the advantage; they are equals before the law.

Served with a Petition? You have only thirty **safe** days to file your Response before Petitioner will be allowed to "take your default." Petitioner can take up to two years, possibly more, to file the Default form, but it can't be done sooner than 30 days after you were served. Once the clerk enters your default, you can't participate in your own divorce without going to a lot of trouble to file a motion (chapter 12) to have the default set aside. So, if you want to take part in your own divorce, play it safe and file a Response within the first thirty days after you were served. You have to pay the filing fee, but it is otherwise easy and we show you how to do it in Book 1, *How to Do Your Own Divorce,* chapter 11.

Is it contested yet? Once a Response is filed, the case is "contested," but only technically, because no legal proceeding has been initiated yet. Nothing is happening in court: no motions, no applications for orders, no demands for discovery. Respondent has merely joined the case. Whether or not there is a lot of legal activity depends on how you go about solving problems and resolving differences, and to what extent either party uses legal tools and protections along the way.

Once the Response is filed, there are only two ways you can get your Judgment:

1) the parties reach an agreement on all legal issues (property, support, children), or
2) the parties take their case to court and let the judge decide any issues they can't agree on.

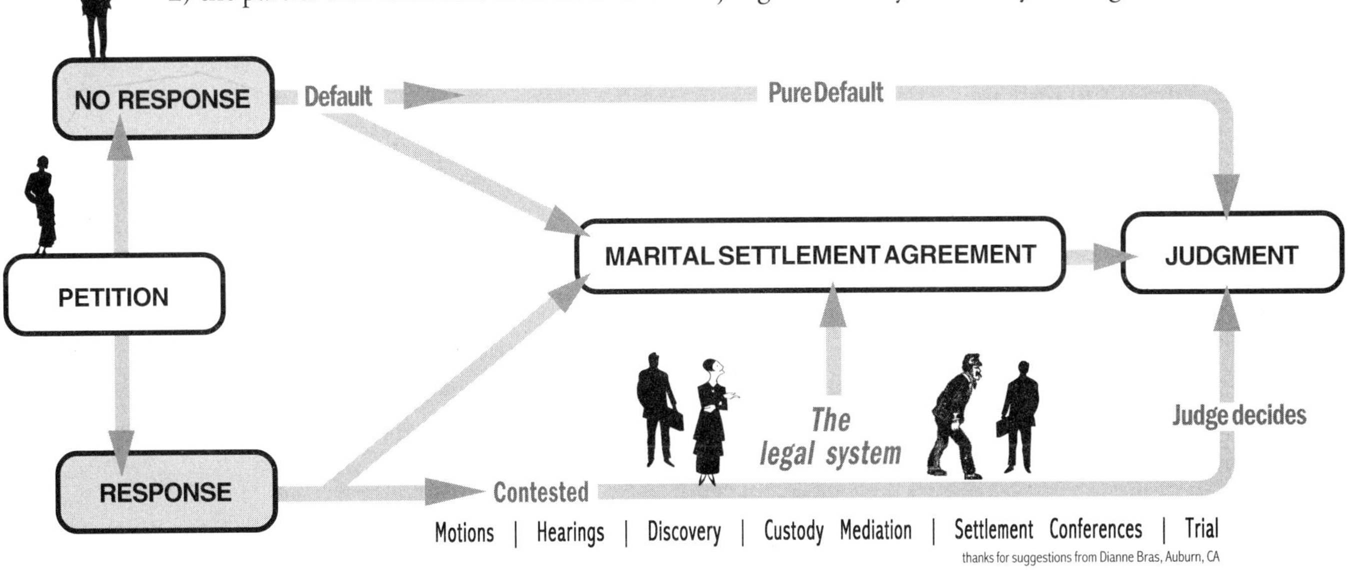

HERE'S ANOTHER VIEW: THE LEGAL DIVORCE ON A TIMELINE

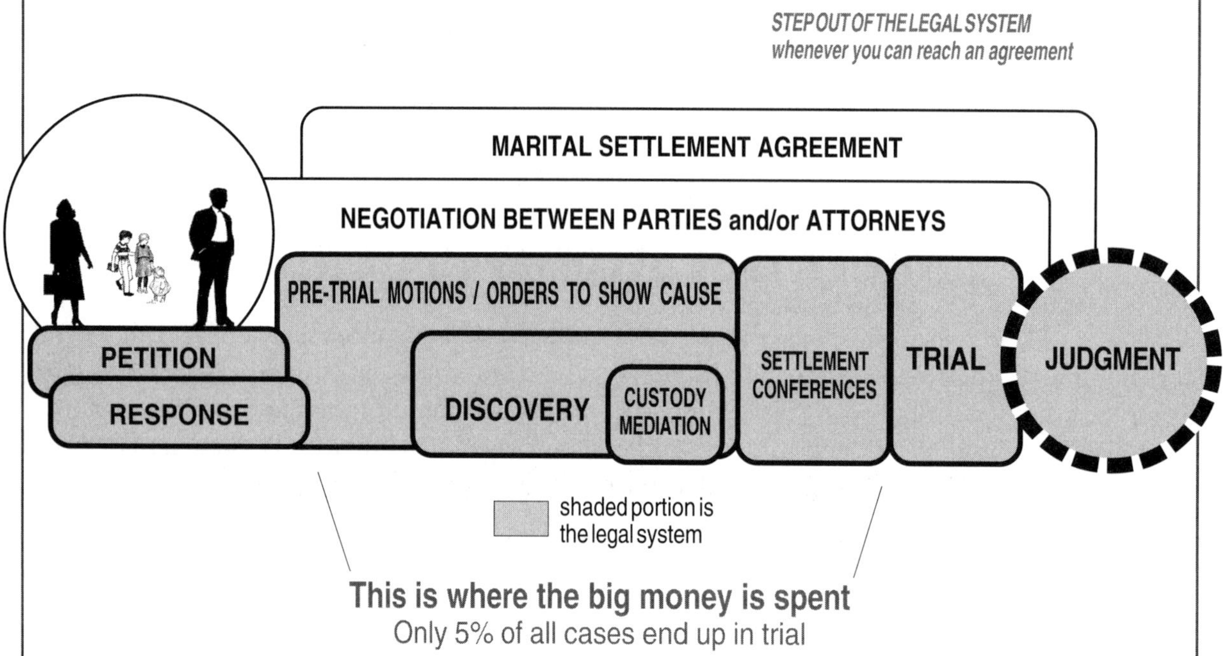

Pre-trial motions / Orders to Show Cause. Requests for court orders to address problems that can't wait for trial—typically for such things as support, custody, visitation, restraining orders, freezing assets and accounts, but almost any problem related to the case can be raised.

Discovery. Legal tools to dig out information and documents: written questions answered under oath, subpoenas to produce documents, taking of statements in person and under oath.

Custody mediation. Required by law in cases where the parties can't agree on parenting arrangements. If that doesn't work, the judge might order a home study and report by a court-appointed counselor.

Settlement Conference. A formal meeting between lawyers, parties, and the judge who will give an opinion on likely rulings and try to persuade or pressure the parties to settle before trial.

The diagram above covers the same thing as the one on the previous page, only this one adds the role of negotiation (which takes place outside the legal system) and all the pieces are organized on a timeline so you can see better how they are related. Later, we will discuss each legal procedure in detail, what it's good for and how to handle it. For now, the important thing is to observe that *outside the legal system,* negotiation and settlement are available at all times. From any point in the legal divorce, you can go into negotiation and work toward agreement. As soon as you get a written marital settlement agreement, the contest is over and all you have to do is complete some forms to get your Judgment.

Agree about what? Be sure to read the first half of *How to Do Your Own Divorce* to learn about the basic rules of divorce in California. You will see that the legal divorce has only three concerns: dividing your property (and debts), care of minor children, and support. In high conflict cases, it is also about orders for keeping the peace. That's it; that's all. Nothing else is involved in the legal divorce. Make an agreement on these subjects and you are done.

We have a saying: "The Real Divorce is Free." The Real Divorce is about redefining yourself, making a new life, finding a new center of balance. There's very little in the legal divorce that will help with your real life work, but it *can* get in the way, wipe out your savings, and delay your ability to move forward. We're going to help you avoid that, but, lawyer or no lawyer, it's up to you.

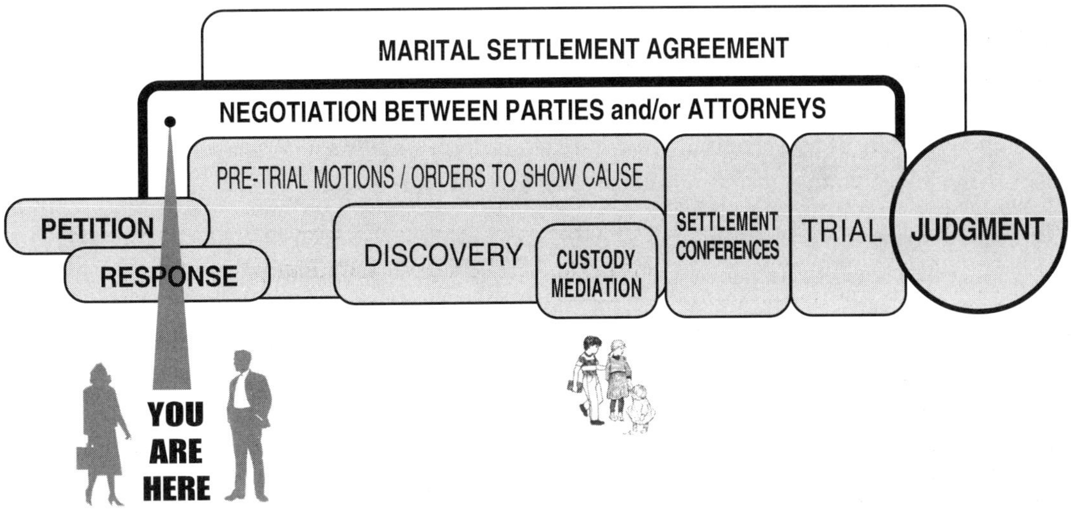

CHAPTER 3

HOW TO GET OUT OF THE LEGAL SYSTEM

–obstacles to agreement and how to overcome them

Unless you are facing an emergency, the most important thing you need to know about the legal system is how to get around it or out of it—how to get your Judgment with as little legal action as possible. Even if you need to take legal action for some specific reason (chapter 1), once you reach a stopping point you should try very hard to negotiate your way through all issues, or as many of them as you possibly can.

Agreement = Out. You already know there are only two ways to get your Judgment: you can make an agreement or you can suffer and struggle your way through the legal system so that a complete stranger (the judge) can decide important issues about your children, your money and your life. Compared to this, a fair agreement with your spouse is worth a great deal of effort and compromise. If you can agree, your written agreement actually sets the terms of your Judgment, so you get to decide everything ahead of time with complete certainty and in far greater detail than any orders some judge might make. Once an agreement is signed, your divorce is essentially finished. More important, divorces settled by good agreements usually work out better afterward: spouses are more likely to comply with terms, have better post-divorce relationships, better co-parenting, and faster healing. Book 1, *How to Do Your Own Divorce,* chapter 6, discusses marital settlement agreements.

Understandably, people tend to shy away from talking to their estranged spouses about the issues of their divorce. You might not believe you can handle it or fear you will get into terrible fights or upset if you try to talk about divorce terms. Hiring an attorney to take over starts to look very attractive—but, ultimately, this might not be the best decision. Many attorneys are not particularly good negotiators, have no training in it, and almost always drag cases into conflict that could have been settled by other means. They do this because the system works that way and they just tend to go along with it.

The truth is that no one can do it better than you . . . if you know how. If you learn a little about how to negotiate, then—unless you are dealing with an abuser or controller, or emotions are out of control—you probably won't be afraid to talk with your spouse and you'll probably be able to face the ups and downs on the road to your agreement. With help and advice from a Divorce Helpline attorney-mediator, you can work with even more comfort and confidence.

That's what these next chapters are about—how to deal with disagreement, from simple difference of opinion to active upset and anger. We show you specific steps to take that will help you talk to your spouse and negotiate effectively. As you will see, the things you can do yourself are often more effective than anything a lawyer can do. If you need help, we show you the best way to go about getting it.

Emergencies. If an urgent or emergency situation comes up while you are trying to work out an agreement, turn immediately to chapters 10–14. Better yet, call Divorce Helpline.

Why you can't agree. At least 95% of all cases are settled before trial, but too many are settled only after the spouses have exhausted their emotional energies on conflict and their financial resources on lawyers. So much time and effort spent battling impairs the ability to get on with life and may cause serious psychic damage to spouses and their children. Sure, spouses can save themselves all that pain and suffering simply by agreeing to settle earlier—so why don't they? Why don't you just go ahead and do it? There are five specific reasons why spouses have trouble negotiating an agreement. Which of these are present in your case?

- Emotional upset and conflict
- Insecurity and fear
- Ignorance and misinformation
- The legal system and lawyers
- Valid disagreement

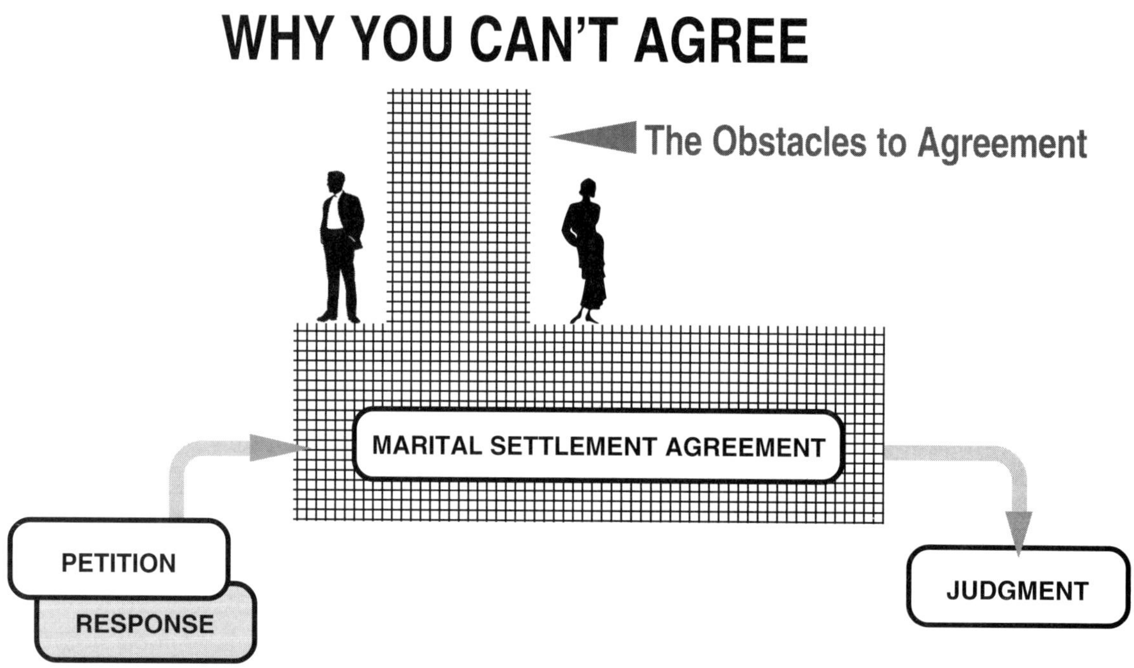

To get an agreement, in or out of the system, with or without an attorney, you have to overcome the five obstacles, and you have to clear away the first four before you can work effectively on the fifth—the valid disagreement. Look what you're dealing with:

1. Emotional upset and conflict. If one or both spouses are upset, you can't negotiate, have reasonable discussions or make sound decisions. What's worse, complex and volatile emotions become externalized and get attached to things or to the children. When emotions are high, reason is at its lowest ebb and will not be very effective *at that time*. The other spouse frequently tries to reason with the upset spouse but it never works—you can't reason with an emotion.

There are many causes of upset: obvious ones such as the divorce itself, financial strain, stress of major change, broken dreams, fear of an unknown future, and so on. But there is one root cause of conflict that appears in almost every case, and this is something you can do something about. Upset and conflict are always more intense when one spouses can't accept the idea of the divorce. The most constructive thing you can do is take the time to work toward mutual readiness and willingness to accept the divorce. Don't push or rush. If you are the one who can't accept the divorce, you have to try to get over it.

Don't try to negotiate when feelings are high. Don't get engaged in emotional arguments and stop discussing who is more wrong; rather, drop out of such conversations as gracefully as possible (sure!) and wait for a better time. We describe below specific things you can do to reduce the causes of upset.

2. Insecurity, fear, lack of confidence, unequal bargaining power. You can't negotiate if either spouse feels incompetent or afraid or believes the other spouse has a big advantage. Divorce is tremendously undermining and tends to multiply feelings of low self-esteem and lack of self-confidence. Often, there are very real causes for insecurity: lack of skill and experience at dealing with business and negotiation, and lack of complete information and knowledge about the process and financial matters. We'll show you some steps you can take to reduce fear and build self-esteem, for you and for your spouse.

3. Ignorance and misinformation. Ignorance about family affairs or the legal system and how it works can make you feel uncertain, insecure and incompetent. You feel as if you don't know what you are doing . . . and you are right.

Misinformation is when the things you think you know are not correct. Misinformation comes from friends, television, movies, even from lawyers who are not family law specialists. It can distort your expectations about your rights and what's fair. It's damn difficult to negotiate with someone who has mistaken ideas about what the rules are. Don't let that someone be you.

Fortunately, both conditions are easily fixed with reliable information. By reading this book, you are well on your way out of the Dumb and Dumber Dilemma.

4. The legal system and lawyers. The legal system does *not* help you overcome obstacles to agreement, but it is itself one of the major obstacles you have to overcome. While there are some valid reasons for going into the legal system, for the most part you want to avoid it as much as possible—and you can. This book shows you how to beat the system.

5. Valid disagreement. Real disagreements are based on the fact that spouses who once had common interests now have different needs and goals. This is a level you can deal with rationally and negotiate cleanly. If you can dispel the influence of the first four obstacles, valid issues that involve property, debts and support can be cleanly negotiated if you get a neutral reading of California's detailed rules of law. If you remain at odds over parenting, you should negotiate for both parents to take counseling for separated parents and get advice from a child development pro who knows what's best for kids after divorce.

Overcoming the obstacles to agreement

The solutions are entirely in your hands. Apart from the legal system—which you can avoid—all obstacles to your agreement are personal, between you and your spouse, and between you and yourself.

Take care. Pay special attention to emotional upset and even more to insecurity and fear. These are the forces that drive people into lawyers' offices. The upset person is saying, "I can't stand this and I won't take it any more! I'm going to get a lawyer to take over my case!" The insecure person is saying, "I can't understand all this and I can't deal with it. I can't talk to my spouse. I want to be safe. I need someone to help me. I'm going to get a lawyer to take over my case."

Try hard to reduce the causes of upset and fear. Avoid doing anything that might increase it for either of you. Try to arrange things so both spouses are comfortable about not retaining an attorney. If you are self-confident but think your spouse may be upset or insecure, you have to be very sensitive and patient. If you are feeling insecure and incapable of dealing with your own divorce, the information in this book will help a lot, and you will see that you can get all the legal help and support you need without retaining an attorney to take over your case.

Please don't just walk up to your spouse and start negotiating. First, you need to do something about the obstacles to agreement. This means that *before* you get down to negotiating your real issues, you must:

- Calm emotional upset, reduce fears, and balance the bargaining power
- Get reliable information and advice
- Learn how to get safe, reliable help if you need it

Ten steps

Before you start negotiating, go through these specific steps you can take to overcome the obstacles to agreement—*then* get down to negotiation. Use this as a checklist to make sure you've built a good foundation for negotiation. If you run into trouble later, come back and double-check these steps.

1. Get safe, stable and secure long enough to work toward an agreement. Your first and most important job is to do whatever you must to arrange short-term safety, stability, and security for yourself, your children, *and your spouse* . . . in that order. This doesn't mean forever—just for a month or a few months at a time. Don't be concerned yet about the long term or the final outcome. And we are talking about *minimum* conditions here, not your original standard of living. But don't attempt to do anything else until minimum conditions are met. You can't negotiate if you don't know where you will live, or how you will pay the rent, or if you feel afraid for your safety or for your children, or if you think your house is about to be foreclosed or your car repossessed. Legal action may be useful to help you reach this goal, but the practical things you can do are usually more important and certainly more reliable.

2. Make some "New Life" resolutions. Start thinking of yourself as a whole and separate person. If the divorce wasn't your idea, try to accept that however painful divorce is, it's better than trying to live with someone who doesn't want to be with you.

If you feel wounded, try to realize that you are healing and on your way to becoming whole and complete. Keep that picture in mind. Try to accept the pain and confusion that are part of healing. Let go of old attachments, old dreams, old patterns that don't work; this is your time to build new ones. You can come out ahead in the end. Decide you will not be a victim of your spouse, the system, or yourself. You can lay down the burden of trying to change or control your spouse—or the burden of being nagged and manipulated. That's all over now, it doesn't work, it's contrary to the meaning of divorce.

Stop trying to make your spouse wrong. You can't negotiate if this is your emotional theme song. The only future down this path is prolonged suffering as you go on hurting yourself. After you get your marital settlement agreement with fair terms, you can do all the blaming you like. Besides, what's the point? Who cares what he/she thinks or realizes? That's over.

Concentrate on yourself, especially on your own actions. You can't change your spouse, but you *can* change who you are and how you act. The best, perhaps only, way you can break out of bad old patterns is by changing what you do and how you react (or don't react) to things your spouse does.

Concentrate on your physical health, your work, children, and friends. Try to become quiet and calm. Keep your life as simple as possible.

3. Insulate and protect your children. Involving your children will surely harm them and upset both parents as well. Keep them well away from the divorce. Tell them the truth in simple terms they can understand but don't discuss the divorce or your problems in front of them. Don't involve the children or pass messages through them. Don't let them hear you argue or hear you criticize their other parent. Let your children know you both love them and will always be their mother and father, no matter what happens between you. Tell them clearly and frequently that the divorce is not their fault and not caused by anything they did or did not do. If possible, let the children see where both parents now live.

4. Agree on temporary arrangements. It can take a long time for things to settle down and for the spouses to work out a final agreement. Meanwhile, you have to arrange for the support of two households on the same old income, the parenting of minor children, making payments on mortgages and debts, and so on. As a matter of routine, most lawyers take almost any case immediately to court to get temporary orders for child custody and support, etc. If they think about it at all, they probably believe this is the professionally correct way to establish stability until the case can be settled or tried. A lot of money can be spent on this step, and the level of conflict is very likely to escalate. But, if you can work out your own temporary arrangements, you won't need legal action to get temporary court orders.

It is very much to the advantage of *both* parties to create stability on *both* sides without involving lawyers and legal action. Start by agreeing that you want a fair result and that you will both act fairly. Agree to communicate before doing anything that will affect the other spouse, the property or the children. Then, agree to some terms that will allow both sides to live and parent in a reasonable degree of stability until things can be permanently worked out. It is best if your temporary arrangements are put in writing. If you have trouble working out temporary arrangements, use techniques discussed here. If nothing else works, consider handling the court action without retaining an attorney to do it.

5. Slow down, take some time. If you can make your situation safe and stable for awhile—even just for a few months—you don't have to be in a panic to push ahead. Think of divorce as an illness or an accident. It truly is a kind of injury, and it takes time to heal. You have to go slow and easy, be good to yourself. Some very important work goes on during this slowdown. Work quietly and patiently toward mutual acceptance of the divorce going forward.

6. Get information and advice. First, organize your facts, records and documents. See chapter 8 about what information you need and how to get it.

Spouses have a right to get a full, open, and honest exchange of information and they have the duty to give it. Even if you don't want to do it, it's the law. Failure to disclose fully can be penalized, so you might as well just go ahead and do it. On the positive side, fairness and openness help to build trust and confidence. If information is not exchanged freely outside of the legal system, you will probably end up in court undergoing expensive time-consuming discovery procedures.

Learn the law as it applies to your case. California has so much law on divorce that almost every conceivable issue has already been decided. Because you can usually get a pretty good idea ahead of time what a judge will do, there's not much to be gained from litigation. The one exception is the terms for parenting of children after divorce, which is still decided on a case-by-case basis.

Start by reading Part One of *How to Do Your Own Divorce.* If you feel it might help, get some advice, but be *very* careful where you get it. Your friends and relatives might be a fountain of free advice, but don't take it—they mean well, but probably don't know what they're talking about. Their cases will have been different from yours, so won't apply to you. If they are wrong, who pays? Use your friends for emotional support, but take advice only from an attorney who specializes in divorce. Be careful about taking advice from paralegals and divorce typing services; they're not trained for it. For a wide range of *reliable* legal advice, practical problem-solving and support services, call Divorce Helpline at (800) 359-7004.

7. **Focus on needs and interests.** Don't take any positions yet. A position is a stand on a final outcome: "I want the house sold and the children every weekend." In the beginning, there's too much upset and too little information to decide what you want for an outcome. Worse, taking a position is bad negotiating and an invitation to an argument. The other side either agrees or they disagree and you're in an argument rather than a discussion. It's better to think and talk in terms of needs and interests. These are your basic concerns: "I need to know I'll have enough to live on. I want to have a good relationship with my children. I want an end to argument and upset." When put this way, these are subjects that you and your spouse can more easily discuss together.

8. **Stick with short-term solutions.** Concentrate on short-term solutions to immediate problems like keeping two separate households afloat for a few months; keeping mortgages paid and cars from being repossessed; keeping children protected, secure, stable, in contact with both parents. These are things you can try to work on together.

9. **Minimum legal activity.** You want to avoid legal activity unless it is necessary—zero is best, or the minimum necessary to protect yourself and create short-term stability. Ideally, you will avoid retaining an attorney, and you won't give your spouse any reason to retain an attorney.

10. **Get help if you need it.** Consider counseling for yourself or your children. For help with talking to your spouse, consider couple counseling or going to see a mediator. Mediators and counselors are low-conflict professionals who can help with emotional issues, defusing upset or, in the case of the mediator, with making agreements for your temporary or final arrangements.

If you follow these steps, you'll be able to clear away the first four obstacles to agreement. The next chapter will show you how to talk to your spouse effectively and negotiate an agreement. Follow those steps and you will be ready and able to negotiate the real issues of your divorce.

It is important that your spouse have the information in these books, too. Give your spouse copies to read, or at least direct your spouse to **www.divorcehelp.com** and **www.nolodivorce.com** for information.

If you slip easily into conflict, read "How to Reduce Conflict" in the Reading Room on the companion CD or at Divorce Helpline's Web site **www.divorcehelp.com**. Even better, get a copy of Nolo's *Divorce Solutions: How to make any divorce better.*

More depth on problem solving . . .

DIVORCE SOLUTIONS: ***How to make any divorce better***

This book deals at length with solutions for practical, emotional and financial problems. Portions of this book that discuss emotional upset and how to negotiate are condensed into two chapters in ***How to Solve Divorce Problems***. Order at **www.nolodivorce.com** or call (800) 464-5502.

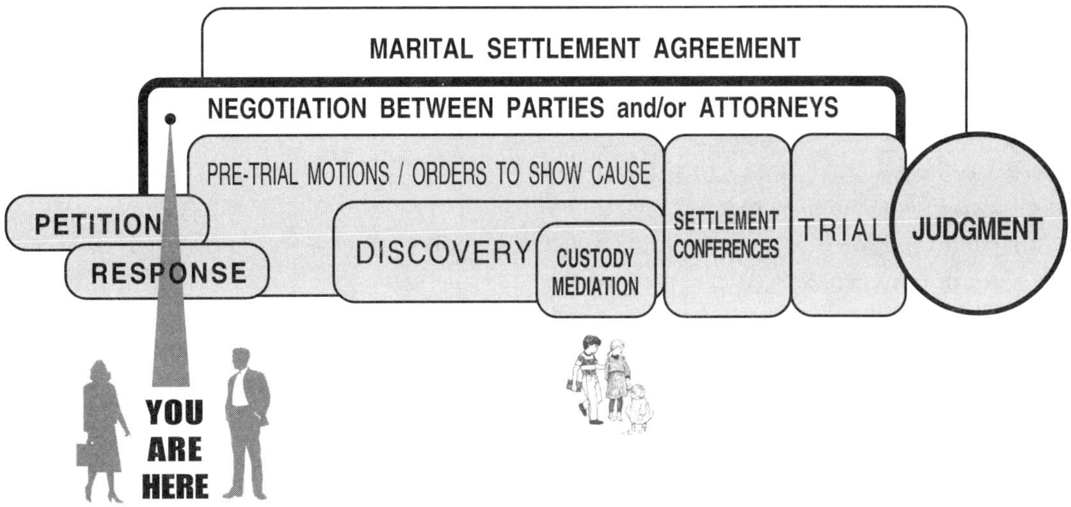

CHAPTER 4

HOW TO NEGOTIATE AN AGREEMENT

The best predictor of a good divorce outcome is *client* rather than attorney control of negotiation. This doesn't mean you should not get help and advice from an attorney when you want it; it means you are better off if you can do most or all of the negotiating yourself. Studies indicate that most clients feel their attorneys don't give them much help or guidance anyway. In a Connecticut study, nearly half of those interviewed reported no more than three contacts with their attorney, *including* phone calls, while 60% said they had worked out all issues without attorney help. In a New Jersey study, where *both* spouses had attorneys, less than 20% felt their lawyers had played a major role in settlement negotiations.

So, you see, you are likely to end up dealing with the negotiation anyway, and there is strong evidence that you are better off if you do. You get a higher degree of compliance with terms of agreement, a much lower chance for future conflict, co-parenting is smoother, support payments are more likely to be made in full and on time, and you get on with your life more quickly.

Negotiating with a spouse is never easy because there are built-in difficulties—so many that you may decide to get professional help from a good mediator, such as those at Divorce Helpline. But, okay, so there are problems—what to do? Here are ten steps you can take to make your negotiations work:

1. Be businesslike. Keep business and personal matters separate. Make it a condition of negotiation that you will not discuss personal matters when discussing business and vice-versa. Only do business by appointments and an agenda. This is so you can both be prepared and composed. Do not discuss either personal or business matters when you exchange the children. Act businesslike: be on time and dress for business. Don't socialize and don't drink; it impairs your judgment. Be polite and insist on reasonable manners in return. If things start to sneak into the personal, get back on track. If talk becomes unbusinesslike, say that you will leave if the meeting doesn't get back on track. Ask to set another date. If matters don't improve, don't argue; be nice about it, but get up and go.

2. Meet on neutral ground. Find a neutral place to meet, not the home or office of either spouse where there could be too many reminders, memories, and personal triggers. Otherwise, the visiting spouse could feel at some disadvantage, and the home spouse can't get up and go if things get out of hand. Try a restaurant, the park, borrow a meeting space or rent one if necessary.

3. Be prepared.

• Get control of the facts of your own case. Use the forms in Book 1, *How to Do Your Own Divorce,* chapters 14–16, to help you organize information and understand if any pieces are missing, or use the worksheets on the CD that comes with that book. Read chapters 8 and 17 in this book about what information you need and how to get it.

• Understand the law. Start by studying Part One of Book 1, *How to Do Your Own Divorce,* particularly the marital settlement agreement in chapter 6. Consider getting advice from Divorce Helpline to help you understand the law, develop options, and form your goals.

• Plan your strategy (chapter 6). Consider getting advice to help you do this.

• It will be useful if you try to understand yourself and your spouse. Try to step out of old patterns that did not work. Break old cycles. See if you can stop doing things that push your spouse's buttons and try to stop letting *your* buttons get pushed, even if your spouse is leaning on it. Just the fact that you are attempting this will help make things a little better. See the article *How to Reduce Conflict* in the Reading Room on the companion CD or at **www.divorcehelp.com**. Read Nolo's *Divorce Solutions: How to Make Any Divorce Better.*

4. Balance the negotiating power.

• If you feel insecure, become informed, be extra well-prepared, use an agenda, get expert advice and guidance. You never need to respond on the spot; state your ideas, listen to your spouse, then think about it until the next meeting. Get advice if you need it, use friends for moral support and venting, then go back in there. Don't meet if you are not calm, and don't continue if the meeting doesn't stay businesslike. Consider using a professional mediator.

• If you are the more confident one, help build your spouse's confidence so he/she can negotiate competently and make sound decisions. Share all information openly with your spouse. Be a good listener: restate what your spouse says to show you heard it; don't respond immediately, just say you'll think about it. Tone yourself back; state your own points clearly but don't try to persuade or "win" a point. Don't argue or repeat yourself. Listen, listen, listen.

5. Build agreement.

• Start with the facts: you should by now have gathered and exchanged all information. If not, complete the information gathering, then try to agree what the facts are. Write down the facts you agree on and list exactly what facts you do not agree on. Note any competing versions, then do research to resolve the difference with research and documents. Compromise, because if you can't prove some fact to each other, you may have a hard time proving it in court.

• Make a list of the issues and decisions you *can* agree on. Write them down. This is how you build a foundation for agreement and begin to clarify the major issues between you. Next, write down the things you don't agree on, always trying to refine your differences—to make them more and more clear and precise. Try to break differences down into digestible, bite-sized pieces.

6. Consider the needs and interests of both spouses. Avoid taking a position. Consider your needs, interests and concerns alongside the facts of your situation. Work *together* on brainstorming and problem solving; look for ways to satisfy the needs and interests of both spouses and try to balance the sacrifices. Call Divorce Helpline for practical problem-solving ideas.

7. State issues in a constructive way. "Reframing" is when you restate things in a more neutral way, to encourage communication and understanding. For example: one spouse says, "I have to have the house." Reframe: "What I would like most is to have the house, that's my first priority. What the house means to me is . . . "

8. Get legal advice. Typically, legal questions come up as you negotiate. Get professional advice from Divorce Helpline or a local family law attorney who specializes in mediation. Find out if the laws provide a clear, predictable outcome on your issue. Don't hesitate to get more than one opinion.

9. Be patient and persistent. Don't rush; don't be in a hurry. Divorces take time and negotiation takes time. It takes time for people to accept new ideas and even longer to change their minds. It may take time to shift your mutual orientation from combative to competitive to cooperative. So don't just *do* something, *stand* there! A slow, gradual approach takes pressure off and allows emotions to cool.

Meanwhile, you may want to work out temporary solutions for certain issues. If the situation of both spouses is stable and secure for awhile, you can afford to take some time. If not, work on that, not the negotiation. Settle in, get as comfortable as you can, go on with building your new life. If the going seems slow, remember, working through attorneys usually takes a *very* long time, many months or even years. You can beat that, for sure.

10. Get help. Negotiating with your spouse may not be easy because you're dealing with old habits, raw wounds, entrenched personality patterns—all the obstacles to agreement all at once. You might decide you just can't face all that alone. Even if you do try and find you aren't getting anywhere, don't struggle *too* long, don't wait until you are both at war from entrenched positions, don't get frustrated, don't get depressed, don't get mad—get help. A third person can really help keep things in focus. Mediators are trained to help you negotiate; they are expert at helping couples get unblocked and into an agreement. Mediation can be very effective, and it usually goes quickly. Call Divorce Helpline for help with your negotiation; it's one of the things we do best.

Negotiate what?

Naturally, when you think about negotiating, you think about getting a final resolution of all issues: division of property and debts, child and spousal support, and parenting arrangements. But, along the way, you can also negotiate temporary living arrangements while working on the final outcome. In court, you can negotiate the resolution of discovery issues, motions, or Orders to Show Cause that might come up during the divorce. The tools for negotiation that we've been discussing can help you in all of these arenas.

Full or partial agreement

Of course, you would rather have a complete resolution of all issues, but if you can't get that, a partial agreement can still be valuable. Agreeing on some, but not all, parts of any disagreement can narrow and focus the scope of your dispute and limit the effort and expense necessary to finish your case. It sets a pattern and builds a degree of confidence that at least some things can be agreed. It gives you stability in some areas of your life and less to worry about.

This does not mean you should give up an important bargaining chip that could be compromised as part of a settlement of some other important issue. For example, you might not want to give up a claim to one piece of property while the division of another is still in dispute.

Never use child custody, visitation, and support as bargaining chips. Not only is this damaging to the children, it is a poor strategy. Orders affecting children are modifiable, meaning they can be changed in the future if circumstances change. Let's say you concede some property in order to gain better support and visitation terms. Later, the child support and visitation can be changed, but the property is gone forever.

Before you start to negotiate

It is *not* a good idea to start working on a final agreement until both spouses have a complete picture of all property, debts, income, and expenses. Ideally, you will first exchange the preliminary and final disclosure documents and any discovery required to complete the picture. Read chapters 8 and 17 about getting information, and *How to Do Your Own Divorce,* chapter 14, about disclosure. If, in the future, one party can show that important financial information was not disclosed, your agreement and Judgment can be revisited, possibly set aside, and penalties could be imposed. You don't want that kind of insecurity hanging over your future, so be sure that your disclosure is open, honest, and full. Make sure your spouse knows these rules, too.

Before you begin to negotiate, give your spouse this book and, if possible, discuss parts of it together. Talk about how you can put these ideas to work and how you can proceed. Go over each step and talk about how it's going and what more can be done.

There are many good books about negotiation, but one of the easiest to read is the 150-page Penguin paperback by Fisher and Ury, *Getting to Yes: Negotiating Agreement Without Giving In,* which is also available on tape and has a workbook. The chapter titles are a checklist for things you need to know:

- Don't bargain over positions
- Separate the people from the problem
- Focus on interests, not positions
- Invent options for mutual gain
- Insist on using objective criteria
- What if they are more powerful?
- What if they won't play?
- What if they use dirty tricks?

When you reach your agreement

Chapter 5 discusses what to do when you reach a full or partial agreement. Chances are very good that you *will* work things out by using the techniques discussed in this book—ideally, before legal action, but certainly before trial. Once you have reached an agreement, you can relax a little bit; your divorce is effectively over—all that's left is to get it drafted in legally correct form and then go through some red tape and paperwork to get your Judgment.

Counseling, mediation and arbitration

There are times when a third person can really help with some words of advice, feedback on how something looks from the outside, another point of view, a new idea for how to handle a situation. In broad terms, there are three kinds of professional help—counseling, mediation and arbitration.

Counseling. The goal of individual counseling is mental health and emotional growth. A counselor can help you understand and accept yourself, or perhaps make constructive changes in your habits and attitudes. Counseling can be very practical and goal-oriented, or it can be directed more toward therapy and personal transformation. Counselors help with the difficult job of digging into your own process and dealing with your life. Couples counseling is practical and oriented toward mutual understanding and better communications. This can be great stuff if you want to work out an agreement or work on better co-parenting.

Mediation. The goal of mediation is to help a couple reach an agreement. A less popular but still useful goal is to bring some order to your disagreements—to narrow and sharpen the issues so if a conflict can't be avoided, it can at least be limited to real issues, which makes any subsequent legal contest more efficient and less expensive. The mediator is an objective, neutral person who is skilled at conflict resolution and negotiation. The mediator works to control upset, calm fears, equalize the bargaining power, and keep you focused on needs and interests. A mediator can help you get unstuck by shedding new light, bringing in new ideas, and other options. If you are unable to work out an agreement on your own, you should definitely try mediation—if the other party is willing—and preferably with a family law attorney-mediator. Family law attorney-mediators will know much more about the laws, likely outcomes of cases, and legal aspects of settlement agreements. Lawyers will tend to be more practical and businesslike.

Perhaps the only disadvantage of mediation compared to court battle or arbitration is that testimony cannot be taken under oath, so you could end up with an agreement based on incomplete information. However, by using disclosure and discovery (see chapter 8E) before mediation, documents and written information can be obtained from either party under penalty of perjury.

Mediation is not just for friendly divorces. Angry, conflicted couples are especially in need of mediation and stand to gain the most, particularly if they have children. Mediation can be very effective, even in cases with high conflict, especially if conducted by experienced family law attorney-mediators like those at Divorce Helpline.

Divorce Helpline offers professional mediation at its offices in San Jose, Sacramento, Walnut Creek, and Santa Cruz. Unlike many mediators, if the parties can't even agree to try mediation, they are willing to contact the other side and try to arrange a meeting. They also do telephone mediation, when necessary, which can be surprisingly effective and a lifesaver when parties can't conveniently meet in one location in person.

Arbitration. If counseling or mediation do not resolve your disagreements, or if you did not want to try one or the other, there is still one more good alternative to going to court. Arbitration is like hiring your own, private judge, except that the proceedings are less formal and much less costly. Arbitrators are typically retired judges or family law attorneys with lots of experience. Divorce Helpline attorneys, for example, are available to act as arbitrators in family law disputes.

The last resort

After all our talk about the advantages of reaching agreement, it is finally time to face the fact that you can't always get one no matter what you do. Or, maybe working with your spouse on an agreement is not something you want to do under any circumstances. If you can't settle, you have to litigate. If you have to litigate, you might as well learn how to do it in the most efficient and cost-effective way possible. So, dust off your briefcase and move on to chapter 6.

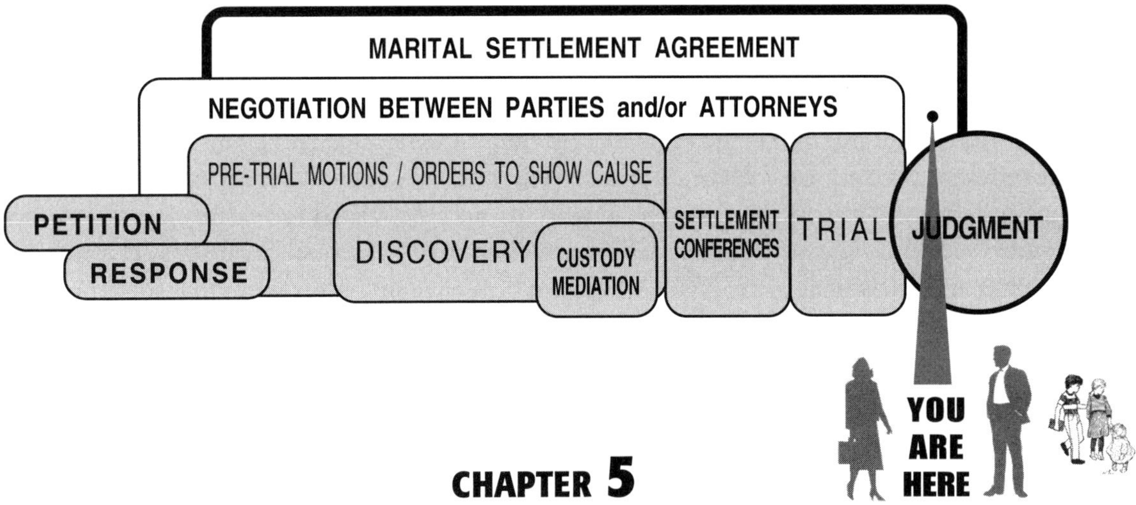

CHAPTER 5

WHAT TO DO WHEN YOU REACH FULL OR PARTIAL AGREEMENT

A Agreements and stipulations

It has to be in writing. The goal of any divorce is to reach agreement on all issues. Whenever this happens, you'll make a written marital settlement agreement (MSA) which defines your Judgment. Case over. Once you sign, your divorce is essentially over except for some red tape and paperwork.

Along the way to a full and final agreement, couples are often able to agree on some things, even in difficult cases. You need to know that a verbal agreement isn't worth much until it is written down in good form and signed. So, whenever you reach an agreement on any matter in your case, large or small, you *always* want to get it in writing. A written contract is better than a signed letter; a signed letter is better than a promise.

Stipulation is a fancy legal way to say agreement, so lawyers and judges love to use it. You can stipulate (agree) to a fact or a procedure, or you can stipulate to an order. In this book, we use "stipulation" when parties sign off on agreed orders. You will use stipulations if you agree to settle all or part of a motion or OSC in your case, and one way you can end your case is by filing a stipulated Judgment.

B Full agreement–do an MSA

Whenever you can reach a full and final settlement of all the issues in your case—division of property and debts, child and spousal support, and parenting arrangements—you will make a written marital settlement agreement. You need to do it quickly, before anyone changes their mind, so it is best to have most of the agreement worked out on your word processor, or typed up and ready to go, with only last-minute changes required. It isn't over until the MSA is signed and, in some counties, notarized. How to prepare an MSA, with a sample agreement, is found in Book 1, *How to Do Your Own Divorce,* chapter 6, and that MSA is also on the CD that comes with Book 1.

You *must* do disclosures before signing an MSA

Do *not* sign a marital settlement agreement (MSA) without making completion of the Preliminary Declaration of Disclosure (PDD) and Final Declarations of Disclosure (FDD) a condition of the agreement, together with a completed declaration of service of the declarations. This is something that *must* be done either before or at the time of signing. Disclosure and the related forms are discussed in Book 1, *How to Do Your Own Divorce,* chapter 14. Getting disclosure is essential because it gets your spouse's sworn statement as to what is in the estate, which can be used later if it turns out that some property was hidden or forgotten. The parties can waive the FDD in the MSA, but unless you are certain there is no property in the marital estate worth worrying about, we recommend that you do *not* do this.

If your spouse hasn't served you with a PDD by the time an agreement is ready to sign, take blank forms and sit there until they are completed and signed. Do *not* sign the MSA until this is done. Do not prepare the forms for your spouse's signature, as it could later be claimed that you exercised undue influence. The forms can be filled out by hand and your spouse can copy your documents if he/she wants to. Don't forget that your spouse must also complete and sign the Declaration Re Service of Declaration of Disclosure, to show that the Declaration was served on you.

Now you can complete your case

Once an MSA is signed, your case is essentially over, and can be completed following the checklist in *How to Do Your Own Divorce,* page 80. Follow the instructions at Step 4 for a case with an MSA where a Response was filed, and carry on through Judgment.

C Partial agreements

If you can reach a partial agreement in your negotiations, it is extremely important to get it in writing using the same format as the sample MSA in Book 1, chapter 6. Make it clear where you still do not agree. If you later change terms or increase your areas of agreement, draft a new agreement that begins, "This agreement supersedes all prior written agreements made between the parties on these issues."

D Stipulated orders

When a motion or OSC is filed, you might be able to negotiate full or partial agreement on issues raised, in which case you prepare a stipulated order that resolves the issues. Let's say your spouse files a motion to get all bank statements over a six-year period. Before the hearing, you send email explaining you have only the last two years, which you are willing to deliver, and you will give your spouse a letter to the bank authorizing them to deliver any documents at your spouse's expense. Your spouse agrees, so you draw up a stipulation in the form of an agreed order that follows your agreement. You either take the stipulation to court before the hearing, get the judge's signature, then have the clerk take the matter off the court's calendar, or you show up at the hearing, submit the stipulation for the judge's signature, and the motion is settled in court. Of course, the content of your stipulation will depend on your issues, but the format will look like the examples in Figures 5.1 and 21.1.

Your wording must be very specific and precise, as you do not want an order that is subject to more than one interpretation. Whenever possible, follow language used in printed forms, adapting it to suit your needs.

Figure 5.1

STIPULATION AND ORDER

YOUR NAME
Your Address
City, State, Zip
Your Phone

Petitioner in propria persona

SUPERIOR COURT OF CALIFORNIA, COUNTY OF [County name]

In re Marriage of)	No.: Your case number
Petitioner: YOUR NAME)	STIPULATION AND ORDER
Respondent: SPOUSE NAME)	

IT IS HEREBY STIPULATED by and between the parties hereto, and their their counsel if represented, that each will comply with all terms and conditions of the following agreement:

[Clearly state all the terms of your agreement]

You only type in the line for the attorney's signature if the party is represented.

______________________	______________________
YOUR NAME, Petitioner	SPOUSE NAME, Respondent
______________________	______________________
Attorney for Petitioner	Attorney for Respondent

The above agreement of the parties having been duly considered by the Court, and good cause appearing therefor,

IT IS ORDERED that the above agreement is approved, and each party is ordered fully to comply with all terms and conditions thereof to be performed on his or her own part.

Dated: ______________________

Judge of the Superior Court

1

Stipulation and Order

Custody stipulations. If your stipulation is for custody and visitation, if you do not state that the parties intend it to be a final judicial determination of the matter, on a later motion to modify the terms of the order, the moving party must only show what is in the best interest of the child. If you did clearly state the intention to make it a full and final judicial determination of custody, the moving party must first show that circumstances have changed, then show the best interest of the child.

E Stipulated Judgment

An agreed Judgment following a marital settlement agreement is discussed in section B, but there are cases where the last stubborn issues can be settled unexpectedly at some meeting, or on the courthouse steps, or in court at recess. That's why you always carry a completed Judgment around with you, so you are can get a stipulated Judgment signed at almost any moment. It's okay if it ends up with a few things written in handwriting or scratched out and changed, so long as both parties initial each place where this happens.

Prepare your Judgment as described in chapter 26 and Book 1, *How to Do Your Own Divorce,* chapter 18. Now, at the end of your Judgment, immediately above the Judge's signature line (which you might have to move to the end of your Further Orders), type in the language below:

The foregoing is agreed to by

Dated: ______________________________
Respondent, in pro per

Dated: ______________________________
Petitioner, in pro per

____
Judge of the Superior Court

Part Two
Preparation:
Where Cases Are Won or Lost

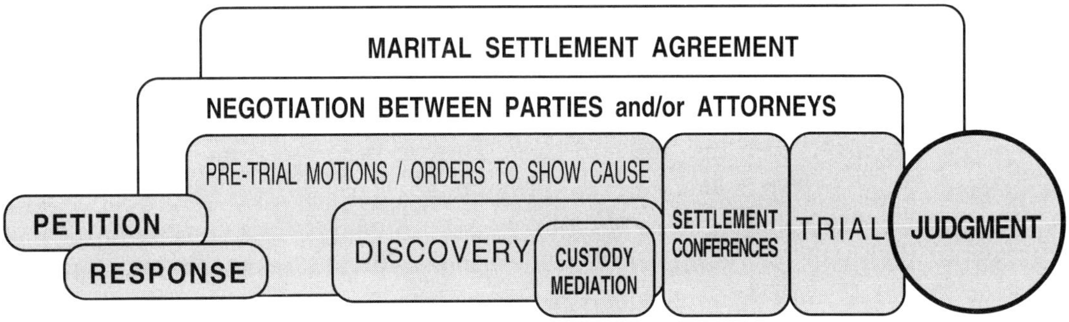

CHAPTER 6
HOW TO PLAN AND PREPARE YOUR CASE

A. Why you need strategy
B. Strategy is based on your goals
C. The effect of events and circumstances
D. Tactics based on who you are dealing with

Plan and prepare

It is very important to *not* be afraid of court, legal documents, or trial. If you are afraid, you are vulnerable to being bullied. A specific remedy for fear is reliable information. You gain a lot of confidence from knowing what can happen, what you have to do, and how to handle things; so, study this book and do the work. If you can afford it, get some advice; get a coach. But right now, the most important thing you can do, assuming you are not urgently pressed by events, is to organize, plan, and prepare your case.

- Learn the rules that apply to your case (Book 1, *How to Do Your Own Divorce,* Part One)
- Form your goals (this chapter)
- Find out what information you need and how to get it (chapter 8)
- Understand what you can do for yourself *outside* the legal system (chapters 3 and 4)
- Understand what you can do for yourself *inside* the legal system (chapters 9–27)
- Plan your strategy for achieving your goals (this chapter)
- Organize your facts and documents (chapter 9G) (a confused file causes *you* to be confused)
- Reevaluate your goals and strategy as you learn and experience more

From now on, think of your case in terms of the facts you can prove

Everything counts in life; lots of things count when you negotiate; but only *facts* count in court—and only those facts that are relevant to specific issues in your case. From now on, think of your case in terms of *facts* that you or your spouse can present in court in the form of documents or statements of witnesses. Documents can always be introduced, but in hearings before trial only written declarations can be used, while in a trial only oral testimony of a witness present in court can be used. Start gathering documents and list the witnesses who can state what each document is and say other relevant things about the issues in your case. Make lists of witnesses who will be willing to sign a written statement of what they know and, if necessary, appear some day in court. We show you how to do written statements in chapter 11.

A Why you need strategy

Your strategy is your plan for achieving your ultimate goals for the divorce. Planning is *essential.* You need a plan—strategy—to define your case and lead it to a fair conclusion. It is more difficult to succeed against someone who has a plan if you don't. Your plan should *not* be based on waiting to see what your spouse does, which is like having no plan at all; or, worse, planning to let your spouse call the shots. Planning is particularly difficult for formerly dependent spouses because they relied for so long on their mates to plan things for them. If you are such a person, you are less likely to succeed if you don't make extra effort to become a planner now. Even if you are in the middle of a divorce, it is not too late. If you have a plan and your spouse does not, you have an advantage that will guide you through every step, even the way you do your documents. For example, in dealing with property you might write a letter with an initial settlement offer. Later you draft a proposed marital settlement agreement which will be similar to your offer. If this fails to result in agreement, you might press towards trial and end up doing a settlement conference statement or a trial brief. Again, you just update and carry on what you were doing before. You don't start from scratch—your strategy is consistent and carries you through it all.

Tactics guided by strategy

Tactics are plans for any single step. Your case can be seen as a sequence of skirmishes: phone calls, letters, discovery, OSCs, or motions. Your strategy will dictate what tactics you use at each step. Let's say your strategy is to resolve child issues before you deal with property issues. If your spouse makes an early motion regarding property, your strategy will tell you to figure out some way—a tactic—to postpone the property issue rather than jumping headlong into it. Strategy will tell you what to focus on—that is, the most important thing to you. Each letter, phone call, discovery, OSC or motion is a tactic dictated by your strategy. You can't do everything, so you have to focus on what is most important.

Factors that affect your strategy and tactics

In any case, there are three factors that determine what, when and how you do things. These are:

- Your goals
- Events in your case and in your life
- Who you are dealing with on the other side

B Strategy is based on your goals

Strategy means making a plan to get what you want most—your goals. You need to ask yourself what, very specifically, are the most important things to you in your divorce. Your strategy will be a plan for achieving those goals. Throughout your case, while putting your plan (strategy) into effect, keep your goals at the front of your mind. Having a well thought out plan is one of the most important aspects of your case. Strangely, most lawyers do *not* tailor plans for any particular case. They tend to simply follow a routine of filing one paper after another, handling all cases in more or less the same routine way. So, even if you have a lawyer, you might need to come up with a plan if your lawyer doesn't. If you plan to hire a lawyer, this is something you should discuss right from the beginning.

It would be a good idea to sit down now, get a general idea of what is in the chapters in this book, then start writing your plan. It might be only a few sentences, but it will set your direction and help carry you through the entire case. Your plan should consist of two things: (1) a short list of two to five of your most important goals listed in order of importance, and (2) a short list of ideas for steps you can take to accomplish each goal. For example, let's say your first goal is to create stable, stress-free parenting for the children, make a list of some steps you can take to achieve this. For example, you could ask your spouse to find another place to live so the kids won't be immersed in constant tension, and propose a comfortable visitation schedule. If your spouse won't agree, you need backup plans for what you will do next, then next after that. Try ideas you get in chapters 3 and 4; see a counselor or mediator; get a restraining order—whatever you think the next steps should be based on what you know about your spouse and your life. Do the same thing for the other goals on your list. You can refine your plan as you learn more.

Next, you need to be certain your goals are realistic, given your circumstances. Because having a good plan from the beginning is so important, you might want to contact Divorce Helpline for help in making a plan for your divorce or evaluating a plan you have already made.

The list of goals and the plan you make will stand behind every step you take and every document you write, particularly the strategically important ones, such as initial motions or OSCs, letters offering to settle, the settlement conference statement, and the trial brief. As you read through this book, you will see that your plan will be the common thread that pulls everything together and keeps you on track. You won't be blown off course by whatever your spouse does; instead, you will stick to your goals.

Short and long-term plans

The long-term plan is the important one, but you also need a short-term plan to cover the immediate future and the time while the divorce is pending. The short-term plan should lead to where you want to end up in the long term. If it doesn't, you need to take a new look at things. For example, let's say your long-term goal is to encourage contact and bonding between the children and their other parent, and your parents are willing to watch the kids for free while you work your halftime job, but they are very antagonistic toward the other parent and say unpleasant things in front of the kids. This is a clear conflict between short-term convenience and long-term goal. You have to figure out which is more important in any situation where the short-term plan and long-term goals are in conflict.

A reliable generic plan

Most people will be well-served if they go after these things in this order:

1. Short-term safety and stability for you, your children, and property
2. Satisfactory parenting arrangements that you can live with indefinitely
3. Full access to financial information and documents
4. Negotiation and reasonable progress toward resolution
5. A fair settlement

1. Create short-term safety and stability

You can't negotiate if either you *or your spouse* are afraid or don't know how food and rent will be paid next week or next month. It is in the interest of both spouses to work at creating short-term safety and stability on *both* sides. While working toward a final resolution, you need to be safe and relatively at peace. You also need to eat, pay bills, parent your children, preserve the marital estate, prevent waste and hiding of assets. No matter what the other side does, you *must* get this for yourself before you do much else. Looking down the road, you can't expect to live at your former level, but inconvenience and compromise should be shared more or less equally. If you can't arrange a reasonable degree of safety, peace, and financial stability for yourself and your children through other means, then legal action might be in order. While waiting for the legal process to kick in on your side, you *still* have to solve problems in a practical way, any way you can. For example, you can:

- File a motion for orders that will address your problem (chapter 12), assuming you can get by for the time it takes to get a hearing on a motion in your county. It might be useful to keep negotiating while the motion is pending, as the looming court date can help move things along. You can file a motion requesting orders on any of the following: child or spousal support; establish custody and visitation rights; freeze assets or accounts, prevent transfers of property; distribute funds your spouse is holding; take possession of a particular asset, such as tools, car, computer.
- If the problem is very urgent and can't wait, you should file an Order to Show Cause (chapter 13) and ask for immediate temporary orders: for any of the above motion subjects; to keep spouse away from you, your house, your job, and to have no contact; to kick your spouse out of the house.

2. Parenting arrangements

When it comes to children, some judges don't like to change the *status quo*—meaning "the way things are." If your spouse is unwilling to cooperate in a stable and reliable parenting arrangement that is agreeable to you, your current reality soon becomes *status quo* and therefore increasingly difficult to change in court; so, you might be better off going straight to court rather than continuing to negotiate to change a situation that you don't want.

Sometimes, getting the right parenting arrangement immediately is very important. If it seems likely that you are eventually going to end up in a custody disagreement anyway, take legal action, but keep negotiating too, if possible, trying to get an agreement for a fair and reasonable status quo that you can live with. The pressure of a pending hearing might help. Many counties can schedule a hearing on a motion fairly quickly, but in others you'll probably want to file an Order to Show Cause (chapter 13) for fastest results. If the court is backed up, you should also request temporary orders pending the hearing.

3. Full access to financial information and documents

Spouses owe each other the highest degree of openness and honesty when dealing with marital affairs. You have a right to all financial information and documents. You can't form goals or negotiate when you don't have complete information about your marital estate or the income and expenses for both spouses.

In chapter 8, we tell you how to get information and records the easiest way possible. However, if your spouse won't cooperate (not a good sign for negotiation), and if you can't get what you need any other way, you will have to use legal discovery (chapter 17) and send out interrogatories and subpoenas. Once you have the information you need, you might be ready to start negotiating.

4. Negotiation and reasonable progress toward resolution

There are many effective things you can do outside the legal system to encourage negotiation, as discussed in chapters 3 and 4. These are fundamental techniques that you use before or along with any legal action you might need to take. But, certainly, there are situations where legal action can be useful as a tool of negotiation. For example:

- **Moving things along.** If you have been patient and given your spouse time to cope with emotions and sudden changes, yet your spouse is dragging his/her feet, not giving the negotiations enough attention, refusing to take care of business, then file a motion and let the pressure of a court date bring some pressure to the situation. Be sure to tell your spouse ahead of time what you are doing and why you are doing it.

- **Breaking impasse.** If there's one small point that seems to stand in the way of moving forward toward a complete settlement, you should consider mediation or arbitration. Another possibility, depending on the subject, is that it might be a valid subject for a motion that will get you a decision far easier than going to trial.

5. Get what's fair, what you have a right to under the law

This is what the rest of the book is about. Go for your goals. Follow your plan.

C The effect of events and circumstances

Tactics must consider events, but events rarely change strategy. Whatever comes up won't sidetrack you for long if you stick to your plan and work toward your primary goals. If your spouse does something, in or out of court, deal with it and move on. Almost any legal action the other side can throw at you is discussed in Part Three, along with actions you can throw back so, when something comes up, you can be ready to respond quickly. If you can afford it, long before trouble starts, get an attorney in your corner who can coach you through tight spots. If something happens, it's too late to start looking for help. Many (most?) traditional attorneys will not do coaching, which is why we invented Divorce Helpline.

D Tactics based on who you are dealing with

The emotional dynamic underlying your case is usually the key to the entire divorce. This does not refer to the reasons you are getting divorced but to the way in which you, your spouse, and your attorneys approach problems. It is always the emotions, personalities, and attitudes of the players that drive the divorce process. Calm, reasonable people can divide up millions in a fairly short time, while an angry spouse can make the divorce drag on for years and consume marital assets along the way.

This means that when you deal with your spouse directly, it is more important than at any time in your life that you pay attention to the kind of person your spouse is—what makes him/her tick. You were married to this person; this is someone you know pretty well. Try to see your spouse objectively, not idealized as when you were in love and not demonized as you might feel right now. Be aware of strengths, weaknesses, patterns of behavior. But even more important, there's the matter of your own feelings and attitudes. If you can't keep business and personal stuff separate, you're going to need help negotiating, maybe a mediator, and you'll want to get advice to see if your plan is emotional or reasonable.

You know better than anyone else what kind of person your spouse is, so don't fight it, use it! Put that knowledge to work; let it be your guide for how to deal with your spouse. When the deal's done, you can do whatever you want, but don't let your emotions get in the way of business. Review chapters 3 and 4 for ideas about how to deal with your spouse and with yourself. Understanding the emotional makeup and processes of your spouse can pay off in a big way. Understanding yourself and breaking bad habits can pay off even bigger. Here are some examples of how the relationship between personalities can affect the way you conduct your case:

Controllers

Controllers are the people who end up in horrible divorces. These are people who need to be in control and to control others. Not being in control—especially for controllers who were abused as children—brings up huge fears, so they fight for control as if they were fighting for their lives. It is very hard to do cost-effective litigation against a serious controller because they will spend a dollar to gain fifty cents. If your spouse has been controlling you, one of your main goals in the divorce process is to break free. This is done not only with restraining orders but also with fair property, support and custody orders.

In extreme cases, you can't make a controller stop fighting, no matter how many times you win in court. They fight on and on, trying to hold on to control. When a custody/visitation battle goes on for years and years, it is often because one spouse is a serious controller. Unless you have a lot of money, it is difficult to be able to afford an attorney throughout this process. Use the tools in this book and get advice when you need it if you can afford it.

Abusive spouses

There is some overlap between abusers and controllers. Normal people hate the legal process and want to get out of it as soon as possible. Abusive people welcome it as a new opportunity to abuse their spouse. This is exacerbated if the abuser has a lot of money to pay counsel to join in the abuse. Unfortunately, these people often masquerade as a "victim," and if the judge does not see through the disguise, the judge may join in the abuse. Then, the real victim finds him/herself the victim of "court abuse." This can be an extremely traumatizing process. Abusers like to pair up with mad-dog attorneys, if they can afford to. If your spouse is a serious controller or an abuser, you could find yourself in a battle that goes on for years and years—long after all your funds for an attorney are used up. This book is designed to help you function in that type of long, drawn-out battle as well as helping people whose cases can be settled after one simple motion.

Insecure, upset spouses

You can't negotiate with someone who is insecure, upset, or fearful. They are likely to fight, or worse, retain a lawyer to fight for them. **If your spouse is insecure**, there's a lot you can do to calm him/her. Let your spouse know you'll be open and fair, follow all laws, make no sudden moves without letting him/her know ahead of time. Make sure both sides have some stability for the time it takes to settle things. Tone yourself back, listen more, don't argue, repeat yourself, or insist. Take it slow and easy and help your spouse gain the confidence to negotiate. Do not try to con your spouse, because if he/she catches on, you're dead meat for the rest of your miserable, expensive, and well-deserved lawsuit. Even years later, if lawyers get into it, the con could come back to haunt you. **If you are the insecure person**, you have to get some backbone or get help. You'll feel a lot better if you understand the laws and other subjects in our books. You'll probably get some advice and learn for certain what you have a right to. You'll come to grips with the financial aspects of life that you let someone else take care of before. This is the new you, kid.

Unresponsive, incompetent or lazy

This looks a lot like being in denial, but it is just plain being slack—mentally, physically, or both. This person is unwilling to take responsibility, make decisions, get on with life. Use motions to encourage them to pay attention.

Spouses in denial, resisting the divorce

Sometimes a spouse does not want a divorce. Under California law they have no legal basis to stop the divorce from being granted, so they focus on obstructing any way they can. Spouses who are in only mild denial will come out of it when they get the first divorce papers and see that the divorce is really going to happen. Then there are spouses who are not in touch with their own feelings and do not realize that they want to stop the divorce, but they fight each step along the way. One purpose of this book is to show you that you can get a divorce without the cooperation of the other side. Meanwhile, discussion or counseling could help undermine the denial and reduce conflict.

Unreal expectations, wrong ideas

People get unreal expectations from a lot of places: TV, friends, relatives or the hairdresser. Wherever it comes from, it is almost impossible to settle with a spouse who is operating on misinformation or bad advice. The cure for this is to make sure he/she gets reliable information in a form that he/she can accept. Start by giving him/her our books, then discuss the parts that apply to your case. If you can afford it, pay for your spouse to get advice from Divorce Helpline attorneys or a local divorce specialist attorney. You might involve a mediator. If all that fails, tell your spouse that you want to let a judge decide, then file a Notice of Motion or OSC on one of the central topics of disagreement. For example, if a spouse believes incorrectly that no judge would award support to the other spouse and he/she has rejected all the computer printouts and advice you've sent to them, then just file a Notice of Motion for support and let the judge decide. In a letter, explain that you are filing the motion so the two of you can get a resolution on the issue from a neutral party (the judge), so you can go ahead and settle the remaining issues. This could open the way for agreement on all other subjects.

Hanging on

This is about negative involvement. Holding up an agreement is a way of not letting go. Keeping the argument going makes the relationship last longer, even if it's no fun. Some people feel, "I'd rather see you in court than not see you at all." Try to minimize your contact with them and insist that the process move forward. Having your spouse's cooperation is certainly to be preferred, but in most cases you do not need your spouse's cooperation to get a divorce. If you have a lawyer who says things are going slowly because your spouse won't cooperate, this is probably a poor reflection on your lawyer. Read this book to learn about ways to get your case finished without cooperation.

Conclusion

Build the foundation for your case by writing down an outline of your goals in order of priority, then plan how to get what you want most. For each goal, write a brief plan for how you are going to reach it.

Your goals and plan will be based on everything you know and understand at the time, including yourself, your finances, and the other people in your family. As you go along, reevaluate your goals when you learn more about the laws, the courts, and details about the facts in your case. You do not want to be chasing goals that are unrealistic in the light of your overall situation or the law.

Stick with your plan throughout the divorce unless there is a major change of circumstances (your spouse getting upset doesn't count). You knew your spouse when you made the plan. If the most important thing in the world to you is not to make your spouse angry, make your plan accordingly. However, if you have other things such as your children or finances or your home that are more important to you, that's what comes first. This is the time for a realistic, true look at what you want. When you are clear on that, your plan will carry you through the divorce, and it will be reflected in all your major moves and documents.

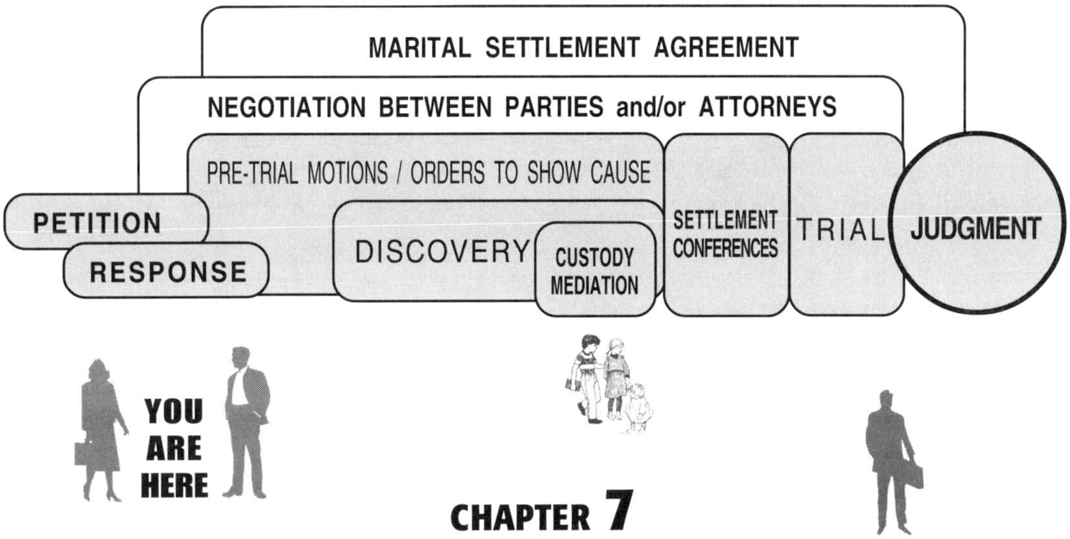

CHAPTER 7
WORKING WITH AND AGAINST AN ATTORNEY

A. What a good attorney can do
B. Should you retain an attorney?
C. How to find a good attorney
D. How to get the most from your attorney
E. How to supervise your attorney
F. It's easy to fire an attorney
G. How to work against your spouse's attorney

Whether you use an attorney or not, in whatever capacity you choose to use one, you can save a lot of trouble and money if you first learn how to choose and use an attorney, and always prepare before you contact them.

A What a good attorney can do

Good attorneys know divorce law in depth and detail, the local rules and practices, and what various judges are like. They can dig information out of the other side, plan strategy, prepare paperwork, defend legal actions from the other side, negotiate with the other side, and prepare your case and witnesses for hearings or trial.

A good attorney should be able to get a case into negotiation and only fight when appropriate. If they need to fight, they can be tough, effective, and efficient, yet always looking for the right time to get back into negotiation. They do not let cases linger without a stated reason. A *really* good attorney would tailor his/her strategy to your goals and deal with you as an individual. They *could* (if they would) help you understand the rules, form your goals, and understand the strategy being followed in the case. They answer your calls within 24 hours and keep you abreast of what's going on at each step. If you know any attorneys like this, we hope you will send us their names.

If the attorney is a trained mediator, he/she probably also knows how to listen and communicate, negotiate effectively, defuse rather than create conflict, balance the negotiating power between the parties, find and suggest alternatives and options the parties haven't thought of, and help the parties get past emotional issues to deal with business.

The problem. We are sorry to tell you this, but most attorneys are below average, or at least below what we think average should be. In part, this book was written because good attorneys are so hard to find and hard to afford even if you *can* find one. We will help you learn how to handle your own case as much as possible, and choose and supervise an attorney if you decide to retain one. We hope to raise the average level of divorce practice by educating our readers to know how to insist on quality representation.

B Should you retain an attorney?

Using an attorney and retaining one are two different things. A retained attorney "takes" your case and becomes professionally responsible for it. You *literally* hand over your power and authority. All papers, contacts and negotiations will go through the attorney. What's worse, the retainer agreement you sign means that the more trouble you have, the more money the attorney will earn.

In general, we believe that a person should *use* an attorney but resist *retaining* one to take over his/her case. However, because our legal system is so excessively complex, if you can find and afford a *good* attorney to represent you throughout the divorce process, that would be a reasonable choice—provided that you use this book to stay in charge of your own case and supervise your attorney to maintain at least the standards established here (see section E, below).

If you find a good attorney but can't afford the high cost of having him/her handle your entire case, consider using that attorney for advice, coaching, and some paperwork—assuming he/she will work in that capacity (many will not). Affording an attorney will be difficult or impossible if there's trouble. A mild divorce involving only one court appearance can cost $5,000 to $8,000 on each side, but with a difficult attorney or party on either side, it could go far higher. For a moderately contested divorce, plan to spend $20–40,000 on each side, while a hotly contested divorce can cost well over $50,000 on each side. We know many couples who have spent hundreds of thousands. If you do not have thousands of dollars sitting in a bank, you cannot afford to have an attorney represent you in a contested divorce.

If your resources are limited and your case might have some trouble, you would do better to spend, say, $4,000 having an attorney advise you while you represent yourself. If you use that same $4,000 to retain the attorney, your money will soon be used up and your attorney will withdraw in the middle of the case when you can no longer pay.

When you should not represent yourself

It is possible that your case will not require a hearing or trial, but even then, you will not negotiate well if you are afraid of legal or verbal conflict, or if you lack the confidence to go for your goals. If you are a very submissive person who always gives in, you might have a hard time speaking up for yourself in court or negotiations. You should not represent yourself in any confrontation unless you can develop confidence and emotional distance. In negotiations, use a mediator. In court, you can bring a support person/assistant to sit with you at the counsel table, but while he/she can help you keep your papers organized and your spirits up, you still have to speak for yourself.

You can only represent yourself if you can speak to the court calmly, firmly, and in an organized, businesslike manner.

- If you are in the grips of upset or anger, you might be better off having an attorney represent you. The judge might hear your emotion rather than the substance of what you are saying. You have a right to your feelings, but if they undermine your presentation, or your ability to handle yourself in court in the presence of your spouse, that could hurt your case.

- If you do not speak or understand English well, this makes it more difficult for you to appear in court. If the judge has to struggle to understand what you are saying, the effect of your words is reduced; so if you can afford it, get an attorney to speak for you. If you can't afford it, bring an interpreter and speak in your own language. If possible, use an interpreter who has been certified by the court, as some judges will not accept a non-certified interpreter in a legal proceeding.
- If you are not very literate in English and do not write well, you probably need an attorney or Legal Document Assistant to prepare papers for you.

C How to get a good attorney

Before you go see any attorney, you are going to get completely prepared, but that comes next. First, let's discuss how to find the attorney you want to use.

The search

Shopping for an attorney is like shopping for melons; check prices and make sure the one you choose "feels" right. You have a right to ask questions and be choosy about whom you hire for such an important role in your life. Don't be intimidated. Call around and ask how much it will cost just to meet the lawyer and see if you want to retain or use him/her. Many attorneys do an initial interview for nothing or a fairly small fee. Ask what their hourly rate is. Rates run from $100 to $500 per hour, but $175 to $350 is common; higher in urban areas, lower elsewhere.

Many attorneys—perhaps most—will only want to work if retained as attorney of record, so if you are looking for advice, coaching, and maybe some paperwork while you handle your own case, you should ask at the very beginning if the attorney will work with you in this capacity and at what rate.

You want a lawyer who specializes, that is, divorce is at least 50% of their case load. We admit to a bias in favor of State Bar-certified specialists, but we know there are many fine divorce attorneys who are not certified. Mediation-minded attorneys are more likely to be trained communicators who can give you problem-solving advice, whereas traditional attorneys tend to be more oriented to conflict and their advice tends to be adversarial. Your attorney must be someone you feel you can trust and work with comfortably. The lawyer you choose to represent you should have handled a lot of divorces in the court where your divorce is or will be filed. Knowing the local rules and judges is important. Watch out for any attorney who seems to make things more complicated or who urges you to do things that could lead to more conflict. Avoid situations where you don't like the way the attorney or staff treat you. Avoid lawyers with a pushy, domineering personality; they may not listen to you or be willing to do things your way.

Holistic Lawyers. A tiny but growing number of lawyers are looking for better, healthier ways to practice. In the vanguard are those who call themselves "holistic lawyers," meaning that they incorporate integrity, humanity and spiritual values in their practices and see themselves as peacemakers, even healers. You might be surprised at how effective they can be. To see if there are any holistic lawyers in your community, check in at **www.nolodivorce.com/links** or go to the lawyer locator at the web site of the International Association of Holistic Lawyers at **www.iahl.org**.

The best way to find a divorce lawyer is on the recommendation of a professional whose opinion you trust—someone who works in a field that gives him/her an opportunity to know about divorce attorneys and their reputations, such as a counselor, accountant, financial planner, etc. Next best is the personal recommendation of someone you trust who has had a divorce in your county and was pleased with a particular lawyer's services. But, if your friend's case was easy and yours isn't, their experience has limited value. If you are looking particularly for a litigator, go to court and watch divorce cases in action. If you see someone who impresses you as being prepared and effective, ask their name. But don't forget: attorneys who mediate effectively are less likely to be found in court. Finally, your local bar association will have a referral service; look them up in the Yellow Pages and ask for a family law specialist.

Be very cautious with recommendations from people you don't know well, especially if they didn't have a divorce similar to yours. It won't help you to know that a certain attorney is good at business, personal injury, or criminal work, nor does the fact that your friend's attorney negotiated brilliantly mean he/she can fight your rabid spouse and the mad-dog attorney.

The attorney you choose will strongly affect the temperature in your case. We suggest that you avoid anyone who seems cynical, unnecessarily aggressive, or moralistic. For most cases, you want someone who prefers to avoid conflict in favor of negotiation and compromise. In some cases, however, you know ahead of time that you want someone who can slug it out if the other side gets ugly.

The interview

When you call for an appointment, ask if the person you are talking to can answer questions about the attorney's rates, background, or practice. Ask some of the following questions meant for the attorney. Questions the staff won't answer, you need to ask the attorney when you get there. Be very well prepared before you go in, as detailed in section D below.

About the attorney's background

- How long have you been in practice? How long with this firm?
- What percentage of your practice is divorce? Are you a Bar-certified specialist?
- What percentage of your divorce cases settle without *any* formal legal activity?
- Do you practice as a divorce mediator? What percentage of your case load is mediation?

About fees

- How much do you charge if you take my case as attorney of record?
- Are you willing to work as my coach or consultant? If so, how much do you charge?
- How am I billed for your secretary's time or research by other staff?
- How much do you need to get started (the retainer)?
- Is the initial retainer applied against future billings? If there's a balance, will it be returned?
- What costs can we anticipate?
- Can I count on you to get your fee from my spouse, or am I going to be responsible for your payment and collection from my spouse?
- Do you bill exactly for time spent, or do you round off to a higher time period?

About other things

- Can I expect you to return my calls within 24 hours?
- Can I expect a copy of all papers and documents and reports on negotiations?
- Do you need any information that you don't have yet?

Tell the lawyer how you want it to be. Being in control of your own case is the single best thing you can do. You have to actually tell the attorney that this is what you want. Tell the lawyer you will rely on his/her advice, but that you expect to make decisions including strategy, and that you want to discuss ahead of time all steps taken in your case. Find out if he/she can work cheerfully on this basis. Optionally, say you want to see copies of letters to the other side *before* they go out. This lets you find out how fast work gets done and if you like the way your points are made. This takes time and costs more, so once you are satisfied with their work, you can eliminate this step.

Ask, "How would you proceed in this case? What are the first steps you would take? What would be your goals?" If the attorney cannot make a plan at the beginning of the case, this is not a good sign.

Finally, ask to have a copy of their standard retainer agreement; then go home, read the agreement, and think about all you have heard and seen. If you want to retain the attorney, it is now time to negotiate the terms of the retainer contract.

The retainer agreement

You might not need one of these if you are only going to use the attorney now and then for advice and service, but the law does require a written retainer contract in any case that is likely to run over $1,000, so some attorneys might insist in any case. A retainer agreement should specify in great detail what work is to be done, under what conditions, and the fee or the manner in which the fee will be calculated.

Chances are, the better you understand the agreement, the less you will like it. You will probably be handed a legalistic document designed to protect the attorney from a lot of things—mostly you—and expected to sign it as is. Don't. Here are some things you can do and terms you can ask to have written into the retainer that will help protect your interests.

A retainer contract is something you negotiate like any other deal, and there is no law that says it has to be a take-it-or-leave-it proposition. Attorneys with that attitude may be otherwise hard to work with, so keep looking. Billing practices can work to your disadvantage, so you want to examine and give careful thought to the details of any retainer you are asked to sign. Take it home, study it, make sure you understand everything in it before you sign. Discuss terms you don't understand and terms you want changed or added. It is okay to request and discuss terms that you want but don't expect to get.

Avoid putting up security for your attorney's fees—that is, don't sign a mortgage or trust deed on your home or other property. That would make it very complicated if you become dissatisfied with the attorney. However, if the attorney is taking your case for little or no cash and is willing to be paid from assets sold when the case settles, this might be the only way you can get legal service. If you have little or no income or other assets, and your spouse has plenty of stable income, savings, or other assets, then you might look for an attorney who will agree in the retainer contract to take your case for out-of-pocket costs and collect all attorney's fees from your spouse, but finding such an attorney would be like winning the lottery; few will do this.

Here are some points you can bring to a retainer negotiation, in order of importance to you:

- Be clear that you do not pay for time spent negotiating the attorney's contract. The attorney is working for himself during that time, so billing should start only after the contract is signed.
- Likewise, you want it written that you never pay for time spent discussing the bill or your contract or problems with their service—only for time spent working your case.
- Make sure the retainer paid will be applied to future billings and not kept as a base fee for taking the case. Specify that all unused portions will be returned.
- Specify that you be sent copies of all documents and letters, either incoming or outgoing. Get a clause that says your phone calls will be answered within 24 hours or the next working day.
- Limit rounding off. Try to avoid the common practice of billing a quarter hour for a five-minute phone call. Say that you want no more than five-minute rounding and you don't care if the software won't do it; that's their problem.
- Request a monthly billing with detailed itemization on each bill that shows the date and time for each task, total time spent, and amount billed. Ask to see a sample bill.
- Ask about charges, if any, for secretary and staff time. Request that amounts for time billed to secretaries, research assistants, paralegals, or associate attorneys be billed separately so you can see exactly what is going on and who is doing what.
- Make it clear that you will not be charged for experts retained without your written consent.

- If your case is not very complex, ask that the contract specify that you will not be billed for research time. A high hourly rate implies that the attorney already knows his business.
- Try to get an agreement that you will not be billed for court time spent on continuances that you do not request or for any court time not actually in trial. You really don't want to pay $250 an hour for time spent sitting around waiting to continue your case to some other day. You aren't likely to get this one, but ask.
- Here's a novel idea: consider offering an incentive fee where the attorney gets paid at a higher rate if your case is settled very quickly, in less than a certain number of hours of attorney time. This rewards the attorney for fast, effective work. Conversely, the rate would go down if your case goes over so many hours or if it goes to trial. This ought to get a reaction.

D How to get the most from your attorney

Whenever you contact an attorney, even the initial interview, be very well prepared. Know your facts, know what you want to ask about, and know exactly what you want the lawyer to explain or do for you. Plan each conversation: make an agenda; write down the things you want to talk about; take notes on the content of every conversation; keep track of time spent on all phone calls and meetings. Keep a file for all your notes, letters, and documents. Do as much as possible on the phone and by mail to keep office time to a minimum. Work with the attorney's staff whenever possible; it's cheaper.

The CD that comes with Book 1, *How to Do Your Own Divorce,* has a set of worksheets like the ones attorneys use when they go over the details of your case with you. Why pay an attorney $200 per hour to develop this information when you can do it for free? Using these worksheets will help you organize and analyze your case, clarify your thinking, and probably save you hundreds of dollars or more. At the initial interview, give the attorney a copy of these worksheets so they won't have to spend hours of expensive time developing this information for you. Use this book to answer your own questions and to bring the discussions with your attorney into sharper focus.

Regard your attorney as a resource, not someone you depend on for emotional support and stability. Lawyers cost too much to use for sympathy and consolation—that's what family, friends, and therapists are for. When you talk to a lawyer, stick to what's important and don't just chat, ramble, or complain about things your spouse did unless you actually want your lawyer to do something about it.

E How to supervise your attorney

If you retain an attorney to handle your case, you still want to be in control as much as possible—after all, it's your life at stake here—and you want to supervise your attorney to be sure you are being represented competently. Read this book to obtain a standard by which to measure your attorney. If the attorney does not perform as least as well as the guidelines described in this book, that would be a red flag.

Some delays are built into the legal system, all documented in this book. Any additional, unexplained delays will be the result of attorney foot dragging and should not be tolerated. Your case should always be going somewhere specific unless there is a conscious plan to wait for a specific reason. There is no good reason why most cases cannot be concluded in about nine months, unless you have a particular reason for taking more time, such as bitter resistance to discovery that you can't work around.

Planning. This is something you might have to bring up, as many attorneys don't do it. After reading chapters 1 and 6, you can tell the attorney your goals and discuss a plan to get what you most want.

Temporary orders. Many attorneys routinely file initial motions or OSCs in every case, but unless there is a specific strategic reason based on your plan, you should tell them not to do this. If not essential, this practice merely runs up fees and creates more conflict.

A case should have definable stages that progress towards a goal without being deflected for long by anything the other side does or doesn't do. If non-cooperation can deflect the case, it is not being pursued with sufficient vigor. Your attorney should have a plan for the case from the beginning, including:

- getting temporary orders *(if required by your plan)*
- getting information and documents
- negotiating toward settlement
- setting the case for trial if settlement isn't forthcoming
- getting experts and evidence ready for trial
- going to trial if settlement proves impossible

The first three steps can be undertaken more or less at the same time, depending on your situation. You need information to negotiate and you can start negotiating about getting information.

Getting information. If you follow chapter 8, you know how to get information without using the legal system. From reading chapter 17, you know the most cost-effective ways to use legal procedures to demand information and documents, and you know how long it takes. At the beginning, discuss with your attorney what information is needed and make sure the process of getting it is underway within a week of the retainer. Monitor the responses from the other side and decide what additional discovery is necessary. If the other side does not respond in a timely manner, a motion should be quickly made. If your attorney can't keep up with the procedures described in this book, start looking around for another attorney.

Negotiating. This is something you might end up doing yourself. Few attorneys have had any training at it, attorney time is very expensive, and, as a statistical fact, most spouses eventually end up settling their own issues themselves. Consider whether or not your case is one that could be taken into mediation.

Delay. In general, the sooner the case is finished, the lower attorney fees will be, so don't let your attorney be slow to request a trial date. After you have pushed through discovery, if negotiations aren't going anywhere, it is probably time to set the case for trial (chapter 22). Ask your lawyer if there is any good reason why this can't be done. If some necessary evidence has not been obtained, the lawyer should be able to tell you precisely what is needed, the plan to get it, and how long that will take.

Legal ability. Use this book as a guide to minimum standards for legal practice. For example, it is not unusual for an attorney to have no idea how to do the records-only deposition package explained here. If they can't subpoena records when you need them, you may need another attorney, or you might do better representing yourself. As you read this book, ask yourself whether your attorney knows about this information and why he/she does not use procedures at least as effective as those described here. If you find that your attorney is unaware of the procedures, you should get a second opinion or change attorneys.

If you feel your attorney is not properly representing you

If you feel your attorney is not doing the right thing, the first thing to do is to get a competent second opinion. Divorcing a difficult person can be very difficult and unpleasant. You need a second opinion to determine whether your attorney is failing you or whether the process is merely horrible. What you do *not* do is tell your attorney you think they are doing a rotten job. If the attorney is really incompetent, saying this will not help; if the attorney is actually okay, they will be offended by your comments.

When you go for a second opinion, have an organized copy of all your information and court papers with you. Without the court papers, the attorney cannot give you any opinion at all. If the second opinion confirms your belief that you are being badly represented, you should get another attorney, or fire your existing attorney and take over the case yourself.

Figure 7.1
SUBSTITUTION OF ATTORNEY
Form MC-050 (page 1)

ATTORNEY OR PARTY WITHOUT ATTORNEY *(Name and Address)*: YOUR NAME, Your Address, City, State, Zip	TELEPHONE NO.: Your phone no.	*FOR COURT USE ONLY*
ATTORNEY FOR *(Name)*:		
NAME OF COURT: SUPERIOR COURT OF CALIFORNIA FOR (YOUR COUNTY) STREET ADDRESS: Court street address MAILING ADDRESS: Court mailing address (if different) CITY AND ZIP CODE: City, State, Zip BRANCH NAME: Name of your branch		
CASE NAME: Marriage of (YOUR LAST NAME) and (SPOUSE LAST NAME)		
SUBSTITUTION OF ATTORNEY—CIVIL **(Without Court Order)**		CASE NUMBER: Your case number

THE COURT AND ALL PARTIES ARE NOTIFIED THAT *(name)*: makes the following substitution:

1. **Former legal representative** ☐ Party represented self ☑ Attorney *(name)*: Attorney's name
2. **New legal representative** ☑ Party is representing self* ☐ Attorney
   a. Name: b. State Bar No. *(if applicable)*:
   c. Address *(number, street, city, ZIP, and law firm name, if applicable)*:
   Your address, city, state, zip
   d. Telephone No. *(include area code)*: Your phone number with area code
3. The party making this substitution is a ☐ plaintiff ☐ defendant ☑ petitioner ☐ respondent ☐ other *(specify)*:

***NOTICE TO PARTIES APPLYING TO REPRESENT THEMSELVES**

- **Guardian**
- **Conservator**
- **Trustee**
- **Personal representative**
- **Probate fiduciary**
- **Corporation**
- **Guardian ad litem**
- **Unincorporated association**

If you are applying as one of the parties on this list, you may NOT act as your own attorney in most cases. Use this form to substitute one attorney for another attorney. SEEK LEGAL ADVICE BEFORE APPLYING TO REPRESENT YOURSELF.

NOTICE TO PARTIES WITHOUT ATTORNEYS

A party representing himself or herself may wish to seek legal assistance. Failure to take timely and appropriate action in this case may result in serious legal consequences.

4. I consent to this substitution.
   Date: Date you sign the form
   YOUR NAME, in pro per
   (TYPE OR PRINT NAME) (SIGNATURE OF PARTY)

5. ☑ I consent to this substitution.
   Date:
   ATTORNEY'S NAME
   (TYPE OR PRINT NAME) (SIGNATURE OF FORMER ATTORNEY)

6. ☐ I accept this substitution.
   Date:
   (TYPE OR PRINT NAME) (SIGNATURE OF NEW ATTORNEY)

(See reverse for proof of service by mail)

Form Adopted by the Judicial Council of California MC-050 [New January 1, 1996]

SUBSTITUTION OF ATTORNEY—CIVIL

Code of Civil Procedure, §§ 284(1), 285 Cal. Rules of Court, rule 376

F It's easy to fire an attorney

You have a right to discharge your attorney at any time for any reason or no reason at all, whether or not any money is owed. It's easy—all you have to do is file a form. Of course, you will continue to owe your former lawyer for time spent working on your case.

If your lawyer is not performing to your satisfaction, you should send a letter (keep copies) setting out very specifically what needs to be changed. If there is no improvement, start shopping for another lawyer. Some things can't be changed. For example, if you lose trust and confidence in your lawyer, get another one or take over the case yourself. Nothing is worse than feeling trapped in a bad relationship with your own attorney.

If you want to fire your attorney, simply fill out the Substitution of Attorney form as shown in Figure 7.1. You have two choices now:

1. Substitute another attorney for your old attorney. In this case, your new attorney will take care of the substitution and get all files transferred.
2. Substitute yourself in as your own attorney and ask that all files be sent to you.

Once the form is filled out and you have signed at item 4, make four copies and have someone (not you) mail a copy to your ex-attorney, your spouse, and your spouse's attorney, if any. That person signs the Proof of Service on the back of the original, then you file it with the court clerk. Proofs of Service are filled out as described in Book 1, *How to Do Your Own Divorce,* Figures 13.3 and 13.4,

The copy that goes to your ex-attorney should be sent with a letter politely explaining that you have taken over your own case, requesting that all files and papers be immediately forwarded to you. Wait a few days and call to see if your files have been sent. After a few more days, mention that you are going to write to the local and state bar associations if you do not get your complete file immediately. An attorney cannot ethically delay turning over files and documents merely to pressure you into payment of amounts owed. Failure to promptly forward files as you request is a breach of the attorney's ethical duty to you. In case of unreasonable delay, fire off a letter of complaint to the local and State Bar associations with copies to your old attorney. Meanwhile, you can always get copies of court documents from the court clerk.

G How to work against your spouse's attorney

If you are represented, it is your attorney's job to handle the other attorney; in fact, the other attorney is forbidden by law to talk to you directly. However, if you are representing yourself, you conduct your own negotiations and contacts with the other side. In all your contacts with the other side, it is *essential* that you always be businesslike and efficient no matter how they act, chummy or ugly.

You have to work against the opposing attorney a bit to see how he/she works. For example, at the beginning of the case, you start off trying to exchange with your spouse the information you need to get through your divorce, trying to do it voluntarily and cheaply as described in chapter 8. If you don't get the information or response you are asking for, possibly your spouse is working with an attorney who is dilatory, or not competent, or a shark who cannot work cooperatively. So, you start some formal discovery (chapter 17) and see what happens. If you end up making motions to compel discovery (chapter 18), you are in for a struggle. Unfortunately, it is not unethical to be a poor attorney or unpleasant, difficult, and confrontational, so attorneys who act like that are not subject to discipline by the Bar.

When your spouse's attorney is the problem

If your spouse has an attorney who you feel is creating conflict, you should say so in a letter to your spouse unless you are already sure that this is what your spouse wants. It is not uncommon for a spouse to blame the "mean" attorney, but if after several events the attorney has not been fired or controlled, you have to assume that the attorney is doing what your spouse wants, or at least with your spouse's consent.

If your spouse's attorney is being a problem, don't back down—press forward. As your own attorney, it is your job to contact the other attorney to try to settle your case or move it forward. So get busy: send letters, make phone calls, file motions. These must all be legitimate efforts to move the case forward or settle some outstanding issue. If the attorney refuses to talk to you, or does something clearly offensive, keep a detailed diary of every event. Some attorneys believe, or claim to believe, that they cannot work with an unrepresented person. This is not the law. Send a letter detailing each event and letters trying to settle each specific issue. You might use these records in court to show that an award of sanctions should be made against the attorney, because the court in a dissolution matter can punish an attorney who frustrates settlement. All of your work can run up your spouse's bills and put pressure on him/her to control or remove the attorney. If not, at least you are vigorously representing yourself. Be careful. If you are perceived by the judge as harassing the attorney and running up fees without good cause, the judge can make you pay sanctions. If you occupy the attorney with ridiculous, little points, you could find yourself in hot water. But, if there are real issues in your case, and you want legitimate attention, you are certainly entitled to try to discuss settlement with opposing counsel.

Sometimes an attorney stands in the way of settlement. The two parties may talk and reach a basic agreement, but every time one returns to his/her attorney, the attorney brings up more issues or writes up the agreement in such a way as to torpedo the agreement. Sometimes this is legitimate because the parties made an agreement that was not thoroughly thought out, so it turns out there really was not a meeting of minds. But other times the attorney is just a troublemaker. When that happens, the only way to get to a settlement is if the party with the confrontational attorney will tell the attorney to cut it out. This is very difficult to accomplish because such attorneys are masters at flaring up people's emotions.

When your spouse is the problem

Sometimes a party wants it to appear that he/she is personally trying to be reasonable, but that mean attorney is doing bad things. This is different from the confrontational attorney causing the problem. In this situation the party is really the one who opposes settlement but is not honest or assertive enough to say so. He/she hides behind the screen of the attorney—but he/she hired the attorney, keeps paying the attorney, and doesn't put a foot down. In this smoke screen sort of situation, it is the party who is the problem. And, the party may never admit it even if everyone can see it. A party is free at any time to fire his/her attorney. If your spouse chooses not to control or fire the attorney, he/she is in fact responsible for what the attorney is doing, and all you can do is let your spouse know that you see through the screen, and you know it is your spouse who is in charge. Let your spouse know that as long as the attorney proceeds in the same fashion, you hold your spouse responsible.

Is your spouse having sex with his/her attorney?

Clients often think their spouse is having sex with his/her attorney and that explains the attorney's enthusiasm for your spouse's cause. This is not impossible, but highly unlikely and even if you're right, there's not much you can do about it. Divorces become problematic in many more cases than a personal affair between lawyer and client. Forget it; stay on track with your case.

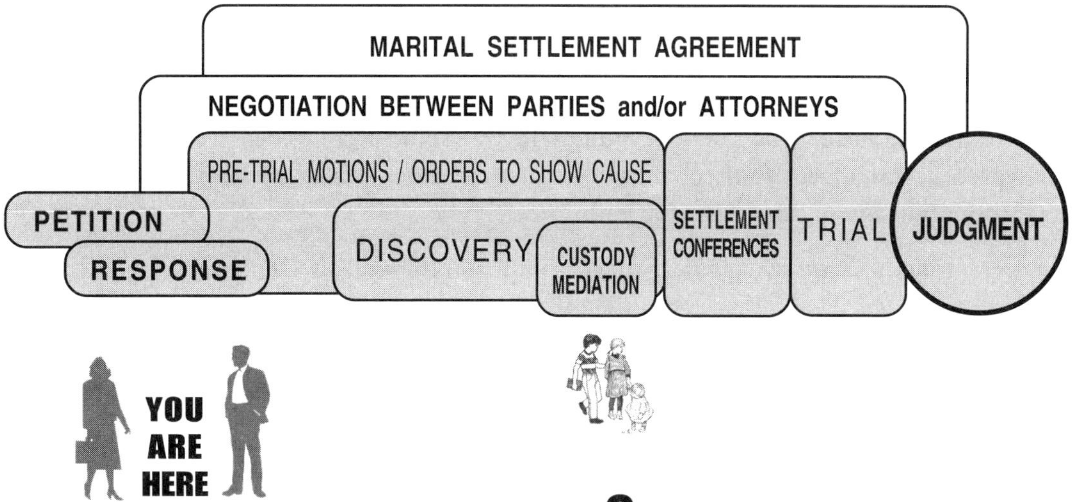

CHAPTER 8
HOW TO GET THE INFORMATION YOU NEED

Guess what will happen if you charge blindly into your own divorce without knowing how the law works, what the legal system is like, and the facts of your marital estate? If you want to play Russian roulette with your life or volunteer to be a victim, then okay, stumble on. Otherwise, prepare your case and prepare yourself. Sure, it takes some time and effort, but it is essential, it is worth it, and we show you how to do it:

- First, read about the legal system (chapter 2);
- Then, read the basics of divorce law (Part One of *How to Do Your Own Divorce*)

If you have already done this much, it's time to make sure you have the facts and documents you need—things you need to know *before* you can form goals and make decisions about what you have a right to, what you want, or negotiate a final settlement, or press your case toward a conclusion in court. In this chapter, we show you what information you need and how to get it without resort to legal action.

Use the worksheets on the companion CD to Book 1 to organize your case. They will make it very clear what information and documents you already have and what you need to get. These worksheets will save you a lot of time and money if you need to use an attorney (chapter 7).

A The information you need

Local rules. One of the first things you *must* do is to get a copy of the local rules of court for your county. State law governs the big picture, but every county has its own rules for little details about how cases are conducted in their courts. In some counties, the rules are out-of-date and not much relied upon, but unless you know this for a fact, you can't take the chance of ignoring them. These rules can change at any time and without notice, so be sure you are using the latest version. See chapter 9B for a discussion of where to find your county's local rules.

Facts and documents. You want to learn everything there is to know about your marital assets and debts, and about the income and expenses of both spouses. If you should ever decide to get legal assistance, any lawyer will need all this information, so you will save a lot of time and money if you collect and organize as much information as you can before you go in.

Start organizing the facts of your case, either by filling out the worksheets on our CD, or the financial forms in *How to Do Your Own Divorce*, chapters 14 and 16, where you will find the Schedule of Assets and Debts (4 pages) and the Income and Expense Declarations (4 pages). Using these forms is like having a checklist of everything you should think about. Make copies to work on and start filling them out. This will help you organize what you already know and what you need to find out.

Here's a partial list of important information and documents you will need:

- Federal and State tax returns for the last three years
- Bank records for three years: passbooks, statements, cancelled checks and checkbooks.
- Credit card statements for the past three years
- Real estate deeds and mortgage papers, lease or rental agreements
- Insurance papers, policies, statements
- Auto license numbers, registration, and insurance information
- Driver's license numbers for both you and your spouse
- Statements and records for stock accounts, mutual funds, pension plans
- Books and records for a private practice or self-employment business
- Books and records for any rental activities
- Birth certificates for you, your spouse, and the children
- Social Security numbers for you, your spouse, and the children
- Health insurance cards, copies of medical records
- Your passport and any immigration documents
- Family address books, calendars

Do you already have these things? If you already have access to the facts and documents of the marriage, then if your spouse doesn't, you have a great opportunity to reduce potential conflict and unnecessary expense. Simply make sure your spouse has open access to all records and information in your possession, but never loan or give away your last copy! Your openness will reduce anxiety and increase trust. No tricks now, because they usually backfire and, the way California law works, any effort you make to hide information will probably leave you vulnerable and cost you a lot.

The bare and basic minimum. You need a copy of your joint income tax returns for the last two or three years. If you own a home or other real property—homes, condos, raw land—you must get copies of all the deeds, purchase papers, and mortgage documents. You need copies of statements from banks and other financial institutions for the present and for a year before your spouse knew there would be a divorce (to make sure nothing tricky was done in anticipation of the divorce).

Some assets are hard to find. Deferred compensation (income your spouse received and put in a savings-type plan on which income tax is not paid) will not appear on tax returns, or in a bank account, and might not appear on pay stubs—for example, if the contributions are not being made currently. These records must be obtained from your spouse or from your spouse's employer through a subpoena. Tax-free income—for example, income from municipal bonds—will probably not appear on an income tax return. To locate an asset that produces tax-free income, including tax-free mutual funds, you probably have to get a copy of the checks used to buy the asset, a statement, or find other written evidence.

B Easy ways to get information

When you collect information, make two or three copies of everything. If you "borrowed" your spouse's records to copy, return originals that you don't personally need. One set goes to your lawyer (if you get one), one set is for your working files, and one set should be put in a very safe place: a safe-deposit box, storage locker, or some other secure place your spouse can't get into. Do not hide things in a house the two of you share or in the trunk of your car.

Ask your spouse. Of course, the simplest thing is to obtain copies of documents from your spouse—just ask nicely. But if you don't want your spouse to know you are collecting documents, or if your spouse is not cooperative, or if you think your spouse can't be trusted, you can obtain a surprising amount of information acting completely on your own.

Collect what you have access to right now. A great deal of information is available to you right now if you just go get it. You have a right to all information about your marital estate and you actually own records related to joint accounts or documents that have your name on them.

The home computer. If your spouse uses a computer and you have access to it, make sure you get a copy of all important or useful data on it. If you don't know how to do this safely, find a computer consultant to do it for you. Make duplicate copies of data and put one copy somewhere safe away from your home or office. If your spouse has put a password on the computer and you can't get into it, take the entire unit, or at least the computer box, and put it where your spouse can't get it. Then, file a motion asking the court to order your spouse to give you the password, or ask the court to order a disinterested third party to hold the computer, receive the password from your spouse, and copy all information from it before the computer goes back into your spouse's control. Use an Order to Show Cause instead of a motion if your spouse has an urgent need for the computer; for example, if the family business runs on it. Taking a computer is a hostile act which you must weigh against the possibility of losing whatever information might be on that computer that could be hidden from you later if things don't go well.

Tax returns. You have a legal right to a copy of any joint income tax return that was signed by both you and your spouse. It is best to have complete, certified copies of your returns and all amended returns, together with all schedules and attachments, not just the form 1040. You can get certified copies of federal returns from the IRS and state returns from the California Franchise Tax Board.

If you used a professional to prepare tax returns, you can ask for copies from recent years, but most do not keep W-2 forms and they cannot certify copies; however, your ex will probably admit to the copies of the returns, so it may not be absolutely necessary to get certified copies. Even if your tax preparer is a great friend of your spouse, he/she is obligated by law to give you a copy of any joint return with your name on it. When you first get your hands on copies, look at the first page of each return and see if it refers to any schedules or attachments. If it does, make sure you have the attachments. For example, if it shows a figure next to "Schedule E," make sure you actually have Schedule E. Ask whoever gave you the return for Schedule E and point out that the return shows that one exists. This is usually sufficient to get someone to cough up the schedule. You want *all* pages of each return.

You can get copies from the Internal Revenue Service of any forms you signed. Use IRS form 4506 and send it with a check for the amount indicated on the form. The IRS sometimes provides copies within a month, but sometimes they send you a letter that basically says, "We can't find your tax return; ask again in 60 days if you really want a copy." Therefore, you need to make your written request to the IRS long before you actually must have the copy in your possession as you may have to make more than one request to get a copy. Even if your name on your tax return was forged, you should be able to get a copy. In case of forgery, you could have to contact your representative in Congress for help in getting a copy, but this would be an extreme case.

If you want a copy of your California income tax return, contact the California Franchise Tax Board. As with the IRS, you must send a check to pay for the copies and for certification.

Locate properties on the Internet. The Internet is a great way to locate people, personal property (such as cars, boats, airplanes), and real estate. Such searches are becoming easier and more useful. This is, of course, of concern, because people are losing their privacy, but it also means that information is easier to come by than ever before. You can ask an attorney who has Lexis-Nexis software or a private investigator to do a search for you, or you can simply check out software and search on your own. With Lexis software, an attorney can look up your spouse's name and locate properties throughout California and in some other states. This method of locating property can be quite inexpensive, and if you have a spouse with hidden wealth, it may come to light by this method.

County Recorder for property deeds. You can get copies of deeds from the County Recorder of the county in which the property is located. You go to the County Recorder's office and look up your and your spouse's names in the "Grantor/Grantee Index." A grantor is the person who gave the deed; a grantee is the person who received the deed. If you buy a property, you are the grantee. On the deed of trust that secures a mortgage, you would be the grantor. The Grantor/Grantee Index gives you the information that you need to obtain a copy of the deed at the Recorder's Office.

Get bank statements. For joint accounts, you can get copies of statements from banks and other financial institutions by asking and paying a fee. Banks keep copies of all deposit slips, deposits, and photocopies of the front and back of all checks for about six years. The bank will not give you copies of statements for accounts that are only in the name of your spouse. Unless your spouse will give them to you voluntarily, you will have to subpoena them (see chapter 17C).

Review documents carefully to locate hidden assets. Once you have copies of tax returns and deeds, read them carefully, even if you have a lawyer. For example, Schedule B of the tax return lists interest income which might help you discover hidden bank accounts. A deed will show which title company recorded the deed, and you can contact the title company to obtain copies of the closing statement issued when you and your spouse bought the property. If you have significant property or complicated finances, these documents might not be sufficient. But without at least this much, you do not have enough information to make intelligent decisions in your divorce.

Personally review all records even if you have a lawyer. If your lawyer gets copies of your spouse's records, such as bank records, you should personally review those records. You might notice things that the lawyer cannot. For example, an accountant working for the wife's divorce lawyer reviewed the husband's business records and concluded that everything was in order. But, when the wife herself reviewed the records, she saw that the husband had his girlfriend, who did not work in the company, on the payroll. The accountant was good, but only the spouse had the vital information that made the difference.

C Rights and duties of a spouse

Under California law, married persons have a very high duty of trust to each other, called a "fiduciary" duty. A banker, for example, owes such a duty of trust to customers. More to the point, business partners owe each other a very high duty. Likewise, spouses are required by law to be open and honest with each other. When a divorce is filed, both spouses are required to give each other a complete accounting of everything they know about property, debts, income, obligations, and anything that might affect the marital estate, both now and in the near future. This is called Disclosure, and the forms used are called "Declarations of Disclosure." Be sure to read about disclosure in *How to Do Your Own Divorce,* chapter 14. Be sure to comply with the requirements of disclosure, as described there.

These fiduciary duties continue throughout the case. Even if your spouse is withholding information, you should comply with your own duty of full disclosure—not because you want to be nice, but because you don't want to lose your discovery request because you acted as badly as your spouse.

The one important lesson you should carry away is this: there are many penalties and sanctions against a spouse who hides information about the marital finances. Any misconduct in this area can come back to haunt you, possibly years in the future. So, if you want your divorce to be final and over forever, be sure you are completely open and honest with your spouse on financial matters.

The duty of one spouse to the other

Family Code §721(b) states:

> [I]n transactions between themselves, a husband and wife are subject to the general rules governing fiduciary relationships which control the actions of persons occupying confidential relations with each other. This confidential relationship imposes a duty of the highest good faith and fair dealing on each spouse, and neither shall take any unfair advantage of the other. This confidential relationship is a fiduciary relationship subject to the same rights and duties of nonmarital business partners, as provided in Sections 15019, 15020, 15021, and 15022 of the Corporations Code, including the following:
> (1) Providing each spouse access at all times to any books kept regarding a transaction for the purposes of inspection and copying.
> (2) Rendering upon request, true and full information of all things affecting any transaction which concerns the community property. Nothing in this section is intended to impose a duty for either spouse to keep detailed books and records of community property transactions.
> (3) Accounting to the spouse, and holding as a trustee, any benefit or profit derived from any transaction by one spouse without the consent of the other spouse which concerns the community property.

D How to respond to requests for information

The primary rule is to be open and honest. It's the law, it's the right thing to do, and failure to do so will come back to haunt you. If your spouse makes a reasonable request, you should respond fully. However, you do not have to produce what you do not have and cannot get with reasonable effort. If you are asked for bank statements, you should call your bank and request them. However, if you are asked for records and making a phone call, writing a letter, or filling out a form cannot get them, it is sufficient just to explain this. Finally, if the other side has made an unreasonable request (such as all cancelled checks during a ten-year marriage), you can send a reasonable amount, say the last three years of the marriage, unless there is some special reason why more documentation is necessary. If they insist, you can balance whether it is easier to give what they want or go to court to resist (chapter 14).

E Disclosure and discovery

There are two legal procedures for obtaining required information: Disclosure, which is *supposed* to be automatic, and Discovery, which requires you to initiate the procedure.

Disclosure

To get a divorce, both spouses are required by law to exchange Declarations of Disclosure listing all information about their property, debts, income and expenses. Disclosure is an extension of the fiduciary duty owed by spouses, discussed above and more completely in Book 1, *How to Do Your Own Divorce,* chapters 3.2, 3.3, and 6. The way you do disclosure is described in detail in *How to Do Your Own Divorce,* chapter 14. Be sure to read it and do it.

No agreement without disclosure. If your spouse has not served you with Preliminary and Final Declarations of Disclosure, do not negotiate a marital settlement without making the completion of them a term of the agreement and getting them both signed and served *before* you sign the agreement. See chapter 5B for discussion and guides for how to get this accomplished.

Discovery

Discovery is a formal legal procedure for getting information from your spouse, possibly under compulsion of law. How to do discovery is discussed in chapter 17. If you need information that you can't get by using the methods described in this chapter, or through disclosure, then you should go to chapter 17 and start discovery as soon as possible.

Part Three
Solving Problems In Court

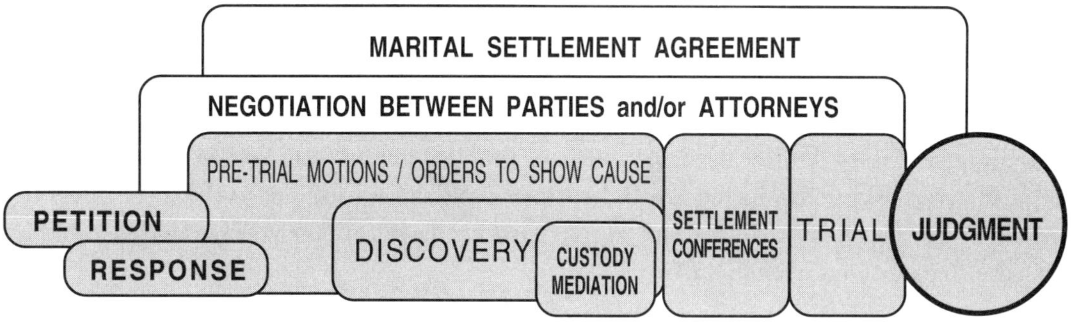

CHAPTER 9
BASICS –local rules, forms, paperwork

A. Petitioner or Respondent –who's who?
B. Learn local rules and conditions
C. Filling out forms
D. How to do typed pleadings
E. How to file papers
F. Keep a case calendar for deadlines
G. How to keep your papers in good order
H. How to serve documents on the other side

The following chapters are about action in the legal system, which involves a fair bit of paperwork. This chapter is about the basics of dealing with all that paper, whatever kind of legal action you might get involved with. Chapter 17 is about formal requests (demands) for information that you can use without going to court. If you can't get information you need from your spouse, you should start work there, too.

A Petitioner or Respondent –who's who?

The person who starts the divorce files a Petition and is called Petitioner. If the other spouse enters the case, that person files a Response and is called Respondent. In every respect their positions are equal—there is no advantage in being either Petitioner or Respondent. Either party can make motions, demand information, move toward trial, and negotiate. Parties keep their titles throughout the case, no matter who starts a particular legal action within the case. For example, if Respondent files a motion, that person is still called Respondent, even though in this instance he/she initiated the motion.

Read discussion for both sides. For any legal procedure, you could be the initiating or the responding party. We show you what to do on both sides, both for the person who is asking the court to do something and the person who is responding. Whichever side you are on, read the information for the other side, too, so you will understand what is coming.

Responders: We write each chapter as if we are talking to the initiating party, but the responding party does almost all of the same things. If (when) you are the responding party, you should read everything that is addressed to the initiating party, because most of it applies to you, too.

B Learn local rules and conditions

Every county has local rules that govern how the courts conduct family law business. If you go to court, you *must* study local rules. The local rules can be your friend. Many people representing themselves have succeeded in tying lawyers up in red tape when they took the time to learn the local rules. In some counties, the rules are out-of-date and not much relied upon, but unless you know this for a fact, you can't take the chance of ignoring them.

In 2000, Los Angeles had about ten pages of local family rules, San Francisco had sixteen pages, and Santa Clara County was tops at thirty-six pages, including local forms. For most counties the rules are short enough that you can actually read through them fairly quickly.

Contact your court clerk and ask where you can get the local rules. Every county posts addresses and phone numbers on a Web site; many post local rules there, too. You can find your county's Web site at **www.nolodivorce.com/links**. Or contact the circulation department of the *Daily Journal* newspaper at (415) 252-0500 or (213) 229-5412. Get these rules early and read them right away. Don't wait.

Observe your judge

Go to court well before your hearing, preferably before you write your motion or OSC, and watch some cases to see how much time you will be allowed and how the court handles things. You want to see how your judge handles cases, especially where parties are representing themselves. You'd like to figure out if the judge is a reader who prefers to get information from the papers, or a listener who likes to be told what the case is about. After you read the chapters on OSCs and motions, you will understand much more about what you are looking for when you go in to observe.

The way cases are assigned to judges will vary from one county to the next and local rules might or might not make this clear. More and more, courts are assigning cases to one judge to handle everything from beginning to end—an all-purpose judge. If your case is assigned to an all-purpose judge, that's the judge you should watch. But you might be in a county where you only find out who your judge will be when you file motion/OSC papers. After the clerk completes your papers, look on page one where it will indicate a department or room number for your hearing. Go find that courtroom. Whenever it is open, you can go in and observe. Ask the clerk when would be a good time to see that judge handling a "law and motion calendar." In other counties, cases are assigned out from a master calendar department to whatever judge happens to be free, so you have no way of guessing ahead of time. In this kind of county, wander around and watch several judges handle family law motions.

C Filling out forms

There are 66 legal documents in this book and CD and 45 that come with Book 1, *How to Do Your Own Divorce*—but relax, you don't use them all, just the ones needed for your case. Thirty-two of the documents in this book are printed Judicial Council forms, plus 34 typed pleadings that you prepare yourself using our templates. The printed forms in the back can be torn out and used, but they are also on the companion CD in a format that you can use on your computer. The typed pleadings are all on the CD in word processor files. It is *essential* that the Judicial Council forms you use be current. Forms are modified from time to time, and clerks are likely to reject any that are not current. If this book was printed more than six months before the print date on page 6, be sure to check **www.nolodivorce.com/alerts** to see if any of the forms in your copy of this book need to be updated.

When you fill out printed forms, read every word *very* carefully—there's a tremendous amount of useful information buried in there. Forms can be very dense, so it would be easy to overlook something important. If you're not doing them on a computer, make a blank copy and go over it in pencil before you type in information. In some places you have to choose words carefully to squeeze your information into the space provided. Use abbreviations if necessary.

The illustrations in this book assume that the user is Petitioner. If you are Respondent, you only have to change the name and address in the caption accordingly.

Captions

Most Judicial Council forms have long captions that are filled out like the illustration below, although you will find some variation among the various forms.

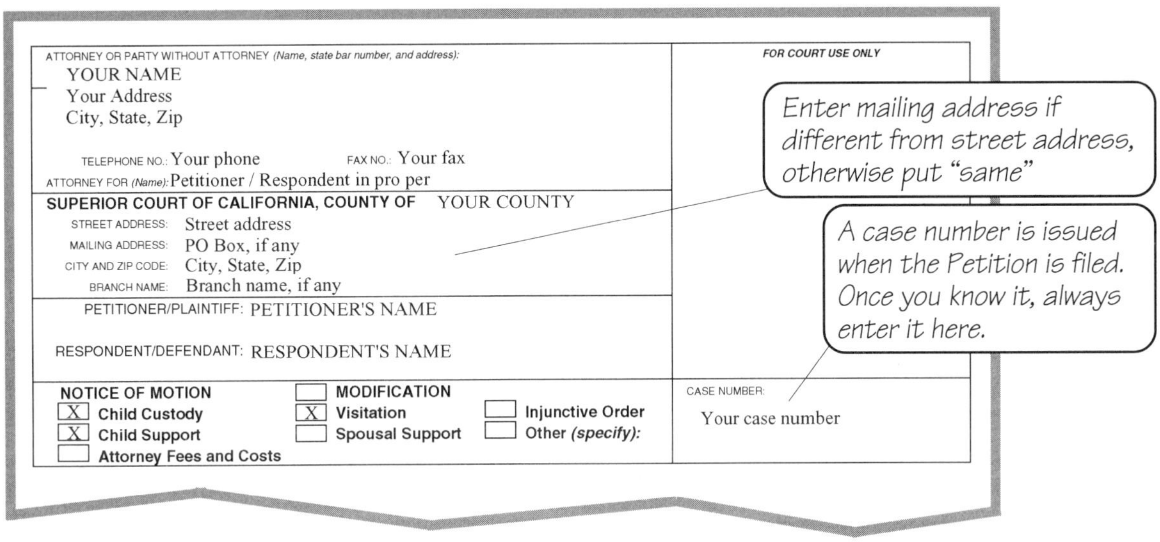
ATTORNEY OR PARTY WITHOUT ATTORNEY *(Name, state bar number, and address):*
YOUR NAME
Your Address
City, State, Zip

TELEPHONE NO.: Your phone FAX NO.: Your fax
ATTORNEY FOR *(Name):* Petitioner / Respondent in pro per
SUPERIOR COURT OF CALIFORNIA, COUNTY OF YOUR COUNTY
STREET ADDRESS: Street address
MAILING ADDRESS: PO Box, if any
CITY AND ZIP CODE: City, State, Zip
BRANCH NAME: Branch name, if any
PETITIONER/PLAINTIFF: PETITIONER'S NAME
RESPONDENT/DEFENDANT: RESPONDENT'S NAME
NOTICE OF MOTION [ ] MODIFICATION
[X] Child Custody [X] Visitation [ ] Injunctive Order
[X] Child Support [ ] Spousal Support [ ] Other *(specify):*
[ ] Attorney Fees and Costs
FOR COURT USE ONLY
CASE NUMBER:
Your case number

On second pages, and some other places, you will find a short caption like the one below. Enter the names as shown. Last name last is typically used, but last name first is okay, too, if you stay consistent.

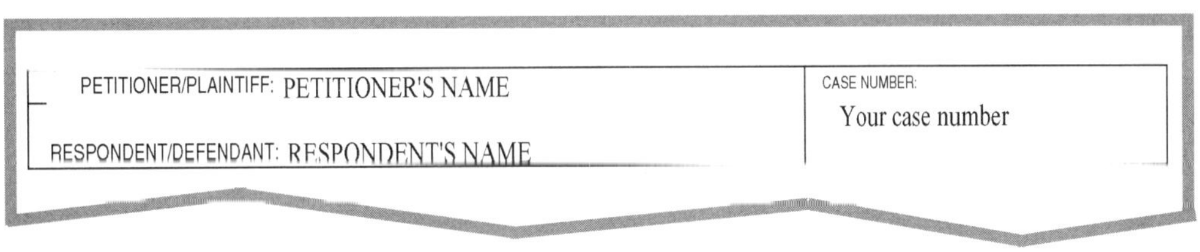
PETITIONER/PLAINTIFF: PETITIONER'S NAME
RESPONDENT/DEFENDANT: RESPONDENT'S NAME
CASE NUMBER:
Your case number

Attaching 'Exhibits' to forms –need tabs

In many forms, you will refer to a list, letter, or a document that proves something, like a receipt or photo, a letter, school records, etc. "See Exhibit C," you might say. All exhibits that are attached to one form—even if there is only one exhibit—are labeled (and referred to) as *Exhibit A, B, C,* etc., starting with A. On top of each exhibit, you put a paper divider page with a tab at the bottom marked with the letter of the exhibit, or even the whole name "Exhibit B." You can buy bottom-tabbed paper divider sheets at a stationery store.

Running out of room

If you have more information for any item than will fit in the space available, no problem; just type in "Continues on Attachment X," where X is the number of the item. Get an Additional Page form (see

How to Do Your Own Divorce, chapter 7), or a sheet of numbered legal paper (on the CD in the Pleadings folder), type a header that reads "CONTINUATION OF ITEM X," then type in all the information for that item. Follow all the rules about homemade documents in the next section. An attachment is not considered an exhibit.

All forms need page numbers

Always staple together multiple pages of any form or document with all of its attachments. For example, the Application and Declaration for a motion, with attachments, declarations, etc. Always number all the pages consecutively at the bottom right.

A few counties require certain papers to be filed on colored paper. Check your local rules and ask your clerk. For example:

- Income and Expense Declarations must be yellow in Contra Costa County and green in San Diego, Santa Barbara and Sonoma Counties
- First page of motion must be green in Contra Costa County
- Judgment must be pink in San Diego, San Joaquin and Santa Barbara Counties
- Response must be gold in San Diego County
- At-Issue Memorandum must be green in Santa Clara County

Number of copies of documents

The number of copies you make depends on what you're doing and who the document goes to. Local rules usually cover this. The original usually gets filed, though not always, then you need one copy for the other side, one for any other parties, such as a joined pension plan or an attorney assigned to children, one endorsed copy (stamped by the clerk) that you will keep, and an extra copy to leave at home in case the clerks lose your forms...yes, it happens.

D How to do typed pleadings

Typed pleadings—papers presented for filing with the court but *not* official printed forms—should be prepared on legal pleading paper with line numbers, as illustrated in many Figures in this book. Lines must be 1.5 or double spaced. More formatting details are in California Rules of Court 201.

- **Typers.** Use a black ribbon and pica-sized type on 8.5 x 11 legal pleading paper with 28 line numbers down the left margin. You can get this at a stationary store. First do drafts on plain paper until you get it right, then type it or use a copy machine to fit it onto the lined paper.
- **Computers.** If you are using the computer forms on our companion CD or word processing, use 8.5 x 11 good quality white paper, black ink, using 12 point Courier, Times, Helvetica, or Arial, double or 1.5 spaced. Our Word 6.0 pleadings have line numbers. If you must use the plain text versions, get legal pleading paper from a stationers and set your margins until your documents print in the right place, more or less matching the numbered lines. Our forms use Times, but the pleadings use Courier, which you may change to Times when you edit them.

They all need footers

Rule of Court 201(g) requires that pages of every document filed with the court must have a footer at the bottom, below the page number, separated from the text by a line, that states the document's title or a clear abbreviation of it. All Judicial Council forms have the footer already printed on them, but when you do your own homemade documents for filing, you must add footers. Clerks can reject papers that do not conform to this rule.

E How to file papers

Good subject, thoroughly discussed in Book 1, *How to Do Your Own Divorce,* chapter 7. Don't miss the tips on dealing with irritable clerks, kickbacks from the clerk's office, and filing for a Fee Waiver. But it bears repeating: never, never, never piss off a clerk, even if they deserve it. Never. There's nothing to be gained, and it can come back to haunt you some day.

F Keep a case calendar for deadlines

Missing deadlines could cause you to lose a motion, OSC, or even your whole case. It is very important to record and honor every deadline for every aspect of your case. You need to keep a calendar for your divorce to keep track of all deadlines, tasks, appointments, and court appearances. If you have a very organized personal calendar, you can use that, but it might be better if you keep a separate case calendar.

Whenever a court date is set, you need to immediately calendar all the tasks that you need to do to be fully prepared at least two days ahead for the hearing, or a week ahead for trial. Work backwards from the court date to set tasks and deadlines based on state law and local rules. For example, if you have a trial date, state law provides that discovery must be completed at least 30 days before trial. Mark the trial on the calendar, count back 30 days and note the deadline for discovery. Then count back an additional amount of days, such as 35, to do one last round of discovery. As you read about various legal procedures in this book, you will be told about relevant deadlines.

If deadlines fall on holidays or weekends. Under California Rule of Court 5.16, if a deadline falls on a weekend or on a court holiday, it is automatically postponed until the next court day. This affects when you must respond to discovery items (chapter 17), but it does *not* affect the date on which you need to serve moving or responding papers—those dates are not postponed by this rule. The best practice is to not wait until the last minute so you don't have to worry about missing the deadline.

G How to keep your papers in good order

It is not unusual for someone with a problem divorce to find themselves almost drowned in a shower of paperwork. If you are not very well organized, you could lose track of things and go under. You are not going to let this happen to you.

Unless your case is quite big, you can keep your papers in three file folders:

- Court papers (in chronological order)
- Letters (also in chronological order)
- Other (such as evidence, bank statement, pay stubs, etc.)

When you do discovery, you will keep each discovery request and all correspondence and other papers related to that particular request in a separate folder, as explained at the beginning of Chapter 17. If your case expands so much that these three files cannot hold it, use three notebooks with the same titles as the files. Get a three-hole punch and keep everything in the notebooks. For both ways of filing, always keep your papers stapled. Staples do not disqualify documents—they have no legal significance—but losing the last few pages of your motion will have significance. Keep things stapled.

As you are working on your papers, you will find that you have various sets made up of several documents and copies of those documents. Always arrange them in sets with the original set on top. When you go to court, clerks are expecting the original on top with two holes punched at the top, using a standard two-hole punch. They will probably have a hole punch you can use at the filing desk.

H How to serve documents on the other side

Whenever you initiate any legal action, you have to give notice to the other side. This is called service of process and is always done by having someone else give the other side a set of documents. Afterward, the person who served the papers must sign a Proof of Service which is then filed with the court. You *must* serve papers correctly *and* file the Proof of Service on time, or your legal action will almost certainly fail. Instructions and forms for how to serve papers in person and by mail, and how to prepare proofs of service, are found in Book 1, *How to Do Your Own Divorce*, chapter 12.

Who can serve papers?

You can't serve papers in your own case, but any friend or relative over 18 can do it, or you can hire a professional process server. Use someone mature and uninvolved; avoid anyone who is openly antagonistic to the other side, unless you have no other choice. Before your papers are filed, your server should be selected, instructed, and your Proof of Service should be ready to be completed and signed by the server.

Who gets served?

The Summons and Petition, subpoenas, and Orders to Show Cause are *always* served personally on the party *and* on the attorney of record, if any. All other papers are served on the attorney of record. The "attorney of record" is the person whose name appears on the caption of the most recent court documents that were served on you. You *must* use that name and address on all proofs of service, *exactly* as it appears in the caption. Just consulting an attorney does *not* make that attorney "of record" unless the attorney's name and address appear on court documents served on you. If your spouse's name appears on the most recent caption, your spouse is his/her own attorney of record.

An attorney who represents your spouse, and is of record, can be served by mail or in person. Personal service on an attorney is easier than on a non-attorney (Code of Civil Procedure 1011). The server can simply (1) go to the attorney's office any time it is open and hand an envelope bearing the attorney's name and containing the papers to a receptionist or any adult in charge, or (2) from 9 a.m. to 5 p.m., if nobody is there, leave the envelope in a conspicuous place in the office. Where the Proof of Personal Service form asks for the name of the person served, type in "Adult in charge at the office of Attorney (name)." If no one was present, type in "Attorney (name), papers left at address in conspicuous place."

Serve first, then file

Generally, the most convenient order of business is to have the papers served first, then filed with the court along with the Proof of Service. Remember, when serving by mail, you *must* include a copy of the Proof of Service with papers served so the recipient can know the date of mailing. An exception to this order of business would be where you have a pressing deadline for filing papers and you are doing personal service the same day (risky, but it happens). The server can't sign the Proof of Service until after the recipient is served, so go ahead and file your papers in court to make sure this happens on time—that's the most important thing—then file the Proof of Service as soon afterward as possible.

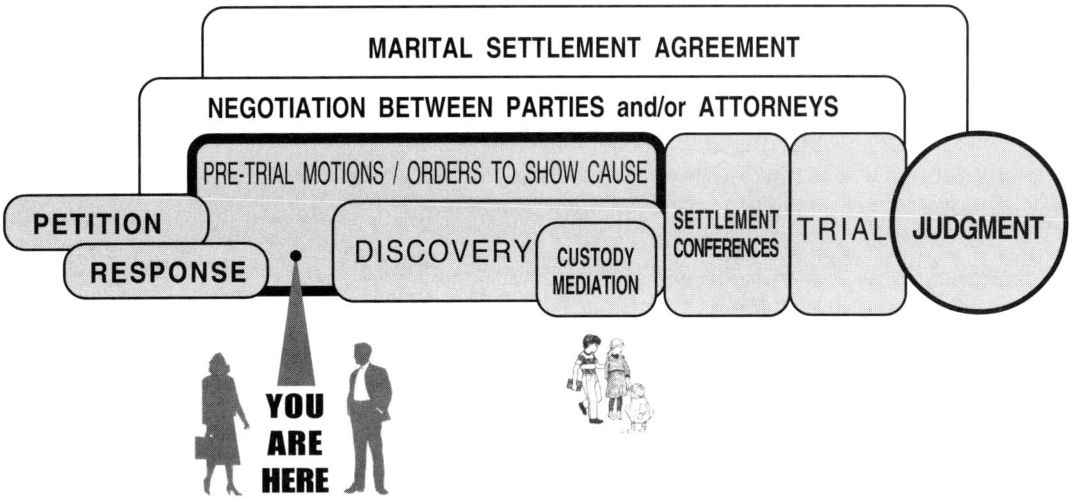

CHAPTER 10
WHEN TO USE AN OSC OR MOTION

Motions and Orders to Show Cause—this is where the action (and expense) is, the heart and guts of any court battle, gentle or harsh. Apart from procedures leading to trial, almost anything that gets done in court is done with a motion or Order to Show Cause (OSC). This is why this part of the book is so long and why it is so important for you to study it carefully. Very few cases end up in trial because most issues get resolved by motion or OSC. But which one should you use? That's what this chapter is about.

In many ways similar

Either a motion or OSC can raise almost any issue. You can use either one to request orders for custody and visitation, child and spousal support, attorney fees and costs, ordering a spouse to vacate the family home, stay-away orders, restraining orders, exclusive possession and use of specific community property (auto, tools, computer, etc.), property restraints and controls (don't transfer, mortgage or waste community assets), payment of bills (car payments, mortgage, credit cards), and almost anything else you can think of for which you can justify the issuance of specific court orders.

For either a motion or OSC, you:

- begin by filing forms and documents that request specific orders from the judge
- state facts that give you a right to the orders you are requesting
- have the clerk set the matter for a hearing
- serve copies of the documents on the other party
- wait to see if the other party responds

You might or might not try to negotiate a settlement before the hearing. In most counties, you present your case by way of documents and written statements from witnesses, trying to get the judge to see things your way and issue the orders you requested. The other side might also file documents and declarations in opposition. After the hearing, if you succeed, you get orders signed by the judge and, if your spouse was not present in court, have the orders personally served.

All orders are temporary. With only a few exceptions, orders obtained through motions or OSCs will be effective only until the Judgment. No order continues past the Judgment unless it is restated in the Judgment itself. However, the effect of your temporary orders can be permanent, because issues resolved this way usually become integrated into a negotiated settlement agreement or a Judgment.

So what's the difference?

Unlike a motion, a judge must sign your OSC, ordering your spouse to come to a hearing if he/she wants to oppose your request for orders. That's not as big a difference as it sounds, because a motion, though not signed by a judge works much the same way—show up or orders might be issued. With a motion, you do not need a judge's signature; all you have to do is file the document.

Emergency TROs. The *really* big difference is that when you file an OSC you can ask the judge to sign Temporary Restraining Orders (TROs) that will go into effect immediately and last until the hearing. When you file a motion, you can't get orders until after the hearing. To get a TRO, the emergency must be one recognized by law, which usually means a party or member of the party's household has a reasonable fear of imminent harm or loss of property unless orders are issued *right now!* Strangely, the law does not consider it an emergency if you have no money to live on and your spouse has money but won't give you any. You can make a motion or OSC for support, but you cannot get a TRO for support.

OSC is more complicated. Because you have to get a judge's signature first, the OSC is more complicated to do than a motion and takes more trips to the courthouse to get it going.

OSC with no TRO is very similar. When you are not asking for a TRO, the only difference between a motion and an OSC is the way you go about doing it—very little difference otherwise.

Which one to use?

Neither one. Never file a motion or OSC unless there is a sound strategic reason for doing so. Being served with notice of legal action is going to have a big and unsettling impact on your spouse, which will almost certainly drive the case deeper into conflict. Is this what you want right now? Is it worth it?

Many attorneys serve the other side with an OSC at the beginning of any divorce as a matter of routine, whether the case requires it or not. This should be discouraged. Make sure there is a clear purpose that *requires* a motion or OSC before you allow your attorney to file either one.

If your spouse is Respondent and has not filed a Response. The OSC should be used if your spouse has not yet filed a Response. You would not file a motion, because if he/she does not respond in time, you are going to take his/her default and get a Judgment. You would use an OSC only because you need emergency orders, whether or not a Response is filed.

Emergency TROs. The OSC is used when you need TROs, that is, when you have an emergency that can't wait for orders until a hearing on a motion can be heard.

OSC/TRO might be heard more quickly. This is only important in a county with a backlogged calendar where OSCs get heard a lot faster than motions. When you have a TRO, the OSC hearing must occur within 20–25 days (Family Code section 242). This is because a TRO can be issued without the other party being present, and in our system the right to have a hearing before orders are issued is very basic. In most counties, this difference in speed will not usually be very important as the court calendars are not clogged. However, in a few counties, such as Santa Clara, the hearing on a motion could well be months after filing, while the hearing of an OSC that has a TRO will occur within three weeks.

Early hearing by trickery. In counties where OSCs are heard much more quickly than motions, lawyers sometimes use a sham TRO to get an early date on the court's calendar. For example, a lawyer's client wants support in a hurry, but support is not considered a legal emergency to justify an OSC/TRO. However, if someone does have technically valid claim for a TRO, a request for support can ride along, so the lawyer plays a trick and requests almost any TRO—say, an order to prevent the other party from disposing of marital property without written consent, which is automatically included with the Summons in every case—when what he/she really wants is a fast hearing on support. An experienced family law judge will catch this and deny the TRO, but others will just sign it.

Either one will work. Other than stated above, either a motion or OSC will do the job. So which?

What the professionals say

If a Response has been filed, and there is no legal emergency, and you don't have a valid legal emergency that requires a TRO, and your county can hear a motion in reasonable time, then it makes little difference whether you use a motion or an OSC. Very good attorneys disagree emphatically on this choice. Many excellent attorneys recommend that you always use an OSC for any purpose. Others prefer the motion unless there's a legal emergency. This could be a matter of local practice and preference, so ask a family law attorney or the Family Law Facilitator in your county. Either one will probably work just fine.

Advantages to filing an OSC/TRO

The OSC allows you to request immediate orders (TROs). If you get your TROs signed, your court hearing *must* occur within about three weeks, but this will only matter in courts with clogged calendars. Without the TRO, the OSC and motion are otherwise fairly equivalent, yet the OSC *feels* stronger because it is signed by a judge and orders the recipient to show up in court or face the requested orders.

Disadvantages to filing an OSC/TRO

In order to obtain a TRO before hearing, you must state very specific facts for the judge to show that you have a valid legal emergency and are entitled to the TRO. If your case actually might proceed by agreement, you can push it over the brink to hostility by things you might have to say in order to get your restraining order. For example, to kick your spouse out of the house, you cannot just say, "I'm afraid of this person, and they're emotionally unstable right now and make me nervous." You have to say that they have engaged in some form of "abuse," giving dates and saying just what happened. A copy of everything you write down has to be delivered to your spouse. If your spouse wasn't enraged before reading your papers, he/she might well be afterwards. On the other hand, if you really need the court's protection, you should go ahead with it.

Advantages to filing a motion

You can file the motion in a routine manner, and you don't have to obtain the judge's signature. Often obtaining the judge's signature will take only about a day, but it's simpler if you don't have to get it. On the other hand, if there is no TRO, clerks often stamp the judge's signature on the OSC, so in that situation an OSC might not take more time to file than a motion. But, in some counties, they are so overworked that occasionally you have to leave OSC papers for the judge to sign, and papers occasionally do get lost. It's rare, but it happens. If you can use a motion and thereby avoid letting your papers out of your control, that might be preferable.

Disadvantages to filing a motion

The main disadvantage is that, not being an emergency, the motion is going to be calendared for the court's next available date. Whether or not this is months or only days away will depend on whether you are in a county where the court has a crowded calendar.

Motions and OSCs both require a court hearing

Many people think that it is possible to present papers to the court and get an order. While you can get a TRO that way, the TRO can last only about 25 days before a hearing must be held. Unless you and your spouse agree (stipulate) to court orders as a way to settle the motion or OSC, you cannot get orders without going to a hearing.

Read all about it

First, read chapter 16—study the Order form and all the printed order attachments to get clear about the kinds of orders that are covered on printed order forms. If you need something different, you can ask for it but you will have to compose your own order language. Then, go on to read about how to do motions and OSCs in chapters 11 and 12, and how to do a hearing in chapter 15.

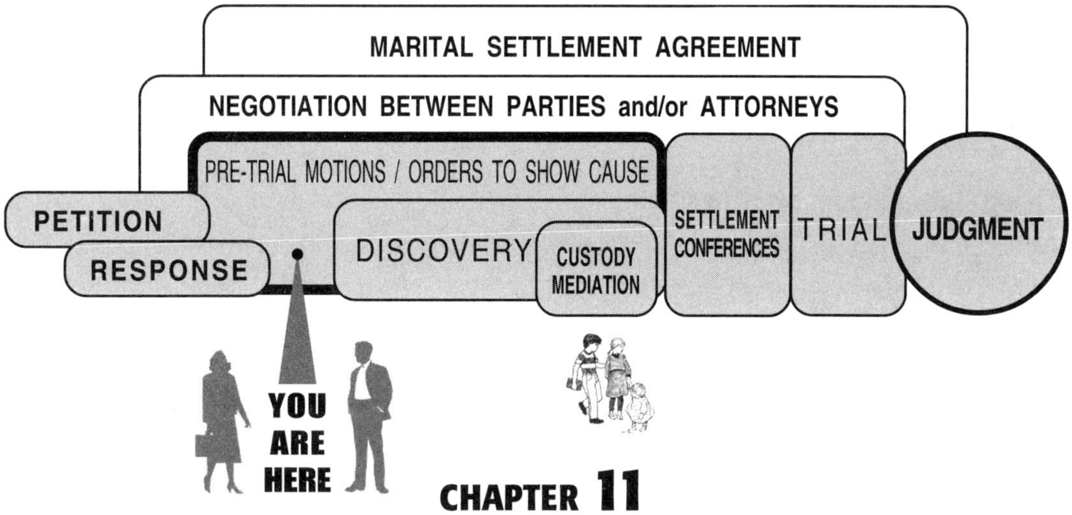

CHAPTER 11
HOW TO PREPARE FOR AN OSC OR MOTION

A. Check local rules and practices
B. Timing is everything
C. Plan how you will serve papers
D. Is oral testimony allowed?
E. Build your case
F. How to write a declaration and authenticate documents
G. Oops, I goofed –relief from error
H. Stipulate if you can agree
I. Child and spousal support preparation

Don't just rush out and start doing forms. First, read chapter 16 to get clear about the orders you can request. Next, read this chapter about deadlines you must meet and how to build your case. Yes, you can definitely file a motion or an OSC by yourself—many people have done it, even without this guide, more or less well—but as you will see in these chapters, it takes clear thinking and an ability to concentrate, study and think. This is a complex, technical area where rules vary somewhat from county to county or judge to judge. We will show you how to get over these hurdles, but we also tell you this: if you can afford it, get help from a good family law specialist attorney. As discussed in chapter 7, it would be better to find one who does more mediation than litigation, in the hope that he/she will be well intentioned, oriented toward problem solving, and trained to communicate. You will save a lot of money if you study this book before you go in, so you can organize your issues and questions, prepare the basic facts of your case in a typed brief, and state your plan and goals clearly.

A Check local rules and practices

Before you start paperwork for a motion or OSC, look for local rules in your county that apply to family law cases. We discuss where to find them in chapter 9B. Local rules might state things you need to know, but it is possible that there are also local practices that must be learned by asking the clerks, observing the court, or asking a local family law attorney. In particular, you need to find out:

- How motions are scheduled for hearing (calendaring)
- Local deadlines related to motions or OSCs
- If parenting programs are required where custody is an issue

- If any forms need to be filed on colored paper
- The filing fee for motions and OSCs (ask court clerk)
- Any forms or information the court wants that are not required by state law

Calendaring -how motions are scheduled

Calendaring refers to how the clerk schedules hearings on the court's calendar. In some, counties, judges might take certain types of cases only on certain days, or shorter matters (called "short cause" cases) might be heard on different days than longer ones ("long cause" cases). Find out how your county organizes its calendar—look in your local rules and discuss it with the calendar clerk. When you bring your papers to court for filing, the clerk will see what kind of case it is and will set it on the right day, but you need to know how things work ahead of time so you can allow for how calendaring might affect your deadlines.

Mandatory custody mediation

If child custody or visitation is an issue in your OSC or motion, you *must* include an order referring the case to Family Services for mediation (see chapter 20). You need to check your local rules or ask the clerks the name, address and phone number of the agency that does this in your county.

Memorandum of Points and Authorities

A Memorandum of Points and Authorities (P&As) is a brief statement to the court, setting forth the statutes and cases showing that you have a right to the orders you requested. In civil practice, Rules of Court 312(a)(3) requires P&As with every motion, but in family law cases Rule 5.118 states that no P&As need be filed unless required by the court, so you are off the hook—sort of. P&As become more important when the orders requested are out of the ordinary or if you get a judge who is not familiar with family law. An example of P&As is shown in Figure 12.5, but the truth is that P&As are very technical and beyond the scope of this book. Check local rules and practices to see if and when P&As are necessary. If you need P&As in your case, you had better get an attorney to help you do them.

B Timing is everything

Deadlines

Knowing the deadlines for serving documents is essential to success—miss a deadline and you lose, or at least you have to start over. Deadline details for OSCs and motions will be covered in their respective chapters, but the general rule is that papers must be served *at least* 21 days before the hearing unless you get an order shortening time (see below). This applies to personal service. If you serve papers by mail—which you can do when your spouse has joined the case by filing a Petition or Response—your deadline for serving papers increases as follows: you must add 5 more days for mail inside California, 10 days for mail to the rest of the U.S., and 20 days for mail outside the U.S. So, if you are pressed for time, or if the other party has not filed a Petition or Response, papers should be served personally.

Order Shortening Time (OST)

This is a court order giving you permission to reduce the number of days' notice you give to your spouse and the number of days before the hearing that your spouse has to respond. Because orders shortening time are requested so often, it is included as a standard item on OSC and Notice of Motion forms. Under ordinary circumstances, you would ask for permission to serve your spouse 5 days before the hearing and have any response from your spouse due 2 days before. However, in a real emergency, or where you have reason to fear what might happen when your spouse is served, you can reduce time to 2 days for service and 1 day for the response.

State facts. When you request an order shortening time, you must state facts that justify your request. In any domestic violence OSC based on facts that look valid to the judge, you are likely to receive an order shortening time. As to other OSCs, the judge may or may not accept that your spouse is going to be difficult to serve. If the judge does not grant your order shortening time, when you get the papers back, look at the hearing date and see whether you can still get your spouse served 21 days before the hearing. If it is already too late when you receive the papers, you will have to resubmit them to the court and add a Declaration page (Figure 12.4) explaining the problem to the judge and again explaining why you need an order shortening time.

In domestic violence cases, fear of reaction to service will almost always justify an OST. Here are some examples of non-DV matters that could also get you one:

- An OSC or motion needs to be heard before a hearing or trial that is already set in the near future, so it can only be heard first if an OST is granted. For example, a motion to compel discovery to get something for the hearing or trial, and the motion won't be heard in time without an OST.
- You need to have a motion heard on the same calendar with another that you served earlier.
- Need to get appraiser into house before a scheduled hearing on the house.
- Escrow is closing and you need to get funds disbursed by court order very quickly or you will lose the sale of the house.

C Plan how you will serve papers

First, read chapter 9H about who can serve papers for you and who gets served. Instructions and forms for how to serve papers in person and by mail, and how to do Proofs of Service, are found in Book 1, *How to Do Your Own Divorce*, chapter 12. This section is specific to OSCs and motions.

Plan service before you file

Before you file your OSC or motion, you need to have a plan for serving papers immediately, if necessary. You need to know ahead of time who gets served, who will do the serving, how they must do it, and where to find the person being served right away if papers are served personally. You do not want to file your papers and suddenly realize that there is too little time to get them served. This can happen with motions and almost always happens when filing an OSC. If you don't make it on time, you have to start over again, so it is important to have plans made and ready to go.

Witnesses

Will you need to subpoena witnesses or records to your hearing? If so, then before you file your motion or OSC, you must have subpoenas ready to go the instant you learn your court date, just in case it comes sooner than you think. See chapter 15, section B.

D Is oral testimony allowed?

Rule of Court 323(a) States, "Evidence received at a law and motion hearing must be by declaration, affidavit, or request for judicial notice without testimony or cross-examination, except as allowed in the court's discretion for good cause shown." What is "good cause" will vary from judge to judge.

When you might have good cause for oral testimony

- There might be a witness who knows something important but will not sign a declaration, although they would tell the truth if subpoenaed. For example, in a custody case a teacher might be unwilling to sign a declaration but would probably answer truthfully in court.
- A witness who made a written statement for the other side happens to be someone who would never be believed in person, or someone who you could undermine if you could ask them some tough questions. Or, you might want to ask questions of an "expert" witness who made a declaration that you think has holes in it or is not backed up by facts.

In some situations, you might not be able to present your case fully or fairly without oral testimony. If the matter is very important and you feel strongly about the need, file a notice to request oral testimony (see below) supported by strong declarations to support your need.

What to do

In every case, prepare the strongest paper case you can and act as if everything will be decided only on documentary evidence. Prepare declarations with care and dig up every document, witness declaration, or tangible evidence you can find that will reinforce your position. If necessary, request permission to present oral testimony, but prepare as if your request will be denied, yet be ready to go the other way if you get what you asked for. If oral testimony is allowed, it is up to you to make sure the witnesses you want to examine or cross-examine show up for the hearing. Learn how to subpoena a witness in chapter 15.

You have to request oral testimony if you want it

If you need oral testimony, you *must* file and serve a written request to be allowed this *privilege* that used to be a birthright, even if the only witness is you. If you do not file and serve this statement, the hearing judge can refuse to let you present any witnesses at all. Rule of Court 323(b) states,

> "A party seeking permission to introduce oral evidence, except for oral evidence in rebuttal to oral evidence presented by the other party, must file, no later than three court days before the hearing, a written statement stating the nature and extent of the evidence proposed to be introduced and a reasonable time estimate for the hearing."

How to do a Notice of Request for Oral Testimony

This typed pleading is prepared as shown in Figure 11.1. The sample requests one witness; if you have more, merely repeat the same information for each witness. It should be served on the other side and filed with a Proof of Service as soon as possible after you decide you need oral testimony. If you know this from the beginning, you can do the Request and serve it along with your OSC or motion. The rule requires you to file it no later than 3 court days before the hearing, but if you file it less than 5 court days before the hearing, you must serve the other party so that they get it at least 2 days before the hearing. So, you could file it 3 court days before the hearing and personally serve a copy on the other side 2 days before the hearing. Of course, it is better to do this earlier if possible.

Figure 11.1
REQUEST TO PRESENT ORAL TESTIMONY

YOUR NAME
Your Address
City, State, Zip
Your Phone

Petitioner in pro per

SUPERIOR COURT OF CALIFORNIA, COUNTY OF [County name]

In re the Marriage of	)	No. [Your case number]
	)	
Petitioner: YOUR NAME	)	NOTICE OF REQUEST TO
	)	PRESENT ORAL TESTIMONY
Respondent: SPOUSE NAME	)	
______________________________	)	

TO ALL PARTIES AND THEIR ATTORNEYS OF RECORD:

PLEASE TAKE NOTICE that at the hearing of the Order to Show Cause filed on [date], petitioner intends to present the following witnesses: [for each witness, give the following information]

Name Telephone number
Address, City, State Zip
Title (such as Ph.D., psychologist, appraiser, CPA, etc.)
A summary of the substance of the expected testimony is as follows: [summarize major points very briefly]

The reason that this testimony cannot be presented by declaration is that [state reason].

Time for the hearing will be __hours (or days, if you have a really complicated matter).

Dated:

____
YOUR NAME, Petitioner

1

Notice of Request to Present Oral Testimony

E Build your case

Before you start working on forms for a motion or OSC, you have to make sure you have a case that you can prove convincingly at a hearing. Go over chapters 12 and 13 to get an idea of the kinds of orders you can ask for and the kinds of statements you must make to justify the orders. Scour the Application and the Order forms; they have lots of information. Now think about how you are going to convince a judge, especially on the basis of written statements and documents, that your facts are correct and you deserve the orders. This is the important part. Thinking is hard, but this is where cases are won and lost. This is case-building.

Just the facts. Make a page for each issue and list all facts you can think of that you can put on the table. Each fact must be relevant and important toward proving your point or undermining your spouse's points. Also write down facts your spouse can present and what points he/she can make with them. For each fact, you *must* have either a document or the declaration of at least one witness (perhaps you) to support your claim, otherwise the judge might think you are unreliable—next case! If it looks like *your* facts don't beat *their* facts, negotiate the best deal you can and get out.

Documents. If any fact can be proved by a record or item, use it. However, *every* record or item must be attached to the declaration of someone who can state of their own knowledge what it is, where it came from, and that it is genuine and accurate. Often, this will be you, but there might be a record or item that requires the declaration of someone else. Let's say someone sent you a photo of your spouse asleep amid beer cans while supposedly taking care of your baby. The person who took the photo would have to state the time, place and circumstances.

Witnesses. You are a witness. Anyone can be a witness who *knows* something relevant and important about your case. This *must* be something they saw or heard, or your spouse told them something that undermines his/her case, or they have a document or thing that proves a point in your case. You need to have what they know in a thoughtful written declaration under oath; otherwise, you have to weigh your chances for getting their oral testimony before the court, which might not happen. Avoid using your children as witnesses unless unavoidable; it's bad for them and can reflect badly on you. Several statements by different witnesses, even on the same point, will show the judge that a variety of people in the community support you. It can make an impression. Add up all the written statements, add whatever documents you have, and see if you have something on each and every essential fact in your case.

Accusations. It is easy to just check a box to accuse your spouse of something, but if you can't prove your allegations with pretty good evidence, you will probably turn the judge against you and possibly get fined as well. You could damage your entire case. If you don't have it already, you need to get proof of anything you want to charge before you make the charge. This is especially true when charging child abuse or neglect. Warning! Do not make accusatory statements in your forms that you are not prepared to prove when you get to your hearing.

Degrees of proof. Your own declaration or testimony is evidence, but for important matters it would be better to have documents or statements of other witnesses to back up your version of the facts. You have to assume the other side is going to claim different facts, and you have to try to anticipate what they know or could come up with to strengthen their view of things.

The degree of proof you need varies, depending upon how intrusive the order will be against your spouse or how strongly it will impact children. If you ask the court to order your spouse not to hit or threaten you, you won't need much proof—perhaps just your own declaration. Likewise, an order prohibiting the transfer of community property would not burden your spouse much unless he/she shows some reason why it would. But, if you want your spouse kicked out of the house, or not to have visitation unless supervised, or change the current and established care pattern of the children, your proof has to be pretty good. If you go to a hearing and say, "She drinks when she's taking care of the children," and she says, "I never did, not once," and there is no objective evidence, how will the judge know what's true? Remember, the judge will probably not see witnesses in person. You need witness statements, arrest reports, or whatever else you can think of to support your allegations.

Case-building tips

Keep a diary and describe every incident, who was present, where the kids were, always noting the date and time of significant events.

Witnesses. Log their names, addresses, phone numbers, email, fax. Ask them to give you a statement under penalty of perjury on a Declaration form (section F below). If they won't do that, try for a signed letter that states, just before their dated signature: "The above facts are true under penalty of perjury under the laws of the State of California."

Medical records related to any injury caused by your spouse. You should get treatment even if it might not be absolutely necessary in order to build a record. Even if you only have a bruise, see a doctor and explain that you want the bruise documented. Be aware that medical people are required by law to report to the police any injuries that seem to have been caused by abuse or a deadly weapon.

Police reports. Call the police, make a report, and get a copy. Get copies of any past reports.

Photographs of property damage caused by your spouse or visible injury to yourself or others. Bruises, especially on dark-colored skin, may be hard to photograph. Try photographing from one side so the light of the flash doesn't bounce back and ruin your picture. Get the photos developed right away so you can retake them before the bruises disappear in case your photos don't come out.

Keep notes, letters, recorded phone messages where your spouse threatens you or apologizes. Don't tape over or erase the message; keep the tape. If it's not a tape, play the message onto a tape recorder and play it back to make sure it recorded right. Keep torn or bloody clothing, small broken things.

Receipts. Keep receipts for all medical expenses, attorney fees, costs, moving and rental expenses if you must move due to your spouse's bad behavior.

Financial records. If support is an issue, you will have to prove the income and debts of you and your spouse, what it costs you to live, and any special needs that you or your children have. You'll need evidence such as pay-stubs, W-2 forms, tax returns, etc. If necessary, consider using a subpoena to get payroll records (chapter 17).

F How to write a declaration and authenticate documents

In a very simple motion, you might be able to fit your entire statement into the small space provided at the end of the Application and Declaration form, but most often you will need to attach a typed declaration. A one page declaration is conveniently prepared on a Declaration form (Figure 12.4). Longer statements are more convenient on plain paper with a caption at the top as illustrated in Figure 12.7. Declarations should be double-spaced and all pages should be numbered as page *x* of *y*, where *x* is the page you are on and *y* is the total number of pages in the Declaration. If using a computer, use a 12 point font, either the traditional Courier (looks like a typewriter), Times, Helvetica or Arial. Our forms use Times to get the most in limited spaces. The pleadings use Courier, but you can change it to Times when you edit them, if you want your papers to all be consistent (not a legal requirement). As explained in chapter 9, every typed paper must have a "footer" on each page. For example, see Figure 12.7.

Often people, even lawyers, write as if the reader already knows or cares about the case. Don't do that. Your declaration should be completely clear to an uninterested stranger, which is exactly who the judge is. You need to work a basic understanding of your case into the declaration. Typically, you need to explain who you and your spouse are, what you do for a living, the length of the marriage, and the ages of your children. If you are seeking to modify an earlier order, you need to explain that and explain how things were and how they have changed. Even though you have a lot to explain, it is important to keep the declaration to the minimum length possible while still including all relevant facts. While this is your only divorce, and you might want to explain everything at length, the judge has too many cases and wants only the bare bones—the basic, essential facts without any elaboration or decoration. You need to strike a balance, where you include all the *necessary* facts and yet do not go on for page after page.

It is particularly bad to go on at great length if you do not use paragraphs and do not underline or bold anything. That makes the judge want to go to sleep instead of reading with interest and understanding. Start each new fact or thought as a new paragraph. In long declarations, separate facts into logical categories and use bold or underlined subject headers to help the reader follow the flow. When a declaration is finished, step back and try to look at it through the eyes of a stranger to see if it is completely clear.

Only state facts

In most counties, your motion or OSC will succeed or fail on the strength of the supporting declarations. So, let the facts speak for themselves—plain, undecorated facts. A fact is something that you or someone else personally observed. It does *not* include what anyone said (other than your spouse) or anyone's opinion. You don't want guessing about what your spouse felt or was thinking unless you are a mind reader, you can't know that. You *can* describe observable facts, such as his face was red, he was yelling, had his fists balled up and was swinging them, and he acted upset and angry.

Include only facts you can prove in court and that justify orders you are requesting, and make sure to state all relevant facts. For example, if you requested temporary possession of your own vehicle, don't just say, "This is my car." Explain that you routinely drive this automobile, that your spouse has another vehicle, that you have custody of the children and need to have a car, or whatever are the facts in your case.

When you are done with your declaration, go back and check every item listed in your Application form. Have you stated facts that would make the judge feel justified in granting each order you requested? If not, add the appropriate information.

The opening

Every declaration you write will start with:

I, the undersigned, declare as follows:

1. My name is ______________________________.
2. I am (petitioner herein / respondent herein / or state relationship to parties or case).
3. I have personal knowledge of every fact herein and could competently testify thereto if called as a witness at trial.

Numbering each separate factual item, go on to state all *relevant* facts known to the declarant. If this is your own declaration, what follows next should let the judge know immediately upon glancing at the beginning of your declaration what the motion and your declaration is about. You need what amounts to a headline in bold or underlined type near the beginning, then a couple of sentences that state what your motion requests and also calls the judge's attention to the most important fact(s). For example:

> 4. **Motion to Compel Vocational Examination.** This declaration is in support of my motion requesting that my spouse be compelled to submit to a vocational evaluation. My spouse has a college degree and works only part-time as a sales clerk.

This reduces the essence of the motion to two sentences. Now you can go on with the details.

Dates and locations

It is important to include a date and location for each fact or event described. The judge can't know how significant an event is without knowing when and where it occurred.

Order of facts

After the opening, it is usually best if the rest of your declaration is written in chronological order or reverse chronological order (with the most recent event immediately after your headline). If you are attempting to do an emergency kick-out request (getting your spouse out of the house) by means of an OSC claiming domestic violence, you need first to tell the judge about the most recent violence, then the worst violence, then the pattern and history of past violence. In this case, you go from most recent to older. If you are trying to file a motion to obtain an order for discovery, you will proceed in chronological order, covering, for example: when you made your initial discovery request and the history of any response and further demand(s) you might have made. If it has been a long time since the events you write about, you should explain why it is that you are now coming to court and why the delay does not show that the matter is not important.

Declarations by others

A good way to get people to make declarations to support your motion or OSC is to use the Declaration form (Figure 12.4). If you are in a county that will accept handwritten papers, it may be a good idea to have each witness write the declaration by hand if it can be made easy to read. If you give the judge a number of declarations by different people in different handwriting, the judge sees that you did not make the words up, the witnesses did. Also, the judge sees that there are members of the community that support you, and this does have an effect. If you do this, you should first fill out the caption of the Declaration form before you give it to the witness. If handwritten papers are not acceptable in your county, you will have to type the declaration for the witness, then get a signature. As much as possible, do it in the witness' own words.

Have the witness state his/her name, then explain who they are and how they know you and/or your spouse and/or children. They need to say something like, "I am _______________, a close neighbor of the Smith family, and I have known the parties to this lawsuit as well as their children for 10 years." This tells the judge how much weight to give to the person's statements. Then the witness should tell the judge whatever relevant facts he/she knows about your case.

Naturally, you would like witnesses to state facts that make you look good, but if they know something negative about your spouse (like they came to your house on the weekend when you were away and found your spouse passed out drunk and the 2 year-old standing there crying), they need to state the facts directly and plainly, without any opinion or emotional decoration. Let the simple facts speak for themselves. You don't want anyone to say what they think anyone felt, thought, or intended. Only what was observed.

Authentication of documents –attachments to declarations

You might have documents or other items that support your case; for example, medical records, pay-stubs, bank statements or photos. These can be essential to your case, but need to be introduced correctly.

Authentication. Every document or item in your case must be "authenticated" by attaching it to the declaration of someone (often you) who states of their own personal knowledge what it is, where it came from, and that is accurate. If the attachment is not the original, state that it is "a true and accurate copy," and bring the original to court unless it has been destroyed or is not available to you. If your request for oral testimony is granted, you could authenticate documents orally, but you should use declarations anyway because a witness might fail to show up or a judge might rush the case and not hear every witness. It is always best to get everything in the written record.

Private documents. There are certain documents that some courts do not want attached to your declarations, feeling they are best kept off the public record, such as sensitive records related to children. Check your local rules. For example, San Francisco rules state that medical, psychological, educational, or other reports about a child should not be attached to the motion but provided at the time of the hearing. If you want to use documents made private by local rule, you are in a bind. You resolve this by making an advance written request to present oral testimony about the documents (section D) or, alternatively, to present them separately to the judge at the time of the hearing. Again, check your local rules.

Identity information. There could be a privacy problem if you attach so much of your personal financial information that someone could steal your identity if they view a copy of your file in the public record, so black out social security numbers, charge card numbers, things like that. If you do this, be sure to take clean originals to the hearing to show the judge.

G Oops, I goofed –relief from error

Running a contested divorce is so complicated that it won't be a shock if somewhere in the process you miss a deadline or make an error or omission in your papers. Fortunately, the law provides the possibility of being excused from almost any error. Code of Civil Procedure section 473 says that the judge can relieve you from a "default" if your error was the result of "excusable neglect." Of course, you never want to find yourself in this position because there is no guarantee that the judge will find your error "excusable." Some judges don't like pro pers and won't cut you much slack.

Excusable neglect is something that to a judge would seem reasonable—not laziness, dumb carelessness, or an attempt to avoid the consequences of legal action. Lawyers make mistakes with calendars and deadlines all the time. The judge will also consider how much the other side will be disadvantaged if you are excused. Judges tend not to respond well to child-centered delays such as your child was sick so you had to take him/her to the doctor. They relate more to business reasons, such as your printer broke down and you could not print documents in a timely manner. Of course, this would only work if you act quickly to correct the error.

As soon as you discover that you missed a deadline or that there has been a mistake, contact your spouse or their attorney immediately and ask for permission to amend, file or serve papers a few days late. If you are making your request in writing, give a specific deadline for their reply. If they agree, you should immediately FAX a letter to them confirming that agreement and indicating that they should contact you immediately in writing if your understanding of the conversation is not correct.

They agree. If the other attorney doesn't object, you just proceed as if things are OK. For example, if you're filing your Responsive Declaration only 8 calendar days before the hearing, then it's late under the law; but generally, if the opponent doesn't object, neither will the court. Of course, a judge could refuse to consider a late pleading even if the opponent doesn't object, but in most situations if the opponent doesn't make an issue of a missed deadline, neither will the court. If the court *does* try to enforce the deadline, you could then make the Oops motion.

They don't agree. If, by the deadline you set, you don't get the consent of the other side to allow you to correct your mistake, file a motion as soon as possible, preferably the very next day. The statute provides six months within which to make the motion, but that is the absolute, outside limit. The court can say that you should have done the motion earlier even if you do it within the six-month limit. Don't wait. Once the problem comes to your attention, move to correct it.

How to do it

This motion is in every respect like motions described in chapter 12, except for what you put in the Notice of Motion and in the Application and Declaration. Fill them out as shown below, but otherwise run your motion exactly as described in chapters 12, 15, and 16.

Notice of Motion

In the caption, check the box "Other," and type: "CCP 473 – Motion for relief from mistake or error."

Application For Order and Supporting Declaration, item 9. Other relief:

1. **Missed a deadline, no orders against you.** All you want is permission to file documents after the missed deadline. At item 9, type in: "The court declare that I may respond to the (motion, OSC, written interrogatories) dated (date), by filing the attached (list the attached papers you want to file)."

2. **Missed a deadline, orders have issued.** This case is more serious because as a result of your missed deadline, the judge has already issued orders which you want the judge to set aside. This takes a stronger set of facts. At item 9, type in: "The court set aside the order filed on (date) and permit me to respond to (papers that were served on you) by filing the attached (list the attached papers you want to file)."

Application For Order and Supporting Declaration, item 10. Facts:

Explain the facts that constitute the mistake, surprise, or excusable neglect such as:

"The motion herein is set for hearing on (date), so my Responsive Declaration should have been served on (date 10 days before hearing). I miscalendared the date for my response, and in error thought that it was due on (date). When I discovered my error on (date), I immediately FAXed to Petitioner a request for permission to file my Responsive Declaration late, but have not yet had a reply. I have been diligent in responding to all other documents in this action for dissolution of marriage, and I request that the court permit me to respond to the motion and accept into the court file the attached proposed Responsive Declaration which was personally served on Petitioner on (date)." You must attach a copy of the document you propose to file/serve.

H Stipulate if you can agree

If a motion or OSC is filed, the person who filed it can dismiss it if no response has been filed. However, if a responsive declaration was filed asking for affirmative relief, the OSC or motion can only be dismissed by the written agreement of both parties. At any time up to and including the time for the hearing, the parties can reach an agreement on issues that were raised. A set of orders—called a stipulation—is drawn up, approved, signed by both parties, then presented for the judge's signature. A stipulation can also be recited orally in court instead of in writing, but afterwards one of you must prepare a written order to reflect the oral stipulation and get the judge's signature on it. How to prepare a stipulation is discussed in chapter 5.

I Child and spousal support preparation

If you are requesting child or spousal support, you should start preparing as far in advance as possible because this requires digging up records, thinking, figuring, and filling out detailed financial forms. First, read Book 1, *How to Do Your Own Divorce,* chapter 5, to get the basic rules on support and terms used. Now, go to the companion CD and print out copies of:

- ☐ Child Support Information and Order Attachment (FL-342) (Fig. 16.3)
- ☐ Non-guideline Child Support Findings Attachment (FL-342(A))
- ☐ Spousal or Family Support Order Attachment (FL-343) (Fig. 16.5)
- ☐ Income and Expense Declaration (FL-150) (in Book 1, chapter 16)

Study the order forms first and create the order you want the judge to make. Whatever facts are required in the order must first be presented to the court in your moving papers and proved with at least FL-150 and attached records such as pay stubs, tax returns, etc. Depending on your case, more might be required.

Computer calculation. When support has been requested, every judge wants to see a printout from support software, like CalSupport, that has been certified by the Judicial Council. Many counties require one. You can get CalSupport for $30 (see front of book), or get an attorney to run a calculation for you, or get one from the Family Law Facilitator for free, if you can get it in time. CalSupport and its help files are a very good place to learn about support and the terms you'll see on the support forms.

Prepare your motion or OSC papers

Go to chapter 12 to learn how to do your motion paperwork, or to chapter 13 for an OSC.

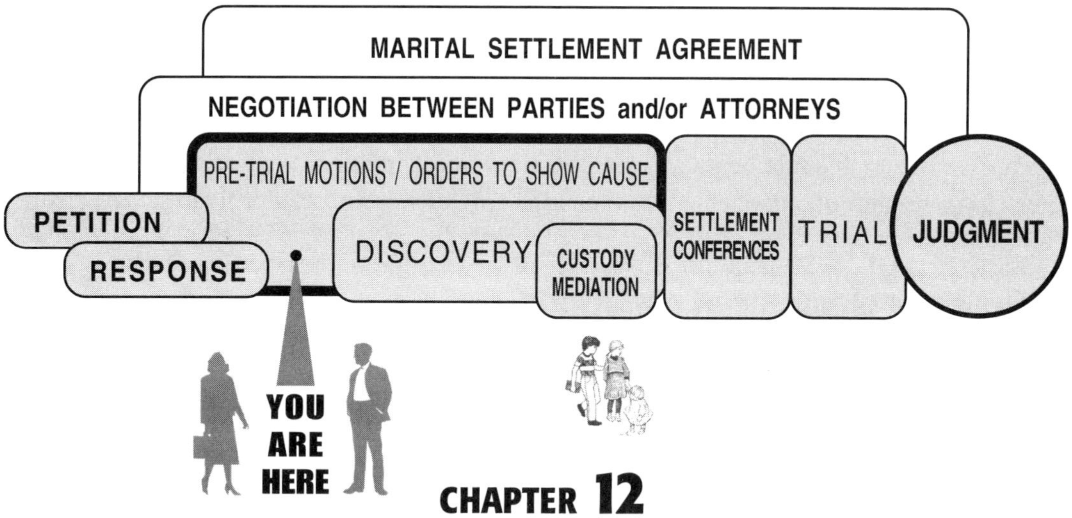

CHAPTER 12
HOW TO DO A MOTION

A. The basic elements of a motion
B. Application for Order and Supporting Declaration
C. How to do the Notice of Motion
D. How to file a motion
E. Service and the Proof of Service
F. If your spouse responds

Read chapter 11 before you start a motion

A motion is a request to the court requesting orders to relieve a specific problem in your case that can't wait until trial. Whether you need to set aside your default, postpone a hearing, obtain documents, try to force your spouse to undergo a drug test, or accomplish a broad range of other things, a motion is probably the tool you need. You can file a motion on any subject, although you do not want to trouble the court with bizarre or unimportant requests.

The motion forms have check-boxes that make it relatively simple to request orders for:

- child custody and visitation (read chapters 11(I) and 20 right away)
- money: child and spousal support, pay debts, attorney fees and costs
- exclusive use and possession of residence, auto, computer, etc.
- property restraints and protections (freeze assets)

You can also use the motion forms to bring any other issue to the court's attention. For example, you might need an appraisal of the family home, but your spouse lives there and won't let the appraiser in. Solution: file a motion requesting an order that, within a specified number of days after the hearing, your spouse must permit the appraiser access to all parts of the home without interference.

Combining issues in one motion

Many attorneys believe you should include all issues that need to be resolved at the time you file your motion, certainly all that appear in check-boxes on the face of the forms. The judge gets a better picture of the whole case, but the down side is that many courts allow only 15-30 minutes to handle a motion. If you run out of time, the judge will hear the most important issues first and reset the matter for another hearing, but the fear is that some issues will be hurried or lost in the rush. This is especially a problem if your case requires oral testimony (if allowed), because testimony takes time. For these reasons, it is often better to file separate motions for matters that are not closely related. For example, if you need to compel your spouse to give you documents and your spouse is also late in paying support, you would file two separate motions, so each could be given separate attention. If in doubt, you could ask the calendar or filing clerk (who might not answer) what is the judge's preference or ask a local family law attorney.

A The basic elements of a motion

All motions consist of the same basic documents, shown here in the order in which you will prepare them. When you go to file your motion, you'll put the Notice of Motion on top.

- ☐ 1. **Application for Order and Supporting Declaration (FL-310)**
  Attachments that might be used:
  - ☐ a. Child Custody and Visitation Attachment (FL-311) (if parenting is an issue) and Declaration Under Uniform Child Custody Jurisdiction Act (FL-105)
  - ☐ b. Income and Expense Declaration (FL-150) (if money requested) and guideline computer report if support requested (optional some counties)
  - ☐ c. Declarations of witnesses, if any (see chapter 11F)
  - ☐ d. Memorandum of Points and Authorities (optional, see chapter 11A)
  - ☐ e. Request for Oral Testimony (optional, see chapter 11D)
- ☐ 2. **Notice of Motion (FL-301)** (goes on top when you file)

B Application for Order and Supporting Declaration (FL-310)

This is where you tell the court and the other side what orders you want, along with a very concise statement of facts that support your requests. For convenience, we'll sometimes shorten the name of this form to "Application and Declaration." Fill it out as shown in Figure 12.1.

Items 1 to 7—Orders requested: The Application and Declaration form sets out a list of the most common orders requested so you only have to put Xs in boxes next to orders you are requesting. Read each item carefully and decide which are important to your case. Check the orders you want to request and fill out each item completely by marking additional boxes and adding required information. Next to each order is a box that says, "To be ordered pending the hearing." Do **not** check these boxes! They can't be used in a motion; these are only used when this form is attached to a "regular" OSC (chapter 13B).

Item 2. If you request child custody, you must also do visitation: check items 2, 2(b), and maybe 2(c). At 2(b), type in, "As specified in attached form FL-311." If your spouse might not go to required mediation, it would be better to use an OSC and have him/her ordered to do it. First, read chapter 20.

Items 3 and 4. If requesting child or spousal support, it is a very good idea to attach a computer printout from support software such as CalSupport (see front of book). Some counties require it in their local rules. If you do, make sure you refer to it in item 10.

Item 5. You can't ask for attorney fees to cover your own time, but you can ask to be reimbursed for any amount paid to an attorney for advice and assistance; for example, if you used Divorce Helpline.

Item 8. Order shortening time: If you want an order shortening time (chapter 11B), check this item and enter the number of days you want to serve papers before the hearing—5 days is a typical number, or 2 days if there's a real emergency. You must state facts to justify this request at item 10.

Figure 12.1
APPLICATION FOR ORDER AND SUPPORTING DECLARATION
Form FL-310 (page 1)

FL-310

PETITIONER/PLAINTIFF: PETITIONER'S NAME RESPONDENT/DEFENDANT: RESPONDENT'S NAME	CASE NUMBER: Your case number

(THIS IS NOT AN ORDER)

☑ Petitioner ☐ Respondent ☐ Claimant requests the following orders be made:

1. ☑ CHILD CUSTODY ☐ **To be ordered pending the hearing**
   a. Child *(name and age)*: Child 1; Child 2
   b. Request custody to *(name)*: YOUR NAME; YOUR NAME
   c. ☐ Modify existing order
   (1) filed on *(date)*:
   (2) ordering *(specify)*:

2. ☑ CHILD VISITATION ☐ **To be ordered pending the hearing**
   a. ☐ Reasonable
   b. ☑ Other *(specify)*: Alternate weekends and 3 wkeeks in summer
   c. ☑ Petitioner ☑ Respondent shall not remove the minor child or children of the parties
   (1) ☑ from the State of California (2) ☐ other *(specify)*:
   d. ☐ Modify existing order
   (1) filed on *(date)*:
   (2) ordering *(specify)*:

3. ☑ CHILD SUPPORT *(A* Wage and Earnings Assignment Order *will be issued.)*
   a. Child *(name and age)*: Child 1; Child 2
   b. Monthly amount *(if not by guideline)* $
   c. ☐ Modify existing order
   (1) filed on *(date)*:
   (2) ordering *(specify)*:

4. ☐ SPOUSAL SUPPORT *(A* Wage and Earnings Assignment Order *will be issued.)*
   a. ☐ Amount requested *(monthly)*: $
   b. ☐ Terminate existing order
   (1) filed on *(date)*:
   (2) ordering *(specify)*:
   c. ☐ Modify existing order
   (1) filed on *(date)*:
   (2) ordering *(specify)*:

5. ☐ ATTORNEY FEES AND COSTS a. ☐ Fees: $ b. ☐ Costs: $

6. ☐ PROPERTY RESTRAINT ☐ **To be ordered pending the hearing**
   a. The ☐ petitioner ☐ respondent ☐ claimant are restrained from transferring, encumbering, hypothecating, concealing, or in any way disposing of any property, real or personal, whether community, quasi-community, or separate, except in the usual course of business or for the necessities of life.
   ☐ and applicant will be notified at least five business days before any proposed extraordinary expenditures and an accounting of such will be made to the court.
   b. ☐ Both parties are restrained and enjoined from cashing, borrowing against, canceling, transferring, disposing of, or changing the beneficiaries of any insurance or other coverage including life, health, automobile, and disability held for the benefit of the parties or their minor children.
   c. ☐ Neither party shall incur any debts or liabilities for which the other may be held responsible, other than in the ordinary course of business or for the necessities of life.

NOTE: TO OBTAIN DOMESTIC VIOLENCE RESTRAINING ORDERS, YOU MUST USE THE FORMS *REQUEST FOR ORDER (DOMESTIC VIOLENCE PREVENTION)* (FORM DV-100) AND *TEMPORARY RESTRAINING ORDER (DOMESTIC VIOLENCE PREVENTION)* (FORM DV-110).

Form Adopted for Mandatory Use
Judicial Council of California
FL-310 [Rev. January 1, 2003]

APPLICATION FOR ORDER AND SUPPORTING DECLARATION

Page 1 of 2
Family Code, §§ 2045, 6224, 6226, 6320–6326, 6380–6383
www.courtinfo.ca.gov

Figure 12.2
APPLICATION FOR ORDER AND SUPPORTING DECLARATION
Form FL-310 (page 2)

PETITIONER/PLAINTIFF: PETITIONER'S NAME RESPONDENT/DEFENDANT: RESPONDENT'S NAME	CASE NUMBER: Your case number

7. [✔] PROPERTY CONTROL [ ] **To be ordered pending the hearing**
   a. [✔] Petitioner [ ] Respondent are given the exclusive temporary use, possession, and control of the following property we own or are buying *(specify)*:
   Residence at (address); 2001 Nissan Altima CA lic. no. 4XYZ987;
   Dell Inspiron 4500 serial no. 123456
   b. [✔] Petitioner [ ] Respondent are ordered to make the following payments on liens and encumbrances coming due while the order is in effect:

Debt	Amount of payment	Pay to
Mortgage	$1234	Acme Mortgage Co.
Car payments	$234	Jiffy Auto Loans

8. [✔] **I request** that time for service of the Order to Show Cause and accompanying papers be shortened so that they may be served no less than *(specify number)*: 5 days before the time set for the hearing. I need to have the order shortening time because of the facts specified in the attached declaration.

9. [ ] OTHER RELIEF *(specify)*:

10. [✔] FACTS IN SUPPORT of relief requested and change of circumstances for any modification are *(specify)*:
[✔] contained in the attached declaration.

If your own statement of facts in support of every order you requested will fit, enter it here.

Or, check the box above, as shown, and attach your declaration. If you have additional documents or declarations to attach, type in something like the following:

Also see attached Exhibits A, B, and C, and declarations of day-care operator John James and children's paternal grandmother Martha Smith.

I declare under penalty of perjury under the laws of the State of California that the foregoing is true and correct.

Date: Date signed

YOUR NAME in pro per ▶ ____________________

(TYPE OR PRINT NAME) (SIGNATURE OF APPLICANT)

FL-310 [Rev. January 1, 2003] **APPLICATION FOR ORDER AND SUPPORTING DECLARATION** Page 2 of 2

Item 9. Other Relief: Check this if you want an order that was not covered in the printed items. Type in the orders you want. If not enough room, enter "Contained in Attachment for Item 9." What you put here must be so clear that anyone can understand exactly what you want. If you are not sure your request is clear enough, show it to a friend who is not involved in your case and see if he/she can understand the order by reading it (not by you explaining it verbally). Don't just say, "Do you understand it?" Have your friend repeat back to you in their own words what they think you are asking for.

Item 10. Facts. This is where you state facts to justify each request you made above. This is your own declaration, or statement of facts. Do not write your declaration before you read chapter 11F. It might be possible for you to fit a simple declaration into the space provided, but if that's not enough room, simply check the second box at this item and attach your typed declaration. If you requested an order shortening time, don't forget to state facts to justify that order.

More facts. If you support your case with declarations of other witnesses or documents, such as receipts, medical records, photos, pay-stubs, or bank statements, you must make this clear at item 10. For example, type "See attached declarations of (Petitioner/Respondent), declarations of (full names of witnesses), and attached documents in support of this motion."

Authentication of documents. Read about attachments in chapter 11F where it explains how every document or item must be attached to the declaration of someone (often you) who states of their own knowledge what it is, where it came from, and that is accurate.

a. Child Custody and Visitation Attachment (FL-311)

This is your request for custody and visitation orders that will stay in effect until your divorce is concluded. Fill it out as shown in Figure 12.3 and the notes below. First, read Book 1, chapter 5. Also attach Declaration Under UCCJEA (see Book 1, How to Do Your Own Divorce, chapter 10, Figure 10.3).

Item 1(b), Visitation. Complete 1(b) to propose a schedule for visitation. Check 1(b)(1) if you want no visitation, which is extremely difficult to get, requiring convincing proof of danger to the child, but if you only want it until the hearing, maybe you can get it. Check 1(b)(2) if you want supervised visitation and have clear evidence that the child cannot safely be left alone with the other parent; for example, if he/she is an alcoholic or has threatened to take the child to another country. Check item 1(b)(3) for supervised exchanges at the beginning and end of visitation. Check 1(b)(4) to specify transportation arrangements. Finally, check 1(b)(5) if you want to restrict removal of the child from California or the United States, or from a particular city. Supervision can be by a friend, relative, or a professional. A professional costs $35 to $100 per hour, so even at the low end it can amount to more than many people can afford. Either party can request a mutually acceptable friend, but the parties would have to agree on this. If you can't locate or agree on someone, check for local supervised visitation programs. Contact Family Court Services or a local family attorney to get names and phone numbers. Find out what they charge and what services they provide for supervising visits or exchanges.

b. Income and Expense Declaration (FL-150)

A motion that asks for money must include a completed Income and Expense Declaration (see *How to Do Your Own Divorce,* chapter 16). **Local rules** might contain requirements in addition to state law, such as pay stubs and P&L statements. **Warning:** court files are public records, so required attachments such as pay stubs could put your social security number where someone could steal your identity. Laws have not yet dealt with this problem, but we assume courts will let you blank out any sensitive information that is not essential to the hearing. **Child or spousal support printout.** Read chapter 11(I). If you request support, every judge would like to see a printout from a computer program like CalSupport (see front of book) that has been certified by the Judicial Council and many counties require one. Get CalSupport for $30, or get an attorney to run a calculation for you, or get one from the Family Law Facilitator for free.

Figure 12.3
CHILD CUSTODY AND VISITATION ATTACHMENT
Form FL-311 (page 1)

Note: These orders are only an example—tailor to suit your own case. **Note:** When making a motion, do not check boxes next to orders that say "until the hearing." You can only do that when using this form with an OSC (chapter 13).

FL-311

PETITIONER: PETITIONER'S NAME
RESPONDENT: RESPONDENT'S NAME

CASE NUMBER: Your case number

CHILD CUSTODY AND VISITATION APPLICATION ATTACHMENT

☑ **to Petition or Application for Order** ☐ **To be ordered now and effective until the hearing.**

1. ☑ **CUSTODY**
I request custody orders as follows:

Child's name	Birth date	Legal custody to *(Person who makes decisions about health, education, etc.)*	Physical custody to *(Person who the child lives with.)*
Child one	birth date	Petitioner	Petitioner
Child two	birth date	Joint	Petitioner

2. ☑ **VISITATION**
I request visitation orders as follows:
a. ☐ Reasonable right of visitation to the party without physical custody. *(Not appropriate in cases involving domestic violence.)*
b. ☐ See the attached ________ page document dated: ____________.
c. ☐ The parties will go to mediation at:
d. ☐ No visitation.
e. ☑ Visitation for ☑ Father ☐ Mother will be:

Fill out to show the details of your proposed schedule

(i) ☐ **WEEKENDS** *(starting)*:
(The 1st weekend of the month is the 1st weekend with a Saturday.)
☐ 1st ☐ 2nd ☐ 3rd ☐ 4th ☐ 5th weekend of the month
from ________________ *(day of week)* at __________ *(time)* ☐ a.m. ☐ p.m.
to ________________ *(day of week)* at __________ *(time)* ☐ a.m. ☐ p.m.
☐ The parents to alternate the 5th weekends, with the ☐ Father ☐ Mother having the first 5th weekend.
☐ Father to have 5th weekends in ☐ odd ☐ even months.
☐ Mother to have 5th weekends in ☐ odd ☐ even months.

(ii) ☑ **ALTERNATE WEEKENDS** *(specify starting date)*: ______________
☑ Father ☐ Mother to have the children with him/her *(specify days and times)*:
from Friday *(day of week)* at 6:00 *(time)* ☐ a.m. ☑ p.m.
to Sunday *(day of week)* at 6:00 *(time)* ☐ a.m. ☑ p.m.

(iii) ☐ **WEEKDAYS** *(starting)*:
☐ Father ☐ Mother to have the children with him/her *(specify days and times)*:
from ________________ *(day of week)* at __________ *(time)* ☐ a.m. ☐ p.m.
to ________________ *(day of week)* at __________ *(time)* ☐ a.m. ☐ p.m.

(iv) ☐ **OTHER** *(specify days and times as well as any additional restrictions)*: ☐ See Attachment 2e.

Form Approved for Optional Use
Judicial Council of California
FL-311 [Rev. January 1, 2004]

CHILD CUSTODY AND VISITATION APPLICATION ATTACHMENT

Page 1 of 2
Family Code, § 6200 et seq.
www.courtinfo.ca.gov

Figure 12.3a

CHILD CUSTODY AND VISITATION ATTACHMENT

Form FL-311 (page 2)

PETITIONER: PETITIONER'S NAME RESPONDENT: RESPONDENT'S NAME	CASE NUMBER: Your case number

CHILD CUSTODY AND VISITATION APPLICATION ATTACHMENT

3. ☐ **SUPERVISED VISITATION**

I request that *(name):* have supervised visitation with the minor children according to the schedule marked above and that the visits be supervised by *(name):* , who is a

☐ professional ☐ nonprofessional supervisor. The supervisor's phone number is *(specify):*

I request that the costs for supervision be paid as follows: Mother: _______ %, Father: _______ %

Fill out to show the details of your proposed schedule

4. ☑ **TRANSPORTATION FOR VISITATION AND PLACE OF EXCHANGE**

a. ☑ Transportation *to* the visits will be provided by *(name):* Petitioner

b. ☑ Transportation *from* the visits will be provided by *(name):* Respondent

c. ☑ Drop-off/Pickup of the children will be at *(specify address):* 1234 5th Street, Moreno, CA

d. ☑ The children will only be driven by a licensed and insured driver. The car or truck must have legal child restraint devices.

e. ☑ During the exchanges, the parent driving the children will wait in the car and the other parent will wait in their home while the children go to the home.

f. ☐ Other *(specify):*

5. ☑ **TRAVEL WITH CHILDREN** ☑ Father ☐ Mother ☑ Other *(name):* Respondent's parents

must have written permission from the other parent or a court order to take the children outside of

a. ☑ the State of California

b. ☑ the following counties *(specify):* Moreno County

c. ☑ other places *(specify):*

Moreno, CA

6. ☐ **CHILD ABDUCTION PREVENTION ORDERS**

There is a risk that one of the parents will take the children out of California without the other parent's permissior the orders set out on form FL-312.

7. ☑ **CHILDREN'S HOLIDAY SCHEDULE**

I request the holiday and visitation schedule set out on attached ☑ form FL-341(C) ☐ Other.

8. ☐ **ADDITIONAL CUSTODY PROVISIONS**

I request the additional orders regarding custody set out on attached ☐ form FL-341(D) ☐ Other.

Take a close look at these additional forms and attach any that are useful to present the details of your requested arrangement.

9. ☐ **JOINT LEGAL CUSTODY PROVISIONS**

I am requesting joint legal custody and want the following additional orders set out on attached ☐ form FL-341(E) ☐ Other.

10. ☐ **OTHER**

I request the following additional orders *(specify):*

FL-311 [Rev. January 1, 2004] **CHILD CUSTODY AND VISITATION APPLICATION ATTACHMENT** Page 2 of 2

c. Declarations of witnesses (where your motion will be won or lost)

Prepare declarations as described in chapter 11F. Also read 11E. Figure 12.4 shows the Declaration form, best for one page declarations, and Figure 12.7 shows a typed declaration that is suitable for longer statements. Your case will be won or lost on the strength of declarations and attached documents. It is not unusual if you are the only declarant/witness, but of course it is more convincing if you can get the declarations of others stating facts that support your case. The facts in your declarations and documents must convince the judge that you have a right to the orders you requested and they must explain or overcome whatever facts the other side can put forward. You have to anticipate as best you can what those facts might be and counter them to begin with, for there is not always time to reply to their response.

d. Memorandum of Points and Authorities (P&As)

As discussed in chapter 11A, a Memorandum of Points and Authorities is not required in a divorce unless the judge requires one or unless your motion or OSC is unusual. Although we include an example in Figure 12.5, doing P&As is work for an experienced lawyer; so, if you need P&As, you'd best get help.

e. Request for Oral Testimony

Read chapter 11D. If you want to oral testimony, attach your request (Figure 11.1).

C How to do the Notice of Motion

You do not prepare this form until all your other documents (see list in section A) are completed and you are ready to file. When you do file your motion, place the Notice of Motion on top of your set of forms. The Notice of Motion form (Figure 12.6) gives the other party notice of basic things such as the subject of the motion and the time, date, and place of the hearing. The back of this form (not shown) is a typical proof of service by mail which you can use if you serve by mail.

Caption. In the heading, check a box or boxes to indicate what kind of orders your motion is requesting. Check "injunctive order" if you asked for any of the items 6–10 in the Application and Declaration. If you requested "Other Relief," then you would check the box "Other" and type in a very brief description of your request, such as "Access of appraiser to home." Because there is so little space available, you might have to abbreviate some words. You check the box "Modification" only if you are requesting an order that changes an existing order.

Item 1. Full name of the party to whom the motion is addressed, just as it appears in the caption.

Getting a hearing date. When you are ready to file your motion, call the clerk of the court to find out what date, time, and department should be typed on the Notice of Motion. **Short or long-cause calendar?** When you call the clerk, you should already know how your county calendars motions (see chapter 11A) so you can give the clerk the required information.

Call the other side first? Some counties require you to clear the date with the other side before filing the motion. If this is required in your county, you must call opposing counsel (or your spouse if not represented) to find an acceptable date. If they refuse to tell you what dates are okay and merely hassle you, use a declaration like the one in Figure 12.7 to inform the court of the problem and get a date without the cooperation of the other side. Once you are sure of your time, date and department, complete the Notice of Motion and file your motion papers with the court. You have to pay a filing fee for each motion. The amount varies from county to county from, say, $15 to $50.

Figure 12.4 DECLARATION

(of self or witness)

Form MC-030 and MC-031 (on back)

Note: This form has two sides. The side below is for statements that are *not* attached to other forms or pleadings, while the reverse side, with a simpler caption, is used only when the declaration is attached to another printed court form. They are both one-page declarations.

Note: For longer statements longer than one page, use a typed declaration like the one illustrated in Figure 12.7 and continue for as many pages as needed.

ATTORNEY OR PARTY WITHOUT ATTORNEY *(Name and Address)*: YOUR NAME, Your address, City, State, ZIp — TELEPHONE NO.: Your phone ATTORNEY FOR *(Name)*: Petitioner/Respondent in pro per	FOR COURT USE ONLY
NAME OF COURT: SUPERIOR COURT OF CALIFORNIA, YOUR COUNTY STREET ADDRESS: Street address MAILING ADDRESS: PO Box, if any CITY AND ZIP CODE: City, State, Zip BRANCH NAME: Branch name, if any	
PLAINTIFF/PETITIONER: PLAINTIFF'S NAME DEFENDANT/RESPONDENT: RESPONDENT'S NAME	
DECLARATION	CASE NUMBER: Your case number

I, the undersigned, state:

1. I am (Petitioner / Respondent / or state relationship to parties or case).

2. I have personal knowledge of every fact herein and could competently testify thereto if called as a witness at trial.

3. (continue stating facts, one number for each individual fact with date and location for each event)

I declare under penalty of perjury under the laws of the State of California that the foregoing is true and correct.

Date: Date signed

YOUR NAME
(TYPE OR PRINT NAME)

▶ ______________________
(SIGNATURE OF DECLARANT)

☐ Petitioner/Plaintiff ☐ Respondent/Defendant ☐ Attorney
☒ Other *(specify)*: witness

(See reverse for a form to be used if this declaration will be attached to another court form before filing)

Form Approved by the Judicial Council of California MC-030 [New January 1, 1987]

DECLARATION

Figure 12.5

MEMO OF POINTS AND AUTHORITIES

(Page 1)

YOUR NAME
Your Address
Your City, State, Zip
Your phone

Petitioner in pro per

SUPERIOR COURT OF CALIFORNIA, COUNTY OF [Your County]

In re the Marriage of)	No. [Your file no.]
Petitioner: YOUR NAME)	MEMORANDUM OF POINTS AND AUTHORITIES IN SUPPORT OF PETITIONER'S DISCOVERY MOTION
Respondent: SPOUSE NAME)	

THE PARTIES HAVE FIDUCIARY DUTIES TO SHARE INFORMATION.

Family Code section 2102 provides in part:

> From the date of separation to the date of the distribution of the community asset or liability in question, **each party is subject to the standards provided in Section 721, as to** all activities that affect the **property and support** rights of the other party, . . . (bold added)
>
> Family Code section 721 provides in part:
>
> . . . . [I]n transactions between themselves, a **husband and wife are subject to** the general rules governing **fiduciary relationships** which control the actions of persons occupying confidential relations with each other. This confidential relationship imposes a duty of the highest good faith and fair dealing on each spouse, and neither shall take any unfair advantage of the other. This confidential relationship is a fiduciary relationship subject to the **same rights and duties of nonmarital business partners, as provided in Sections 15019, 15020, 15021, and 15022 of the Corporations Code** . . . . (bold added)

It should be noted that the mentioned sections of the Corporations Code have been repealed and replaced by Corporations Code section 16100 and sections following it. However, it seems that the successor sections should be applied, and no modification of section 721 was intended by the legislature in enacting these new sections of the Corporation Code. Section 16403 of the Corporations Code provides in part that any partnership (which,

1

Memo of Points and Authorities in Support of Petitioner's Discovery Motion

Figure 12.5a

MEMO OF POINTS AND AUTHORITIES

(Page 2)

based on Family Code section 721, includes the marital partners):

> shall provide partners and their agents and attorneys **access to books and records** pertaining to the period during which they were partners. The right of access provides the opportunity to inspect and copy books and records during ordinary business hours. . . .
>
> (c) Each partner . . . shall furnish to a partner, . . . both of the following:
>
> (1) **Without demand, any information concerning the partnerships' business and affairs reasonably required for the proper exercise of the partner's rights and duties** under the partnership agreement or this chapter [of the law]; and
>
> (2) **On demand, any other information** concerning the partnership's business and affairs, except to the extent the demand or the information demanded is unreasonable or otherwise improper under the circumstances. (bold added)

The above statutes place on partners, including spouses, a heavy obligation to share information, sometimes even without a request being made. Certainly, if a formal discovery request is made, the burden to disclose information is very great.

In the present case petitioner served a Request to Produce on the Respondent, and it was ignored. Respondent has a duty to disclose the requested information, and the court should order Respondent to pay Petitioner sanctions as this motion would not have been necessary if Respondent had complied with the statutory fiduciary obligations.

Dated:

Respectfully submitted,

____
YOUR NAME, Petitioner

2

Memo of Points and Authorities in Support of Petitioner's Discovery Motion

D How to file a motion

Checklist of documents for a motion

- ☐ Notice of Motion
- ☐ Application and Declaration (with whatever attachment forms you used)
- ☐ Declarations by witnesses (if any)
- ☐ Memorandum of Points and Authorities (optional)
- ☐ Request for oral testimony and/or cross-examination (if you want oral testimony)
- ☐ Check or cash for filing fee (call clerk to ask the amount)

Arrange originals and copies in sets in the order above. Leave a copy set at home as backup. Put the original set on top of two copy sets and take them to the court clerk with a check for the motion filing fee. The originals need to have two holes punched in them at the top of the page. There will probably be a hole punch at the filing desk. The clerk should put on a date, stamp all copies and hand you your copies back, keeping the originals. Make sure that your copies have the hearing date on them. You then carry out your plan for serving the papers. When service has been completed, file the Proof of Service.

E Service and the Proof of Service

If you serve your motion by mail, use the Proof of Service by Mail that is on the back of the Notice of Motion form. However, in counties or situations where you must first file your motion and then serve it, that form will not be available to you, so you will use the Proof of Service by Mail found in Book 1, *How to Do Your Own Divorce,* chapter 13. If you serve the motion personally, use the Proof of Personal Service form found in the same chapter. **Add phone numbers.** The forms do not have a blank for your server's phone number. You are encouraged to add the phone number along with his/her name and address even though there is no blank. If you are in a hostile divorce, you never know what obscure rule of court might end up getting applied in your case.

Deadlines

If a motion is served personally, it must be given to the other party or his/her attorney of record at least 21 calendar days before the hearing. If served by mail, to this 21 day deadline you must add:

- 5 days if mailed within California = 26 days before the hearing
- 10 days if mailed to another state in the U.S. = 31 days before the hearing
- 20 days if mailed outside the U.S. = 41 days before the hearing

You count all days, including holidays and weekends, but you do *not* count both the day of mailing (or hand delivery) and the day of the hearing; just one of them is counted. It is best to give yourself extra days if you can, just to be sure you did not miscount.

Order shortening time. If time to serve was shortened by an order (chapter 11B), then of course you would serve your spouse personally the number of days indicated before the hearing, and for service by mail you would add the number of extra days indicated above.

Serve the motion package

After the motion is filed and you have a hearing date, have someone serve a copy of the filed papers on the other side. If your spouse has filed a Petition or Response, you can serve the papers by mail. Service *must* be completed within the deadline period detailed above. If you are pressed for time, or if the other party

Figure 12.6

NOTICE OF MOTION

Form FL-301 (Page 1)

FL-301

ATTORNEY OR PARTY WITHOUT ATTORNEY *(Name, state bar number, and address):*
YOUR NAME
Your Address
City, State, Zip

TELEPHONE NO.: Your phone FAX NO.: Your fax
ATTORNEY FOR *(Name):* Petitioner / Respondent in pro per

FOR COURT USE ONLY

SUPERIOR COURT OF CALIFORNIA, COUNTY OF YOUR COUNTY
STREET ADDRESS: Street address
MAILING ADDRESS: PO Box, if any
CITY AND ZIP CODE: City, State, Zip
BRANCH NAME: Branch name, if any

PETITIONER/PLAINTIFF: PETITIONER'S NAME

RESPONDENT/DEFENDANT: RESPONDENT'S NAME

Check boxes to indicate what kind of orders you are requesting.

NOTICE OF MOTION
[X] **Child Custody**
[X] **Child Support**
[ ] **Attorney Fees and Costs**
[ ] **MODIFICATION**
[X] **Visitation**
[ ] **Spousal Support**
[ ] **Injunctive Order**
[ ] **Other *(specify):***

CASE NUMBER:
Your case number

1. TO *(name):* SPOUSE NAME
2. A hearing on this motion for the relief requested in the attached application will be held as follows:
   a. Date: Hearing date Time: Hearing time [X] Dept.: Dept. number [X] Rm.: Room no.
   b. Address of court [X] same as noted above [ ] other *(specify):*
3. Supporting attachments:
   a. Completed *Application for Order and Supporting Declaration* (form FL-310) and a **blank** *Responsive Declaration* (form FL-320)
   b. [X] Completed *Income and Expense Declaration* (form FL-150) and a **blank** *Income and Expense Declaration*
   c. [ ] Completed *Financial Statement (Simplified)* (form FL-155) and a **blank** *Financial Statement (Simplified)*
   d. [ ] Completed *Property Declaratio*[n] and a **blank** *Property Declara*[tion]
   e. [ ] Points and authorities
   f. [X] Other *(specify):*
      Computer support calculatio[n]
      Declaration of Joe Smith

Check boxes to indicate all attached documents

Date: Date signed

YOUR NAME
(TYPE OR PRINT NAME) ▶ (SIGNATURE)

ORDER

4. [X] Time for [X] service [X] hearing is shortened. Service must be on or before *(date):* date
5. Any responsive declaration must be served on or before *(date):* date
6. *If child custody or visitation is an issue in this proceeding, Family Code section 3170 requires mediation before or concurrently with the hearing listed above.* The parties are ordered to attend orientation and mandatory custody services as follows:

Fill in this section if you are requesting an order shortening time.

Date:
JUDICIAL OFFICER

NOTICE: If you have children from this relationship, the court is required to order payment of child supp[ort based on] **the income of both parents. The amount of child support can be large. It normally continues until the child is 18. You should supply the court with information about your finances. Otherwise, the child support order will be based on the information supplied by the other parent.**
You do not have to pay any fee to file responsive declarations in response to this *Notice of Motion* (including a completed *Income and Expense Declaration* (form FL-150) or *Financial Statement (Simplified)* (form FL-155) that will show your finances). In the absence of an order shortening time, the original of the responsive declaration must be filed with the court and a copy served on the other party at least ten calendar days before the hearing date.

Page 1 of 2

Form Adopted for Mandatory Use
Judicial Council of California
FL-301 [Rev. January 1, 2003]

NOTICE OF MOTION

Government Code, § 26826
www.courtinfo.ca.gov

has not filed a Petition or Response, papers must be served personally, as explained in detail in Book 1, *How to Do Your Own Divorce,* chapter 12.

Motions before judgment are always served on the "attorney of record" (see chapter 9H). The name and address of the person you serve will show on the caption of the latest court documents that have been filed by your spouse. You must use that same name and address on all your proofs of service, exactly as it appears in the captions.

Make sure your case name and number are on the proof of service and your server signed it. Now file the Proof of Service and ask the clerk to endorse a copy, which you will keep. This is of *extreme* importance, because if your spouse doesn't show up at the hearing and you don't have a completely filled out and endorsed Proof of Service, you could be thrown out of court and have to begin your motion all over.

F If your spouse responds

If your spouse files a response to your motion, it is *essential* that you reply in writing to every new issue or fact that your spouse raises so you get your points into the written record. You must serve and file your reply at least 5 calendar days before the hearing if personally served, or 7 days if served by overnight courier (where local rules permit), so the papers to your spouse or the attorney are received by the close of business on the next business day after they are filed.

Usually it is best to go through the response paragraph by paragraph and respond specifically to each item. Make sure you respond to every single allegation, otherwise the judge will assume it is true. Do not repeat what you said in your moving papers. Judges do not like reading the same old thing twice to learn nothing new. Don't waste their time. You can use the Declaration form (Figure 12.4) and attach additional pages, typed on plain white bond (with footers and page numbers) if you need more space.

You might want to consider also filing a motion to strike out everything in declarations presented by the other side that is technically not supposed to be considered by the judge. This brings the matter very forcefully to the judge's attention. For example, a nonexpert witness is only allowed to state things he/she personally observed that are relevant to the issues in dispute, so you would ask the court to exclude specific statements that lack foundation, are hearsay (about which the witness had no personal knowledge), or speculation or an opinion of a witness who is not an expert, etc. You could certainly use the assistance of an attorney to prepare this kind of motion.

If you obtained an order shortening time and served your spouse, say five days before the hearing, and your spouse's papers are filed one or two days before court, as a practical matter you might be unable to produce a reply and file it before the hearing. You can try bringing your reply to the hearing and see whether the judge will accept it. If you have time to respond to their response, do it. Use the generic Declaration form illustrated at Figure 12.4.

Request for a continuance

If the other side contacts you and requests a continuance, you can agree or not. Either way, you should follow the procedures discussed in chapter 24, section B.

Get ready for the hearing

Go quickly to chapter 15 to learn how to prepare for the hearing and how to present your case in court.

Figure 12.7

DECLARATION RE ATTEMPT TO OBTAIN MUTUALLY CONVENIENT HEARING DATE

YOUR NAME
Your Address
City, State, Zip
Your Phone

Petitioner in pro per

SUPERIOR COURT OF CALIFORNIA, COUNTY OF [Your county]

In re the Marriage of)	No. [Your case number]
Petitioner: YOUR NAME)	DECLARATION OF ___________ RE: ATTEMPT TO OBTAIN MUTUALLY CONVENIENT HEARING DATE
Respondent: SPOUSE NAME)	

I, the undersigned, state:

1. I am the petitioner herein.

2. I have personal knowledge of every fact herein and could competently testify thereto if called as a witness at trial.

3. I phoned the office of the attorney for respondent on the following dates and at the following times and asked the staff to let me know on what date the attorney for respondent would be available for a motion in this matter to be heard:

<u>Date</u> <u>Time</u> <u>Person I spoke to</u>

3. On each occasion, they refused to inform me of any convenient dates. In fact [person you spoke to] said, [fighting words]. I request that the court set this matter for hearing at the earliest available date which is at least 30 days away.

Executed at [City], California on [date].

I declare under penalty of perjury under the Laws of the State of California that the foregoing is true and correct.

____
YOUR NAME, Petitioner

1

Declaration of ________________ re: Attempt to Obtain Hearing Date

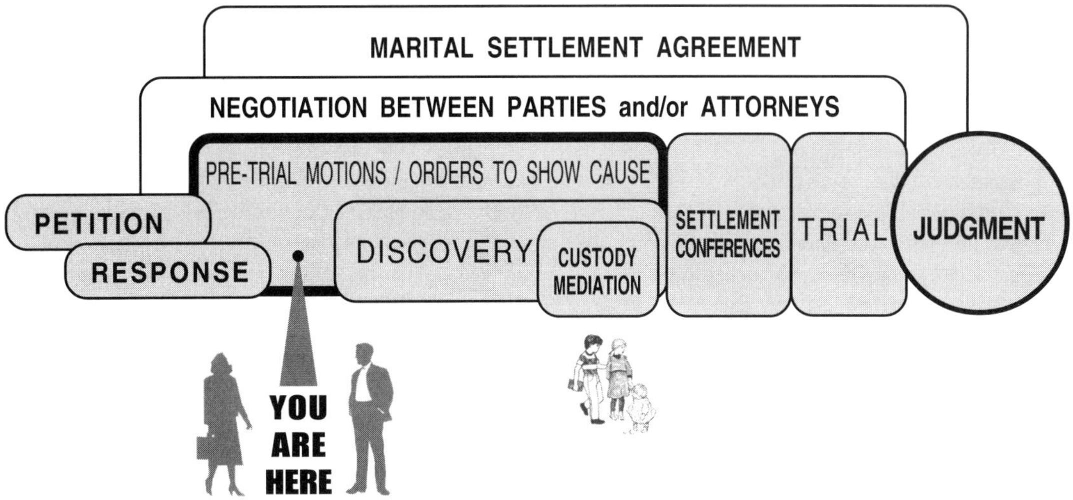

CHAPTER 13
HOW TO DO AN ORDER TO SHOW CAUSE
–creating safety and stability

A. Deadlines and timelines
B. How to do a regular OSC
C. How to file and serve your OSC
D. If there's a response
E. How to do a domestic violence OSC

Read chapter 11 before you start an OSC

An Order to Show Cause (OSC) is an order signed by a judge directing the named party to come to court to give a reason—show cause—why the judge should not make the orders you requested in your OSC forms. If the person served does not respond and come to court, the judge will probably issue the orders.

Orders last only until Judgment. OSC orders are intended to stabilize and protect parties, their children, or their property until the Judgment is entered. Then they expire. Your OSC does *not* get you permanent protective orders—for that, you must either stipulate (agree) to include such orders in your Judgment or at trial ask the judge to include them in your Judgment. An OSC generally does not divide up property—that is done later by agreement or by trial.

Automatic restraining orders. On the back of the Summons, you will see that when a Petition is served, both parties become bound by certain orders. You would use an OSC if you want orders that are different than those or if you want to call your spouse's attention very forcefully to the matter.

Two types of OSC –regular and domestic violence (DV)

There is a set of forms for an OSC that involves domestic abuse and another set for everything else. If your problem involves domestic abuse, you use the domestic violence (DV) set of forms. Family Code §6203 says that "abuse" is any conduct that causes bodily injury or a reasonable fear of *imminent* bodily injury to you, your child, someone you do or did live with, or a member of your household. While emotional abuse can be devastating, particularly if it occurs over a long period, it alone does not support the use of the domestic violence OSC. If your problem involves abuse as defined by the Family Code, use the domestic violence OSC (see section E). If you do not have a clear case of abuse, use the regular OSC.

AN ORDER TO SHOW CAUSE CAN BE USED TO REQUEST	
Orders for	**Orders against**
Child custody, visitation, support	Violence, harassment, contact
Spousal support (but not in a DV OSC)	Visitation until after the hearing
No contact with persons protected	Drugs/alcohol during or before visits
Exclusive possession of family home	Possession of firearms
Possession of family auto or other property	Entering into any new major obligations
Pay bills such as car payment, mortgage, or credit cards	Transferring, hiding, or wasting community property
Refer to Family Court Services to deal with custody/visitation	

You can file a DV OSC at any time by itself. The regular OSC, as used in this book, is part of your divorce and can be filed with the Petition or Response or at any time afterward. We assume that your divorce has already started. If not, use Book 1, *How to Do Your Own Divorce* to prepare a Petition or Response to file along with your OSC.

Child and spousal support

With a regular OSC, you can request orders for both child and spousal support. However, with a DV OSC, you can request only child support but not *spousal* support. Don't ask why. If you want both a DV OSC and a spousal support order, you are going to have to file (1) a domestic violence OSC and a regular OSC or (2) a domestic violence OSC and a motion for support. If you are going to request child or spousal support, go read chapter 11(I) right now and start preparing.

Temporary Restraining Orders (TROs)

When you file either type of OSC, you can also request immediate Temporary Restraining Orders, effective until the date of the OSC hearing, to give you some protection until the case can be fully heard. An OSC is the *only* way to get a TRO. The emergency that justifies a TRO has to be a legally recognized emergency, not just something that seems desperate to you. For example, the law does not recognize lack of support as the kind of emergency that would justify a TRO. It usually has to involve an immediate and credible threat of harm to you, your children, or your property.

Requesting a TRO for support

You cannot get a TRO with either type of OSC *solely* for money requests, such as support. A TRO is only for legal emergencies and, for some reason, being totally without funds is not considered a legal emergency. However, if you have a valid action on any of the OSC matters listed above, you can also include money requests, including child and spousal support, in your OSC. However, if you are using the Domestic Violence procedure, you can't request spousal support. Don't ask why; we can't figure it out either.

Put it another way: if you have a valid reason to file a regular OSC (no domestic abuse), you can also include a request for child and spousal support orders. However, if you file a Domestic Violence OSC, you can only request child support. In that case, if you also want to obtain spousal support, you have to file a separate motion for spousal support. Neither you nor the court want two separate hearings on support, so be sure to request that the OSC and the motion be calendared for the same date and time. If for some reason they cannot be calendared for the same time, if motion hearings are not being set too far in the future, consider removing your child support request from the domestic violence OSC and filing a separate Notice of Motion for both child and spousal support.

A Deadlines and timelines

Local rules and deadlines

First, study your local rules and look for anything that applies to Orders to Show Cause. Be sure to read chapter 11A on important things you have to find out before you start an OSC and 11B on timing.

If you are requesting a TRO, you must give notice or explain why you didn't

If you ask for TROs, you *must* file a declaration stating that (1) notice was given to your spouse *personally* (not his/or her attorney) of when and where TROs would be requested, and whether he/she plans to appear in opposition; or (2) you tried but were unable to give notice, specifying what efforts were made; or (3) there is a very good reason not to give notice, detailing why this is so (Rule of Court 379).

When and how. Notice must be given to your spouse *personally* no later than 10 a.m. on the *court* day before you go to court to request TROs. If notice was given later than this, you must explain exceptional circumstances that justify it. The person giving notice must state specifically what relief is being requested and the date, time, and place TROs will be requested, and *must* ask if the other party plans to appear to oppose the application. Have someone telephone your spouse, give notice, and ask if he/she plans to appear in opposition. Get this person's declaration as to what was done. Absent reason not to, also have all the OSC/TRO papers served on your spouse and get a Proof of Personal Service.

Excuses. For a court to issue orders without notice to the other side, you have to *prove* that giving notice would create a real threat of harm; for example, your spouse lives in the house and is prone to violence, so if he learns of the TRO, he will be likely to harm you or the children. Or, your spouse has threatened to take the children to another country and is likely to do so if she has notice that you are asking for a TRO. One last possibility: if giving notice is likely to cause your spouse to hide, you might be able to use this to avoid giving notice, especially if he/she has done anything like it before. **Failed excuses.** If the judge does not accept your reason for not giving notice, your papers will be returned and you will be expected to go give notice. However, if you feel that your spouse truly is dangerous but you just didn't express it clearly enough, you could resubmit the papers and explain the problem better; but, if you do this, you have to tell the judge that this is the second submission and explain that your request to skip the notice had previously been denied.

Responders! If you get notice that a TRO is going to be requested, if at all possible prepare a Responsive Declaration and file it immediately or take it to court at the time and place indicated to present your side of the case. See chapter 14E. At least show up if you want to oppose the TROs.

Plan service of papers before taking OSC to court - deadlines

Read chapter 11C on who and how to serve. You won't have much time to serve papers, so you need a plan all set up and ready to go *before* you file your OSC. If you don't serve your spouse on time, you'll have to have your OSC reissued. Worse, if your spouse was served late and the judge refuses to hear the matter, your spouse might hide to avoid getting served again. Always have an Application for Reissuance (Figure 13.4) on hand to present to the court in case a hearing is continued.

Order shortening time (OST). Read chapter 11B about orders shortening time. If you request an OST as described in section B1, it will make your job a lot easier. For urgent matters, ask that time for service be shortened to 5 days before the hearing and the responsive declaration be due 2 days before the hearing. If there is a specific emergency, you can request that service be shortened to 2 days before the hearing and the responsive declaration be due one day before the hearing.

Timeline for OSC without TROs (CCP § 1005)

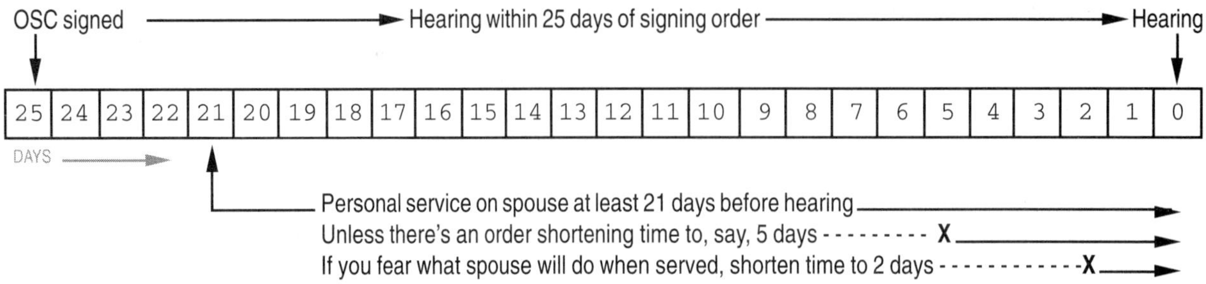

So, after filing, you have a little over 4 days to get papers served. However, it is not unusual for OSC papers to be delayed at court, or for the court to set the hearing in less than 25 days, so you might end up with only 1 to 3 days to get it served.

Order shortening time

If you get an order shortening time of service to 5 days before the hearing, that gives you 10–14 days to serve.
If you have reason to fear what your spouse will do when served, you can get order shortening time to 2 days' notice.

Timeline for OSC with TROs (Fam. Code §§ 240–243)

When a temporary restraining order (TRO) is issued, the timetable above is modified by Family Codes 240 to 243, as follows: the hearing must be held as soon as the court calendar permits, but no later than 20 days, or 25 if the court finds good cause to extend the time.

TRO granted *with* notice given to the other side. You must personally serve your spouse with a full set of OSC/TRO papers (checklists B and C below) at least 15 days before the hearing.

TRO granted *without* notice given to the other side. You must personally serve your spouse with a full set of OSC/TRO papers (checklists in B and C below) at least 5 days before the hearing.

B How to do a regular OSC

First, read chapter 16 to get clear about the orders you can request and chapter 11 about how to prepare and build your case. When you are clear about the orders you want to request, the facts you can prove to justify those orders, and how you are going to serve the papers, you are now ready to do the forms. Don't worry—just be patient and methodical. Read every word on every form, including fine print, and try to see the whole package. Look to see the various orders they provide and what information they ask for.

The OSC forms provide check-boxes and language for mainstream divorce issues related to property and debts, child or spousal support, custody and visitation. However, if your non-abusive spouse is constantly phoning or harassing you, or worse, you might want to add more exotic protections like move-out, no contact, and stay-away orders. This sort of thing is already built into the DV OSC, but if there is no actual physical harm or reasonable fear of physical harm involved, you can't use it. In the regular OSC, you have to type in your own special language for such orders; but, no problem, we'll show you how to add additional orders to your forms.

Checklist of documents for a regular OSC

- ☐ 1. **Order to Show Cause (FL-300)**
  Possible attachment:
  - ☐ a. Temporary Orders (FL-305) (if TROs requested)
- ☐ 2. **Application for Order and Supporting Declaration (FL-310)**
  Attachments that might be used:
  - ☐ a. Child Custody and Visitation Attachment (FL-311) (if kids are in the request) and Declaration Under Uniform Child Custody Jurisdiction Act (FL-105)
  - ☐ b. Income and Expense Declaration (FL-150) (if money requested) and guideline computer report if support requested (optional some counties)
  - ☐ c. Declarations of witnesses, if any (see chapter 11F)
  - ☐ d. Memorandum of Points and Authorities (optional, see chapter 11A)
  - ☐ e. Request for Oral Testimony (optional, see chapter 11D)
- ☐ 3. **Declaration re Notice of Ex Parte Application for Orders**
  (Only if you request immediate temporary orders)
  (After all forms are completed, this one goes on top)
- ☐ 4. **Application and Order for Reissuance of OSC (FL-306)**
  (Used if you can't serve the OSC by the deadline. Good idea to have one ready.)

1. Order to Show Cause (FL-300)

Complete as shown in Figure 13.1 and the notes below. Read every word.

Item 2a. Leave the date and time blank. The court clerk will fill them in later.

Item 2c. If custody or visitation is an issue, you have to mediate (see chapter 20). Call the clerk to get the name, address, and phone number for Family Court Services in your county. If the court wants mediation ordered to occur before the court hearing, as in San Diego, Contra Costa, and some others, the court clerk will probably make sure that you do this. Check box 2(c) and complete it as shown.

Item 3b. If you want an order shortening time (see chapter 11B), check this box and enter the number of days before the hearing that documents must be served and the number of days before the hearing that the Responsive Declaration must be filed. **Note:** you must also check and complete item 8 on the Application for Order form and state facts there to justify the order shortening time.

Item 3c. If you want immediately effective protective orders (TROs), check this box and attach the Temporary Orders form (Figure 13.2).

a. Temporary Orders (FL-305)

This form is used only when you want temporary orders (TROs) that become effective *immediately* when signed and last only until your hearing. Fill it out as shown in Figure 13.2.

Items 1–3. Check boxes to show the temporary orders you are requesting. Read and choose carefully.

Item 2. This is for payment of debts that fall due before the hearing and for immediate exclusive possession and control of property such as a car or computer. **Move-out:** Asking for immediate exclusive possession of the family home is extreme, so don't do this without convincing evidence that (a) you have a right to be there because you are on the deed or lease, and (b) your spouse has somewhere to go, and (c) harm to a child is likely if your spouse remains, say due to drinking or drug use. If you do ask for

Figure 13.1
ORDER TO SHOW CAUSE
Form FL-300

FL-300

ATTORNEY OR PARTY WITHOUT ATTORNEY *(Name, state bar number, and address):*
YOUR NAME
Your address
City, State, Zip

TELEPHONE NO. *(Optional):* Your phone FAX NO. *(Optional):* Your fax
EMAIL ADDRESS *(Optional):* Your email
ATTORNEY FOR *(Name):* Petitioner / Respondent in pro per

FOR COURT USE ONLY

SUPERIOR COURT OF CALIFORNIA, COUNTY OF YOUR COUNTY
STREET ADDRESS: Street address
MAILING ADDRESS: PO Box, if any
CITY AND ZIP CODE: City, State, Zip
BRANCH NAME: Branch name, if any

PETITIONER: PETITIONER'S NAME

RESPONDENT: RESPONDENT'S NAME

ORDER TO SHOW CAUSE FOR [ ] **MODIFICATION**
[X] **Child Custody** [X] **Visitation** [X] **Injunctive Order**
[X] **Child Support** [X] **Spousal Support** [X] **Other *(specify):***
[ ] **Attorney Fees and Costs** Possession of residence, move-out

CASE NUMBER:
Your case number

1. TO *(name):* SPOUSE NAME
2. YOU ARE ORDERED TO APPEAR IN THIS COURT AS FOLLOWS TO GIVE ANY LEGAL REASON WHY THE RELIEF SOUGHT IN THE ATTACHED APPLICATION SHOULD NOT BE GRANTED. **If child custody or visitation is an issue in this proceeding, Family Code section 3170 requires mediation before or concurrently with the hearing listed below.**

   a. Date: Time: [ ] Dept.: [ ] Room:

   b. The address of the court is [X] same as noted above [ ] other *(specify):*

   c. [X] The parties are ordered to attend custody mediation services as follows:
   Immediately contact Family Court Services at (phone number) and schedule mediation.

3. THE COURT FURTHER ORDERS that a completed *Application for Order and Supporting Declaration* (form FL-310), a **blank** *Responsive Declaration* (form FL-320), and the following documents be served with this order:
   a. (1) [X] Completed *Income and Expense Declaration* (form FL-150) and a **blank** *Income and Expense Declaration*
   (2) [ ] Completed *Financial Statement (Simplified)* (form FL-155) and a **blank** *Financial Statement (Simplified)*
   (3) [ ] Completed *Property Declaration* (form FL-160) and a **blank** *Property Declaration*
   (4) [ ] Points and authorities
   (5) [X] Other *(specify):* Temporary Orders

   b. [X] Time for [X] service [X] hearing is shortened. Service must be on or before *(date):* date
   Any responsive declaration must be served on or before *(date):* date
   c. [X] You are ordered to comply with the temporary orders attached.
   d. [ ] Other *(specify):*

Date:

JUDICIAL OFFICER

NOTICE: If you have children from this relationship, the court is required to order payment of child support based on the incomes of both parents. The amount of child support can be large. It normally continues until the child is 18. You should supply the court with information about your finances. Otherwise, the child support order will be based on the information supplied by the other parent.
You do not have to pay any fee to file declarations in response to this order to show cause (including a completed *Income and Expense Declaration* (form FL-150) or *Financial Statement (Simplified)* (form FL-155) that will show your finances). In the absence of an order shortening time, the original of the responsive declaration must be filed with the court and a copy served on the other party at least ten calender days before the hearing date.

Page 1 of 1

Form Adopted for Mandatory Use
Judicial Council of California
FL-300 [Rev. January 1, 2003]

ORDER TO SHOW CAUSE

Family Code, §§ 215, 270 et seq., 3000 et seq., 3500 et seq., 4300
www.courtinfo.ca.gov

Figure 13.2
TEMPORARY ORDERS
Form FL-305

Enter case no. if you have one, otherwise one will be issued when you file.

FL-305

PETITIONER/PLAINTIFF: PETITIONER'S NAME RESPONDENT/DEFENDANT: RESPONDENT'S NAME	CASE NUMBER: Your case number

TEMPORARY ORDERS
(Attachment to Order to Show Cause)

NOTE: TO OBTAIN DOMESTIC VIOLENCE RESTRAINING ORDERS, YOU MUST USE FORMS *REQUEST FOR ORDER (DOMESTIC VIOLENCE PREVENTION)* (FORM DV-100) AND *TEMPORARY RESTRAINING ORDER (DOMESTIC VIOLENCE PREVENTION)* (FORM DV-110).

1. [X] PROPERTY RESTRAINT
   a. [ ] Petitioner [X] Respondent is restrained from transferring, encumbering, hypothecating, concealing, or in any way disposing of any property, real or personal, whether community, quasi-community, or separate, except in the usual course of business or for the necessities of life.
      [X] The other party is to be notified of any proposed extraordinary expenditures and an accounting of such is to be made to the court.
   b. [X] Both parties are restrained and enjoined from cashing, borrowing against, canceling, transferring, disposing of, or changing the beneficiaries of any insurance or other coverage including life, health, automobile, and disability held for the benefit of the parties or their minor child or children.
   c. [X] Neither party may incur any debts or liabilities for which the other may be held responsible, other than in the ordinary course of business or for the necessities of life.
2. [X] PROPERTY CONTROL
   a. [X] Petitioner [ ] Respondent is given the exclusive temporary use, possession, and control of the following property the parties own or are buying *(specify):*
      Family residence at (address), 1999 Nissan Altima, CA license 4XYZ123, Dell Laptop serial 12345
   b. [ ] Petitioner [X] Respondent is ordered to make the following payments on liens and encumbrances coming due while the order is in effect:

Debt	Amount of payment	Pay to
Mortgage	$1234	Ace Mortgage
Auto payments	$345	Jiffy Auto

3. [X] MINOR CHILDREN
   a. [X] Petitioner [ ] Respondent will have the temporary physical custody, care, and control of the minor children of the parties, [X] subject to the other party's rights of visitation as follows: Per attachment FL-
   b. [ ] Petitioner [X] Respondent must not remove the minor child or children of the parties
      (1) [X] from the State of California.
      (2) [X] from the following counties *(specify):* Your county
      (3) [X] other *(specify):* Your City
4. [X] OTHER ORDERS *(specify):*
   (1) (Spouse Name) must take only personal clothing and belongings needed until the hearing and move out immediately from (address). (2) Supervised visitation as specified in Attachment for Item 4. (3) The parties are ordered to contact Family Court Services at (phone) and schedule orientation and mandatory mediation.

Date:

JUDGE OF THE SUPERIOR C

5. **The date of the court hearing is** *(insert date when known)*: Date of hearing

If you need to use attachments for any items on this page, indicate this is page 1 of (total number).

CLERK'S CERTIFICATE

I certify that the foregoing is a true and correct copy of the original on file i

[SEAL]

Date: Clerk, by ____________________, Deputy

Page 1 of 1

Form Adopted for Mandatory Use
Judicial Council of California
FL-305 [Rev. January 1, 2003]

TEMPORARY ORDERS

Family Code, §§ 2045, 6224, 6226, 6302, 6320–6326, 6380–6383
www.courtinfo.ca.gov

possession of the home, it makes sense to also add a move-out order at item 4: "(Name) must take only personal clothing and belongings needed until the hearing and move out immediately from (address)."

Item 3. If you need *immediate* orders for custody, check box 3 and indicate which party gets physical custody until the hearing. If you can't wait until the hearing for visitation to be specified as to time and place, or that it be supervised, check the box for visitation and type in, "As specified in item 4, below."

Item 4. Any order you request in your Application or its attachments (see below) that is not found in items 1–3, type them here. If you need more than three lines, attach a typed page with the heading "Item 4, Other Orders," and under box 4 type, "See orders attached hereto and made part hereof by reference; the parties are directed to obey all terms and conditions of those orders." Then, in the lower right corner of the form, indicate that this is page 1 of *x* pages. Number attached pages 2 of *x*, 3 of *x*, and so on.

Children. If your OSC involves custody/visitation issues and your county requires mediation or a parenting program, this is where you type in an order that the parties must go at a certain time and place to attend mediation or some parenting program. Read chapter 20. **Visitation.** The hearing is not very far away, but you might want to specify when and how visitation will be handled until then. Take your language from FL-311 (Figure 12.2) and type a schedule in the form of an order that begins, "Pending the hearing, (Spouse Name) shall have the following temporary visitation rights." **Supervised visitation.** If you have convincing evidence that your spouse cannot safely be left alone with the children because, for example, he/she is alcoholic, you can type in language borrowed from FL-311, item 1(b)(3), but in the form of an order rather than a request, e.g., "(Spouse Name) shall have supervised visitation as follows."

No contact. If your spouse is constantly phoning or harassing you, or worse, you might want a temporary order for absolutely no contact. If so, type in the following language:

> "(Spouse) shall not contact, molest, harass, attack, strike, threaten, sexually assault, batter, telephone, send any messages to, follow, stalk, destroy the personal property of, disturb the peace of, keep under surveillance, or block movements in public places or thoroughfares of (Your Name), who shall have the right to record communications made by (Spouse) that violate this order."

Read it carefully to see what you are asking. **In pro per.** If you are both representing yourselves, a no-contact order could interfere with the conduct of your case, so you should modify the order to work around this. For example, (1) remove the words "contact" and "telephone;" or (b) after the word "contact" add "except by email." Email is non-intrusive and it gives you documentary evidence of the communication. At the end, you can add, "except for peaceful written contact through a process server or another person to serve legal papers." **Children.** If you have kids, you should add at the end, "and except for brief and peaceful contact as required for court-ordered visitation."

A no-contact order is pretty much one way as the person who is protected can still contact the other party. Also, these orders are not necessarily forever. Typically, such orders begin very strong early in the case and can be eased up later for most people as they accept the reality of the divorce.

Stay away. In some cases, you will want the following: "(Spouse Name) is ordered to stay at least 300 yards from (Your Name) and (Your Name)'s residence, vehicle and place of work." If your spouse works near you, reduce the distance to 10 or 30 yards, whatever will allow you to both keep working without violation of the order. You will need to add a provision for visitation if there are kids.

2. Application for Order and Supporting Declaration (FL-310)

This is where you request all the orders you want and any TROs that you put in your OSC for the judge to sign. The same form is used for motions, so fill it out as shown in Figures 12.1 and 12.2, following the notes below. The main difference is that when applying for an OSC, you can ask for immediately effective orders by checking the box at each order that says "until the hearing."

Items 1–7. Read very carefully and be sure to ask for every order that you checked or typed in your Order to Show Cause (Fig. 13.1). If you also used the Temporary Orders form (Fig. 13.2) to get immediately effective orders, you *must* request the same orders on this form and you *must* check the boxes that say, "To be ordered pending the hearing," otherwise you won't get them. Finally, you must state facts at item 10, or in attached documents and declarations, that justify every order you are requesting. In other words, this is your entire case. Read chapter 11D–F on preparing a case and writing declarations.

Item 2. If you requested custody in item 1, check items 2, 2(b), and maybe 2(c). At 2(b), type in, "As specified in attached form FL-311."

Items 3 and 4. If requesting child or spousal support, it is a very good idea to attach a computer printout from support software such as CalSupport (see front of book). Some counties require it in their local rules. If you do, make sure you refer to it in item 10.

Item 5. You can't ask for attorney fees to cover your own time, but you can ask to be reimbursed for any amount paid to an attorney for advice and assistance; for example, if you used Divorce Helpline.

Item 8. To request an order shortening time (see section A and chapter 11B), check this box, enter the number of days before trial that documents must be served and days before trial that the response must be filed. At item 10, or in an attached declaration, you *must* state facts that justify the shortened time (see chapter 11B). **Note:** you *must* also complete item 3b on the Order to Show Cause form above.

Item 10. This is where you state facts to justify each order you request the court to make. This is your own declaration or statement of facts. Do not write your declaration before you read chapter 11F. It might be possible for you to fit a simple declaration into the space provided, but if there's not enough room, simply check the second box at this item and attach your typed declaration that includes facts you want to state to the court. If you also attach the declarations of other witnesses, or other documents, refer to them here. For example, "See attached declarations of (Petitioner/Respondent), declarations of witnesses, and attached documents in support of this Order to Show Cause."

a. Child Custody and Visitation Attachment (FL-311)

This is your request for custody and visitation orders that will stay in effect until your divorce is concluded. Fill it out as shown in Figure 12.3 and the notes in that chapter. First, read Book 1, chapter 5. Also attach FL-105, Declaration Under Uniform Child Custody Jurisdiction and Enforcement Act. That form and instructions for using it are in Book 1, *How to Do Your Own Divorce*, chapter 10, Figure 10.3.

b. Income and Expense Declaration (FL-150)

A motion that asks for money must include a completed Income and Expense Declaration (see *How to Do Your Own Divorce,* chapter 16). **Local rules** might contain requirements in addition to state law, such as pay stubs and P&L statements. **Warning:** court files are public records, so required attachments such as pay stubs could put your social security number where someone could steal your identity. Laws have not yet dealt with this problem, but we assume courts will let you blank out any sensitive information that is not essential to the hearing. **Child or spousal support printout.** If you request support, every judge would like to see a printout from a computer program like CalSupport (see front of book) that has been certified by the Judicial Council and many counties require one. Get CalSupport for $30, or get an attorney to run a calculation for you, or get one from the Family Law Facilitator for free.

c. Declarations of witnesses (where your motion will be won or lost)

Prepare all declarations as described in chapter 11F. Also read 11E. Figure 12.4 shows the Declaration form, best for one or two page declarations, and Figure 12.7 shows a typed declaration that is suitable for longer statements. Your case will be won or lost on the strength of declarations and attached documents. It is not unusual if you are the only declarant/witness, but of course it is more convincing if you can get the declarations of others stating facts that support your case. The facts in your declarations and documents must convince the judge that you have a right to the orders you requested and they must explain or overcome whatever facts the other side can put forward. You have to anticipate as best you can what those facts might be and counter them to begin with, for there is not always time to reply to their response.

d. Memorandum of Points and Authorities (P&As)

As discussed in chapter 11A, a Memorandum of Points and Authorities is not required in a divorce unless the judge requires one or unless your motion or OSC is unusual. Although we include an example in Figure 12.5, doing P&As is work for an experienced lawyer; so, if you need P&As, you'd best get help.

e. Request for Oral Testimony

Read chapter 11D. If you want to oral testimony, attach your request (Figure 11.1).

3. Declaration re Notice of Ex Parte Application for Orders

If you are going to request TROs (see section A), you *must* file this declaration. If no TROs, you don't need it. Some counties have a local form, one example of which is shown in Figure 13.3. If your county doesn't have a local form for this, you'll have to type one up according to local requirements, if any. You'll find a typed notice in the companion CD, Figure 13.3 in the Pleadings folder. Check your local rules to see if you have to indicate the date and time that you intend to present the OSC in court. This form is the last thing you do, but it goes on top of the stack when you present your forms to the clerk.

4. Application and Order for Reissuance of OSC

If you do not serve your OSC by the deadline described in section A, then you either start all over again or ask to have your OSC reissued. You do this by filing the Application and Order for Reissuance of OSC (FL-306) (Figure 13.4). Although the form does not require you to attach a copy of your OSC, the court clerk might want that, so take an extra set of papers along. When the Order for Reissuance is signed, a new hearing date will be written on it. Attach this form to the package of papers you are serving and proceed to serve papers on the other side. In some counties, we've heard, the clerk will simply write a new date on the old OSC and recalendar the hearing.

Review and file

Review the checklist on page 103. Make sure you have listed everything you attached and attached everything you listed. Arrange originals in the order in the checklist, but put item 3 on top if you used it. Make three copies of everything: the court keeps the originals, one copy is for your spouse, one is for you, and one is for you to keep at home, just in case. Make another copy if you need to give notice of intent to request a TRO, plus one more if your spouse has an attorney of record. Punch two holes at the top of originals. The clerk's office will probably have a two-hole punch you can use before filing. Staple all the originals together, in order, into one OSC set, then staple all the copies together into similar sets. Keep all sets of papers firmly clipped together and in order, including any statements and exhibits. At the hearing, don't try to work with disorganized papers or you will increase your chances for error.

Figure 13.3

DECLARATION RE: NOTICE UPON EX PARTE APPLICATION FOR ORDERS

(Local form—Santa Clara County)

Attachment M

NAME AND ADDRESS OF PARTY OR ATTORNEY FOR PARTY: YOUR NAME, Your address, City, State, Zip
TELEPHONE NUMBER: Your phone
ATTORNEY FOR (Name): Petitioner / Respondent in pro per

FOR COURT USE ONLY

SUPERIOR COURT OF CALIFORNIA, COUNTY OF SANTA CLARA
MAILING ADDRESS: 170 PARK CENTER PLAZA
CITY AND ZIP CODE: SAN JOSE CALIFORNIA 95113
BRANCH NAME:

PETITIONER: PETITIONER'S NAME
RESPONDER: RESPONDENT'S NAME

Case Number: Your case number

DECLARATION IN SUPPORT OF EX PARTE APPLICATION FOR ORDERS

Department Number:
FCS Number:

I, the undersigned, declare:

1. **I am (choose one):**
   (1) ☐ **attorney for** Petitioner ☐ **attorney for** Respondent ☐ **attorney for** child(ren)
   (2) ☒ **self-represented** Petitioner ☐ **self-represented** Respondent
   (3) ☐ **other** (explain):
2. **The opposing party or minor child(ren) is represented by an attorney:** ☐ Yes ☒ No
   (If you checked "yes", fill in the attorney's name, address, and telephone number. If you checked "no", fill in the other party's name address, and telephone number.
   Party/Attorney name: SPOUSE NAME
   Address/Telephone number: Spouse's address, City, State, Zip
   Child's attorney name and address:
3. **OTHER CASES:** Have the parties to this case been involved in another Family, Probate Juvenile, or Criminal Court Case? ☐ Yes ☒ No If there has been another case, fill in the case number:
4. **NOTICE**

   A. **I HAVE given notice to the opposing party and/or their attorney by the following method:**
   ☒ Personal delivery ☐ Fax ☐ Overnight Carrier ☐ First Class Mail ☐ Other:
   Date: Date Time: Time
   I have received confirmation that the other party has received my papers as follows: (Check one below)
   ☒ In person/telephone (describe): Per attached Proof of Service and declaration of (person giving notice)
   ☐ Confirmation of receipt.

   B. **I HAVE NOT given notice of the ex parte request for orders because (Check *all* that apply. You must explain below):**
   ☐ This is an application for Domestic Violence Prevention Act (DVPA) restraining orders.
   ☐ Great or irreparable injury will result to me before the matter can be heard on notice.
   ☐ It is impossible to give notice.
   ☐ The other party agrees to the orders requested.
   ☐ No significant burden or inconvenience to the responding party will result fro the orders requested.
   ☐ Other:

   C. **Explanation::**
   ☐ A hearing between the parties is already set I am asking that this motion be heard at the same time.
   ☐ I am unable to serve the other party 21 days before the hearing.
   ☐ I fear for my physical safety (and that of my children, if applicable).
   ☐ Other:

I declare under penalty of perjury that the forgoing is true and correct.

Date		YOUR NAME
Date	Signature of Declarant	Print Name

Rev. 01/01/02 **DECLARATION IN SUPPORT OF EX PARTE APPLICATION FOR ORDERS** Page 1

C How to file and serve your OSC

1. If you are going to request TROs, give notice first

Before asking for TROs, you first need to give notice that you intend to do so (see section A). If your spouse has an attorney of record, serve the attorney—it's easier. In counties where you present papers directly to the judge, wait at least 24 hours after service to take your OSC package to court. If you are not requesting TROs, file your papers, then skip to number 4 and get them served.

2. Take the OSC package to court

Take your OSC package and copies to the court clerk for filing. If you are requesting TROs, you'll also need a judge's signature. Although you can theoretically mail your papers or hire a court runner to file them for you, it is best to take them to court in person. This is a crucial step in your divorce, time is short, and you want to make sure everything goes smoothly.

In some counties (like Santa Clara), a person who is not a judge might review your papers before the judge sees them; this could be a court clerk, document examiner, legal examiner, etc. In those counties you might not see the judge. In other counties, you take your OSC papers to a judge at the time you told your spouse you would, and the judge reviews them and may speak to you and to your spouse if he/she shows up. Either way, the judge signs the OSC and makes a decision on requests for TROs.

Never give away your last copy. In counties where you turn your original OSC over to a clerk, it is always possible that the papers might get lost. If this happens, it could be hard to prove what happened or who lost what. That is why you keep a copy. Never, never give away your last copy of your papers.

Filing fee. Call the clerk to find out how much the filing fee for an OSC is and whether or not they will take your personal check. If they'll take your check, it *must not bounce.* Period. If there is any chance it will bounce, use cash. The cost of filing a motion or OSC is typically $15 to $50.

3. Pick up the signed OSC

Documents must be conformed. In counties where you do not see the judge, give the clerk the original plus two copies of your papers and the filing fee. In counties where you take your papers to a judge, give the judge the *original* papers. When the package is returned to you, give it and all copies and the filing fee to a clerk to file. In both types of counties, all copies must be "conformed," that is, if the judge changed anything such as part of the TRO, all copies must be changed to be exactly like the original before they are filed. Sometimes a clerk does this, and in other counties you must do it.

Check the hearing date. As soon as you get your papers, look at page one of the OSC to check the hearing date. Did the judge give you an Order Shortening Time? Figure the deadline for you to serve the OSC and decide if it is possible for you to serve your papers on time. Sometimes the judge does not sign the OST, and your papers get delayed at the clerk's office, and by the time they return your papers to you, it is already too late to serve them and you have to resubmit them to be reissued right away (below). If you do have time to serve the papers, get going on it immediately.

4. Serve the OSC package

Although people generally mail motions, you should have an OSC served personally. If your spouse has an attorney *of record* (see 9H), also serve a copy on the attorney. You can do this by mail if you have time to add 5 extra days to the deadline for service, or personally. You need a signed Proof of Service for each person served, which you file in court immediately (safest) or in court when you appear at the hearing.

5. How to get your OSC reissued

If you can't serve your OSC by the deadline (section A), quickly file the Application and Order for Reissuance of OSC (FL-306) as described in section B(4). When the Order for Reissuance is signed the clerk will write a new hearing date on it. Attach it to the package of papers you are serving and proceed to serve papers on the other side before your new deadline.

D If there's a response

If your spouse served you with a Responsive Declaration, it is *essential* that you respond in writing to every *new* issue or fact. You must serve and file your reply at least 5 calendar days before the hearing if personally served, or 7 days if served by overnight courier (where local rules permit). Also, these papers *must* be received by the close of business on the next business day after they are filed.

Go through the Responsive Declaration carefully and reply specifically to each item that you think is untrue or misleading. The judge can assume that any fact you do *not* reply to is true. Do not repeat what you said in your moving papers—judges don't like reading the same thing twice to learn nothing new. Use the Declaration form (Figure 12.4) or type one up as in Figure 12.7, and attach additional pages, typed on plain white bond (with footers and page numbers) if you need more space.

You might also want to do a written motion to strike (using the motion forms), asking the court to strike out everything that is technically not supposed to be considered by the judge. A nonexpert witness is only allowed to state things he/she personally observed that are relevant to the issues in dispute, so you would ask the court to exclude anything that lacks foundation, is hearsay (about which the witness had no personal knowledge), is speculation or an opinion of a witness who is not an expert, etc. You could certainly use the assistance of an attorney to do this.

If you obtained an order shortening time and served your spouse, say, five days before hearing, and your spouse's papers are filed one or two days before court, you might be unable to produce a response and file it before the hearing. If you have time to respond to their response, do it; otherwise, try bringing it to the hearing and see whether the judge will accept it. Use the generic Declaration form (Figure 12.4).

Request for a continuance

If the other side contacts you and requests a continuance, you can agree or not. Either way, you should follow the procedures discussed in chapter 24B.

Get ready for the hearing

Go quickly to chapter 15 where you will learn how to prepare for the hearing and how to present your case when you are in court.

Figure 13.4
APPLICATION AND ORDER FOR REISSUANCE OF ORDER TO SHOW CAUSE
Form FL-306

FL-306/JV-251

ATTORNEY OR PARTY WITHOUT ATTORNEY *(Name and Address)*: YOUR NAME, Your address, City, State, Zip
TELEPHONE NO.: Your phone

ATTORNEY FOR *(Name)*: Petitioner / Respondent in pro per

SUPERIOR COURT OF CALIFORNIA, COUNTY OF YOUR COUNTY
STREET ADDRESS: Street address
MAILING ADDRESS: PO Box, if any
CITY AND ZIP CODE: City, State, Zip
BRANCH NAME: Branch name, if any

PETITIONER/PLAINTIFF: PETITIONER'S NAME
RESPONDENT/DEFENDANT: RESPONDENT'S NAME
OTHER:

FOR COURT USE ONLY

APPLICATION AND ORDER FOR REISSUANCE OF ORDER TO SHOW CAUSE

CASE NUMBER(S): Your case number

1. Applicant is *(specify)*: Petitioner / Respondent
2. Applicant requests the court to reissue the *Order to Show Cause* [X] *and Temporary Restraining Order* originally issued as follows:
   a. Order to Show Cause was issued on *(date)*: Date first OSC signed by judge
   b. Order to Show Cause was last set for hearing on *(date)*: Date set for hearing on 1st OSC
   c. Order to Show Cause has been reissued previously *(number of times)*: 0
3. Applicant requests reissuance of the order because:
   a. [X] Respondent/Defendant [ ] Petitioner/Plaintiff [ ] Other party could not be served as required before the hearing date.
   b. [ ] The hearing was continued because the parties were referred to court mediator or family court services.
   c. [ ] Other *(specify)*:

I declare under penalty of perjury under the laws of the State of California that the foregoing is true and correct.
Date: Date signed

YOUR NAME
(TYPE OR PRINT NAME) (SIGNATURE)

ORDER

4. IT IS ORDERED that the *Order to Show Cause* issued as shown in item 2 above is reissued and reset for hearing in this court as follows:

Date:	time:	dept.:	room:
at the street address of the court shown above.			

   a. A copy of this order must be attached to documents that must be served on the [ ] Respondent/Defendant [ ] Petitioner/Plaintiff [ ] Other party as directed in the *Order to Show Cause*.
   b. All other orders contained in the *Order to Show Cause* and [ ] *Temporary Restraining Order* remain in full force and effect unless modified by this order. **THE *ORDER TO SHOW CAUSE* AND THIS ORDER EXPIRE ON THE DATE AND TIME OF THE HEARING SHOWN IN THE BOX ABOVE UNLESS EXTENDED BY THE COURT.**
   c. [ ] Other *(specify)*:

Date: ▶ JUDICIAL OFFICER

Page 1 of 1

Form Adopted for Mandatory Use
Judicial Council of California
FL-306/JV-251 [Adopted January 1, 2003]

APPLICATION AND ORDER FOR REISSUANCE OF ORDER TO SHOW CAUSE (Family Law—Governmental—Uniform Parentage—Custody and Support—Juvenile)

Code of Civil Procedure, § 527(d)
www.courtinfo.ca.gov

E How to do a domestic violence OSC

You would use a DV OSC only if there has been physical harm in your family, or conduct that gives you a good reason to fear imminent harm to you or anyone in your family. Otherwise, use the regular OSC.

The domestic violence OSC is a special set of forms that are relatively easy to use. They come with instructions for both the applicant and responding party that are kind of basic and out of order (see below), but still adequate—especially with help from this book. The way a DV OSC works is very similar to the regular OSC, so first read the DV help pages in the list below, then study this chapter and chapter 14 about how to respond. It will help you understand things better. Be sure to read chapter 15 on presenting your case at a hearing and chapter 16 on what to do after the hearing. The DV set is designed to be used without an attorney and can be filled out in handwriting as well as typed. Typing or computer printing is better because it makes a good impression and is easier for the judge to read.

A complete set of DV forms is on the companion CD in a format that you can fill out and use on your computer. If you don't have a computer, get them free from your clerk's office or take the CD to a copy shop like Kinkos or an Internet cafe and rent a computer long enough to print out all the forms and instructions. Here are the key forms in the set:

Information and instructions

- ☐ DV-210 What is "Proof of Service"?
- ☐ DV-500 Can a Domestic Violence Restraining Order Help Me?
- ☐ DV-505 Forms You Need for a Temporary Restraining Order
- ☐ DV-510 I Filled Out the Forms — What Now?
- ☐ DV-520 Get Ready for Your Hearing (For Protected Person)
- ☐ DV-530 How to Enforce Your Order
- ☐ DV-540 Information for the Restrained Person
- ☐ DV-550 Get Ready for Your Hearing (For Restrained Person)
- ☐ DV-560 How Can I Make the Order Permanent?
- ☐ DV-570 Which Financial Form—FL-155 or FL-150?

Forms for doing a DV OSC

- ☐ DV-100 Request for Order
- ☐ DV-101 Description of Abuse
- ☐ DV-105 Child Custody, Visitation, and Support Request
- ☐ DV-108 Request for Order: No Travel With Children
- ☐ DV-110 Temporary Restraining Order and Notice of Hearing
- ☐ DV-120 Answer to Temporary Restraining Order
- ☐ DV-130 Restraining Order After Hearing
- ☐ DV-140 Child Custody and Visitation Order
- ☐ DV-145 Order: No Travel With Children
- ☐ DV-150 Supervised Visitation Order
- ☐ DV-160 Child Support Order
- ☐ DV-170 Other Orders
- ☐ DV-200 Proof of Service (In Person)
- ☐ DV-250 Proof of Service by Mail
- ☐ DV-260 Confidential Information
- ☐ DV-290 Request for Free Service of Restraining Order
- ☐ DV-800 Proof of Firearms Turned In or Sold

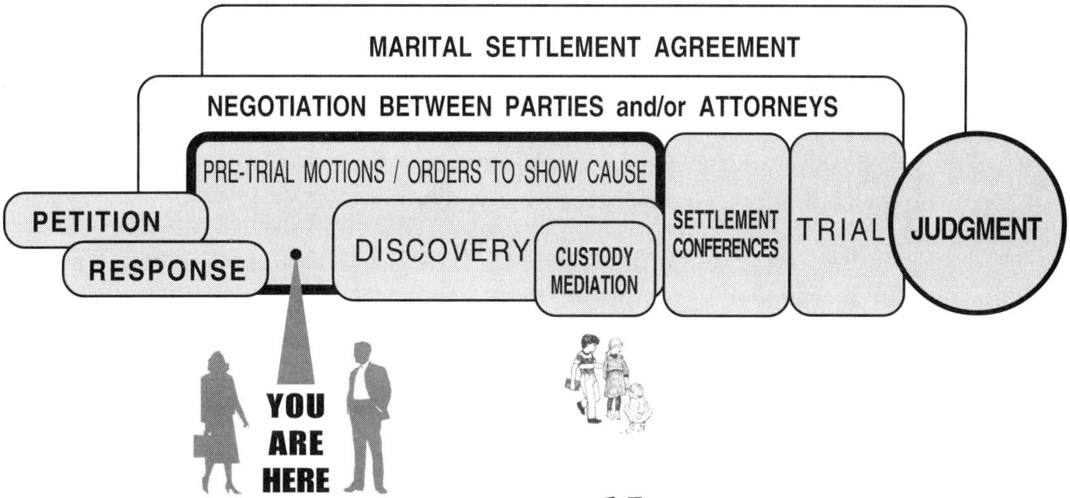

CHAPTER 14
RESPONDING TO A MOTION OR OSC

A. First things
B. Respond or settle?
C. How to object if served at the last minute
D. Asking for a continuance (postponement)
E. How do a Responsive Declaration

Read chapter 11 before you do your response.

Every action to change marital status starts with a Summons and Petition. It is not unusual for a motion or OSC to be served at the same time or shortly afterward. Many attorneys file a motion or OSC at the start of a case as a routine matter. It's poor practice to take legal action without a sound strategic reason, but this is nonetheless a common way for attorneys to enter a case and get things going. If you were served a motion or OSC at the start of a case, you can't be sure if the papers you were served are routine or a real battle brewing. Either way, you should treat the matter very seriously. The outcome of most cases is determined at this level—OSCs and motions—rather than later at trial.

A First things

Whenever you are served with legal papers, read *every* word of *every* paper, even the fine print (skip the Spanish if you read English), including anything that is rubber-stamped. It is all important.

- If you were served with nothing but a Summons and Petition, go to item 4.
- If you were served with a Notice of Motion, go to item 2.
- If you were served with notice of intention to request temporary restraining orders, read item 1.
- If you were served with an OSC, look immediately for two things:
  1. Does the OSC form show a hearing date? See item 1, below.
  2. Are any orders effective against you immediately? See item 2, below.

1. Does the OSC show a hearing date? Have you been given notice of intent to request TROs?

Here's how it works: unless the other side can convince a judge that there is a good reason not to give notice, the judge *must* require at least 24 hours' notice that immediate TROs are going to be requested.

No hearing will have been set yet, so if you received an OSC and the time and date of the hearing have been left blank, although you should also have been given explicit notice with the time and place, this *probably* means you have just received your 24 hours' notice that your ex is seeking orders effective even before the hearing (TROs). Of course, if you received a notice of intention to request immediate orders (TROs) there is no doubt about it. So now here's what you do:

First, look to see what orders are being requested and what facts have been stated to support the requests. Do you want to oppose the request? If you do, ask yourself if you have facts to state on your behalf and any evidence (declarations, witnesses or documents) to present that might contradict or undermine facts stated in your spouse's papers. If you do, you have to move with extreme speed. It's probably too late to get an attorney to help you unless you already have one who happens to have nothing else to do that day. You might have to do this yourself.

- Read all the papers carefully—every word, even fine print and things that have been rubber-stamped on the papers—to see if they say when and where your spouse will submit papers to a judge. Some counties require that you be told this and others do not, so look carefully.
- If the papers say when they will be presented to the court, you can show up and be heard before the judge signs. It will be much better if you can also file a Responsive Declaration ahead of time, but at least show up with something prepared to say.
- If you are not told when and where the papers will be presented for signature, you still file a Responsive Declaration within 24 hours. If you can get your side of things in the file before the judge considers the case, you might do some damage control from the beginning.
- Even if you can't get a Responsive Declaration completed and filed before the judge considers the TROs, you have to start work right away to get one filed before the date of your hearing.
- If this is the first document you have filed in the case, be prepared to pay the filing fee for a Response, about $200. If you have already paid that fee, filing this time is free.

Now, go on to item 2, to see if orders have *already* been signed into effect against you.

2. Orders that are effective when you are served

Motions. The orders requested in a motion are *never* effective until after the hearing on the motion and an Order After Hearing or a stipulation is entered. However, mistakes get made, and this paperwork is over the heads of some attorneys and judges. If your motion came with the Temporary Orders form attached and signed (shouldn't happen) read this next bit about the regular OSC.

Orders to Show Cause. If an OSC has been served on you, it is very possible that some orders have already been made that become effective the moment you are served personally. Check carefully—here's how to tell:

- **Domestic Violence OSC.** If form DV-110 was *not* signed by a judge at the bottom of page 3, there are no orders against you until after the hearing, if ever. If it *was* signed by a judge, then certain orders became effective when you were served. The temporary orders are those checked on form DV-110 at items 6–18. All other forms contain only requests, not immediately effective orders. If you are subject to any orders at all, read page 4 of the OSC *very* carefully. Also carefully read the section on firearms, below.
- **Regular OSC.** If the Temporary Orders form FL-305 is attached to the OSC and signed by a judge, the orders are in effect when you are served. Otherwise, they will not go into effect until after the hearing, if at all.
- Nothing in the Application and Declaration is an order.

If orders are in effect. First, look to see what orders are being requested and what facts have been stated to support the requests.

- Do you want to oppose the request?
- If you do, ask yourself if you have facts to state on your behalf and any evidence (documents, witnesses or declarations of witnesses) to present to the court that might contradict or undermine facts stated in your spouse's papers.
- If you do, you have to move fast. It could be too late to get an attorney to help you unless you already have one lined up and ready to move quickly. You might have to do this yourself. You can object to inadequate notice or request a continuance (sections C and D, below), but even if you do, you still want to get a Responsive Declaration on file as soon as possible.

Do not violate any orders. Read each order very, very carefully and be very careful not to violate any order, no matter how unreasonable or unfair it might seem. To do so could destroy your credibility in court and wreck your case. Orders made at this stage are only "temporary," but they can have a tremendous impact on your case and on your life. You should consider getting some quick, competent advice.

Got guns? If you were served with a Domestic Violence OSC and item 11 is checked, you must go to a police department or sheriff's office within the period of time indicated. Be sure to get a receipt, because within 72 hours of the time you were served with the OSC, you need to take your OSC with the receipt so you can file the receipt with the court clerk. Note that you cannot purchase firearms as long as you have such a restraining order against you. If your employment requires use of firearms, this may be very serious and you should get an attorney to help you. If you end up criminally charged with a domestic violence offense, you should contact an attorney. Even if you are convicted of only a misdemeanor, you can never own a firearm again. If you own any firearms, even if item 11 is not checked, you should turn them over to a relative or friend to get them out of your house until the divorce has settled down.

3. If child custody or visitation is an issue

If the orders requested include child custody/visitation, there could be a date for you to attend an appointment with Family Court Services for mediation, screening or a parenting program. Whatever kind of action you are served with, this information will appear on item 9 of a Domestic Violence OSC (DV-110), item 2c on a regular OSC, or item 6 on a Notice of Motion. Write this date on your calendar. You should also put a note where you can't help seeing it. You do not want to miss this, even though participating in the process can be upsetting. Read about parenting programs in chapter 20.

4. How much time do you have to respond?

Response to the Petition. You need to file a Response to the Petition within 30 days of the day you were served in order to protect your rights and get equal standing in the case with Petitioner. If you do not respond, you can lose your right to participate and a "default" judgment can be entered against you. It is a lot of trouble to have the default set aside later.

The Response is a separate document from the Responsive Declaration to an OSC or motion, and they have different deadlines, so be careful! If you were served with both a Petition and an OSC or motion, you *must* respond to both. Sometimes self-represented people—and even some lawyers—will file a Responsive Declaration to an OSC or motion and forget to file the Response to the Petition. The opening stages of a divorce can be upsetting, so it is easy to forget about the Response. Don't do that.

More about responding to a Summons and Petition, including forms, instructions, and things to look for, is found in Book 1, *How to Do Your Own Divorce,* chapter 10.

Response to Petition and OSC or motion

Petition	is opposed by	**Response** filed and served personally within 30 calendar days of service
OSC or motion	is opposed by	**Responsive Declaration** filed and served personally at least 10 calendar days before the hearing (unless OST changes the deadline)

Response to motion or OSC. If you were served with a Notice of Motion or OSC, examine the papers you were served with to see when your matter is set for a hearing and mark that date on your calendar. Unless the judge signed an order shortening time, you need to file and serve your Responsive Declaration at least 10 calendar days before the hearing, including weekends and holidays, so mark that date, too. It is very important not to be late, but it is better to file late than to not file at all. Papers should be served personally, no later than by the end of the next business day after they were filed.

Custody issue? If there is an appointment with a mediator, it would be best to get your Responsive Declaration on file as much ahead of time as possible, in hopes that the mediator will see the other side of the story. For sure, take a copy of your papers to the appointment.

Order shortening time? If there is an Order Shortening Time (OST), your hearing might be in a day or two, so your Responsive Declaration will have to be done with the speed of light. To find out if there is an OST, look at item 4 on the Notice of Motion, item 18 on the Domestic Violence OSC, or item 3b on a regular OSC.

Make a case calendar

You need to organize and keep track of all activities and deadlines in your case, so set up a calendar that covers the next year or so. Mark the date you were served with the Summons, then count 30 days later and write down "Deadline for Response." A week before that write, "Prepare Response." If you were served with a Notice of Motion or OSC, you will need to calendar the date for your hearing and the deadline for your Responsive Declaration, as explained below.

Get help?

Your spouse could have been planning the divorce for months, but now you have to run around in a mad rush to plan, gather evidence, file a formal responsive paper, and appear in court. It might take an attorney to even up this position, whether or not your spouse has one. Consider calling Divorce Helpline or a local attorney for assistance.

Continuances

Because time is so short and you are under so much pressure, it would be only natural to think about getting your hearing postponed by asking the other side or the judge for a continuance. In either case, you might or might not get one. Asking for a continuance is discussed in section D, below.

Filing fees

The first time you file papers in court, you must pay approximately $200 for becoming a party to the case. Call the court clerk to get the exact amount in your county. If you have already filed a Response and paid the filing fee, there is no additional fee for a Responsive Declaration to a motion or OSC. But if you have not previously paid the Response filing fee, then your Responsive Declaration will trigger the response filing fee and you will have to pay it at that time. Later, when you file your Response to the Petition, there will be no additional cost.

B Respond or settle?

If you can enter into an agreement *in writing* and avoid the necessity of responding to a motion or OSC, that is always desirable, assuming it can be done on reasonably fair terms. However, *never* let a deadline to respond go by just because you are talking. This is a time when you need to proceed on two tracks at the same time: (1) work on a negotiated settlement and hope for a fair agreement, and (2) prepare for the worst—a contested court hearing. Start your response now. Another possibility is where both parties agree to take the matter off-calendar or reset it for a specific later time while they attempt to negotiate the matter. If this happens, you have to file a written stipulation with the court, or have the moving party take the matter off-calendar or set for a later date. The other party should call the clerk to verify.

Review chapter 1, item 2, about reasons not to negotiate. If it makes sense to negotiate, then start talking to the other side by letter, telephone, or email. At the same time, you should immediately begin preparing (1) a Responsive Declaration to any motion or OSC and (2) a Response to the Petition. Particularly if financial requests have been made, it could take some time to do your Income and Expense Declaration, so you can't wait until the last minute then madly scramble to get the documents done. Prepare and file them well in advance. Being prepared will impress the other side and give you a secure feeling for your negotiations. If you reach a settlement, be sure that it is in the form of a written agreement or a stipulation (a formal agreement to be signed by the judge) as described in chapter 5. Even if you agree to terms for a motion or OSC, you might want to go to court on the date of the hearing to be sure the agreement is submitted to the court and there isn't any funny business behind your back.

C How to object if you were served at the last minute

You are entitled to 21 days' notice of any motion or *regular* OSC against you (Code of Civil Procedure section 1005), unless the court has issued an Order Shortening Time reducing the required number of days' notice. If the papers were served on you less than 21 days before the hearing—or, if there is an order shortening time, fewer days than it specifies—at the beginning of the hearing you might want to verbally object that you did not receive adequate notice. If the judge agrees, he/she will refuse to proceed with the hearing and this will give you more time. Now we'll discuss how to make a written motion to object, which can be difficult.

If you object, should you also file your response? If you want to object that you had inadequate service, but you file a good and thorough Responsive Declaration, the judge will feel that you do not need more time because you managed to respond. Even if your papers are pretty sketchy, a lot of lawyers file papers that are equally poor, so they may not look bad to the judge. If you do not file a Responsive Declaration at all, even if there was inadequate notice, the judge could mistakenly proceed by default or refuse to accept your papers or testimony in the courtroom at the time of the hearing. If you do not attend, the judge may forget to check the proof of service to be sure you had twenty-one days' notice.

There is no clear answer to this dilemma. Your choices are: (1) don't do anything (dangerous, as the judge may not pick up the problem); (2) don't file papers but go to the hearing and verbally object that you had inadequate time to prepare so it should go off-calendar or be continued (dangerous, because the judge may proceed, as you evidently had enough notice to get to court); (3) do papers but don't file them and go to the hearing and object to inadequate notice and file the papers only if the judge proceeds (dangerous, as the judge could refuse to accept your papers or testimony if he/she feels you got adequate notice); or (4) fully and timely prepare and file papers and attend hearing (and risk that the judge will probably think your notice was adequate as you did such a good job of preparing). Given all these lousy choices, it is probably best to do (4) if you can, as it is safest.

D Asking for a continuance (postponement)

You may want to go to the hearing on the OSC/motion and verbally ask the judge for a postponement, which in court is called a continuance. Often, especially for OSCs, your hearing will be calendared for a date so near in the future that you will not have time to make a written motion to continue. Whether the judge grants your verbal request for a continuance will depend on so many factors that we cannot predict if it will be granted. Getting a continuance is described in more detail in chapter 24. Read it now.

In general, the judge will expect you to have a good reason why you need a continuance. An example related to motions and OSCs (not trials) would be if there was an order shortening time so that you got only a few days' notice of the hearing. Other good reasons are in chapter 24.

Always hope for the best and prepare for the worst. You must be fully prepared to proceed with the hearing if it turns out that your request is denied.

Got orders? The judge is likely to leave restraining orders in force until the next hearing. So if your spouse got an immediate stay-away order against you, it could be used to deny you contact with your children. You will need to call this problem to the judge's attention at the hearing, as he/she might not be aware that an order made for safety is being used to determine visitation.

E How to do a Responsive Declaration

If you are opposed to any of the orders requested by your spouse in an OSC or motion, file a Responsive Declaration to present your side to the court. The way you state facts and build your case is discussed in chapter 11. Much of what applies to doing a motion or OSC also applies to your response, so be sure to review chapters 12 and 13, too. It will help you understand what the other side is doing, as well as what you are going to do.

Order of business

First, complete your papers, then file them, then have someone serve them on your spouse and his/her attorney of record, if any (see chapter 9H), then file a Proof of Service. Your papers must be filed and served personally on your spouse at least 10 calendar days before the hearing, but if there was an order to shorten time, follow that. Count all days including weekends and holidays. It is very important not to be late, but it is better to file late than not to file at all. Do not wait until the last minute. The sooner you file your Responsive Declaration, the more likely it is that your side of the story will be in the judge's file by the time of the hearing. However, if you are relying on some sort of surprise tactic, or want to put time pressure on the other side, have papers served personally 10 calendar days before the hearing and file them on the same day. Be careful, though; this type of brinksmanship is dangerous as your plans can be destroyed by a traffic jam on the freeway or a dozen other things. We cannot recommend serving your response at the last minute.

Checklist of response documents

- ☐ **Responsive Declaration to OSC or Notice of Motion (FL-320)**
  Attachments that might be used:
  - ☐ a. Child Custody and Visitation Attachment (FL-311) (if parenting is an issue) and Declaration Under Uniform Child Custody Jurisdiction Act (FL-105)
  - ☐ b. Income and Expense Declaration (FL-150) (if money requested) and computer report if support requested and you want a different result (optional)
  - ☐ c. Declarations of witnesses, if any (see chapter 11F)
  - ☐ d. Memorandum of Points and Authorities (optional, see chapter 11A)
  - ☐ e. Request for Oral Testimony (optional, see chapter 11D)

Which Responsive Declaration to use

There are two different Responsive Declaration forms: one for domestic violence cases, and another that is used to respond to a regular OSC or a motion.

- If you were served with a Regular OSC (FL-300) or a Notice of Motion (FL-301), you respond with the Responsive Declaration to Order to Show Cause or Notice of Motion (FL-320) (Figure 14.1).
- If you were served with a Domestic Violence OSC, DV-110, respond with DV-120, Answer to Temporary Restraining Order. Instructions on this and all DV forms are found in the DV forms set on our CD (see page 113). Also read this chapter for general information and chapter 15 on how to prepare for and do a hearing.

Attachments. See discussion on the attachments in chapter 12 (motion) or 13 (OSC). The same information can be useful to you, too. Basically, if the motion or OSC includes such attachments and you want to oppose or alter the orders they support, or have a different version of the facts, then you must file your own attachments in response.

How to do the Responsive Declaration

First, think about what facts you are going to state and how you are going to convince the judge that you are in the right. Plan your case and get witness declarations, if there are going to be any. Read chapter 11D–F about how to build your case and make written declarations. The Responsive Declaration form is filled out as sown in Figure 14.1.

Reply to every order requested. You *must* respond to *every* order requested by your spouse, or it will be assumed that you consent to it. You do this by checking boxes on your Responsive Declaration that correspond to the orders requested in the OSC or motion.

Suggest an alternative order. The response to the regular OSC offers you an opportunity to suggest an alternative order that you would accept. On any item, you can check the box that says "I would consent to the following order," and put down what you want on this particular order. For example, for spousal support or attorney fees, you can enter an amount that you would pay, or you could even request that the moving party pay you instead. Or, if your spouse wants control of the family's 2001 Lexus, you could offer the equally serviceable 1992 Honda Civic, pointing out in your declaration that you have to drive buyers while he/she drives your two children around. Or, say supervised visitation was requested; you can oppose or you can suggest other visitation arrangements than the ones requested. If you can't afford supervision, say so, and say that you don't want to be cut off from your kids just because you don't have money for supervision.

State facts. Item 9 is where you state facts and attach documents that justify each position you have taken. This is your own declaration or statement of facts. Do not write your declaration before you read chapter 11F. It might be possible for you to fit a simple declaration into the space provided, but if there's not enough room, simply check the second box at this item and attach your typed declaration that includes facts you want to state to the court. If you also attach the declarations of other witnesses, or other documents, refer to them here. For example, "See attached declarations of (Petitioner/Respondent), declarations of witnesses, and attached documents in support of this Order to Show Cause."

Asking for something new that was not in the OSC or motion

Sometimes you want the court to consider something new and different than what was requested in the OSC or motion. Perhaps the moving party wants you kicked out of the house, and you want him/her to pay the mortgage if he/she stays. Or maybe he/she didn't ask for attorney fees, and you want attorney fees ordered so you can afford to hire a lawyer.

Domestic violence OSC. If you want a domestic violence restraining order against your spouse, you must file your own OSC, not just a Responsive Declaration. Even if your spouse filed a domestic violence OSC against you, you cannot use your Responsive Declaration to obtain a protective order against him/her. You must do your own domestic violence OSC if you are fearful for your own safety. Mutual restraining orders are becoming rare.

Everything else. Sate law is not perfectly clear on the subject of what is new matter and when it can be raised, so results tend to vary from court to court. Most judges will let you raise issues that are closely related to (or part of) the requests in the moving papers, but they will not let you bring up completely new issues in your Responsive Declaration.

If your spouse wants to increase support, and you want to decrease it, you should say so in your Responsive Declaration because it is the same subject. But, if your spouse wants support and you want attorney fees, you will probably have to file your own OSC or motion.

When you are not sure, the safest thing is to do both: include the (possibly) new matter in your response *and* file your own motion or OSC at the same time. You can always take it off-calendar later if the issue is handled in the first hearing. You need to do this because it is possible for the judge that hears your new OSC or motion might think the issue was properly part of the first OSC or motion and decide that you gave up your right by not raising it in your Responsive Declaration in the first place. If the first judge already decided it was a new matter, this can't happen.

How to file and serve your Responsive Declaration

Because time is so short, your Responsive Declaration should be filed first, then served personally no later than by the end of the next business day after filing. Prepare a proof of service and have the server sign it. Make copies, then file the original proof of service with the court. If you file your Responsive Declaration late, bring an extra copy to court to give to your spouse in case your papers haven't gotten to the other side by the time of the hearing.

Figure 14.1

RESPONSIVE DECLARATION TO ORDER TO SHOW CAUSE OR NOTICE OF MOTION

Form FL-320 (page 1)

FL-320

ATTORNEY OR PARTY WITHOUT ATTORNEY *(Name, state bar number, and address):*	FOR COURT USE ONLY
YOUR NAME Your address City, State, Zip TELEPHONE NO.: Your phone FAX NO.: Your fax ATTORNEY FOR *(Name):* Petitioner / Respondent in pro per	
SUPERIOR COURT OF CALIFORNIA, COUNTY OF YOUR COUNTY STREET ADDRESS: Street address MAILING ADDRESS: PO Box, if any CITY AND ZIP CODE: City, State, Zip BRANCH NAME: Branch name, if any	
PETITIONER/PLAINTIFF: PETITIONER'S NAME RESPONDENT/DEFENDANT: RESPONDENT'S NAME	
RESPONSIVE DECLARATION TO ORDER TO SHOW CAUSE OR NOTICE OF MOTION HEARING DATE: Hearing date TIME: Hearing time DEPARTMENT OR ROOM: Department no.	CASE NUMBER: Your case number

1. [X] CHILD CUSTODY
   - a. [ ] I consent to the order requested.
   - b. [X] I do not consent to the order requested but I consent to the following order:

     Joint legal and joint physical custody

2. [X] CHILD VISITATION
   - a. [ ] I consent to the order requested.
   - b. [X] I do not consent to the order requested but I consent to the following order:

     Unsupervised visitation according to the attached schedule, Attachment for Item 2(b)

3. [X] CHILD SUPPORT
   - a. [ ] I consent to the order requested.
   - b. [ ] I consent to guideline support.
   - c. [X] I do not consent to the order requested, but I consent to the following order:
     - (1) [ ] Guideline
     - (2) [X] Other *(specify):* $1234, as shown in attached computer calculation based upon correct financial data and rebuttal factors described in attached declarations and documents

4. [X] SPOUSAL SUPPORT
   - a. [ ] I consent to the order requested.
   - b. [ ] I do not consent to the order requested.
   - c. [X] I consent to the following order: Petitioner pay to respondent $123 per month as and for spousal support

5. [ ] ATTORNEY FEES AND COSTS
   - a. [ ] I consent to the order requested.
   - b. [ ] I do not consent to the order requested.
   - c. [ ] I consent to the following order:

Check only boxes that correspond to requests made by the other side. If you want to request something else, you have to file your own OSC or Notice of Motion. See page 122.

Form Adopted for Mandatory Use
Judicial Council of California
FL-320 [Rev. January 1, 2003]

RESPONSIVE DECLARATION TO ORDER TO SHOW CAUSE OR NOTICE OF MOTION

Page 1 of 2
www.courtinfo.ca.gov

Figure 14.2

RESPONSIVE DECLARATION TO ORDER TO SHOW CAUSE OR NOTICE OF MOTION

Form FL-320 (page 2)

PETITIONER/PLAINTIFF: PETITIONER'S NAME RESPONDENT/DEFENDANT: RESPONDENT'S NAME	CASE NUMBER: Your case number

6. [X] PROPERTY RESTRAINT
   a. [ ] I consent to the order requested.
   b. [ ] I do not consent to the order requested.
   c. [X] I consent to the following order:
   Restraints to be made mutual

7. [X] PROPERTY CONTROL
   a. [ ] I consent to the order requested.
   b. [ ] I do not consent to the order requested.
   c. [X] I consent to the following order:
   Parties to vacate residence and put it up for sale
   Petitioner to have possession of 1987 Toyota Van, CA license 2ZXY321

8. [ ] OTHER RELIEF
   a. [ ] I consent to the order requested.
   b. [X] I do not consent to the order requested.
   c. [ ] I consent to the following order:

9. [X] SUPPORTING INFORMATION
   [X] contained in the attached declaration.

See attached declaration of Respondent, computer support calculation, supporting documentation, and declarations of pediatric nurse John Smith and day-care provider Susan Jones.

NOTE: To respond to a request for domestic violence restraining orders requested in the *Request for Order (Domestic Violence Prevention)* (form DV-100) you must use the *Answer to Temporary Restraining Order (Domestic Violence Prevention)* (form DV-120).

I declare under penalty of perjury under the laws of the State of California that the foregoing is true and correct.

Date: Date signed

YOUR NAME ▶ ______________________

(TYPE OR PRINT NAME) (SIGNATURE OF DECLARANT)

FL-320 [Rev. January 1, 2003] **RESPONSIVE DECLARATION TO ORDER TO SHOW CAUSE OR NOTICE OF MOTION** Page 2 of 2

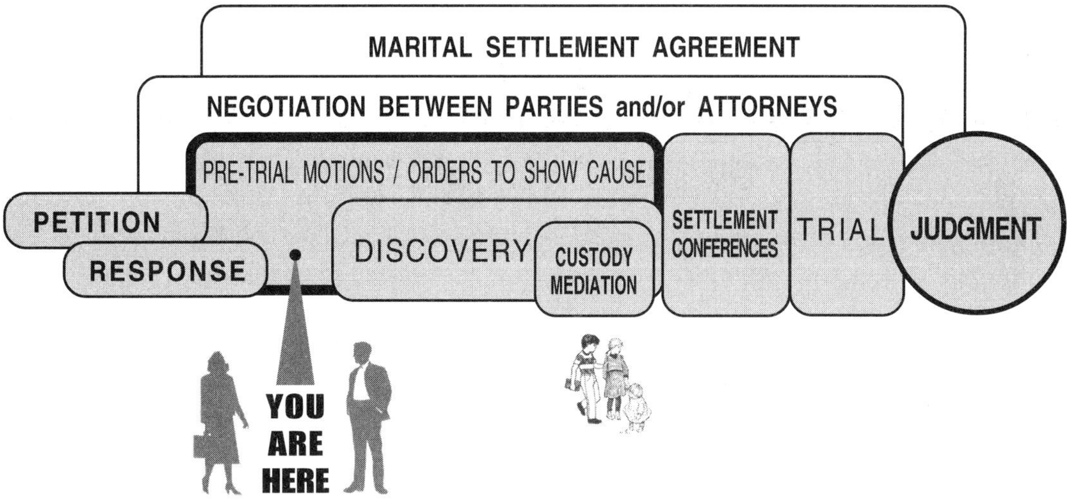

CHAPTER 15
PRESENTING YOUR CASE AT THE HEARING

A. Preparing for the hearing
B. How to subpoena witnesses or records
C. How to do the hearing
D. Expired TROs
E. At the end of the hearing

A Preparing for the hearing

Also read chapter 25, preparing for and conducting a trial, since much of the discussion there is also useful for hearings, especially if you have gained permission to present witnesses. Except for the absence of oral testimony, a hearing is just a teeny trial. Well before your hearing, make sure your case is well-organized and you have notes for what you are going to say, what documents you are going to introduce, and what witnesses, if any, will need to be subpoenaed to be present. Much of this is covered in chapter 25.

Subpoena witnesses or documents to court. If you need a witness to come to court to testify, or bring records, or both, you must be prepared to get subpoenas out as soon as you get a hearing date. How you do this is covered in section B. Deadlines are in B(f).

Go at least one day to visit court and watch divorce motions being heard. Ask the clerk if you can determine ahead of time what judge is likely to hear a motion that you might file in your own case. Observe how attorneys and individuals conduct themselves, what works and what doesn't. Observe the judge's behavior. Try to determine if the judge responds better to written or oral information and plan your own presentation accordingly.

Organize your presentation in writing by bringing a legible outline of what you are going to say and a list of the evidence you want to have introduced. Experienced attorneys often type their presentations to the court, at least in outline. If they need to do this, you certainly do, too, particularly given that you might be under emotional stress. If you have an attorney who comes unprepared to your hearing and just speaks from what he/she remembers, this would not be a good sign. Read the discussion in chapter 25 about how to organize documents and witnesses.

Meet and confer. Many counties have local rules that require parties to meet and confer before the court hearing to try to reach an agreement, unless there is an allegation of domestic violence. You may know in your heart that meeting with your spouse is hopeless, but if the court rules require it, you should figure out a safe way to do it. Many people meet in a 24-hour restaurant where they know there will be other people. You don't want your spouse to come to court and say, "Your Honor, my spouse refused to meet with me and to discuss settlement; he/she only wants to drag me into court." You want to look and act like the good guy, even if the only benefit is to show the judge it's hopeless.

Exchange documents. Many counties have a local rule requiring an exchange of every document you intend to show the court some number of days before a hearing. If yours does, find out the deadline and do it. If you included a copy of everything in your original OSC/motion, as we recommend, you're already covered. Even if your spouse shows you nothing, you should comply because you don't want to risk the judge refusing your evidence because you didn't follow the rules. Sometimes there is an exception for "impeachment" evidence; that is, evidence whose purpose is only to show the other person is a liar. It may not be necessary to exchange that in advance. Check local rules.

Request for oral testimony. If you want oral testimony, you need to file a written request to be allowed this privilege at least 3 days ahead of the hearing as described in chapter 11D. Because this is a state rule, it applies in all counties. Even though you make a request, this does not ensure that it will be granted, so the safest thing is still to put everything into your moving papers.

Does your judge read papers? Since hearings generally do not have oral testimony or cross-examination, you would think judges would read the papers in advance. Wrong. Because almost all cases settle or continue, judges don't want to read papers for cases that are not going to be heard. Call the clerk in the courtroom that will hold your hearing and ask what the judge's practice is. Anything other than a confident, "Judge X always reads papers," then you should prepare as if the judge will not have read your papers. At the hearing, if you are not sure, ask the judge if he/she has read the papers. If not, you need to ask the judge to please read them or allow you enough time to orally describe every detail that is in them.

Ask for a pre-read. Some counties, like Ventura and San Diego, specifically provide in local rules that if you want the judge to read your papers, you should phone the clerk a certain number of days before the hearing. In any county, it can't hurt to ask the clerk if you can request a "pre-read," especially if your motion is not simple.

If you know who your judge will be and whether he/she wants visual or oral information, how to prepare is fairly clear. However, assuming you do not know, you need to be prepared for both possibilities in case (1) the judge will have read your papers and will get irritated if you repeat everything in them, or (2) the judge will want you to present every detail of the case orally. If oral testimony was permitted, you need both a short version and a long version of what you will say at the hearing. Both versions begin with a list of issues that are before the court. This part of your talk recites the headings the moving party used in the motion. After that, you should have (1) a short oral statement with only *new* facts for a judge who reads papers, and (2) for a judge who does not read papers, a longer statement that summarizes the strong points in favor of your position plus any new facts. You should type your statements double spaced or print them very clearly. This way, when you go to court, even if you become so frightened that you can't think of anything to say, you can simply read what you have written. Having everything written will probably keep you from panicking.

Bring extra copies of your papers to court. Court filings can get backlogged, so your papers might not be in the judge's file by the time of the hearing. Your judge might prefer written information, so always bring an extra set of your papers to the hearing so you have one for yourself and one for the judge.

B How to subpoena witnesses or records to court

A subpoena has the power of a court order, requiring the person addressed to come to court. Use the **Civil Subpoena** for Personal Appearance to direct a witness to appear in court to give testimony when you do not need them to bring records or items with them. Use the **Civil Subpoena (Duces Tecum)** to direct a witness to bring something to court (*"Duces tecum"* is Latin for "with you," that is, the witness is to bring something with him/her to court).

How subpoenas are issued. A subpoena must be "issued" by the court clerk—i.e., stamped with the seal of the court. In some counties, you can get blank forms that have already been issued from the place that provides court forms in your area. If you are in a county where the clerk does not issue Subpoenas in blank, fill out your Subpoena first, then take it to court to have the clerk issue it. If you have an attorney, the attorney can issue the Subpoena merely by signing it, without having to involve the court clerk.

Checklist of documents

☐ a. Civil Subpoena, or ☐ b. Civil Subpoena (Duces Tecum)
☐ c. Phone notice agreement (if witness is on phone standby)
☐ d. Consumer/Employee Notice (if seeking anything other than a police report)
☐ e. Proof of Service (part of the Subpoena form)

a. Civil Subpoena for Personal Appearance

Fill it out as shown in Figure 15.1.

Caption. Enter name, address and phone of the person subpoenaed in the space above item 1.

Item 1. Enter the date, time and courtroom where the witness is to appear. If you have an all-purpose judge, subpoena your witnesses to that judge's courtroom; but, if your case is going to be assigned out from a master calendar department, you enter the number of the master calendar department and add "or other department to which assigned for trial."

Item 2. Enter your name and phone number, so the subpoenaed party knows how to contact you.

b. Civil Subpoena (Duces Tecum) for Personal Appearance

Fill it out as shown in Figure 15.2.

Caption. Enter name, address and phone of the person who has control of the things you want.

Item 1. Same as for item 1 on the Civil Subpoena, in (a), directly above.

Item 3. Put an x in box 3(a) to compel the person subpoenaed to bring the records to your hearing. If you are requesting records from a hospital or large business, they may be used to the process in Item 3(b). In fact, they might try to insist on it. Unfortunately, there are two problems with the 3(b) process: first, records are sometimes delivered to court but then can't be located for the hearing; second, the process is fairly complicated and witnesses sometimes do it wrong. So check item 3(a).

Item 4. Enter your name and phone number, so the subpoenaed party knows how to contact you.

Figure 15.1

CIVIL SUBPOENA FOR PERSONAL APPEARANCE AT TRIAL OR HEARING

Form 982(a)(15)

982(a)(15)

ATTORNEY OR PARTY WITHOUT ATTORNEY *(Name, state bar number, and address)*:	FOR COURT USE ONLY
YOUR NAME Your Address City, State, Zip TELEPHONE NO.: Your phone FAX NO.: Your fax (optional) ATTORNEY FOR *(Name)*: Petitioner in pro per	
NAME OF COURT: SUPERIOR COURT, COUNTY OF YOUR COUNTY STREET ADDRESS: Court Street Address MAILING ADDRESS: Court Mailing Address CITY AND ZIP CODE: City, State, Zip BRANCH NAME: Branch name (Norther, Family, Main, etc.)	
PLAINTIFF/ PETITIONER: PETITIONER'S NAME DEFENDANT/ RESPONDENT: RESPONDENT'S NAME	
CIVIL SUBPOENA **For Personal Appearance at Trial or Hearing**	CASE NUMBER: Your case number

THE PEOPLE OF THE STATE OF CALIFORNIA, TO *(name, address, and telephone number of witness, if known)*:
Name of subpoenaed witness
Witness address, City, State, Zip

1. **YOU ARE ORDERED TO APPEAR AS A WITNESS in this action at the date, time, and place shown in the box below UNLESS you make an agreement with the person named in item 2:**

   a. Date: Hearing/Trial date Time: Time ☑ Dept.: number ☐ Div.: ☐ Room:
   b. Address: Court street address
   City, State, Zip

2. **IF YOU HAVE ANY QUESTIONS ABOUT THE TIME OR DATE FOR YOU TO APPEAR, OR IF YOU WANT TO BE CERTAIN THAT YOUR PRESENCE IS REQUIRED, CONTACT THE FOLLOWING PERSON BEFORE THE DATE ON WHICH YOU ARE TO APPEAR:**

   a. Name of subpoenaing party or attorney: YOUR NAME b. Telephone number: Your phone

3. **Witness Fees:** You are entitled to witness fees and mileage actually traveled both ways, as provided by law, if you request them at the time of service. You may request them before your scheduled appearance from the person named in item 2.

DISOBEDIENCE OF THIS SUBPOENA MAY BE PUNISHED AS CONTEMPT BY THIS COURT. YOU WILL ALSO BE LIABLE FOR THE SUM OF FIVE HUNDRED DOLLARS AND ALL DAMAGES RESULTING FROM YOUR FAILURE TO OBEY.

Date issued:

(TYPE OR PRINT NAME) ▶ (SIGNATURE OF PERSON ISSUING SUBPOENA)

(TITLE)

(Proof of service on reverse)

Form Adopted for Mandatory Use
Judicial Council of California
982(a)(15) [Rev. January 1, 2000]

CIVIL SUBPOENA FOR PERSONAL APPEARANCE AT TRIAL OR HEARING

Code of Civil Procedure, §§ 1985, 1986, 1987

Figure 15.2
CIVIL SUBPOENA (DUCES TECUM) FOR PERSONAL APPEARANCE

Form 982(a)(15.1) (page 1)

982(a)(15.1)

ATTORNEY OR PARTY WITHOUT ATTORNEY (Name, state bar number, and address):

YOUR NAME
Your Address
City, State, Zip

TELEPHONE NO.: Your phone FAX NO.: Your fax
ATTORNEY FOR (Name): Petitioner in pro per

FOR COURT USE ONLY

NAME OF COURT: SUPERIOR COURT, COUNTY OF YOUR COUNTY
STREET ADDRESS: Court Street Address
MAILING ADDRESS: Court Mailing Address
CITY AND ZIP CODE: City, State, Zip
BRANCH NAME: Branch Name (Norther, Main, Family, etc.)

PLAINTIFF/ PETITIONER: PETITIONER'S NAME

DEFENDANT/ RESPONDENT: RESPONDENT'S NAME

CIVIL SUBPOENA (DUCES TECUM) for Personal Appearance and Production of Documents and Things at Trial or Hearing AND DECLARATION

CASE NUMBER: Your case number

THE PEOPLE OF THE STATE OF CALIFORNIA, TO *(name, address, and telephone number of witness, if known)*:

Witness' name, address, telephone number

1. **YOU ARE ORDERED TO APPEAR AS A WITNESS in this action at the date, time, and place shown in the box below UNLESS your appearance is excused as indicated in box 3b below or you make an agreement with the person named in item 4 below.**
   a. Date: Hearing date Time: Time ☑ Dept.: number ☐ Div.: ☐ Room:
   b. Address: Court Address, City, State, Zip
2. **IF YOU HAVE BEEN SERVED WITH THIS SUBPOENA AS A CUSTODIAN OF CONSUMER OR EMPLOYEE RECORDS UNDER CODE OF CIVIL PROCEDURE SECTION 1985.3 OR 1985.6 AND A MOTION TO QUASH OR AN OBJECTION HAS BEEN SERVED ON YOU, A COURT ORDER OR AGREEMENT OF THE PARTIES, WITNESSES, *AND* CONSUMER OR EMPLOYEE AFFECTED MUST BE OBTAINED BEFORE YOU ARE REQUIRED TO PRODUCE CONSUMER OR EMPLOYEE RECORDS.**
3. YOU ARE *(item a or b must be checked)*:
   a. ☑ Ordered to appear in person and to produce the records described in the declaration on page two or the attached declaration or affidavit. The personal attendance of the custodian or other qualified witness and the production of the original records are required by this subpoena. The procedure authorized by Evidence Code sections 1560(b), 1561, and 1562 will not be deemed sufficient compliance with this subpoena.
   b. ☐ Not required to appear in person if you produce (i) the records described in the declaration on page two or the attached declaration or affidavit and (ii) a completed declaration of custodian of records in compliance with Evidence Code sections 1560, 1561, 1562, and 1271. (1) Place a copy of the records in an envelope (or other wrapper). Enclose the original declaration of the custodian with the records. Seal the envelope. (2) Attach a copy of this subpoena to the envelope or write on the envelope the case name and number: your name; and the date, time, and place from item 1 in the box above. (3) Place this first envelope in an outer envelope, seal it, and mail it to the clerk of the court at the address in item 1. (4) Mail a copy of your declaration to the attorney or party listed at the top of this form.
4. **IF YOU HAVE ANY QUESTIONS ABOUT THE TIME OR DATE YOU ARE TO APPEAR, OR IF YOU WANT TO BE CERTAIN THAT YOUR PRESENCE IS REQUIRED, CONTACT THE FOLLOWING PERSON BEFORE THE DATE ON WHICH YOU ARE TO APPEAR:**
   a. Name of subpoenaing party or attorney: YOUR NAME b. Telephone number: Your phone
5. **Witness Fees:** You are entitled to witness fees and mileage actually traveled both ways, as provided by law, if you request them at the time of service. You may request them before your scheduled appearance from the person named in item 4.

DISOBEDIENCE OF THIS SUBPOENA MAY BE PUNISHED AS CONTEMPT BY THIS COURT. YOU WILL ALSO BE LIABLE FOR THE SUM OF FIVE HUNDRED DOLLARS AND ALL DAMAGES RESULTING FROM YOUR FAILURE TO OBEY.

Date issued:

(TYPE OR PRINT NAME) (SIGNATURE OF PERSON ISSUING SUBPOENA)

(TITLE)

(Declaration in support of subpoena on reverse)

Page one of three

Form Adopted for Mandatory Use
Judicial Council of California
982(a)(15.1) [Rev. January 1, 2000]

CIVIL SUBPOENA (DUCES TECUM) FOR PERSONAL APPEARANCE AND PRODUCTION OF DOCUMENTS AND THINGS AT TRIAL OR HEARING AND DECLARATION

Code of Civil Procedure, § 1985 et seq.

Figure 15.3
CIVIL SUBPOENA (DUCES TECUM) FOR PERSONAL APPEARANCE

Form 982(a)(15.1) (page 2)

PLAINTIFF/PETITIONER: PETITIONER'S NAME DEFENDANT/RESPONDENT: RESPONDENT'S NAME	CASE NUMBER: Your case number

The production of the documents or the other things sought by the subpoena on page one is supported by *(check one)*:
☑ the attached affidavit or declaration ☐ the following declaration:

DECLARATION IN SUPPORT OF CIVIL SUBPOENA (DUCES TECUM) FOR PERSONAL APPEARANCE AND PRODUCTION OF DOCUMENTS AND THINGS AT TRIAL OR HEARING
(Code Civ. Proc., §§ 1985, 1987.5)

1. I, the undersigned, declare I am the ☐ plaintiff ☐ defendant ☑ petitioner ☐ respondent ☐ attorney for *(specify)*: ☐ other *(specify)*: in the above-entitled action.

2. The witness has possession or control of the following documents or other things and shall produce them at the time and place specified in the *Civil Subpoena for Personal Appearance and Production of Documents and Things at Trial or Hearing* on page one of this form *(specify the exact documents or other things to be produced)*:

   List with specific identity of every item to be produced

   ☐ Continued on Attachment 2.

3. Good cause exists for the production of the documents or other things described in paragraph 2 for the following reasons:

   The information in the subpoenaed records is relevant to issues herein and not available to me by other means.

   ☐ Continued on Attachment 3.

4. These documents or other things described in paragraph 2 are material to the issues involved in this case for the following reasons:

   The subpoenaed records will show (for example: Respondent's assets, income, and ability to make payments, which is relevant to issues of support and payment of debts herein).

   ☐ Continued on Attachment 4.

I declare under penalty of perjury under the laws of the State of California that the foregoing is true and correct.

Date: Date signed

YOUR NAME in pro per
(TYPE OR PRINT NAME)

▶
(SIGNATURE OF ☑ SUBPOENAING PARTY ☐ ATTORNEY FOR SUBPOENAING PARTY)

(Proof of service on page three)

982(a)(15.1) [Rev. January 1, 2000] **CIVIL SUBPOENA (DUCES TECUM) FOR PERSONAL APPEARANCE AND PRODUCTION OF DOCUMENTS AND THINGS AT TRIAL OR HEARING AND DECLARATION** Page two of three

Back of form—Declaration in Support of Civil Subpoena (Duces Tecum):

Item 1. Check box for petitioner or respondent to indicate who you are.

Item 2. List each and every item that you want the witness to bring to court. There can be no ambiguity or doubt as to what is being subpoenaed. If there's not enough room on the form, check the box "continued on Attachment 2" and do your list on another sheet as described in chapter 9C. See Figures 17.2 and 17.3 for examples, except the footer would read "Attachment 2."

Item 3. Make a concise declaration showing that there is a good reason why you need the subpoenaed items. Typically, this will be your statement that "The information in the subpoenaed records is relevant to the issues herein and not available to me by other means."

Item 4. Make a concise declaration stating in what way the information is material (important) to an issue before the court. For example, "The subpoenaed records will show Respondent's assets, income, and ability to make payments which are relevant to the issue of support herein."

d. Phone notice agreement

Cases frequently start late. Call the clerk the day before and ask about the schedule. The best thing is to put the witnesses on phone-call standby. Have him/her sign a written agreement to appear on phone notice (Figure 15.4). You *must* explain that this does not mean the witnesses will testify by phone—witnesses need to be in court. Get each witness to agree to show up no later than an agreed amount of time after he/she is called, say on 30 or 60 minutes' notice. Impress upon each that he/she *must* respond without excuse or the judge will probably get angry and issue a bench warrant for his/her arrest. As soon as your case is assigned to a courtroom, have an assistant call the witnesses and tell each at what time he/she should appear, estimating the time you think each will take. Be very careful not to have gaps in time when you have no witnesses. If you have to wait 20 minutes for a witness, the judge could declare your trial over. Be prepared to testify yourself or have a friendly witness on hand who can testify in a pinch.

If a witnesses refuses to sign the phone-call notice, they are required to appear in court at the time and place on the subpoena. When the case is called, if it is assigned to another courtroom, you *must* ask the judge to order witnesses for your case to go there. If you are in either the master calendar department or the trial department and a witness is missing, you must either do without that witness or immediately ask the court to issue a bench warrant. This tends to make witnesses unhappy, so consider whether you really need the witness and whether this angry witness will say what you want. If you think he/she will be truthful though angry, and if you need the witness, ask for the bench warrant. Usually, if someone phones the witness and mentions the bench warrant, he/she will scurry to court. If the case is called, the witness is not there, and you do not immediately establish that fact on the record and ask for a bench warrant, the court loses power to punish the witness. You have to act immediately or lose the witness.

e. Consumer/Employee Notice

When requiring records that are about anyone but the witness, you must first serve a Consumer or Employee Notice on your spouse as discussed in chapter 17, section C(d). See Figure 17.22.

f. Service deadlines and the Proof of Service

Each subpoena form includes a Proof of Service on page 2 or 3. Have someone *personally* serve *copies* of the subpoena on the witness and sign the *original* form. Keep the original and be *very* careful not to misplace it. Subpoenas are not filed with the court unless you have problems getting compliance. Take it to court with you in case you need to prove the subpoena was served.

Figure 15.4

PHONE NOTICE AGREEMENT

MARRIAGE OF YOUR LAST NAME & SPOUSE LAST NAME

CASE NUMBER: Your case number

ACKNOWLEDGMENT OF RECEIPT OF SUBPOENA AND AGREEMENT TO APPEAR UPON PHONE CALL NOTICE

I acknowledge receipt of a subpoena to appear in Department [Dept. No.], Superior Court of [your county] County, [name of branch or district].

Instead of appearing at the time stated in said subpoena, I agree to appear upon telephone request of at least one half hour.

I understand that my failure to appear pursuant to this agreement may be punished as contempt of court, and I will make myself available for receipt of notice to appear through the following telephone numbers:

_________________ Home Phone

_________________ Business Phone

_________________ Cell Phone

_________________ Pager

_________________ Message Phone

Dated:_________

____
Signature

1

Acknowledge Receipt of Subpoena and Agreement to Appear Upon Phone Call

Deadline for personal appearance. When you subpoena a witness to court, you only need to give him/her "reasonable" notice, and what is reasonable depends on who the person is and how far from court. A judge would probably find less than a week's notice to be unreasonable unless the person subpoenaed was very involved in the case already or there was some good reason for late notice.

Deadline for subpoena duces tecum. For police records, serve the subpoena a reasonable time before trial. For records of a consumer or employee, see chapter 17(C)(d) for special deadlines. Before you subpoena a witness to bring records that concern a third person—bank records, statements, etc.—you must first prepare the Consumer/Employee Notice (Figure 17.22) and serve it on the person whose records have been subpoenaed (typically, your spouse). You must serve the witness at least 16 days before trial, but five days before *that* you must serve your spouse (or spouse's attorney) personally.

Server must be prepared to pay witness fees. Whenever you serve a subpoena on anyone other than your spouse, you must pay a witness fee, but only on demand. The amount of the witness fee is set by law at $35 plus twenty cents a mile one-way. Your server should have a check for $35 plus mileage in hand, in case the witness asks for it. If you are subpoenaing an expert, you must be prepared at the beginning of the appearance to pay the expert for about two hours of preparation plus the hours he/she actually spends testifying. If you subpoena someone from Family Court Services, that expert can charge only his/her usual hourly rate, say $35 per hour, not the $200–400 per hour that private experts would charge.

C How to do the hearing

Also read chapter 25 on going to trial, as much of what's there is relevant to presenting a case at a hearing.

Don't be late, not even by one minute. Plan to arrive 30 minutes early. Check out the parking situation in advance. Allow for terrible traffic. Make sure you have the phone number of the clerk in the courtroom so you can call the court if you are late. Don't take *any* chances. Arriving late could put the judge in a bad mood toward your case. If it is your motion or OSC, it could get your matter thrown out of court, which would mean you'll have to start over from the beginning with a spouse on full alert.

Calendar call. In some counties, you show up at the courtroom where the hearing will be heard. In other counties, you show up at a master calendar court where cases are assigned out for hearing. In either case, when court begins, the judge "calls the calendar" either to see who is present or to actually hear each case. When your case name is called, if you do not have a lawyer, stand up and walk to the railing and say loud and clear, "Ready, Your Honor!" The judge might ask how much time your case will take, then either hear your case or assign it to another court. You'll be happy now if you followed our advice and visited court previously to observe some cases so you'll know how things go.

Judge pro-tem? You might be offered an "opportunity" to have your hearing with a commissioner acting as judge pro-tem (an attorney acting as temporary judge). If you know and like your real judge, you can refuse the judge pro-tem. If you dislike your judge, maybe you should take your chances with a judge pro-tem. If you don't know the pro-tem and are neutral towards your judge, refuse the judge pro-tem if you want to stall your hearing. If you want to hurry up and get it done, accept the judge pro-tem. If you object and are sent to the commissioner anyway, you have to object on the record both *before* and *after* the hearing. Then you are entitled to have your case heard all over again by a real judge.

If your spouse asks for a continuance. Your spouse or his/her attorney might come to court and request a continuance (postponement). This will usually occur during the calendar call. You will want to tell the judge (1) why you very much need the matter heard right now, and (2) your spouse had plenty of time to respond and prepare, and (3) reasons, if you have any, for why having to return to court would work a hardship on you, your kids, your employer, or any witnesses you have with you. Always bring your calendar to court and be aware of your own and your children's schedules for the next several months. Even if you don't expect a postponement, sometimes the case ends up getting continued by the court itself. Be prepared to pick a future date.

Abusive spouse? If you and your spouse don't have attorneys, and your spouse is physically dangerous to you—meaning that he/she has physically hurt you in the past—then a day or two before your hearing, go in and ask the bailiff how your safety can be ensured at the hearing.

Ask to keep TROs in effect. TROs expire at the time of the hearing. If your case is continued, and you had restraining orders through an OSC, you *must* ask the judge to keep those orders in effect until the next hearing. Otherwise, your orders are gone and you will be unprotected.

Pressure to settle. The judge might insist that you and your spouse (or attorneys if there are any in your case) go into the hallway and try to reach a settlement. No matter how hopeless you think this is, you have to go out and talk. If your spouse is abusive and is likely to yell at you or worse, then (1) ask the judge to send a bailiff to ensure civility and safety, or (2) try to talk, and if he/she starts yelling, go back to court and, when your case is called, explain to the judge what happened. You don't have to agree. The judge is there to decide cases for people who don't agree. Who knows, many cases do settle "on the courthouse steps" when both parties see the hearing staring them in the face. If you settle, you must either do it in writing (see chapter 5 about stipulations) signed by the judge or orally in the courtroom and approved by the judge. Never tell the judge the case settled, then get up and start arguing over "just one issue that's not settled." If you have only a partial settlement, say so. You can agree to some issues and ask the judge decide the others. State your partial agreement first and get the approval of the parties and the judge on the record, then have your hearing on remaining matters.

The format of the hearing. In most cases, neither direct nor cross examination will be permitted and the case will be decided on the basis of documents and written statements. The judge can allow oral testimony only if you make a written request in advance (see chapter 11D). If you or the other side has been granted permission to present oral testimony, you have the right to cross-examine witnesses and to present oral testimony of rebuttal witnesses (perhaps you) without prior permission, but you can't go beyond the issues in the oral testimony you are rebutting.

Because family court can get very informal, some (not very good) judges make decisions without any evidence at all. This is not legally acceptable. Statements of lawyers are not evidence (unless there is a formal offer of proof). If you are whirled through a courtroom and find yourself subject to a bad order, ask yourself whether there was evidence to support the specific order the judge made. An order *must* be supported by documents and declarations or oral testimony. If an order is made against you and there isn't anything in any testimony or declaration on the subject of the order, you can file a motion to reconsider within 10 days of the order—although this does not technically meet the requirements of Code of Civil Procedure 1008 re grounds for reconsideration—or you can appeal. The proper procedure is appeal or a writ, but that is beyond the scope of this book.

Make sure everything is covered. Every order you want and all evidence in support of those orders should be in your paperwork. But, if the judge is doing business with the parties or attorneys orally, you *must* be sure to quickly mention each order and its supporting facts orally. Use your Application and Declaration as a checklist and take each item in order. After the hearing, if the judge announces his/her orders from the bench, you get exactly and only what the judge says. Details can get lost in the shuffle, so if the judge did not say anything about some particular request, you do not have an order for it. When the judge announces the decision, if any order you requested is not mentioned, you *must* respectfully remind the judge that you requested the order, and you would like a decision on it.

Is your visitation to be supervised? If it looks like the judge is going to order supervised visitation, make sure the order includes details about who pays how much of the fee and a deadline is set for your spouse to contact the supervisor. You don't want him/her to delay visitation by not contacting the supervisor. Getting a detailed, specific order will help make your visits more likely to actually happen.

Get it on the record. If you have a difficult judge and want to keep open the option of filing an appeal, the key thing is to get everything on the record—that is, with a court reporter or video camera recording every word. Statements in papers filed with the court, including attachments to declarations, are on the record. Letters are not part of the record. Things said in chambers without a reporter or in the hallway are nothing—they are not part of the record. Also, evidence is often returned after a hearing. If you want a full record for appeal, you need to carefully retain all evidence or ask the court clerk to retain the evidence until the order becomes final, which is 60 days after the order was made. If you want letters to become a part of the record, attach them to a declaration and file them with the court before your hearing. It is not unusual for people to have valid complaints about how their case was handled, yet not be able to prove a thing because the problem events occurred off the record. Get everything on the record!

D Expired TROs

You might face a period of time when you are unprotected. All temporary restraining orders end at the date and time of the hearing and you can't be certain your restraining orders will be signed at the hearing. If the judge takes the case under submission, or if orders need to be prepared for the judge's signature, no orders are in effect until the written orders are signed and during that time you are unprotected. Depending on what TROs you had, you might have good reason to be concerned about this.

What to do. Try to keep the time between the end of the hearing and signed orders at zero by bringing several copies of proposed orders to court with you (see chapter 16), already filled out. Prepare them assuming the judge will grant all of your orders. If the judge does not grant them all, cross off the denied parts and ask the judge to sign the order right there. Of course, if the judge takes the case under submission or changes a lot of your requests, this won't work. In that case, ask the judge to extend your TROs until written orders are signed. Local rules often require that after the hearing, you have to get your spouse's (or his/her lawyer's) signature on your proposed orders. If you have a violent spouse who has no attorney, ask the judge to sign your DV order without your spouse's signature.

E At the end of the hearing

If the judge takes the case "under submission," you'll get a decision in writing and what happens next is covered in chapter 16. However, the judge might give the decision verbally, in which case you must be ready to write down every detail. If you missed something, or if your spouse is the sort to cause trouble over almost everything, go immediately to the court reporter and order a copy of the part of the transcript that contains the judge's decision. Be clear that you do not want a full transcript.

Get the reporter's business card. Be sure to get the court reporter's business card, either before or after your hearing. Later, if there is a dispute over wording of the order, you will need to contact the reporter to order a transcript (or videotape, if a camera was used) to resolve the dispute. The reporter keeps the word-for-word record of your hearing, not the clerk. Someone at your court keeps track of the court reporters. If your reporter has gone to another court or retired, you might have to find this person to locate the reporter. Of course, it is much easier to buy the video or arrange for a transcript immediately after the hearing instead of trying to locate the reporter later. So, if you are in the kind of case where a dispute seems likely, go ahead and order it before you leave the courtroom. But, do not leave court without getting the business card and phone number of the reporter.

You have to pay for any transcript or videotape. A videotape will cost from $25 to $50 for a short hearing, more for longer ones, and the tape might be available immediately after the hearing, so you want to bring money with you to court for that purpose. If there was no video, order a partial transcript containing only the ruling of the judge rather than the entire hearing. This will be far cheaper, but not nearly so cheap as a videotape. You have to ask ahead of time for the cost.

Take your things. Don't get flustered and forget to take your papers and things with you when you leave the courtroom. There are probably a lot of things in your file that the other side would love to get a look at.

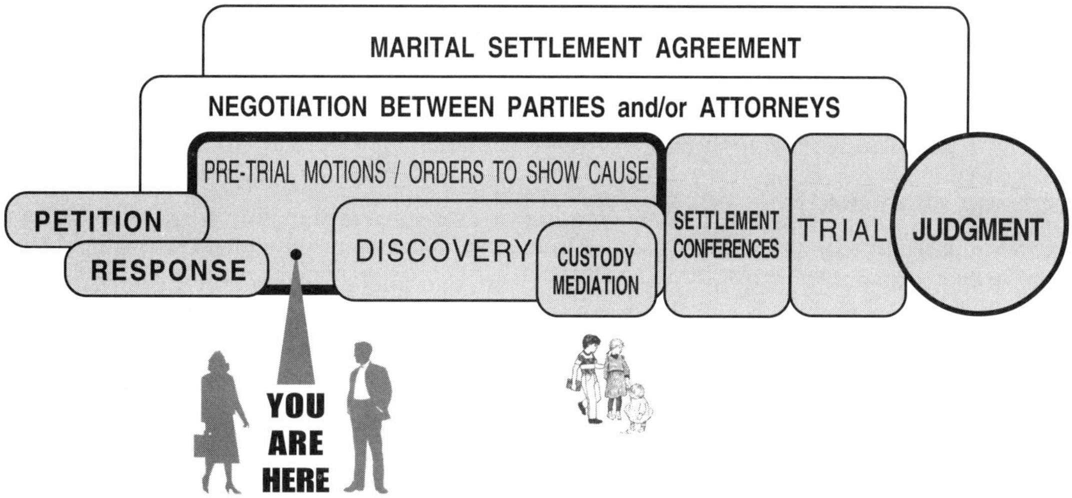

CHAPTER 16
HOW TO DO ORDERS AFTER THE HEARING

A. Prepare the Findings and Order After Hearing
B. Getting the orders signed
C. Serving the orders

The decision might be announced orally at the hearing, but if the judge takes the matter "under submission," a written decision will be sent out later. (If 90 days pass without a decision from the judge, contact both your own judge and the presiding judge of the court.) Either way, verbal or written, once you have the decision, one of the parties (or their lawyer) has to prepare a written order and get it signed by the judge. It is possible the judge will send out an order with or instead of a decision, in which case there's nothing left to do. If your spouse was not present at the hearing, have the order served personally.

Be precise

For some orders, all you do is check a box and completes some blanks, but for others you have to type the order out yourself, in which case your wording must be very precise, as you do not want an order that is subject to more than one interpretation. Whenever possible, follow language used in printed forms, adapting it to suit your needs. Your order must match *exactly* the decisions the judge made, otherwise it will be returned to you unsigned and you will have to fix it. If you are in doubt about any detail, contact the court reporter who recorded the hearing and buy a partial transcript of the hearing to get the judge's orders exactly.

Preparing orders in advance

If you have only a few uncomplicated issues, or think your spouse might not show up, or can't successfully oppose your request, then it is a good idea to bring the prepared orders with you and hand them to the judge at the end of the hearing for signature if you get mostly what you requested.

Who prepares the order and when?

In some counties, local rules resolve this, so look there. Typically, the moving party or the prevailing party prepares the order. Our suggestion is that if you want the order, *you* prepare it, and do it as soon after the hearing as possible, preferably the same day. Local rules often set out deadlines for preparing the order, a process for sending it to the other party, and a deadline for them to respond. Those deadlines are the latest you can do things, but it's better if you go as fast as possible. The local rules often contain a procedure for what to do if one party fails to sign the order. Read them. You want to know what to do if your opponent sends an incorrect order to the judge and gets it signed without your approval.

The forms and attachments

Orders are prepared by using the Findings and Order After Hearing (Figure 16.1) plus whichever additional order attachments are relevant to your case. Most attachment forms are in the back of this book and all of them are on the companion CD that comes with this book.

Checklist for Orders After Hearing

☐ Findings and Order After Hearing (for a motion or regular OSC) (FL-340) (Figure 16.1)

ATTACHMENTS—use only those that are relevant to the judge's decision

- ☐ a. Child Custody and Visitation Order Attachment (FL-341)
- ☐ b. Children's Holiday Schedule Attachment (FL-341(C))
- ☐ c. Additional Provisions—Physical Custody Attachment (FL-341-(D))
- ☐ d. Joint Legal Custody Attachment (FL-341(E))
- ☐ e. Supervised Visitation Order Attachment (FL-341(A))
- ☐ f. Child Abduction Order Attachment (FL-341(B))
- ☐ g. Child Support Information and Order Attachment (FL-342)
- ☐ h. If child support ordered is not the guideline amount, use Non-Guideline Child Support Findings Attachment (FL-342(A))
- ☐ i. Spousal or Family Support Order Attachment (FL-343)
- ☐ j. Property Order Attachment (FL-344) (Figure 16.6)
- ☐ k. Typed attachment if needed for orders not covered on the printed attachments

These are discussed in Book 1, *ch.18—19, and come with that book*

- ☐ l. If child support ordered, attach Notice of Rights and Responsibilities (FL-192)
- ☐ m. If child support ordered, file but *do not attach* Child Support Case Registry (FL-191)
- ☐ n. A wage assignment order must be used if *any* kind of support is ordered. Choose one:
  - Order/Notice to Withhold Income for Child Support (if child support is ordered use this, and include spousal support on it) (see Book 1, chapter 19)
  - Wage and Earnings Assignment Order for Spousal Support (use this if there is only spousal support, no child support) (see Book 1, chapter 19)

A Prepare the Findings and Order After Hearing (FL-340)

This form is used after the hearing on your motion or regular OSC. Study the checklist above and use whichever of the attachment forms are relevant to the orders you are preparing. Fill it out as shown in Figure 16.1, then complete your order attachments and clip them together behind this form. On all order attachments, check the box at the top for "Findings and Order After Hearing."

Item 1. Fill in the date and time of the hearing and the department or room where it was held. Put in the judge's name and indicate if this was a temporary judge (Pro Tem). Check boxes to show who was present at the hearing. If a party was represented, type in the attorney's name.

Items 3–7. For each item, check a box to show that orders for that subject are attached. Otherwise, check the box that shows the category is not applicable.

Figure 16.1

FINDINGS AND ORDER AFTER HEARING

Form FL-340

FL-340

ATTORNEY OR PARTY WITHOUT ATTORNEY *(Name and Address)*: YOUR NAME, Your address, City, State, Zip — TELEPHONE NO.: Your phone	FOR COURT USE ONLY
ATTORNEY FOR *(Name)*: Petitioner in pro per	
SUPERIOR COURT OF CALIFORNIA, COUNTY OF YOUR COUNTY STREET ADDRESS: Street address MAILING ADDRESS: PO Box, if any CITY AND ZIP CODE: City, State, Zip BRANCH NAME: Branch name, if any	
PETITIONER/PLAINTIFF: PETITIONER'S NAME RESPONDENT/DEFENDANT: RESPONDENT'S NAME CLAIMANT:	
FINDINGS AND ORDER AFTER HEARING	CASE NUMBER: Your case number

1. This proceeding was heard
   on *(date)*: Hearing date at *(time)*: Hearing time in Dept.: Dept. no. Room:
   by Judge *(name)*: Judge's Name ☐ Temporary Judge

   ☒ Petitioner/plaintiff present ☐ Attorney present *(name)*:
   ☐ Respondent/defendant present ☐ Attorney present *(name)*:
   ☐ Claimant present ☐ Attorney present *(name)*:
   On the order to show cause or motion filed *(date)*: Date filed by *(name)*: YOUR NAME
2. THE COURT ORDERS
3. Custody and visitation: ☒ As attached ☐ Not applicable
4. Child support: ☒ As attached ☐ Not applicable
5. Spousal-Family support: ☒ As attached ☐ Not applicable
6. Property orders: ☒ As attached ☐ Not applicable
7. Other orders: ☐ As attached ☐ Not applicable
8. ☐ Attorney fees *(specify amount)*: $
   Payable to *(name and address)*:

   Payable ☐ forthwith ☐ other *(specify)*:
9. All other issues are reserved until further order of court.

Date:

JUDGE OF THE SUPERIOR COURT

Approved as conforming to court order.

SIGNATURE OF ATTORNEY FOR ☐ PETITIONER / PLAINTIFF ☒ RESPONDENT / DEFENDANT

Date and signature of other party approving orders. See section B. Check box to show whose signature.

Page 1 of

Form Adopted for Mandatory Use
Judicial Council of California
FL-340 [Rev. January 1, 2003]

FINDINGS AND ORDER AFTER HEARING
(Family Law—Custody and Support—Uniform Parentage)

www.courtinfo.ca.gov

Total number of pages with order attachments.

Item 7. If you requested an order that doesn't have a logical place on one of the attachments, check this box and type your order on a separate page with the heading, "Attachment 7 to FL-340." Use the Additional Page form or numbered pleading paper (see chapter 9C). For example, if the judge made an order on a motion to require your spouse to participate in child custody mediation, there's no logical place on the printed attachments to put such an order, so it would have to go here.

a. Custody and Visitation Order Attachment (FL-341) and related attachments (FL-341A–E)

If child custody or visitation orders were made, fill out this form as shown in Figures 16.2 and 16.2a and attach it to FL-340. Be sure to get every detail of the judge's decision on this form or the related attachments to it. Take a close look at the related child custody and visitation attachments, FL-341(A) through (E) (not illustrated), which can all be found in the forms folder on the companion CD. These are all listed and identified on page 140. If any of those forms are relevant to the judge's orders, they must also be attached along with FL-341. If supervised visitation was ordered and **if you are the one to be supervised**, make sure item 1(b)(3) on FL-341(A) is completely filled out so it is clear who pays how much of the fee and a deadline is set for your spouse to contact the supervisor.

b. Child Support Information and Order Attachment (FL-342) – and attachment (FL-342A)

If child support was ordered, read chapter 11(I). This form is where the judge decides what the facts are that go into the calculation of your support order—in other words, what data one enters into support software to get the guideline result. Fill out this form as shown in Figure 16.3 and attach it to FL-340. Note that at item 1, the judge can decide that an attached computer printout is incorporated in place of some or all of the remaining items. You have to get every detail exactly as the judge determined it in the decision. **Non-guideline order:** If the child support ordered is different from the guideline amount, you must also attach the Non-Guideline Child Support Findings Attachment (FL-342(A)) (not illustrated), which is a finding of the facts that caused the result to differ from guideline. The departure from the guideline could be based on an agreement of the parties, or the judge's finding of any of the statutory factors set out on the form. Make sure to follow the judge's decision exactly. Note that the correct guideline amount must be stated at item 2.

c. Spousal or Family Support Order Attachment (FL-343)

Fill it out as shown in Figure 16.5. Item 3(c) is used when the judge makes findings on the marital standard of living as part of the decision on spousal support. These orders last only until the Judgment in your case is entered, either by written agreement or trial, so it is unlikely that a termination date will be established at this point. At 4(a), one almost always enters "until further order of the court."

d. Property Order Attachment (FL-344)

Fill it out as shown in Figure 16.6 according to the decision of the judge.

Figure 16.2

CHILD CUSTODY AND VISITATION ORDER ATTACHMENT

Form FL-341 (page 1)

FL-341

PETITIONER / PLAINTIFF: PETITIONER'S NAME RESPONDENT / DEFENDANT: RESPONDENT'S NAME	CASE NUMBER: Your case number

CHILD CUSTODY AND VISITATION ORDER ATTACHMENT

Attachment to [✔] **Findings and Order After Hearing** [ ] **Judgment** [ ] **Other**
[ ] **Stipulation and Order for Custody and/or Visitation of Children**

Show who gets custody. See Book 1, chapter 5.

1. [✔] **CUSTODY** Custody of the minor children of the parties is awarded as follows:

Child's name	Date of birth	Legal custody to (Person who makes decisions about health, education, etc.)	Physical custody to (Person the child lives with.)
Child one	birth date	Joint	Petitioner
Child two	birth date	Joint	Petitioner

Fill out item 2 to show what schedule the judge ordered

2. [✔] **VISITATION**
   a. [ ] Reasonable right of visitation to the party without physical custody. *(Not appropriate in cases involvi*
   b. [ ] See the attached ________ page document dated: ____________.
   c. [✔] The parties will go to mediation at: Address of mediation service (ask clerk)
   d. [ ] No visitation.
   e. [✔] Visitation for [ ] Father [✔] Mother will be:

   (i) [ ] **WEEKENDS** *(starting)*:
   (The 1st weekend of the month is the 1st weekend with a Saturday.)
   [ ] 1st [ ] 2nd [ ] 3rd [ ] 4th [ ] 5th weekend of the month
   from ____________ *(day of week)* at ________ *(time)* [ ] a.m. [ ] p.m.
   to ____________ *(day of week)* at ________ *(time)* [ ] a.m. [ ] p.m.
   [ ] The parents will alternate the 5th weekends, with the [ ] Father [ ] Mother having the first 5th weekend.
   [ ] Father to have 5th weekends in [ ] odd [ ] even months.
   [ ] Mother to have 5th weekends in [ ] odd [ ] even months.

   (ii) [✔] **ALTERNATE WEEKENDS** *(specify starting date)*: date
   [✔] Father [ ] Mother will have the children with him/her *(specify days and times)*:
   from Sunday *(day of week)* at 9 *(time)* [✔] a.m. [ ] p.m.
   to Sunday *(day of week)* at 6 *(time)* [ ] a.m. [✔] p.m.

   (iii) [ ] **WEEKDAYS** *(starting)*:
   [ ] Father [ ] Mother will have the children with him/her *(specify days and times)*:
   from ____________ *(day of week)* at ________ *(time)* [ ] a.m. [ ] p.m.
   to ____________ *(day of week)* at ________ *(time)* [ ] a.m. [ ] p.m.

   (iv) [ ] **OTHER** *(specify days and times as well as any additional restrictions)*: [ ] See Attachment 2e(iv).

Page 1 of 2

Form Approved for Optional Use
Judicial Council of California
FL-341 [Rev. January 1, 2004]

CHILD CUSTODY AND VISITATION ORDER ATTACHMENT

Family Code, §§ 3020, 3022, 3040–3043, 3048, 3100, 6340, 7604
www.courtinfo.ca.gov

Figure 16.2a

CHILD CUSTODY AND VISITATION ORDER ATTACHMENT

Form FL-341 (page 2)

PETITIONER / PLAINTIFF: PETITIONER'S NAME RESPONDENT / DEFENDANT: RESPONDENT'S NAME	CASE NUMBER: Your case number

3. [x] **SUPERVISED VISITATION**
until [x] further order of the court [ ] other
[x] Father [ ] Mother will have supervised visitation with the minor children according to the sche[dule]
set forth on page 1. *(You must attach form FL-341(A).)*

If supervised visitation was ordered, check item 3 and attach FL-341(A).

4. [x] **TRANSPORTATION FOR VISITATION**
   a. [x] Transportation *to* the visits will be provided by [ ] Father [x] Mother [ ] Other *(specify):*
   b. [x] Transportation *from* the visits will be provided by [x] Father [ ] Mother [ ] Other *(specify):*
   c. [x] Drop-off/Pickup of the children will be at *(address):* 1234 5th Street, Moreno, CA
   d. [x] The children will be driven only by a licensed and insured driver. The car or truck must have legal child restraint devices.
   e. [x] During the exchanges, the parent driving the children will wait in the car and the other parent will wait in their home while the children go to the home.
   f. [ ] Other *(specify):*

Fill out items 4 and 5 if these terms were part of the judge's order.

5. [x] **TRAVEL WITH CHILDREN** [x] Father [ ] Mother [x] Other *(name):* Father's parents
must have written permission from the other parent or a court order to take the children outside of
   a. [x] the State of California
   b. [x] the following counties *(specify):* Moreno County
   c. [x] other places *(specify):*
   Moreno, CA

Use items 6 - 9 and the related attachments if any of these terms were part of the judge's order.

6. [ ] **CHILD ABDUCTION PREVENTION**
There is a risk that one of the parents will take the children out of California without the other parent's permissi[on.]
FL-341(B) is attached and must be obeyed.

7. [x] **HOLIDAY SCHEDULE**
The children will spend holiday time as listed in attached [x] form FL-341(C) [ ] Other.

8. [ ] **ADDITIONAL CUSTODY PROVISIONS**
The parents will follow the additional custody provisions as listed in attached [ ] form FL-341(D) [ ] Other.

9. [ ] **JOINT LEGAL CUSTODY**
The parents will share joint legal custody as listed in attached [ ] form FL-341(E) [ ] Other.

10. [ ] **OTHER** *(specify):*

Check item 13 and indicate the country in which the child habitually resides.

11. **JURISDICTION:** This court has jurisdiction to make child custody orders in this case under the Uniform Child Custody Jurisdiction and Enforcement Act (part 3 of the California Family Code commencing with section 3400).

12. **NOTICE AND OPPORTUNITY TO BE HEARD:** The responding party was given notice and an opportunity to be heard as provided by the laws of the State of California.

13. **COUNTRY OF HABITUAL RESIDENCE:** The country of habitual residence of the child or children in this case is
[x] the United States [ ] Other *(specify):*

14. **PENALTIES FOR VIOLATING THIS ORDER:** If you violate this order you may be subject to civil or criminal penalties, or both.

FL-341 [Rev. January 1, 2004] **CHILD CUSTODY AND VISITATION ORDER ATTACHMENT** **Page 2 of 2**

Figure 16.3

CHILD SUPPORT INFORMATION AND ORDER ATTACHMENT

Form FL-342 (Page 1)

FL-342

PETITIONER / PLAINTIFF: PETITIONER'S NAME
RESPONDENT / DEFENDANT: RESPONDENT'S NAME
OTHER PARENT:

CASE NUMBER: Your case number

CHILD SUPPORT INFORMATION AND ORDER ATTACHMENT

Attachment to [✔] **Findings and Order After Hearing** [ ] **Restraining Order After Hearing (CLETS)** [ ] **Judgment** [ ] **Other**

THE COURT USED THE FOLLOWING INFORMATION IN DETERMINING THE AMOUNT OF CHILD SUPPORT

1. [✔] A printout of a computer calculation and findings is attached and incorporated in this order for all required items not filled out below.

2. [✔] **INCOME**

   a. Each parent's monthly income is as follows:

	Gross monthly income	Net monthly income	Receiving TANF/CalWORKS
Mother:	$ 2,345	$ 1,234	[ ]
Father:	$ 3,456	$ 2,345	[ ]

   b. Imputation of Income. The court finds that the [ ] Mother [ ] Father has the capacity to earn: $ per: and has based the support order upon this imputed income.

3. [✔] **CHILDREN OF THIS RELATIONSHIP**

   a. Number of children who are the subjects of the support order *(specify):* 2

   b. Approximate percentage of time spent with: Mother 74 % Father 26 %

4. [✔] **HARDSHIPS**

   Hardships for the following have been allowed in calculating child support:

	Mother	Father	Approximate ending time for the hardship
a. [✔] Other minor children:	$ 456	$	
b. [ ] Extraordinary medical expenses:	$	$	
c. [ ] Catastrophic losses:	$	$	

THE COURT ORDERS

5. [ ] **LOW INCOME ADJUSTMENT**

   The court finds that the net income of the parent who will pay support is less than $1,000 per month. Based on the facts presented to the court, the principles provided in Family Code section 4053, and the impact of the contemplated adjustment on the respective net incomes of the mother and father, the court makes the following determination:

   a. [ ] There shall be no low income adjustment.

   b. [ ] There shall be a low income adjustment of: $ per month based upon *(specify):*

6. [✔] **CHILD SUPPORT**

   a. **Base child support**

   [✔] Mother [ ] Father must pay child support beginning *(date):* date payments begin and continuing until further order of the court, or until the child marries, dies, is emancipated, reaches age 19, or reaches age 18 and is not a full-time high school student, whichever occurs first, as follows:

Child's name	Date of birth	Monthly amount	Payable to *(name)*
Child 1	birth date	456	Name of recipient
Child 2	birth date	789	Name of recipient

   Payable [✔] on the 1st of the month [ ] one-half on the 1st and one-half on the 15th of the month [ ] other *(specify):*

   b. [ ] **Mandatory additional child support**

   (1) [✔] Child care costs related to employment or reasonably necessary job training.

   [ ] Mother must pay: % of total or [ ] $ per month child care costs.

   [✔] Father must pay: 50 % of total or [✔] $ 234 per month child care costs.

   [ ] Costs to be paid as follows *(specify):*

THIS IS A COURT ORDER

Form Adopted for Mandatory Use
Judicial Council of California
FL-342 [Rev. January 1, 2003]

CHILD SUPPORT INFORMATION AND ORDER ATTACHMENT

Page 1 of 2

Family Code, §§ 4055-4069
www.courtinfo.ca.gov

Figure 16.4
CHILD SUPPORT INFORMATION AND ORDER ATTACHMENT
Form FL-342 (Page 2)

PETITIONER / PLAINTIFF: PETITIONER'S NAME RESPONDENT / DEFENDANT: RESPONDENT'S NAME OTHER PARENT:	CASE NUMBER: Your case number

THE COURT FURTHER ORDERS

6. b. **Mandatory additional child support *(continued)***
   (2) ☐ Reasonable uninsured health care costs for the children
   ☐ Mother must pay: % of total or ☐ $ per month.
   ☐ Father must pay: % of total or ☐ $ per month.
   ☐ Costs to be paid as follows *(specify)*:

   c. ☐ **Additional child support**
   (1) ☐ Costs related to the educational or other special needs of the children
   ☐ Mother must pay: % of total or ☐ $ per month.
   ☐ Father must pay: % of total or ☐ $ per month.
   ☐ Costs to be paid as follows *(specify)*:

   (2) ☐ Travel expenses for visitation
   ☐ Mother must pay: % of total or ☐ $ per month.
   ☐ Father must pay: % of total or ☐ $ per month.
   ☐ Costs to be paid as follows *(specify)*:

Total child support per month: $ 1,234

7. **HEALTH CARE EXPENSES**
   a. Health insurance coverage for the minor children of the parties must be maintained by ☐ Mother ☑ Father, if available at no or reasonable cost through their respective places of employment or self-employment. Both parties are ordered to cooperate in the presentation, collection, and reimbursement of any health care claims.
   b. ☐ Health insurance is not available to ☐ Mother ☐ Father at a reasonable cost at this time.
   c. ☑ The party providing coverage must assign the right of reimbursement to the other party.
8. **EARNINGS ASSIGNMENT**
   a. An *Order/Notice to Withhold Income for Child Support* (form FL-195) must issue. Note: The payor of child support is responsible for the payment of support directly to the recipient until support payments are deducted from the payor's wages, and for any support not paid by the assignment.
9. ☐ **NON-GUIDELINE ORDER**
   This order does not meet the child support guideline set forth in Family Code section 4055. A *Non-Guideline Child Support Findings Attachment* (form FL-342(A)) is attached.
10. ☐ **EMPLOYMENT SEARCH ORDER (Fam. Code, § 4505)**
   ☐ Mother ☐ Father is ordered to seek employment with the following terms and conditions:

11. **OTHER ORDERS:**
12. **REQUIRED ATTACHMENTS**
   A *Notice of Rights and Responsibilities — Health Care Costs and Reimbursement Procedures* and *Information Sheet on Changing a Child Support Order* (form FL-192) must be attached and is incorporated into this order.
13. **CHILD SUPPORT CASE REGISTRY FORM**
   Both parties must complete and file with the court a *Child Support Case Registry Form* (form FL-191) within 10 days of the date of this order. Thereafter, the parties must notify the court of any change in the information submitted within 10 days of the change by filing an updated form.

NOTICE: Any party required to pay child support must pay interest on overdue amounts at the "legal" rate, which is currently 10 percent per year.

THIS IS A COURT ORDER

Page 2 of 2

FL-342 [Rev. January 1, 2003] **CHILD SUPPORT INFORMATION AND ORDER ATTACHMENT**

B Getting the orders signed

Submit them to the other side. If your spouse or spouse's attorney *did* attend the hearing, the proposed *original* Order After Hearing, with any attachments, is then mailed to your spouse (or his/her lawyer) with a letter requesting that it be signed at the bottom of the first page and returned within two weeks. If your order correctly states the judge's decision, it *must* be signed by the other party even if he/she does not like the decision. If a party does not like the judge's decision, that is not a good reason to refuse to sign the order.

How to resolve disputes about the wording. If there is a dispute as to whether the order correctly reflects what the judge decided, each party must prepare his/her own version of the order and explain his/her position to the other in writing. Of course, you will keep copies of all letters. If this does not resolve the matter, get a transcript from the court reporter to establish exactly what the judge ordered.

If the other side ignores you. Wait 14 days after you send the order to the other side, then send the order to the judge along with a copy of the judge's decision or a transcript of the order part of the hearing and a letter explaining what happened. A copy of the letter should also be sent to your spouse (and your spouse's attorney, if any) as well as to the judge, and the judge's copy should have "cc: (name of your spouse and attorney, if any)" typed below your signature to show that copies were sent to the other side.

If all fails, the judge will decide. Sometimes, even with a transcript, the parties cannot agree on the wording of the order. In that event, either party can ask the judge to sign the order. Usually, this can be done by sending the judge a letter explaining the problem and including copies of the written decision or transcript (including videotape, if any) and correspondence from the opposing party or attorney. If the judge wants a hearing or a written motion, he/she will let you know. Of course, at the same time you must send the other party copies of everything you send to the judge.

Do not tolerate delay. There is no valid reason that it should take many months to obtain an order after a hearing, particularly if you have an attorney. Even if the other side is completely unreasonable, your attorney can use the process described above to get an order without the other party's cooperation. The only valid excuse for delay, other than medical or personal problems, is that a court reporter might take a long time to get a transcript prepared. If this happens, you or your attorney must keep contacting the court reporter to ensure that the transcript gets done.

File the order. Once the judge signs the original Findings and Order After Hearing, make copies and take the original to the clerk of the court for filing and, at the same time, get two copies stamped (clerks call this "endorsed") to show they were filed. Get three copies stamped if the court has appointed an attorney for the children. You should mail a copy of the order to the other party (or his/her attorney).

C Serving the orders

If the other party was not present when the decision was announced, or if the decision was sent by mail, then in order to enforce the judge's orders, you need to have the entire order package of forms personally served on your spouse. Do it as explained in *How to Do Your Own Divorce,* chapter 12, then file the Proof of Personal Service (FL-330) signed by the server, and keep an endorsed (stamped) copy for yourself. This way, if later you have to prove your spouse was aware of the orders so you can enforce them, you'll have little trouble doing it.

Figure 16.5
SPOUSAL OR FAMILY SUPPORT ORDER ATTACHMENT
Form FL-343

FL-343

PETITIONER / PLAINTIFF: PETITIONER'S NAME RESPONDENT / DEFENDANT: RESPONDENT'S NAME OTHER PARENT:	CASE NUMBER: Your case number

SPOUSAL OR FAMILY SUPPORT ORDER ATTACHMENT
Attachment to [X] Findings and Order After Hearing or [ ] Judgment or [ ] Other

THE COURT FINDS

1. A printout of a computer calculation of the parties' financial circumstances is attached for all required items not filled out below.

2. **NET INCOME** *(Complete at least one):*
The parties' monthly income and deductions are as follows:

	Total gross monthly income	Total monthly deductions	Total hardship deductions	Net monthly disposable income
a. Petitioner: [ ] receiving TANF/CalWORKS	amount	amount	if any	amount
b. Respondent: [ ] receiving TANF/CalWORKS	amount	amount	if any	amount

3. **OTHER FACTORS REGARDING PERMANENT SPOUSAL SUPPORT:**
a. [X] The parties were married for 15 years 7 months.
b. [X] The Family Code § 4320 factors were considered, as listed in Attachment 3b.
c. [ ] The marital standard of living was *(describe):*
[ ] Continued in Attachment 3c.

d. [ ] Other *(specify):*

THE COURT ORDERS

4. a. [ ] Petitioner [X] Respondent must pay to [X] Petitioner [ ] Respondent
as [X] spousal support [ ] family support

$ amount per month, beginning *(date):* date after order signed , payable until *(specify duration):*
further order of the court

[X] payable on the *(specify):* first day of each month
[ ] payable other *(specify):*

b. Support must be paid by check, money order, or cash. The support payor's obligation to pay support will terminate on the death or remarriage of the support payee.
c. An earnings assignment for the foregoing support must issue. Note: The payor of spousal/family support is responsible for the payment of support directly to the recipient until support payments are deducted from the payor's earnings and for any support not paid by the assignment.
d. [ ] Service of the earnings assignment is stayed provided the payor is not more than days late in the payment of spousal/family support.

Page 1 of 2

Form Approved for Optional Use
Judicial Council of California
FL-343 [Rev. January 1, 2003]

SPOUSAL OR FAMILY SUPPORT ORDER ATTACHMENT
(Family Law)

Family Code, §§ 150, 3651, 3653, 3654, 4320, 4330, 4337
www.courtinfo.ca.gov.

Page Two

Items 5 and 6. Boilerplate. Read it; understand it; check the boxes.

Item 7. Check this if the judged ordered family support rather than child or spousal support. If you don't know what we're talking about, it probably wasn't ordered.

Figure 16.6
PROPERTY ORDER ATTACHMENT
Form FL-344

FL-344

PETITIONER: PETITIONER'S NAME RESPONDENT: RESPONDENT'S NAME	CASE NUMBER: Your case number

PROPERTY ORDER ATTACHMENT TO FINDINGS
AND ORDER AFTER HEARING

THE COURT ORDERS

1. ☑ **Property restraining orders**
   a. ☐ Petitioner ☑ Respondent ☐ Claimant is restrained from transferring, encumbering, hypothecating, concealing, or in any way disposing of any property, real or personal, whether community, quasi-community, or separate, except in the usual course of business or for the necessities of life.
   b. ☐ Petitioner ☑ Respondent must notify the other party of any proposed extraordinary expenses at least 5 business days before incurring such expenses, and make an accounting of such to the court.
   c. ☐ Petitioner ☑ Respondent is restrained from cashing, borrowing against, cancelling, transferring, disposing of, or changing the beneficiaries of any insurance or other coverage including life, health, automobile, and disability held for the benefit of the parties or their minor child or children.
   d. ☐ Petitioner ☑ Respondent must not incur any debts or liabilities for which the other may be held responsible, other than in the ordinary course of business or for the necessities of life.
2. ☑ **Possession of property**
   a. The exclusive use, possession, and control of the following property the parties own or are buying is given to:

Property	Given to
1999 Nissan Altima, CA license 4XYZ123	Petitioner
Dell Dimension 8200 desktop ser.# HGX334455	Petitioner

   b. ☐ As attached.
3. ☑ **Payment of debts**
   a. Payments on the following debts coming due while this order is in effect must be paid as follows:

Total debt	Amount of payments	Pay to	Paid by
6,543	125	Visa	Respondent
4,321	89	Levits Furniture	Respondent

   b. ☐ As attached.
4. ☐ These are temporary orders only. The court will make final orders at the time of judgment.
5. ☐ Other *(specify)*:

Page 1 of 1

Form Adopted for Mandatory Use
Judicial Council of California
FL-344 [Rev. January 1, 2004]

PROPERTY ORDER ATTACHMENT TO FINDINGS
AND ORDER AFTER HEARING
(Family Law)

Family Code, §§ 2045, 6324
www.courtinfo.ca.gov

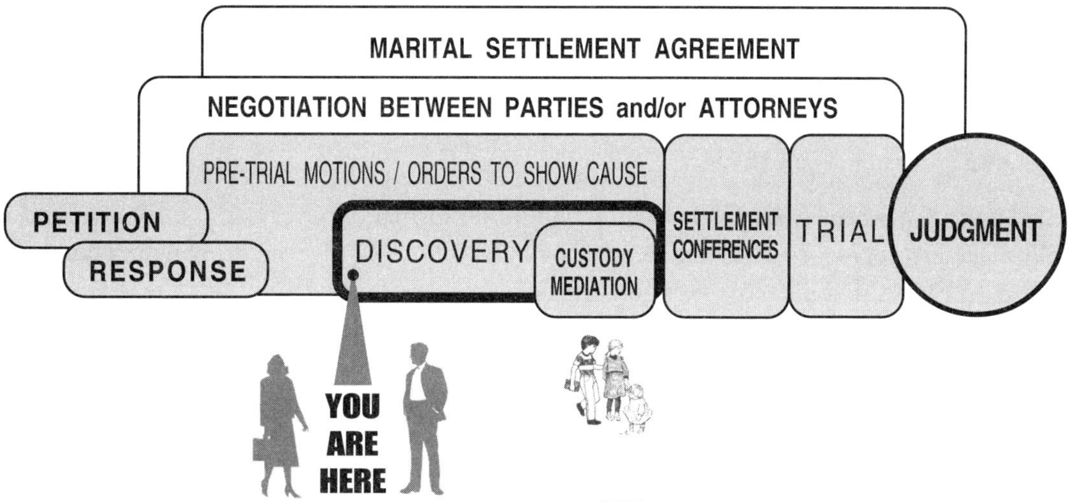

CHAPTER 17
DISCOVERY –formal requests for information

A. Requests for production
B. Written interrogatories
C. Deposition subpoenas for business records
D. Depositions

How to collect information without using legal forms and procedures is discussed in chapter 8. If you tried those methods and still need certain information, you now turn to legal actions we discuss below. In each section, we also discuss how to respond if that particular type of document is served on you.

Do formal discovery early. When a case is near the trial date, it is too late to do discovery. Discovery *must* be completed by 30 days before the *first* trial date set in your case (Code of Civil Procedure section 2024). If the trial is postponed, the discovery cutoff is *not* also postponed. Check local rules on this, too. If, for example, you send interrogatories (section B) to your spouse by mail, your spouse has 35 days to answer. If he/she does not answer or gives incomplete or evasive answers, you need to file a motion to compel and your spouse is entitled to at least 21 days' notice plus time after any hearing to prepare answers. So, just this one part of discovery could require two to three months and, if you have to complete it by 30 days before trial, you must start almost a half year before the trial to accomplish this one thing alone. Start now!

Okay, there is an exception to the "start now" rule. Petitioner can't start discovery within the first 30 days after service of the Summons and Petition. However, Petitioner *can* serve Respondent with a subpoena to bring documents to the first court hearing on a motion or OSC (chapter 15B).

If your spouse has not filed a Response. If you are Petitioner then you only do discovery after your spouse files a Response. If your spouse does not respond and lets the divorce go by default, normally no discovery occurs—you just go to court and get whatever you ask for within reason. A problem can occur if you can't give the judge enough information to make an order. The most typical example is when you want support and thus need to prove your spouse's actual income. You could simply state in a declaration that when you were married, your spouse was in X occupation earning $Y per month and he/she is still doing that, probably with a raise, so his/her income must be at least $Y. However, if you have zero information about your spouse's income and never filed joint income tax returns together, you will have to subpoena your spouse's employer (see chapter 15) to come to the default hearing with records to show your spouse's wages. If you can't do even that, contact the Department of Child Support Services.

To divide unknown property, such as bank accounts, you can obtain a Judgment directing that all accounts either party had with any financial institution as of date of separation (specifying the date) shall be divided 50/50 including interest, and accounting for market fluctuation. Then you will be doing your discovery after entry of Judgment.

Do not use discovery for harassment. You should do formal discovery only for information that you really need. Do not request filing cabinets full of papers just to harass or to vent anger. There are three reasons for this. First, if you later have to file a motion to have the court enforce discovery, the judge might deny everything if it was so broad as to appear oppressive and burdensome. Second, the judge can make you pay sanctions or attorney fees to your spouse if it appears you were engaging in harassment. Finally, it is not unusual for a spouse to change the names on the papers and re-send the entire request back to you, so you could find yourself burdened by the very same requests you created.

Start with a letter. The easiest and cheapest way to get information is to simply ask for it. If he/she cooperates, the discovery process can be inexpensive. If your spouse is secretive and controlling, writing a letter is probably going to be a waste of time, but you now have a written record showing that your spouse has been stonewalling and this can be used later if you ask the court to order your spouse to pay your attorney fees incurred in obtaining information through more formal means. The best approach is to set a short deadline for sending the information you request—like two weeks from the date of the letter. Wait just that long, then start formal discovery as described below. This way, you show good-faith effort not to incur attorney fees. If you have a lawyer who writes letter after letter unsuccessfully begging your spouse for information, get another lawyer. If you wanted to grovel, you could have stayed married.

What to do first. Generally, you do the cheapest discovery first and hope that you will not have to do expensive discovery. Start with requests for production and written interrogatories. If your spouse starts stonewalling, it is probably easier to get the information from another source, so you do "deposition subpoenas" to get records from banks and employers. The most expensive discovery is taking your spouse's deposition. Depositions have an advantage over interrogatories in that the answers you get are more spontaneous. If you send interrogatories and your spouse has a lawyer, the lawyer will probably write or heavily edit the answers, but with or without a lawyer, written answers can be evasive or narrowly defined. In depositions, you (or your lawyer) ask your spouse direct questions in detail and your spouse must respond on the spot. You can ask the same question many different ways to try to eliminate evasion.

The order of discovery is typically:

1. Requests for production
2. Written interrogatories
3. Deposition subpoenas for records
4. Personal depositions
5. Subpoenas to bring records to court

How to organize your discovery papers. Make a separate file for each item of discovery—one for each set of interrogatories, one for each request to produce, and one for each subpoena. When you receive anything related to an item, put it in that specific file. This way, if you find it necessary to file a motion to compel a response, you will have everything together in one place. You should keep one good, clean, non-marked-on copy of any documents you receive. If you want to make notes, either make a copy to write on, or use post-it notes, but do not write on what you have received. You keep the original of each discovery request, and you attach the original proof of service to the document whose service it reflects.

Responding to discovery requests. In each section, we discuss how to respond to that type of discovery. If you find you cannot meet the time limit, you may need to obtain an extension of the time to respond. If so, you must act before the deadline runs, otherwise, you will have to use the Oops motion under Code of Civil Procedure section 473 described at the end of chapter 11. You don't want to find yourself in that position. If you cannot meet a time limit, before the deadline runs, either (1) write to your spouse or his/her attorney, and get an extension of time, and write a letter confirming that your time is extended to a specific date, or (2) file a Notice of Motion requesting more time to respond.

A Requests for production

You can use this method to inspect and copy *relevant* documents in your spouse's possession, but only if your spouse is a party to the case (Petitioner or Respondent). Mail your spouse (or attorney, if there is one) a Request for Production, prepared as shown in Figure 17.1. An Exhibit A is attached, listing all the things you want. See Figures 17.2 and 17.3 for an example, showing a variety of things you might ask for. To determine whether any property has been misappropriated by your spouse (such as if he/she took funds from a bank account), you need to see account balances before your spouse began fiddling around with them. You should ask for statements from the period starting with the present, back to at least a year ago, or even better, at least one month before you think your spouse thought there would be a divorce.

If your spouse is self-employed and you want business records to show his/her income or to assess the value of the business, sending the business a Deposition Subpoena (section C, below) is, in effect, the same thing as a Request to Produce. The Request to Produce is easier, so you should use it first and see what turns up. The example Exhibit A shown in Figure 17.4 shows a request for employment records.

Time and place. In your request, you have to set a date for production at least 35 days away. The Code of Civil Procedure, section 2031, requires only that the production be made at a "reasonable place." Of course, you want a place where you can make copies. If you have a lawyer, production will be made at your lawyer's office. If you do not have a lawyer, you need to list some other office that has a copy machine you can use. If you do not have access to an office with a copier, try to do it at a copy store which is open 24 hours a day, 7 days a week. Chances are your spouse will respond by sending copies, especially if represented by an attorney, but do it this way just in case someone shows up with a box of records.

What you can request and how to request it. You can request to copy any item that is relevant to your case, including writings, audio tapes, video tapes, photographs, etc. The most commonly copied items are bank statements, IRA and 401k statements, stock accounts, credit card statements, deeds to real estate, closing statements for realty, tax returns, paycheck stubs, W-2 forms, and 1099 forms. Your spouse does not have to produce things over which he/she has no custody or control. On the other hand, if he/she can get a copy with a phone call and you can't, then he/she *must* make the phone call to his/her accountant, bank, attorney or whoever. Just giving documents to an attorney does not bring them within the attorney-client privilege; you can still get a copy. Similarly, "Those documents are with my accountant" is not an excuse for nonproduction.

The Request for Production must be clear enough that your spouse can tell exactly what you are requesting. Also, you cannot ask for so many records that it will be unfair, such as all bank statements and all canceled checks during a 20-year marriage. You should specify a time frame that is reasonably related to issues in your case. It is as if you were shooting at a target. If the target is too small (your request is too specific and limited), you will probably miss it. But if the target is too broad, the judge will not make the other side produce it. You have to try for a happy medium request.

Proof of service. You must have someone serve the Request on your spouse (or spouse's attorney) by mail, sign a proof of service by mail, and attach a copy of the proof to the Request being served. Proofs

Figure 17.1

REQUEST FOR PRODUCTION

YOUR NAME
Your Address
City, State, Zip
Your Phone

Petitioner in pro per

SUPERIOR COURT OF CALIFORNIA, COUNTY OF [County]

In re the Marriage of	)	No. [Your case number]
	)	
Petitioner: YOUR NAME	)	REQUEST FOR PRODUCTION
	)	OF DOCUMENTS
Respondent: SPOUSE NAME	)	
______________________________	)	

SET NUMBER: ONE

PROPOUNDING PARTY: PETITIONER/ RESPONDENT

RESPONDING PARTY: RESPONDENT/ PETITIONER

Petitioner/ Respondent requests that on [date] at [time], or before, at [City], California you identify, produce, and permit the inspection and copying or photographing, by or on behalf of said party, of the following documents, papers, books, photographs, objects, or tangible things: All items listed in Exhibit A attached hereto and made part hereof.

You are requested to produce all documents, objects, and things in your possession, custody or control, and in the possession, custody or control of your agents, employees and attorneys.

Dated: ________________

____
YOUR NAME, Petitioner

1

Request for Production of Documents

Figure 17.2
EXHIBIT A –ITEMS TO PRODUCE
(page 1)

EXHIBIT A

ITEMS TO PRODUCE

1. Copies of federal income tax returns (including all returns and all amended returns) of the party or parties for the years [year] through [year], including all attached schedules, W-2 forms, 1099 forms and K-1 forms and requests for extensions and all amended returns.

2. Details of pension or retirement plans, savings plans, insurance plans, profit sharing plans, and stock option and/or participation plans provided by employer of the responding party, whether or not employee contributions are made.

3. All monthly statements reflecting balances as of [date] and [date] through date of production in all savings, checking, credit union, certificate of deposit, mutual funds, IRA's, stock accounts (such as with Charles Schwab) and other types of accounts on which responding party is or has been a signer, regardless of the alleged separate or community nature thereof, and regardless of whether held solely or jointly and regardless of whether held as an individual or as trustee for another and regardless of whether domestic or foreign.

4. All passbooks, check registers, carbon copies of checks and other similar documents relating to the accounts described in the immediately preceding paragraph.

5. All documents relating to the purchase, ownership, and/or sale of real property by the parties or either of them, including deeds, deeds of trust, escrow instructions, statements showing the amount of the encumbrance(s) thereon, date of purchase or sale, and amount of purchase or sale price.

6. All documentation reflecting the lease/ownership of each vehicle owned/leased by the parties as of [date of separation] or either of them, including the registration, any encumbrance thereon, purchase/lease statement, date of purchase/ lease, amount of purchase/lease price, and all documents regarding financing of the purchase/lease price of such vehicles, or, if purchase was not financed, receipt for cash purchase price.

7. All documents relating to any interest of the parties or either of them in any stocks or bonds, including the form of ownership, date of purchase, initial costs, current market value, and a statement regarding the location of the certificates reflecting each stock, bond, or other security.

8. All evidence of ownership or possession or other beneficial interest in or to any safe deposit box or boxes.

Exhibit A page 1 of 2

Figure 17.3

EXHIBIT A –ITEMS TO PRODUCE

(page 2)

EXHIBIT A (continued)

9. Documents of all ownership or beneficial interest by the parties or either of them in any kind of promissory note and other documents relating to a right or claim to money or property, whether or not secured, including the names and addresses of the makers of such notes or documents, and the amounts thereof, along with writings reflecting payment history under each such note.

10. Documents evidencing any and all business entities in which the parties or either of them have any ownership or interest, including the percentage of the interest and the nature of any party's participation, if any, in such business entity and the name and address of the entity and its owner, president, and/or CEO.

11. All writings relating to stock and bond brokers with whom the parties or either of them has had an account or accounts since the date of the marriage if not listed in 7 above.

12. All documentation of all loans and indebtedness of any kind incurred by the responding party from [date], through the date of production/hearing, including copies of any and all loan applications.

13. Statements, notices, and other similar documents reflecting the balance or status of any insurance policies or plans which have an accrued cash value from the date of their inception, in the names of the parties or either of them.

Exhibit A page 2 of 2

Figure 17.4
EXHIBIT A –EMPLOYMENT RECORDS

EXHIBIT A

ITEMS TO PRODUCE

(1) Payroll records pertaining to [Employee Name] (hereinafter "Employee") whose social security number is [S.S. Number], and whose date of birth is [Date], including the following:
(a) gross pay, net pay, itemization of all deductions from gross pay, and expense account or other reimbursement to Employee for out-of-pocket expenses; all payments to Employee are to be shown, including any thing of value received by Employee such as stock options or stock or savings plan and bonuses and deferred compensation;
(b) Employee's W-2 and W-4 form(s) for the year(s)[Year(s)].

(2) Savings plans, 401(k) plans, ESOP plans, profit sharing plans, bonuses, sick pay accounts, vacation pay accounts, and every account of each and every kind held by employer on behalf of Employee;

(3) Stock options, including for each grant: date of grant, number of grant, number of shares, option price, all writings regarding re-pricing of options, date of exercisability/vesting and dates on which options were actually exercised and all funds received by Employee from exercise;

(4) Codes: If any codes are used in the above records, a copy of the booklet or other material needed to understand the meaning of the codes and their applicability to Employee.

The term "Employee", is used for convenience of designation and is not intended to limit production only to records regarding employment as this subpoena includes all payments of any type to [Name], regardless of whether he/she is an employee, partner, independent contractor, or some other legal relationship.

Exhibit A page 1 of 1

of service having to do with discovery are not filed with the court unless a dispute arises, when they are attached to the motion to enforce the discovery. Meanwhile, attach the original of each proof of service to the related Request and keep it safe in your file.

Verified Response due in 30 days. You are entitled to a written response, under oath, from your spouse. If your spouse did not sign a verification (Figure 17.7) swearing that the contents of the document are true, and attach it to the Response to Request to Produce, the Response is inadequate and you cannot rely on it. The response must be personally served on you 30 days after you served your Request, or 35 days if mailed. If the response is late, you could choose to let the technical defect go. However, if there is no response, or if it is unverified or otherwise inadequate, you can file a motion to compel production or to compel the verification (see section B, below).

Time limit to make motion to compel production. If your spouse completely ignores the Request to Produce, you do not have a legal time limit to file a motion to compel. But if he/she makes an evasive, inadequate or unverified Response, you have only 45 days after the inadequate production in which to make *and serve* a motion to force him/her to produce. And if you want to serve your motion by mail, you must do so within 40 days from the date you were served with the Response. Making a motion to compel production is discussed in chapter 18.

Prerequisite to making motion to compel production. Before making the motion, you must write your spouse (or his/her attorney) a letter (Figure 17.8), keeping a copy, and explain why the Response was inadequate and demand further response. If the letter does not produce an adequate response, you need to file a motion to compel production (chapter 18, section E). After the hearing, prepare an Order After Hearing (chapter 16), just as with any other motion. Be sure the order includes a deadline for production, such as saying that the records should be produced within 20 days after the hearing.

How to respond to a Request to Produce

Code of Civil Procedure section 2031(f) prescribes the exact language that you must use in responding to a Request to Produce. The reason the language is so specific is that, over the years hoards of clever lawyers have attempted to evade legitimate requests. Although sloppy lawyers do not use the language of the statute in making their responses (one way to tell how much a lawyer knows), you should do yours right so you don't find yourself caught up in a legal buzzsaw. You must read section 2031(f) in detail (see CD) and be sure to comply with *every* requirement *exactly*.

Each item of the request must be responded to separately, and there are only three acceptable responses: (1) will comply; (2) inability to comply, which requires a particularly detailed statement; and (3) a legal objection that, for some stated reason, there is no obligation to produce the item. Each of these three responses has exact language that *must* be used. The sample response (Figure 17.5) contains examples of the precise language you should use. It is not acceptable, for example, to say, "I have looked through my documents, and I have produced everything that I found." The statute requires much more than that, and the forms in this book will help you comply with the legal requirements for the wording of your response. You should read these forms and read Code of Civil Procedure section 2031(f). This will not only help you reply correctly but also to detect an improper response if you receive one.

Must be served by mail or personally. Your Response to a Request to Produce must be served on the initiating party, and a copy of the Proof of Service should be sent to the recipient and the original kept in your file attached to your response. You must serve your response either (1) personally within 30 days after the date the Request was served on you, or (2) within 25 days if you serve it by mail.

Figure 17.5

RESPONSE TO REQUEST TO PRODUCE

(page 1)

YOUR NAME
Your Address
City, State, Zip
Your Phone

Respondent in propria persona

SUPERIOR COURT OF CALIFORNIA, COUNTY OF [County]

In re Marriage of Petitioner: SPOUSE NAME Respondent: YOUR NAME	No.: Your case number RESPONSE TO REQUEST FOR PRODUCTION OF DOCUMENTS

TO: Petitioner and his/her attorney of record:

Respondent responds as follows to Petitioner's request for production of documents served on [date].

[Note: For every demand you must choose one of the following responses.]

RESPONSE (if you have only some of the requested documents): Respondent hereby complies in part with demand No. [No.] by producing the following documents that are in Respondent's possession, custody or control:

After a diligent search and reasonable inquiry, Respondent is unable to further comply with said request as such items have been lost, misplaced, never have been, or no longer is, in Respondent's possession, custody, or control.

RESPONSE (if you have all the requested documents): Respondent hereby complies in full with demand No. [No.] by producing the following that are in Respondent's possession, custody or control:

1

Response to Request for Production of Documents

Figure 17.6
RESPONSE TO REQUEST TO PRODUCE
(page 2)

RESPONSE (if you have none of the requested documents): After a diligent search and a reasonable inquiry by the Respondent in an effort to comply with Demand No. [No.], Respondent is unable to comply with this demand as the requested documents never existed OR have been destroyed OR have been lost, misplaced, or stolen, OR have never been, or are no longer, in the possession, custody, or control of the Respondent. The name and address of any natural person or organization known or believed by Respondent to have possession, custody, or control of said documents is:[Name and Address].

RESPONSE (if you object to a demand):

[Note: If only part of an item is objectionable, the response must contain one of the three above responses (a statement of compliance, or a representation of inability to comply) with respect to the unobjectionable part; as to the balance, you object as shown below.]

The particular document to which objection is made is: (for example, doctor's letter to Respondent regarding medical condition). The specific objection to this item is:[Objection] (for example, It is a letter from doctor to patient and is within the physician-patient privilege.).

Dated: [Date]

YOUR NAME, Respondent

[Reminder: You must also attach a signed Verification.]

Figure 17.7

VERIFICATION FOR RESPONSE TO REQUEST TO PRODUCE

Marriage of YOUR LAST NAME & SPOUSE LAST NAME

Case No. [Your Case Number]

VERIFICATION

STATE OF CALIFORNIA, COUNTY OF [County]

I am the petitioner/ respondent in the above-entitled action or proceeding. I have read the foregoing [name of document] and know the contents thereof, and I certify that the same is true of my own knowledge, except as to those matter which are therein stated upon my information or belief, and as to those matters I believe it to be true.

Executed at [City], California, on [date].

I declare under penalty of perjury under the Laws of the State of California that the foregoing is true and correct.

____
YOUR NAME

1

Verification

Figure 17.8
LETTER REPLY TO THE RESPONSE
(page 1)

Date

Spouse or his/her Attorney
Address
City, State, Zip

Re: Marriage of [Name]

Dear [Name]:

I have reviewed your Response to our Request for Production of Documents and find that your Responses do not comply with various sections of CCP §2031 which requires specific language when responding to document productions.

(Use next paragraph if production comes without labels and tags.)
First, I attempted to make sense of the documents you sent (reviewing them for almost an hour); however, I have no obligation to do so. The way they were produced did not comply with CCP §2031(f)(1) which states, that the documents must be produced "organized and labeled to correspond with the categories in the demand." Therefore, I am asking that you provide me with another copy of the production with the attachments clearly labeled to correspond to my production request.

(Use the next paragraph if they did not produce documents and did not properly make a statement of inability to comply with the demand.)
Second, your Responses to Requests number [number] and [number] fail to meet with statutory language of CCP §2031(f)(2) which states:

"A representation of inability to comply with the particular demand for inspection shall affirm that a diligent search and a reasonable inquiry has been made in an effort to comply with that demand. This statement shall also specify whether the inability to comply is because the particular item or category has never existed, has been destroyed, has been lost, misplaced, or stolen, or has never been, or is no longer, in the possession, custody, or control of the responding party. . . ."

(Use the next paragraph if the other side says they are still looking for documents and they will produce when they find them.)
Third, your Responses to Requests number [number] and [number] fail to meet the statutory language of CCP §2031(f) due to the fact that the statements are not actual responses to the production requests. The statements do not state that you are producing or not producing in compliance with CCP §2031. Stating that you are still looking for documents and that you will produce if you find them is not sufficient. Please comply with the statute.

Figure 17.9
LETTER REPLY TO THE RESPONSE
(page 2)

(Use the next paragraph if there was no verification.)
Fourth, there was no verification with your purported responses. Case law indicates that an unverified response is the same as no response. Therefore, your response is late, and you have waived all objections. Nonetheless, you must still supply me with a formal, signed verification.

I expect you to redo the Response to Request for Production of Documents as well as clearly label the actual documents produced so that they comply with CCP §2031 and provide us with same on or before [Date].

Very truly yours,

YOUR NAME
Your Address
City, State, Zip
Your Phone

Your response must be verified. A verification is a statement under oath that what you have said is true (Figure 17.7). A response made without a verification is legally the same as no response, so don't forget to do the verification.

Burdensome requests. If your spouse requests something ridiculous like every single canceled check from a 20-year marriage (assuming the two of you are not wealthy), you should object. Of course, the other thing to do is to bring the records to the place where they are due, and refuse to leave them. One way to punish people who make burdensome requests is to give them everything they are asking for and interpret the request as broadly as possible.

Motion for protective orders. Litigants and their lawyers have been known to abuse the discovery process, using it for harassment, more to beat the other party into submission rather than for actual discovery. Any time you receive a discovery request, you can file a motion for a protective order, but we think that is unnecessarily complicated. Better to comply with reasonable parts of their discovery and put your objections to unreasonable discovery in your Responsive Declaration, then wait to see what they do. If your spouse files a motion to compel discovery, you can resist it as described in the next chapter.

B Written interrogatories

Interrogatories are written questions that you can send to your spouse which he/she is required to answer in writing under oath. Sometimes you simply want some answers; other times you are seeking information that will help you prepare for further discovery, such as depositions or subpoenas.

Form interrogatories. The Judicial Council has prepared standard form interrogatories that you can serve on your spouse (Figure 17.10) to ask standard divorce questions. Simply put an X in the box of each question you want answered. If you check the item asking your spouse to fill out a Schedule of Assets and Debts, you must include a blank copy of that form when you serve the interrogatories. Oddly, there is no place for your signature. This and the Summons are about the only forms that do not get signed.

Specially drafted interrogatories. In addition to the printed form interrogatories, you can also send up to 35 questions that are not already included in the form interrogatories. Each subpart of each question counts as a separate interrogatory. If you need to ask more than 35 special questions, you *must* do a declaration explaining the necessity (Figure 17.15). On the companion CD, there is a 10-page set of special interrogatories to cover a wide range of good questions to ask. Please print it out and study all the suggested questions. Edit it to suit your needs. Three pages of that document are at Figures 17.12 to 17.14, to illustrate the general form for specially drafted interrogatories.

If you do special interrogatories, the main thing is to keep them simple and break them into small, precise bits that are unambiguous. Study the style of the form interrogatories. For example, if you ask, "Do you have any bank accounts?" your next question is, "If your answer to the preceding interrogatory is affirmative, as to each such account, state the name of the bank, the address of the bank, and the account number." If you ask, "On May 17, 1999, at 6:00 PM, did you come to the home and remove the stereo and TV?" you might get the answer, "No," simply because the person was there at 6:01 PM, not 6:00. That question has too many parts. It needs to begin, "At any time after (date of separation) did you ever enter the home at (address)? If so, as to each such instance: (a) state the date and time of such entry; and, (b) list any items you removed when you left the premises."

Figure 17.10

FORM INTERROGATORIES

Form FL-145 (page 1)

FL-145

ATTORNEY OR PARTY WITHOUT ATTORNEY *(Name and Address)*: YOUR NAME Your address City, State, Zip	TELEPHONE NO.: Your phone
ATTORNEY FOR *(Name)*: Petitioner / Respondent in pro per	
SUPERIOR COURT OF CALIFORNIA, COUNTY OF YOUR COUNTY	
SHORT TITLE OF CASE: PETITIONER'S NAME RESPONDENT'S NAME	
FORM INTERROGATORIES—Family Law **Asking Party:** YOUR NAME **Answering Party:** SPOUSE NAME **Set No.:** One	CASE NUMBER: Your case number

Start with "One." If you send written interrogs, that will be "Two." Each time, add 1.

Sec. 1. Instructions to Both Parties

These interrogatories are intended to provide for the exchange of relevant information without unreasonable expense to the answering party. They do not change existing law relating to interrogatories nor do they affect the answering party's right to assert any privilege or make any objection. **Privileges must be asserted.**

Sec. 2. Definitions

Words in **BOLDFACE CAPITALS** in these interrogatories are defined as follows:

(a) **PERSON** includes a natural person, partnership, any kind of business, legal, or public entity, and its agents or employees.

(b) **DOCUMENT** means all written, recorded, or graphic materials, however stored, produced, or reproduced.

(c) **ASSET or PROPERTY** includes any interest in real estate or personal property. It includes any interest in a pension, profit-sharing, or retirement plan.

(d) **DEBT** means any obligation including debts paid since the date of separation.

(e) **SUPPORT** means any benefit or economic contribution to the living expenses of another person, including gifts.

(f) If asked to **IDENTIFY A PERSON**, give the person's name, last known residence and business address, telephone numbers, and company affiliation at the date of the transaction referred to.

(g) If asked to **IDENTIFY A DOCUMENT**, attach a copy of the document unless you explain why not. If you do not attach the copy, describe the document, including its date and nature, and give the name, address, telephone number, and occupation of the person who has the document.

Sec. 3. Instructions to the Asking Party

Check the box next to each interrogatory you want the answering party to answer.

Sec. 4. Instructions to the Answering Party

You must answer these interrogatories under oath within 30 days, in accordance with Code of Civil Procedure section 2030.

You must furnish all information you have or can reasonably find out, including all information (not privileged) of your attorneys or under your control. If you don't know, say so.

If an interrogatory is answered by referring to a document, the document must be attached as an exhibit to the response and referred to in the response. If the document has more than one page, refer to the page and section where the answer can be found.

If a document to be attached to the response may also be attached to the *Schedule of Assets and Debts* (form FL-142), the document should be attached only to the response, and the form should refer to the response.

If an interrogatory cannot be answered completely, answer as much as you can, state the reason you cannot answer the rest, and state any information you have about the unanswered portion.

Sec. 5. Oath

Your answers to these interrogatories mu[st be under oath,] dated, and signed. Use the following form a[t the end of your] *answers:*

"I declare under penalty of perjury unde[r the laws of the] State of California that the foregoing answers are true and correct."

Don't date and sign here. It's an instruction to the the responder.

______________ (DATE)   ______________ (SIGNATURE)

Page 1 of 2

Form Approved for Optional Use
Judicial Council of California
FL-145 [Rev. January 1, 2003]

FORM INTERROGATORIES
(Family Law)

Code of Civil Procedure, §§ 2030(c), 2033.5
www.courtinfo.ca.gov

Figure 17.11
FORM INTERROGATORIES
Form FL-145 (page 2)

Note: If you check item 10, you must also serve a blank Schedule of Assets and Debts (Book 1, *How to Do Your Own Divorce*, chapter 14).

[X] 1. ***Personal History.*** State your full name, current residence address and work address, social security number, any other names you have used, and the dates between which you used each name.

[X] 2. ***Agreements.*** Are there any agreements between you and your spouse made before or during your marriage or after your separation that affect the disposition of **ASSETS, DEBTS,** or **SUPPORT** in this proceeding? If your answer is yes, for each agreement, state the date made and whether it was written or oral, and attach a copy of the agreement or describe its content.

[X] 3. ***Legal Actions.*** Are you a party or do you anticipate being a party to any legal or administrative proceeding other than this action? If your answer is yes, state your role and the name, jurisdiction, case number, and a brief description of each proceeding.

[X] 4. ***Persons Sharing Residence.*** State the name, age, and relationship to you of each **person** at your present address.

[X] 5. ***Support Provided Others.*** State the name, age, address, and relationship to you of each **PERSON** for whom you have provided **SUPPORT** during the past 12 months and the amount provided per month for each.

[ ] 6. ***Support Received for Others.*** State the name, age, address, and relationship to you of each **PERSON** for whom you have received **SUPPORT** during the past twelve months and the amount received per month for each.

[X] 7. ***Current Income.*** List all income you received during the past 12 months, its source, the basis for its computation, and the total amount received from each. Attach your last three paycheck stubs.

[X] 8. ***Other Income.*** During the past three years have you received cash or other property from any source not identified in 7? If so, list the source, the date, and the nature and value of the property.

[X] 9. ***Tax Returns.*** Attach copies of all tax returns and schedules filed by or for you in any jurisdiction for the past three calendar years.

[X] 10. ***Schedule of Assets and Debts.*** Complete the *Schedule of Assets and Debts* (form FL-142) served with these interrogatories.

[X] 11. ***Separate Property Contentions.*** State the facts that support your contention that an asset or debt is separate property.

[X] 12. ***Property Valuations.*** Have you had written appraisals or offers to purchase during the past 12 months on any of the assets listed on your completed *Schedule of Assets and Debts*. If your answer is yes, **IDENTIFY THE DOCUMENT**.

[X] 13. ***Property Held by Others.*** Is there any **PROPERTY** held by any third party in which you have any interest or over which you have any control? If your answer is yes, indicate whether the property is shown on the *Schedule of Assets and Debts* completed by you. If it is not, describe and identify each such asset and state its present value and the basis for your valuation, and **IDENTIFY THE PERSON** holding the asset.

[X] 14. ***Retirement and Other Benefits.*** Do you have an interest in any disability, retirement, profit sharing, or deferred compensation plan? If your answer is yes, **IDENTIFY** each plan and provide the name, address, and telephone number of the administrator and custodian of records.

[X] 15. ***Claims of Reimbursement.*** Do you claim the legal right to be reimbursed for any expenditures of your separate or community property? If your answer is yes, state all supporting facts.

[X] 16. ***Credits.*** Do you claim reimbursement credits for payments of community debts since the date of separation? If your answer is yes, **IDENTIFY** the source of payment, the creditor, the date paid, and the amount paid. State whether you have added to the debt since the separation.

[X] 17. ***Insurance.*** **IDENTIFY** each health, life, automobile, and disability insurance policy or plan that you now own or that covers you, your children, or your assets. State the policy type, policy number, and name of company. **IDENTIFY** the agent and give the address.

[X] 18. ***Health.*** Is there any physical or emotional condition that limits your ability to work? If your answer is yes, state each fact on which you base your answer.

[X] 19. ***Children's Needs.*** Do you contend your children have any special needs? If so, identify the child with the need, the reason for the need, its cost, and its expected duration.

[X] 20. ***Attorney Fees.*** State the total amount of attorney fees and costs incurred by you in this proceeding, the amount paid, the source of money paid, and describe the billing arrangements.

[X] 21. ***Gifts.*** List any gifts you have made without the consent of your spouse in the past 24 months, their value, and the recipients.

FL-145 [Rev. January 1, 2003] **FORM INTERROGATORIES (Family Law)** Page 2 of 2

How to do it

Have someone serve the other party (or his/her attorney) by mail with these documents:

1. Written interrogatories (form, specially drafted, or both)
2. Declaration for more interrogatories (if more than 35 specially drafted)
3. Blank verification form
4. Blank Schedule of Assets and Debts (if filling it out was requested)
5. Copy of proof of service by mail

When you have someone serve your interrogatories, you must prepare a proof of service by mail (POS) for your server to sign. Keep the original interrogatories and the original proof of service by mail and send a copy of the interrogatories and proof of service to your spouse or his/her attorney if he/she has one. Whenever you serve someone by mail, you must send them a copy of the POS. The reason for this is that the date of mailing, not the date of receipt, sets off the other party's deadlines, and without the POS they can't determine the date of mailing. Keep the original documents in a safe place until six months after Judgment. At that time, originals can be destroyed unless the court, on motion, orders them preserved for a longer time (Code of Civil Procedure section 2030).

Answers are due 35 days from the date the interrogatories are mailed. If you don't get a written, verified response on time, immediately send a letter to the other side requesting answers within a specified number of days. If you still get no response, file a motion to compel (chapter 18).

Verified response and why you insist on it. A verification is a statement under oath that a document is true, meaning that any false statements would be perjury. One hopes a spouse will hesitate to lie under oath and face possible penalties. Without verification, the answers to the interrogatories are no more legally significant than an informal statement in a letter.

Motion to compel. If your spouse refuses to respond or gives incomplete or evasive answers, or fails to provide a signed verification, you should file a motion to compel answers, which is discussed in chapter 18. Code of Civil Procedure section 2030(l) provides that a motion to compel answers must be made within 45 days of any answers you received. If you didn't get any answers at all, but were just ignored, you don't have a time limit, but you should probably make the motion within 45 days, anyway, just to be safe.

How to respond to interrogatories

Responding to interrogatories can be fairly simple. Use a face page (Figure 17.17), type your answers to every question using a format similar to the interrogatories you received (but any clear format will work), and attach the verification form (Figure 17.7). Have your response served by mail and get a proof of service that you keep in your files. The main thing is to *answer the questions,* all of the questions, and only the questions that are asked. Don't volunteer any information that was not requested. It can't help you, and it may get you into trouble. This is not the time to start spewing opinions and related or unrelated details. If a question calls for a "yes" or "no" answer, and you don't feel comfortable with that, you can add a one-sentence explanation, but don't get carried away. If the question asks for privileged material, such as your private medical information, your counseling information or what an attorney told you, you object and state the legal basis of the objection. If the questions are really a problem for you, you may have to see an attorney, but you have do it fast enough to meet the 30 or 35 day deadline.

Figure 17.12

SPECIALLY DRAFTED INTERROGATORIES

(page 1)

Note: We display the first three pages of this eight-page document which is found on the companion CD. Please print it out and study all of the example questions.

YOUR NAME
Your Address
City, State, Zip
Your Phone

Petitioner in propria persona

SUPERIOR COURT OF CALIFORNIA, COUNTY OF [County]

In re Marriage of	No.: [Your case number]
Petitioner: YOUR NAME	FIRST SET OF WRITTEN INTERROGATORIES (Specially drafted)
Respondent: SPOUSE NAME	

SET NUMBER: ONE

PROPOUNDING PARTY: PETITIONER

RESPONDING PARTY: RESPONDENT

Petitioner requests that Respondent answer under oath, pursuant to Section 2030 of the California Code of Civil Procedure, within thirty (30) days of the date of service hereof, the following Interrogatories.

Each answer must be as complete and straightforward as the information reasonably available to you permits. If an interrogatory cannot be answered completely, answer to the extent possible.

If you do not have enough personal knowledge to fully answer an interrogatory, say so, but make a reasonable and good faith effort to get the information by asking other persons or organizations, unless the information is equally available to the asking party.

Whenever an interrogatory may be answered by referring to a document, the document may be attached as an exhibit to the response and referred to in the response. If the document has

Figure 17.13
SPECIALLY DRAFTED INTERROGATORIES
(page 2)

more than one page, refer to the page and section where the answer to the interrogatory can be found.

Whenever an address and telephone number for the same person are requested in more than one interrogatory, you are required to furnish them in answering only the first interrogatory asking for that information.

Your answers to these interrogatories must be verified, dated, and signed.

Dated: [Date]

____
YOUR NAME, Petitioner

1. **Identification.** State:

a. Your present name and all former names.

ANSWER:

b. Your present residence address.

ANSWER:

c. Your social security number.

ANSWER:

d. Your drivers license number and state of issuance.

ANSWER:

2. **Employment.**

a. State your present occupation.

ANSWER:

b. State the address of your present workplace and/or employer's name and address, the date you commenced work there, and your employee identification number, if any.

ANSWER:

2

First Set of Written Interrogatories (Specially drafted)

Figure 17.14
SPECIALLY DRAFTED INTERROGATORIES
(page 3)

c. What is your present gross monthly income (including all things of value received by you each month from all sources before deducting expenses)?

ANSWER:

d. State your net monthly income, and specifically itemize all deductions from gross income.

ANSWER:

e. If, during the past 12 months, you have worked any overtime, please state the number of hours per month and the overtime rate of pay.

ANSWER:

f. If you will do so without a notice to produce, please attach copies of your four (4) most recent paystubs or other documentation of monthly income along with your most recent W-2 form.

STATE WHETHER ATTACHED:

g. Have any bonuses or commissions been paid to you during the past 12 months, and, if so, what was the amount and source of each?

ANSWER:

h. Do you expect any bonuses or commissions to be paid to you within the coming 12 months, and, if so, what is the amount and source of each?

ANSWER:

i. As of the date of separation from your spouse, did you have the right to any vacation fund, and, if so, state the company or entity holding the fund, the amount of money payable to you upon vacation and the earliest date on which you may draw the money.

3

First Set of Written Interrogatories (Specially drafted)

Figure 17.15
DECLARATION FOR ADDITIONAL INTERROGATORIES
(page 1)

YOUR NAME
Your Address
City, State, Zip
Your Phone

Petitioner in propria persona

SUPERIOR COURT OF CALIFORNIA, COUNTY OF [County]

In re Marriage of Petitioner: YOUR NAME Respondent: SPOUSE NAME	No.: [Your case number] DECLARATION PERMITTING ADDITIONAL INTERROGATORIES [CCP 2030]

I, the undersigned, declare:

1. I am the Petitioner herein.

2. I am propounding to Respondent, the attached set of interrogatories.

3. This set of interrogatories will cause the total number of specially prepared interrogatories propounded to the party to whom they are directed to exceed the number of specially prepared interrogatories permitted by Paragraph 1 of subdivision (c) of 2030 of the Code of Civil Procedure.

4. I have previously propounded a total of [number] interrogatories to this party of which [number] interrogatories were not official form interrogatories.

OR

4. I have not previously propounded any interrogatories to Respondent which were not official form interrogatories.

5. This set of interrogatories contains a total of [number] specially prepared interrogatories which are supplemental to Form Interrogatories.

1

Declaration Permitting Additional Interrogatories [CCP 2030]

Figure 17.16

DECLARATION FOR ADDITIONAL INTERROGATORIES

(page 2)

6. I am familiar with the issues and the previous discovery conducted in the case.

7. I have personally examined each of the questions in this set of interrogatories.

8. The number of questions is warranted under Paragraph 2 of the subdivision (c) of 2030 of the Code of Civil Procedure because the complexity of this matter involving dissolution of marriage requires information which cannot be gained within the statutory limits of thirty-five specially prepared interrogatories.

9. None of the questions in this set of interrogatories is being propounded for any improper purposes, such as to harass the party, or the attorney for the party to whom it is directed, or to cause any unnecessary delay of needless increase in the cost of litigation.

I declare under penalty of perjury under the laws of the State of California that the foregoing is true and correct and that this declaration was executed on [Date] at [City], California.

____

YOUR NAME, Petitioner

2

Declaration Permitting Additional Interrogatories [CCP 2030]

Figure 17.17

RESPONSE TO INTERROGATORIES

YOUR NAME
Your Address
City, State, Zip
Your Phone

Respondent in propria persona

SUPERIOR COURT OF CALIFORNIA, COUNTY OF [County]

In re Marriage of	)	No.: [Your case number]
	)	
Petitioner: SPOUSE NAME	)	RESPONSE TO
	)	WRITTEN INTERROGATORIES
Respondent: YOUR NAME	)	
______________________________	)	

TO: Petitioner and his/her attorney of record:

Respondent responds as follows to Petitioner's written interrogatories, first set, (form OR specially drafted) served on [date].

[Note: As all questions are different, we can't give you examples of answers that will help your specific case. Just answer each question, exactly as asked, not volunteering additional information and not leaving out any parts.]

Dated: [Date]

____
YOUR NAME, Respondent

[Reminder: You must also attach a signed Verification.]

1

Response to Written Interrogatories

C Deposition subpoenas for business records

A subpoena is a court order directing a witness to appear to give testimony, either at an office for a deposition or in court. When the subpoena directs the witness to produce records or things, it is called a "subpoena *duces tecum*" (*duces tecum* is Latin for "with you," that is, bring something to the appearance).

What we are now going to discuss is a specialized form of subpoena called a "Deposition Subpoena for Business Records." This is a cheap and effective way to get routine business records from a third party, such as a bank or employer. By using the Deposition Subpoena, you can get, for example, bank records or employer records regarding wages, retirement benefits (including stock options and stock savings plan), and deductions for 401(k) or other savings plans. If your spouse quit working for a company, you can still get his/her personnel file. In large companies, you might need to serve one set of papers on the payroll department and a second set on the personnel department. If the company has separate payroll and personnel departments, just assume you have to do two separate subpoenas.

Only inside California. You cannot subpoena records outside California unless you (1) are using the business-records subpoena that does not require an appearance, or (2) get the help of an attorney.

The "deposition." In the forms, all reference to a deposition is actually a fiction, an historical artifact of legal evolution. There is no deposition. For this particular form of subpoena, the deposition is only the date the documents must be produced.

How to do it

Checklist of documents for records-only deposition

- ☐ a. Notice of Taking Deposition—Records Only—No Appearance (Figure 17.18)
- ☐ b. Interrogatories to Custodian of Records (blank, to be filled out and returned) (Fig. 17.19)
- ☐ c. Deposition Subpoena – Business Records (Figure 17.21)
- ☐ d. Consumer/Employee Notice (if seeking anything other than a police report) (Fig. 17.22)
- ☐ e. Proof of Service (on back of Deposition Subpoena—Business Records)

How subpoenas are issued. In order to command someone to bring documents to court or at a deposition, including a records-only deposition, a Subpoena must be "issued" by the clerk, that is, stamped with the seal of the court to give it the power of the court. Subpoenas are "issued in blank," which means you can get blank forms from the usual outlet that provides court forms in your area. If you are in a rare county where the court clerk does not make Subpoenas available that are issued in blank, you will fill out the Subpoena and then take it to court to have the court clerk issue it. If the Subpoena needs to be accompanied by a declaration, the declaration would have to be attached to it. If you have an attorney, the attorney can issue the Subpoena merely by signing it, without having to involve the court clerk.

Understand the timing. Before you start, study section e, below, to make sure you understand the timing (deadlines) for serving the subpoena and getting documents in response.

a. Notice of Taking Deposition–Records Only

Fill it out as shown in Figure 17.18. Choose dates that allow you to comfortably comply with deadlines. The most common errors made by individuals and by lawyers are (1) forgetting to serve the consumer/employee 5 days before serving the witness and the opposing party (who may be the consumer/employee and then you only serve him/her once) and (2) forgetting that a subpoena must always be personally served, so it cannot be mailed to the witness. However, it *can* be mailed to the consumer/employee.

Figure 17.18

NOTICE OF TAKING DEPOSITION–RECORDS ONLY

YOUR NAME
Your Address
City, State, Zip
Your Phone

Petitioner in propria persona

SUPERIOR COURT OF CALIFORNIA, COUNTY OF [County]

In re Marriage of)	No.: [Your case number]
Petitioner: YOUR NAME)	NOTICE OF TAKING DEPOSITION–RECORDS ONLY–NO APPEARANCE
Respondent: SPOUSE NAME)	

TO ALL PARTIES AND THEIR ATTORNEYS OF RECORD:

PLEASE TAKE NOTICE that the deposition of the custodian of records of [name of company or organization] will be taken in the above-entitled action before a Notary Public at the following address: [City], California, on [date], at [time], and continued from day to day thereafter, Sundays and holidays excepted, until completed, on behalf of petitioner.

Dated: [Date]

____
YOUR NAME, Petitioner

1

Notice of Taking Deposition — Records Only — No Appearance

b. Interrogatories for custodian of records (the witness)

You are using this subpoena to obtain records that you can use in court without having to bring a witness to court. That would be simple and inexpensive, but there is only one way to get records that can be introduced into evidence at a hearing or trial without the presence of a witness. You must have the custodian of records copy the records and deliver them to you along with a declaration that meets all the legal requirements to authenticate the records and to show that the records are within the business-records exception to the hearsay rule.

Use the typed form at Figure 17.19, which has been very carefully prepared to meet legal requirements. Documents can be excluded at court if the custodian of records returns the form and fails to fill in every single question (and saying "not applicable" is not acceptable). The Interrogatories for the custodian of records are very important and must be complied with in every detail. The custodian of records, by filling out this form, becomes a witness.

c. Deposition Subpoena–Business Records

Fill it out as shown in Figure 17.21.

The deposition officer. At item 1, enter the name of the deposition officer. At a regular deposition, this would be the court reporter. However, a records-only deposition will not have a meeting or a court reporter. Businesses are used to having professional photocopiers handle this, but to save money you can first ask that records be mailed directly to you. Most businesses will comply, but some might insist on a professional photocopier. Rather than fight them, reissue the subpoena naming a professional. To find a professional photocopier in your area, call a local attorney's office and ask the staff who they use. Then call to make sure the service is available to you and discuss fees and logistics for obtaining the documents.

Where? Always check box a, and although it says "delivering," businesses will mail the documents or send them by a courier.

Records to be produced. The two types of records that you are most likely to request are records of financial institutions and employment records. As to how to draft a list of items to be produced, you can apply the same general rules discussed in section A, above, for a Request to Produce. Also see Figures 17.2–17.4.

Sticky situation. If your spouse is employed in a small company or is very high up in a big company or has friends in the payroll department, the company might ignore or resist your request, in which case you will have to file a motion to compel (chapter 18). However, if they are really resisting, you could end up with a couple of rounds of hassling with motions, so in this situation—if the records are really important—you should consider getting a lawyer to do the motion.

d. Consumer/Employee Notice

In order to protect privacy, the law has special requirements if you want to obtain personal records of a consumer (Code of Civil Procedure section 1985.3) or employment records (CCP section 1985.6). In either case, you *must* let the consumer/employee know what you are doing by having someone personally serve a notice (Figure 17.22) 5 days before you actually subpoena the records. Almost anything you are likely to subpoena will be a consumer/employee record except for police reports or the personal records of the witness being subpoenaed, like a calendar or journal. For everything else, you have to give notice.

Figure 17.19
INTERROGATORIES TO CUSTODIAN OF RECORDS
(page 1)

INTERROGATORIES
(Attachment to Notice of Deposition)

1. What is your name?

ANSWER:

2. By whom are you employed?

ANSWER:

3. What is your job title?

ANSWER:

4. Are you the duly authorized custodian of records, and do you have in your care, custody and control all records listed below?

ANSWER:

5. List all attached records:

6. Are these records kept in the regular course of your employer's business?

ANSWER:

7. Are the entries in the records made at or near the time of the event to which they relate?

ANSWER:

8. In response to subpoena duces tecum served on you, have you produced any and all records mentioned in that subpoena?

ANSWER:

9. Has any portion of any record or records mentioned in that subpoena ever been altered or removed from your records prior to this time; if so, explain.

ANSWER:

1

Interrogatories to Custodian of Records

Figure 17.20
INTERROGATORIES TO CUSTODIAN OF RECORDS
(page 2)

10. Are the copies attached true copies of your records?

ANSWER:

11. Are the sources of information and method and time of preparation of the records such that the information is trustworthy?

ANSWER:

12. Explain briefly how the records were prepared:

ANSWER:

13. What information was used to prepare the records?

ANSWER:

14. Would you please turn over at this time to the Deposition Officer of the subpoenaing party, or to the court, all the records, documents and writings which were made a subject of this subpoena duces tecum (and for the purposes of this subpoena, photocopies will be sufficient)?

ANSWER:

I, [your name], am the duly authorized custodian of records for ________________________________ and have authority to certify that I have answered the above questions, and that the documents enclosed are true, legible, and durable copies of the records described in the subpoena duces tecum.

I declare under penalty of perjury under the laws of the State of California that the above, including any attachments, is true and correct and that this declaration is executed on [date] at [City], California.

____
CUSTODIAN OF RECORDS

Note: This document must be notarized if the documents are being sent from outside the State of California.

2

Interrogatories to Custodian of Records

Figure 17.21

DEPOSITION SUBPOENA FOR PRODUCTION OF BUSINESS RECORDS

Form 982(a)(15.2)

982(a)(15.2)

ATTORNEY OR PARTY WITHOUT ATTORNEY *(Name, state bar number, and address):* YOUR NAME Your Address City, State, Zip TELEPHONE NO.: Your phone FAX NO.: Your fax ATTORNEY FOR *(Name):* Petitioner in pro per	*FOR COURT USE ONLY*
NAME OF COURT: SUPERIOR COURT, COUNTY OF YOUR COUNTY STREET ADDRESS: Court Street Address MAILING ADDRESS: Court Mailing Address CITY AND ZIP CODE: City, State, Zip BRANCH NAME: Branch (Main, Norther, Family, etc.)	
PLAINTIFF/ PETITIONER: PETITIONER'S NAME DEFENDANT/ RESPONDENT: RESPONDENT'S NAME	
DEPOSITION SUBPOENA **For Production of Business Records**	CASE NUMBER: Your case number

THE PEOPLE OF THE STATE OF CALIFORNIA, TO *(name, address, and telephone number of deponent, if known)*:
Custodian of Records of ____________________,
Address, City, State, Zip   Telephone number

1. **YOU ARE ORDERED TO PRODUCE THE BUSINESS RECORDS described in item 3, as follows:**

To *(name of deposition officer)*: DEPOSITION OFFICER NAME
On *(date)*: Deposition date   At *(time)*: Deposition time
Location *(address)*: Location of deposition

Do not release the requested records to the deposition officer prior to the date and time stated above.

a. ☑ by delivering a true, legible, and durable **copy** of the business records described in item 3, enclosed in a sealed inner wrapper with the title and number of the action, name of witness, and date of subpoena clearly written on it. The inner wrapper shall then be enclosed in an outer envelope or wrapper, sealed, and mailed to the deposition officer at the address in item 1.

b. ☐ by delivering a true, legible, and durable **copy** of the business records described in item 3 to the deposition officer at the witness's address, on receipt of payment in cash or by check of the reasonable costs of preparing the copy, as determined under Evidence Code section 1563(b).

c. ☐ by making the **original** business records described in item 3 available for inspection at your business address by the attorney's representative and permitting **copying** at your business address under reasonable conditions during normal business hours.

2. *The records are to be produced by the date and time shown in item 1 (but not sooner than 20 days after the issuance of the deposition subpoena, or 15 days after service, whichever date is later). Reasonable costs of locating records, making them available or copying them, and postage, if any, are recoverable as set forth in Evidence Code section 1563(b). The records shall be accompanied by an affidavit of the custodian or other qualified witness pursuant to Evidence Code section 1561.*

3. **The records to be produced are described as follows:**
All items listed in Exhibit A attached hereto

☐ Continued on Attachment 3.

4. **IF YOU HAVE BEEN SERVED WITH THIS SUBPOENA AS A CUSTODIAN OF CONSUMER OR EMPLOYEE RECORDS UNDER CODE OF CIVIL PROCEDURE SECTION 1985.3 OR 1985.6 AND A MOTION TO QUASH OR AN OBJECTION HAS BEEN SERVED ON YOU, A COURT ORDER OR AGREEMENT OF THE PARTIES, WITNESSES, *AND* CONSUMER OR EMPLOYEE AFFECTED MUST BE OBTAINED BEFORE YOU ARE REQUIRED TO PRODUCE CONSUMER OR EMPLOYEE RECORDS.**

DISOBEDIENCE OF THIS SUBPOENA MAY BE PUNISHED AS CONTEMPT BY THIS COURT. YOU WILL ALSO BE LIABLE FOR THE SUM OF FIVE HUNDRED DOLLARS AND ALL DAMAGES RESULTING FROM YOUR FAILURE TO OBEY.

Date issued:

. . . .   ▶ ______________________________
(TYPE OR PRINT NAME)   (SIGNATURE OF PERSON ISSUING SUBPOENA)

____
(TITLE)

(Proof of service on reverse)

Form Adopted for Mandatory Use
Judicial Council of California
982(a)(15.2) [Rev. January 1, 2000]

DEPOSITION SUBPOENA FOR PRODUCTION OF BUSINESS RECORDS

Code of Civil Procedure, §§ 2020, 2025;
Government Code § 68097.1

Figure 17.22

NOTICE TO CONSUMER OR EMPLOYEE

Form 982(a)(15.5)

982(a)(15.5)

ATTORNEY OR PARTY WITHOUT ATTORNEY *(Name, state bar number, and address)*:

YOUR NAME
Your Address
City, State, Zip

TELEPHONE NO.: Your phone   FAX NO.: Your fax

ATTORNEY FOR *(Name)*: Petitioner in pro per

NAME OF COURT: SUPERIOR COURT, COUNTY OF YOUR COUNTY
STREET ADDRESS: Court Street Address
MAILING ADDRESS: Court Mailing Address
CITY AND ZIP CODE: City, State, Zip
BRANCH NAME: Branch (Main, Northern, Family, etc.)

PLAINTIFF/ PETITIONER: PETITIONER'S NAME

DEFENDANT/ RESPONDENT: RESPONDENT'S NAME

CASE NUMBER: Your case number

NOTICE TO CONSUMER OR EMPLOYEE AND OBJECTION
(Code Civ. Proc., §§ 1985.3, 1985.6)

NOTICE TO CONSUMER OR EMPLOYEE

TO *(name)*: YOUR SPOUSE'S NAME

1. PLEASE TAKE NOTICE THAT **REQUESTING PARTY *(name)*:** YOUR NAME SEEKS YOUR RECORDS FOR EXAMINATION by the parties to this action on *(specify date)*: date
   The records are described in the subpoena directed to **witness** *(specify name and address of person or entity from whom records are sought)*: Name of person or entity holding the records
   A copy of the subpoena is attached. Address, City, State, Zip
2. IF YOU OBJECT to the production of these records, YOU MUST DO ONE OF THE FOLLOWING BEFORE THE DATE SPECIFIED IN ITEM a. OR b. BELOW:
   a. If you are a party to the above-entitled action, you must file a motion pursuant to Code of Civil Procedure section 1987.1 to quash or modify the subpoena and give notice of that motion to the **witness** and the **deposition officer** named in the subpoena at least five days before the date set for production of the records.
   b. If you are not a party to this action, you must serve on the **requesting party** and on the **witness**, before the date set for production of the records, a written objection that states the specific grounds on which production of such records should be prohibited. You may use the form below to object and state the grounds for your objection. You must complete the Proof of Service on the reverse side indicating whether you personally served or mailed the objection. The objection should **not** be filed with the court. **WARNING:** IF YOUR OBJECTION IS NOT RECEIVED BEFORE THE DATE SPECIFIED IN ITEM 1, YOUR RECORDS MAY BE PRODUCED AND MAY BE AVAILABLE TO ALL PARTIES.
3. YOU OR YOUR ATTORNEY MAY CONTACT THE UNDERSIGNED to determine whether an agreement can be reached in writing to cancel or limit the scope of the subpoena. If no such agreement is reached, and if you are not otherwise represented by an attorney in this action, YOU SHOULD CONSULT AN ATTORNEY TO ADVISE YOU OF YOUR RIGHTS OF PRIVACY.

Date: Date

YOUR NAME in pro per
(TYPE OR PRINT NAME)

(SIGNATURE OF ☑ REQUESTING PARTY ☐ ATTORNEY)

OBJECTION BY NON-PARTY TO PRODUCTION OF RECORDS

1. ☐ I object to the production of all of my records specified in the subpoena.
2. ☐ I object only to the production of the following specified records:

3. The specific grounds for my objection are as follows:

Date:

(TYPE OR PRINT NAME)

(SIGNATURE)

(Proof of service on reverse)

Form Adopted for Mandatory Use
Judicial Council of California
982(a)(15.5) [Rev. January 1, 2000]

NOTICE TO CONSUMER OR EMPLOYEE AND OBJECTION
(Code Civ. Proc., §§ 1985.3, 1985.6)

Code of Civil Procedure, §§ 1985.3, 1985.6, 2020

e. Proof of Service

For each subpoena, you serve a *copy* of each document in the checklist above. Keep originals in your file. For each subpoena, you usually end up serving two or three people:

1. The custodian of records (the witness) is served *personally*, using the Proof of Service on the back of the subpoena form. You can't serve a witness by mail.

2. Your spouse (the consumer/employee) using the Proof of Service on the back of the Notice to Consumer or Employee form, and

3. Your spouse's attorney of record, if any, using a generic Proof of Service form.

If you have time to meet all deadlines, you can serve your spouse and attorney by mail, otherwise, serve everyone personally. Make sure you have a separate Proof of Service for each person served.

If you use personal service.

In choosing a date for the "date" box of the Subpoena and Notice of Taking Deposition, use a date that gives the custodian of records at least 15 days after service to produce. In practice, this means your date for the deposition—that is, the date you are to receive records—must be at least 22 days after the date you issue the Subpoena. It won't hurt to give yourself some extra days and set the deposition, say, 25 or 30 days after the date on which you issue the Subpoena. Once you've done the Subpoena, check the dates below and the deposition date, and make sure they aren't on weekends. If a date falls on a weekend, put it on the next workday, and add days to anything following it accordingly. Here's a summary:

Prepare the subpoena (issued in blank, or fill it out and take to clerk to issue)
1 day later serve your spouse or, if he/she has an attorney, serve the attorney
6 days later serve the custodian of records (the witness)
22 days later the records are due to you

If you serve your spouse by mail.

Remember, you must still serve the witness personally. In choosing a date to put in the "date" box of the Subpoena form and Notice of Taking Deposition form, you must use a date that gives the custodian of records at least 15 days after service to produce. In practice, this means that your date for the deposition must be at least 27 days after the date you issue the Subpoena. It won't hurt to give yourself some extra days and set the deposition, say, 30 or 35 days after the date on which you issue the Subpoena. Once you've done the Subpoena, check the dates listed below and the deposition date, and make sure they aren't on weekends. If a date falls on a weekend, put it on the next workday, and add days to anything following it accordingly. Here's a summary:

Prepare the subpoena (issued in blank, or fill it out and take to clerk to issue)
1 day later serve your spouse or, if he/she has an attorney, serve the attorney
12 days later serve the custodian of records (the witness)
27 days later the records are due to you

Theoretically, you could issue a subpoena and get documents a minimum of 20 days later, either to court or to a deposition, if you serve the subpoena the same day you issue it. But practically, unless there is a deadline or a court appearance compelling you to use an earlier date, you should select a date about 30 days away for production in order to avoid any possible problem with deadlines.

Payment of fees

Because the custodian of records (the witness) does not have to travel to a hearing there can be no witness fee or travel charge, but they are entitled to a clerical fee of up to $16 per hour plus ten cents a page.

D Depositions

You've probably seen depositions being taken on TV shows. The parties (and attorneys if they are represented) meet face-to-face in the presence of a court reporter for question-and-answer testimony that is taken under oath. It is typically done in the office of one of the attorneys, or in a rented or borrowed conference space if the initiating party does not have counsel. It is very similar to testimony in court, but there is no judge present. Afterwards, the testimony is typed up so it can be reviewed by the parties and used in court.

Depositions are very expensive. You must have a court reporter present who will prepare a transcript of every word uttered during the deposition. If you want a copy, you tell the court reporter at the end, "I want a copy of the transcript." You only order one copy. A typical cost would be about $4.50 per page for the original (with a copy being about $1.50 per page), and it is not unusual for a deposition to cover 150 pages for a total of $676 for the original. This is the most expensive book you will ever own! Therefore, depositions are used only when the information cannot be obtained in some less expensive manner.

One shot. You can only compel a witness (including the other party) to submit to one deposition. If your spouse has previously taken one deposition from you or some other witness, he/she cannot take a second one without a good reason, and you can stop an attempt to do it. This is one reason why you should prepare well before taking a deposition; you probably won't get a second chance.

Whose deposition? You can take the deposition of your spouse and anyone who is a witness to anything relevant to your divorce. For example, you might want the testimony of a person who would know how a self-employed spouse is diverting money from his/her business to personal use, or you could take the deposition of your spouse's live-in mate or roommate if you have a custody/visitation issue.

Where to do it. The place where a witness' deposition is taken must be within 75 miles of where the witness lives. If your spouse has a lawyer, you can schedule the deposition at the attorney's office, but you might feel at a disadvantage there, so you might want to arrange for a conference room in some place that rents meeting space to the public, such as Kinko's or a convenience office center. Wherever you do it, if documents have been subpoenaed to the deposition, it could be important to have access to a copier.

Who may be present. Both parties (the husband and the wife) are entitled to be present at the deposition as well as their lawyers. In cases such as those involving domestic abuse, a support person would be allowed to sit at the conference table with an abused spouse. Anyone can attend a deposition, just as anyone can attend a public trial. On the other hand, under Code of Civil Procedure section 2025, a party may file a motion to the court requesting an order that designated persons, other than the parties to the action and their lawyers, be excluded from attending the deposition. The judge would decide such a motion on an individual basis, based on past histories, present circumstances, and the types of issues involved. Certainly if there were an issue of child molestation, the judge might readily exclude persons other than the parties. Or, if one spouse has been abused, and now the abuser wants to exclude a support person, the judge would hopefully see through this tactic and refuse it.

Get a court reporter. You must arrange for a court reporter to record the deposition. You can locate a court reporter through the phone book yellow pages under "Reporters—Court." Call around and ask their rates and when they are available. You must either find a reporter who can be present on the day you choose to do the deposition, or arrange for your deposition on a day a reporter can be present.

Video and audio taping. There must always be a court reporter at a deposition (unless it is a records-only deposition, discussed below), but you can also videotape or audiotape the deposition if you put that

Figure 17.23

NOTICE OF TAKING DEPOSITION

YOUR NAME
Your Address
City, State, Zip
Your Phone

Petitioner in propria persona

SUPERIOR COURT OF CALIFORNIA, COUNTY OF [County]

In re Marriage of	)	No.: [Your case number]
	)	
Petitioner: YOUR NAME	)	NOTICE OF TAKING DEPOSITION
	)	
Respondent: SPOUSE NAME	)	
______________________	)	

TO ALL PARTIES AND THEIR ATTORNEYS OF RECORD:

PLEASE TAKE NOTICE that the deposition of [Name] will be taken in the above-entitled action before a Notary Public at the following address: [City], California, on [date], at [time], and continued from day to day thereafter, Sundays and holidays excepted, until completed, on behalf of petitioner. In addition to being stenographically recorded, the deposition will be videotaped/ audiotaped.

[If the person whose deposition is being taken is your spouse, you can also state:] YOU ARE DIRECTED TO BRING WITH YOU TO THE DEPOSITION THE FOLLOWING DOCUMENTS AND ITEMS: All items listed in Exhibit A attached hereto and made part hereof. [Use Exhibit A in Figures 17.2- 17.4, or create one of your own.]

Dated: [Date]

____
YOUR NAME, Petitioner

1

Notice of Taking Deposition

Figure 17.24

DEPOSITION SUBPOENA—PERSONAL APPEARANCE

Form 982(a)(15.3)

982(a)(15.3)

ATTORNEY OR PARTY WITHOUT ATTORNEY *(Name, state bar number, and address):* YOUR NAME Your Address City, State, Zip TELEPHONE NO.: Your phone FAX NO.: Your fax ATTORNEY FOR *(Name):* Petitioner in pro per	*FOR COURT USE ONLY*
NAME OF COURT: SUPERIOR COURT, COUNTY OF YOUR COUNTY STREET ADDRESS: Court Street Address MAILING ADDRESS: Court Mailing Address CITY AND ZIP CODE: City, State, Zip BRANCH NAME: Branch (Norther, Main, Family, etc.)	
PLAINTIFF/ PETITIONER: PETITIONER'S NAME DEFENDANT/ RESPONDENT: RESPONDENT'S NAME	
DEPOSITION SUBPOENA **For Personal Appearance**	CASE NUMBER: Your case number

THE PEOPLE OF THE STATE OF CALIFORNIA, TO *(name, address, and telephone number of deponent, if known)*:
Witness' name, Address, City, State, Zip Telephone number

1. **YOU ARE ORDERED TO APPEAR IN PERSON TO TESTIFY AS A WITNESS in this action at the following time and place:**

Date: Deposition date	Time: Time	Address: Address of deposition City, State, Zip

a. [✔] As a deponent who is not a natural person, you are ordered to designate one or more persons to testify on your behalf as to the matters described in item 2. (Code Civ. Proc., § 2025, subd. (d)(6).)

b. [✔] This deposition will be recorded stenographically [ ] through the instant visual display of testimony, and by [ ] audiotape [✔] videotape.

c. [✔] This videotape deposition is intended for possible use at trial under Code of Civil Procedure section 2025(u)(4).

2. [✔] If the witness is a representative of a business or other entity, the matters upon which the witness is to be examined are as follows: Example: Respondent's history of employment with Witness, including Respondent's reasons for leaving employment and various violent altercations between Respondent and fellow employees.

3. *At the deposition, you will be asked questions under oath. Questions and answers are recorded stenographically at the deposition; later they are transcribed for possible use at trial. You may read the written record and change any incorrect answers before you sign the deposition. You are entitled to receive witness fees and mileage actually traveled both ways. The money must be paid, at the option of the party giving notice of the deposition, either with service of this subpoena or at the time of the deposition.*

DISOBEDIENCE OF THIS SUBPOENA MAY BE PUNISHED AS CONTEMPT BY THIS COURT. YOU WILL ALSO BE LIABLE FOR THE SUM OF FIVE HUNDRED DOLLARS AND ALL DAMAGES RESULTING FROM YOUR FAILURE TO OBEY.

Date issued:

(TYPE OR PRINT NAME) ▸ (SIGNATURE OF PERSON ISSUING SUBPOENA)

(TITLE)

(Proof of service on reverse)

Form Adopted for Mandatory Use
Judicial Council of California
982(a)(15.3) [New January 1, 2000]

DEPOSITION SUBPOENA
FOR PERSONAL APPEARANCE

Code of Civil Procedure,
§§ 2020, 2025;
Government Code, § 68097.1

request into the notice of taking deposition. The taping of a deposition might curb a lot of bad behavior that would not be picked up by a written transcript, such as shouting and nasty tones of voice. People tend to behave better in front of a camera or microphone. Also, you might catch some telling eye-contact between witness and attorney. If you decide to tape, you will need a separate person present to handle the video or audio equipment. Ask the court reporter if he/she knows someone who can provide this service.

Bring documents. If you also want to compel your spouse to bring certain documents to the deposition, you will use either (1) a notice to attorney in lieu of subpoena (Figure 17.27), which can be used only if your spouse has an attorney of record, or (2) a Deposition Subpoena (Figure 17.25) if your spouse has no attorney. The notice to attorney in lieu of subpoena can be mailed to the attorney 25 days before the deposition, but the subpoena must be served personally on your spouse as explained in item 1 below.

Pay up. When you take the deposition of an expert witness, you must be ready to pay an expert witness fee by the beginning of the deposition. The witness can also insist on being paid for a couple of hours of preparation for the deposition.

1. How to prepare and serve the papers

This package is easier than the other subpoena packages, consisting only of:

(1) Notice of Taking Deposition (Figure 17.23), and

(2) The Deposition Subpoena for Personal Appearance (Figure 17.24), or
The Deposition Subpoena for Personal Appearance and Production of Documents and Things (Figure 17.25), and

(3) If you are directing the witness to bring documents or things to the deposition, you must attach a declaration showing good cause (reasonable need) for the items subpoenaed. See the discussion on page 151, items 3 and 4, and see Figure 17.26. Staple the declaration to the Subpoena—a subpoena duces tecum without the declaration is void.

Want documents from your spouse? If the witness is your spouse, a party to the action, it is not necessary to serve a subpoena. You just do the Notice of Taking Deposition and in it state, "Under CCP section 2025(h) Respondent/Petitioner is directed to bring the following items to the deposition: [list all items to be produced]." This must be served at least 20 days before the deposition or 25 if served by mail.

You must serve the witness a reasonable time before they must appear. The witness and the party may be the same person if you are subpoenaing your spouse. In that case, your spouse as a witness must be served a reasonable time before the appearance, but as a party your spouse is entitled to ten days' notice of a deposition and 21 days' notice of the hearing of an OSC or motion. In any event, your service of them must comply with both of these time limits. If the witness is a different person or entity from your spouse, you must serve the witness a reasonable time before the appearance. You must also serve any deposition notice on your spouse (or his/her attorney) at least 10 days before deposition if served personally and 15 days if mailed to them within California.

2. How to take someone's deposition

Here are some tips on the practical aspects of taking a deposition, known to experienced trial attorneys, that you probably can't find in any other book.

There are two approaches to a deposition, but you can only use one: (a) scare your spouse into settling by asking all the difficult questions and confronting him/her openly with the serious conflicts in his/her case, or (b) be nice and gentle so you don't scare your spouse into clamming up, and so you don't prepare him/her for the hard questions you will ask at trial when they are in front of the judge.

Figure 17.25

DEPOSITION SUBPOENA FOR PERSONAL APPEARANCE AND PRODUCTION OF DOCUMENTS AND THINGS

Form 982(a)(15.4)

982(a)(15.4)

ATTORNEY OR PARTY WITHOUT ATTORNEY (Name, state bar number, and address):
YOUR NAME
Your Address
City, State, Zip

TELEPHONE NO.: Your phone FAX NO.: Your fa:
ATTORNEY FOR (Name): Petitioner in pro per

FOR COURT USE ONLY

NAME OF COURT: SUPERIOR COURT, COUNTY OF YOUR COUNTY
STREET ADDRESS: Court Street Address
MAILING ADDRESS: Court Mailing Address
CITY AND ZIP CODE: City, State, Zip
BRANCH NAME: Branch (Main, Northern, Family, etc.)

PLAINTIFF/ PETITIONER: PETITIONER'S NAME

DEFENDANT/ RESPONDENT: RESPONDENT'S NAME

DEPOSITION SUBPOENA
For Personal Appearance and Production of Documents and Things

CASE NUMBER:
Your case number

THE PEOPLE OF THE STATE OF CALIFORNIA, TO *(name, address, and telephone number of deponent, if known)*:
Name of witness being subpoenaed Witness' telephone number

1. **YOU ARE ORDERED TO APPEAR IN PERSON TO TESTIFY AS A WITNESS in this action at the following date, time, and place:**

Date: Date of deposition Time: Time Address: Address of deposition
City, State, Zip

a. ☐ As a deponent who is not a natural person, you are ordered to designate one or more persons to testify on your behalf as to the matters described in item 4. (Code Civ. Proc., § 2025, subd. (d)(6).)
b. You are ordered to produce the documents and things described in item 3.
c. ☐ This deposition will be recorded stenographically ☐ through the instant visual display of testimony, and by ☐ audiotape ☐ videotape.
d. ☐ This videotape deposition is intended for possible use at trial under Code of Civil Procedure section 2025(u)(4).

2. The personal attendance of the custodian or other qualified witness and the production of the original records are required by this subpoena. The procedure authorized by Evidence Code sections 1560(b), 1561, and 1562 will not be deemed sufficient compliance with this subpoena.
3. The documents and things to be produced and any testing or sampling being sought are described as follows:
Items listed in Exhibit A attached hereto. (See samples in Figures 17.2—17.4)

☐ Continued on Attachment 3.

4. If the witness is a representative of a business or other entity, the matters upon which the witness is to be examined are described as follows:
Authentication of items in Exhibit A and facts relating thereto. (Explain if there is more. For example if witness is Respondent's employer: work history, ability to work, reasons for termination of employment.)
☐ Continued on Attachment 4.
5. **IF YOU HAVE BEEN SERVED WITH THIS SUBPOENA AS A CUSTODIAN OF CONSUMER OR EMPLOYEE RECORDS UNDER CODE OF CIVIL PROCEDURE SECTION 1985.3 OR 1985.6 AND A MOTION TO QUASH OR AN OBJECTION HAS BEEN SERVED ON YOU, A COURT ORDER OR AGREEMENT OF THE PARTIES, WITNESSES, *AND* CONSUMER OR EMPLOYEE AFFECTED MUST BE OBTAINED BEFORE YOU ARE REQUIRED TO PRODUCE CONSUMER OR EMPLOYEE RECORDS.**
6. *At the deposition, you will be asked questions under oath. Questions and answers are recorded stenographically at the deposition; later they are transcribed for possible use at trial. You may read the written record and change any incorrect answers before you sign the deposition. You are entitled to receive witness fees and mileage actually traveled both ways. The money must be paid, at the option of the party giving notice of the deposition, either with service of this subpoena or at the time of the deposition.*

DISOBEDIENCE OF THIS SUBPOENA MAY BE PUNISHED AS CONTEMPT BY THIS COURT. YOU WILL ALSO BE LIABLE FOR THE SUM OF FIVE HUNDRED DOLLARS AND ALL DAMAGES RESULTING FROM YOUR FAILURE TO OBEY.

Date issued:

(TYPE OR PRINT NAME) ▸ (SIGNATURE OF PERSON ISSUING SUBPOENA)

(TITLE)

(Proof of service on reverse)

Form Adopted for Mandatory Use
Judicial Council of California
982(a)(15.4) [New January 1, 2000]

DEPOSITION SUBPOENA FOR PERSONAL APPEARANCE AND PRODUCTION OF DOCUMENTS AND THINGS

Code of Civil Procedure, §§ 2020, 2025; Government Code, § 68097.1

Figure 17.26

DECLARATION IN SUPPORT OF SUBPOENA DUCES TECUM

Note: You must attach an Exhibit A to this declaration, listing items that are being subpoenaed. Examples for Exhibit A can be seen at Figures 17.2–17.4.

Marriage of YOUR LAST NAME & SPOUSE LAST NAME

Case No. [Your case number]

DECLARATION IN SUPPORT OF SUBPOENA DUCES TECUM
(TO HEARING OR TRIAL)

The undersigned states:

I am petitioner in the above-entitled action; said cause has been set for hearing at the date, time and location specified in the attached subpoena duces tecum.

On information and belief, the subpenaed witness has in his/her possession or under his/her control the following documents: All items listed in Exhibit A, attached hereto and made part hereof.

[Note: Create an Exhibit A based on Figures 17.2-17.4]

On information and belief, the above documents are relevant to a proper presentation of petitioner's case by reason of the following facts: This is an action for dissolution of marriage, involving issues of support and community property.

The respondent's assets, income and ability to make payments are relevant to the issues herein. The requested records are relevant to said matter.

Executed at [City], California, on [Date].

I declare under penalty of perjury under the laws of the State of California that the foregoing is true and correct.

____
YOUR NAME, Petitioner

1

Declaration in Support of Subpoena Duces Tecum

Figure 17.27
NOTICE TO ATTORNEY IN LIEU OF SUBPOENA

YOUR NAME
Your Address
City, State, Zip
Your Phone

Petitioner in propria persona

SUPERIOR COURT OF CALIFORNIA, COUNTY OF [County]

In re Marriage of	No.: [Your case number]
Petitioner: YOUR NAME	NOTICE TO ATTORNEY IN LIEU OF SUBPOENA
Respondent: SPOUSE NAME	

To [name], attorney for Respondent herein:

NOTICE IS HEREBY GIVEN that Petitioner requests that Respondent attend before a Notary Public at a deposition at the following address: [address], California, on [date], at [time], to testify as a witness in this action. Respondent has in his/her possession or under his/her control the items listed in Exhibit A attached hereto and made part hereof.

Said party is requested to bring to the deposition said items. This request is made pursuant to sections 1987(b) and 1987(c) of the Code of Civil Procedure which provide that the giving of this notice has the same effect as the service of a subpoena, and that, in the event of noncompliance with this notice, the parties shall have the rights, and the Court may make such orders, including imposition of sanctions, as in the case of a subpoena for attendance before the Court.

Dated: [Date]

____
YOUR NAME, Petitioner

[Note: See example Exhibit A at Figures 17.2-17.4 showing sample items to produce.]

1

Notice to Attorney in Lieu of Subpoena

The traditional purpose of a deposition is to obtain information that will be used at trial or in settling the case. The second purpose is to psych out the other side so they'll give up and settle. This is much more real than the first purpose, as very few cases actually get to trial. The two purposes conflict. Generally, if you really want information, the best thing is to quietly accept whatever information the witness is giving you and keep trying to draw him/her out more, hoping he/she will fall into a tangle of contradictions. There's a rule: "Don't educate the witness," which means that if you confront the witness directly with the weakness in his/her testimony, they won't repeat it at trial. But there probably won't be a trial. What you really want is to get a settlement as rapidly and favorably as possible, and maybe confronting the witness with his/her contradictions and posturing will, in fact, settle the case faster.

Notes. You should have a typed outline of what you're going to ask, and you take notes on that same outline. You have to focus more on the witness and what he/she says, not on taking notes. The court reporter does that. But you will take some notes, mostly because you'll be thinking of other questions you want to ask or remarks of the witness that you want to follow up. Keep the left-hand margin of your outline clear except for follow-up questions you are going to ask, so you don't overlook them. In other words, clearly separate notes that are follow-up questions from other notes, and be sure you ask all the follow-up questions you have.

Seating. Experienced trial lawyers will sit right next to their clients so they can kick the client to stop them from doing something or to coach them. If it is your deposition being taken, you will want to sit next to your attorney where opposing counsel and his/her client cannot catch any signals. If you are taking your spouse's deposition, you will want to try to sit so that you can see if your spouse has an attorney who kicks him/her. If that happens, you say, "Let the record reflect that opposing counsel just kicked the Petitioner/Respondent." If you are taking your spouse's deposition and can do it at a glass-topped table, that is the best because it permits you to observe any under-the-table note-passing, kicking, or other hanky-panky.

What you see is what you see. Do not sit where the other side can steal looks at your papers or notes, although it is okay if you can get a look at theirs. Or you could purposely leave something out for "disinformation," if you can think of anything that might be effective. Some people might bring a huge case of notes and records just to impress the other side with their determination and preparation. It could be files from Sunday school, but they wouldn't know that.

Getting started. Remember to have the court reporter swear the witness! You don't need to do the long introductory remarks that some lawyers engage in. Just be sure to start by asking, "If I say anything that is unclear in any way, or that you don't understand, will you ask me to clarify this?" You need an audible response from the witness, affirming that they will ask you to clarify any unclear question. Don't just say, "Ask me to clarify anything you don't understand," which doesn't require a response; make it a question they have to answer. You should also ask, "Is there any reason, physical, emotional or medical, why you cannot answer my questions today?"

Pissing contests. Often, at the beginning of a deposition, the lawyer will test you by seeing if he/she can dominate you and engage in improper conduct. It is not unusual to have to begin a deposition with a verbal battle in which you assert yourself. If the other lawyer says, "For the record, (your name) was screaming," you say, "For the record, no I was not." A written record doesn't show who was or was not screaming. You cannot avoid the pissing contest by trying to back off and be rational. The other lawyer is testing you, and the only thing to do is to leap at the opportunity, not to shrink from the contest. This is *not* an instruction to yell, scream, and have an angry scene (which is what the other lawyer may want). You need to remain calm and rational but very, very firm.

Swearing. Often a man will test a woman by swearing at the deposition, testing to see what he can get away with. Even if you swear yourself in private, act outraged and demand that the conduct immediately cease. Insist that you will adjourn the deposition if there is any more swearing.

Priming the pump. One approach is to get the witness to answer some easy questions first: name, address, etc., etc., so that they get used to talking and feel comfortable and less guarded by the time you get to something that counts. Of course, on occasion you use the opposite approach and pop your most devastating question first to take advantage of your spouse's initial nervousness.

Questions. Each question has to stand alone. You must refer to an item clearly by its name each time, never by "it." For example, if you are asking about the witness' employment application, you want to ask about "your employment application" every time, never "it." This sounds quite stilted when you do it, but when you get your transcript and want to use it at court, you'll see why you got this advice.

When you ask a question, it is very common for the witness not to answer it. They often deflect you by answering some other question or by offering an enticing tidbit of information. You must be able to follow up the enticing tidbit, go clear around, and return to your original question. Notes are imperative to accomplish this.

You need a balance between preparing specific questions versus an outline of what you want to know, to ensure thoroughness and non-deflection, balanced against your need to be able to follow up new items spontaneously. Without an outline, you will not be thorough and will miss many areas into which you should inquire. With an outline, you might be tempted to stick mechanically to your list and not follow up on new things that arise. You need to be both thorough and spontaneous.

Sometimes a witness will say that they didn't "really" or "actually" do something. Words like that are clues that you need to do some follow-up. If you ask the witness, "Did you tell Mr. Jones X?" and the witness says, "Not really," you must ask, "Did you tell Mr. Jones anything at all?" or "What exactly *did* you say to Mr. Jones?"

Hmmmm. When a deponent first answers, "Um-hmm," in response to a question, explain that the court reporter can't write "um-hmm," and the witness needs to say, "Yes," or "No," in answer to every question. Never fail to correct this kind of response.

Nod. You pay for deposition transcripts by the word, so you don't want to load it up with unnecessary words. If you want to agree with the witness to encourage them to keep talking, just smile and nod instead of saying "Yes," or "Go on, please."

Spell hard words. If a witness says a name or a place or a hard word or a foreign word, interrupt and ask to have it spelled out.

What do you mean? If you have just done a long, complicated question, the witness may ask what you mean or ask you to repeat the question because the witness doesn't like the question and doesn't want to answer that question. If you like the question and went to some mental effort to phrase it and don't have it written down, ask the court reporter to read back the question.

Don't let the witness ask you questions. A witness may try to go on the offensive against you and start grilling you. You don't let this happen. If a witness asks you a question (other than to clarify legitimate confusion about deposition procedure), say pleasantly but firmly, "It's not my deposition; please answer my questions," and do not answer.

Don't let opposing counsel kibitz. If opposing counsel confers with your spouse, particularly if it is after you ask an important question, the court reporter will not write anything down if it is not audible.

Therefore, you have to say, "Let the record reflect that counsel is conferring with his/her client." Do this every time.

Don't let the witness step on your questions. If the deponent doesn't let you get to the end of your question before jumping in with an answer, explain, "The court reporter can't write down what both of us are saying. You need to wait for the end of my question before you answer." *Every* time the witness steps on your question, go through this. Use it also to show your regard for the court reporter, who will like you for this. (You want everyone to like you: you want the reporter to do your transcript as soon as possible; you want clerks to want to help you; so you are going to be charming to everyone and suppress any feelings of anger, hostility, or irritability.) You can also point out that the witness may not know what your question will be and may answer something other than what you end up asking. This way you make the witness want to cooperate and not talk over the end of your questions.

Going off the record. Your spouse's lawyer might say, "Off the record" to the court reporter. Some lawyers are constantly going off the record to minimize the cost of the deposition. It is not a good practice and minimizes the clarity and value of the deposition. You don't want to go off the record unless you are just dealing with purely mechanical items such as what time to return after lunch. Often a witness will continue remarking on evidence, and if you're off the record, the remark is lost. Also, if the other lawyer is engaging in harassment or improper conduct, they may try to get that off the record. If there is a conflict as to whether to go off the record or stay on the record, you loudly instruct the court reporter, "Don't go off the record unless both parties agree to it." When you want to go back on the record, you say, "Back on the record," and be sure the court reporter heard you and starts writing.

Documents produced at the deposition. You often will have served a notice to produce documents at the deposition. The best practice is to have an extra copy of the notice to produce at the deposition and have the court reporter mark it as an exhibit; then you can refer to it in your questions. For example, "What did you bring with you in response to item number 1 of Exhibit A?" You should mark everything the witness produces as an exhibit, and at the end of the deposition, have the court reporter take the exhibits with him/her. Or, if your spouse wants to take the original, copies can be made at the time of the deposition, and you can return the original to your spouse. For that reason you want to set the deposition at a place where you have access to a copier. The exhibits will be at the end of the booklet when the deposition is typed up.

At the end of the testimony as to what was produced in response to each item, you ask, "Did you bring anything else with you in response to request number X of Exhibit A?" If the witness produces something more, after you have them testify about it, ask, "Did you bring anything else with you in response to request number X of Exhibit A?" You don't want to leave the witness open to contend later that he/she produced documents, but you didn't bother to ask for them. No matter how detailed and far afield the discussion of the produced documents goes, don't forget to end this way for each item.

The other attorney often wants to copy the documents and *not* attach them as exhibits to the deposition to save money, but the result of this will be hassles later over what was or was not produced. It is much better to attach the stuff to the deposition, unless it is incredibly voluminous and non-probative. Explain to the other attorney that you appreciate his/her desire to save money, but say you really want to be sure the record is entirely clear. If something produced is really junk and you don't want to copy it or mark it, clearly orally identify it on the record and say that you are returning the originals to the witness.

End of deposition. At the end of the deposition, hang around and see if you hear anything in casual conversation. As long as the court reporter is still there, if you think of one last brilliant question, you can ask the reporter to stay and set up again. Alternatively, this is a good opportunity to casually ease into a settlement discussion, if you want to, without seeming weak for doing so. When you do leave, make sure you have every scrap of paper and notes with you; don't leave anything for the other side to find, even in the wastebasket, unless you intend for them to find it.

Having your deposition taken

In addition to the notes above, here are some tips for what to do if *they* take *your* deposition.

Don't bring documents. If the other side is taking your deposition, and you bring files to the deposition with you, the opposing counsel can ask you to provide documents right there, and you will find yourself opening up your file, looking for papers, and giving them to opposing counsel or to your spouse with no opportunity to review those papers carefully in advance. It is better practice to bring only documents you have been legally notified to produce, a legal pad and court papers to the deposition and, if you are asked to provide documents later that should have been produced by the time of the deposition, make a note of it, and send them to counsel later. (You are keeping your papers in separate files or notebooks as this book instructed, so you already have your court papers separated from other papers.) If opposing counsel abuses the opportunity and asks you to bring in a whole lot of stuff, or if it is a high-conflict case, you may want to tell them to send you a formal written request to produce so there will be no misunderstandings as to what is to be produced. If you say it this way, sounding like you're working to ensure clarity and full production, you won't sound like you're being oppositional.

Never guess. You don't want the other side to lead you down the "primrose path." The lawyer gets the witness to guess at what was observed or said in a conversation, then acts as if the answer is absolutely true, whereas it was only an attempt to say what might have been, then the lawyer asks about a zillion details about it and gets you all flustered, sounding like a liar. Never guess what probably happened or might have been said.

Objections. If you do not make an objection at the deposition, it will be considered to have been waived. If your deposition is being taken, and you have an objection that you feel firmly about, you might have to refuse to answer the question. This is most important when it comes to questions that could possibly include communications between you and an attorney you might have consulted on your case.

Invasions of attorney-client privilege. If you have consulted an attorney at any time about your case, you must be very vigilant to protect the secrecy of those communications. If a question touches in any way on attorney-client privilege, you can lose that privilege by answering in any way. If the privilege gets waived, the other side can take your attorney's deposition and examine your previously secret files. One lawyer trick is to drop in surprise questions like, "Did anyone ever tell you (anything about your rights or your property or your case)?" "When?" "What did they tell you exactly?" "Who told you?" If you answer the first question in the string, you might have waived the attorney/client privilege. If you are asked, "Did anyone ever tell you . . ." you answer, "Do you mean, 'Except for my attorney'?" You intervene to protect the privilege immediately. The same is true of the question, "Have you discussed your case with anyone?" You say, "Do you mean 'Other than my attorney'?"

Don't answer non-questions. If opposing counsel is questioning you and makes a statement, don't answer it. Sit there and wait for a question. This will avoid being baited by opposing counsel.

End of deposition. At the end of the deposition, gather up all of your papers and leave immediately. As long as the court reporter is still there, if opposing counsel thinks of one last brilliant question, they can ask you to stay and have the court reporter set up again. Be sure you did not leave one scrap or note that the other side can get their hands on.

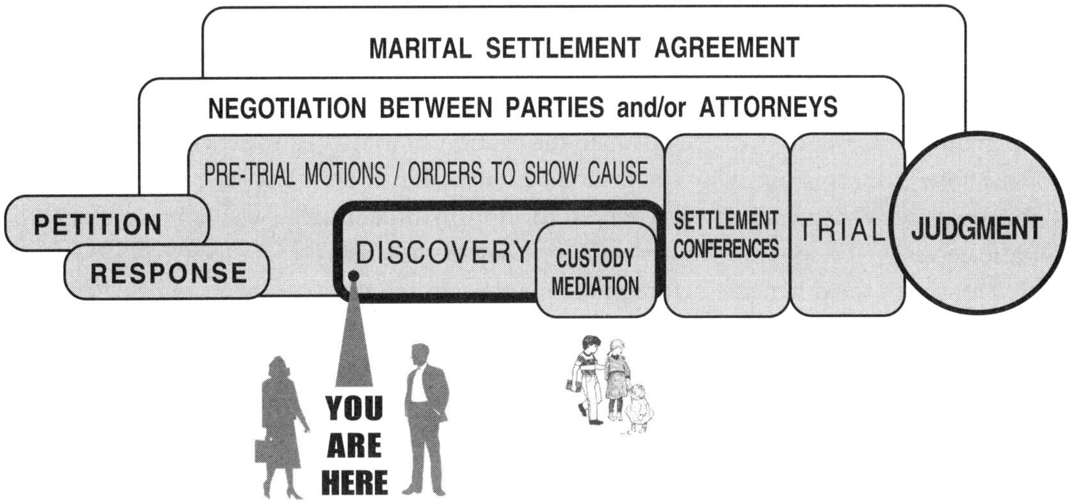

CHAPTER 18
COMPELLING DISCOVERY IN COURT

These motions are much like any other motions. Use the notes here to adapt the basic motion, discussed in chapter 11, to a specific purpose, then follow the other procedures described there.

A Motions to compel discovery

If your demands for discovery were ignored, or the responses were inadequate, you must file a motion to compel discovery. However, this can backfire if it is denied because the judge thinks what you were asking for was totally unrelated or out of proportion to the size of the issue. Another ground for denial would be where the judge feels someone's right to privacy outweighs the usefulness of the records; for example, asking for banking records of a new live-in of your spouse where your spouse and the live-in kept their finances separate. If a judge denies your motion to compel discovery, sanctions (that is, money fines) *shall* be awarded (Code of Civil Procedure sections 2025, 2030, 2031).

If you are not confident you will win your discovery motion, maybe you should not make it. On the other hand, your spouse has a duty to disclose all relevant information, so the court should support legitimate requests and not punish you for asking for information.

Anything relevant to marital finances is discoverable without a showing of good cause (Family Code 721(b)). If you are trying to compel discovery and you decide to file an optional Memorandum of Points and Authorities (see example, Figure 12.5), you can cite the Family Code there. In the hearing, you might get a chance to orally cite the statute to the court at the hearing. Of course, an experienced judge will already know this statute.

Preliminaries –things you must do before making your motion

Before you can compel discovery by motion in court, you first have to make a reasonable and good faith attempt at an informal resolution of each issue in the motion. This usually means that you have to write a letter to the other side explaining why you need the information and/or how their response (if they sent one) is not adequate. If they ignored your request for information entirely, write them and call to their attention the necessity of responding by a certain date, say ten days away. Some local rules require you to meet and confer with the other side before making a motion to compel. Check your local rules. Your discovery motion must be accompanied by a declaration stating what you did to try to resolve the issue by agreement. The sample forms discussed in this chapter show how to do this.

Procedures for discovery motions

If you end up negotiating with the other side about what is due and when, you have to be very careful not to get distracted from the various deadlines (discussed below) for when something must be produced and when you have to file a motion to compel production if you don't get full compliance. In other words, don't get distracted; keep the paperwork deadlines religiously or get them extended.

Order after hearing. If you are compelling the other side to answer questions, produce documents or do any specific act, be sure to include a deadline in your order, such as saying that records should be produced within 20 days after the hearing.

The Code of Civil Procedure permits the judge to send your discovery matters out to a "referee" or "special master," in which case you would have to pay that person to decide your discovery issues. One recent case, *Hobbs v. Superior Court,* 72 CA4 446 (May, 1999), indicates that the courts should not send routine discovery matters out for decision by others but only cases that involve more complicated or lengthy issues.

Requesting attorney fees

The courts want discovery statutes to be self-enforcing; that is, they don't want you to have to come to court to pry information out of the other party, so, if you make a successful discovery motion, the court may award you attorney fees and costs. If you are requesting attorney fees, you must attach an Income and Expense Declaration to your motion. To request attorney fees, check that box on the first page of your Application for Order and Supporting Declaration. If you do not have an attorney of record, you can request attorney fees only if you paid an attorney to advise or assist with the motion, in which case you attach a statement or letter from the attorney to prove the amount billed for that particular service.

B Responding to a discovery motion

Your spouse is clearly entitled to all financial information in your possession related to marital property and your income and expenses. If the other side wants something, unless it is hugely and obviously unreasonable, just give it to them. If they file a discovery motion because you failed to send information or documents, or you sent incomplete information or documents, you should comply with all reasonable requests as soon as possible. You need to minimize attorney fees that might be awarded and try to keep the judge from getting angry for unnecessarily taking up the court's time.

You use a Responsive Declaration form to respond to a discovery motion (Figure 14.1), where you need to address separately each and every item that your spouse claims you haven't produced. You need to explain why such documents never were in your possession (such as you don't get canceled checks with your type of checking account), or they no longer exist (such as you throw away your tax returns after 7 years, which we don't recommend), or some other excuse (such as you moved last week, everything is in boxes, and it will take time to locate the records). It would be best if you were to follow the format of Code of Civil Procedure section 2031 in connection with responding to the request to produce. This statute is on the CD that comes with this book.

Each type of legal action below, sections D–G, also includes notes on how to respond.

C Compelling Declaration of Disclosure

Both parties are required to serve each other with (but not file with the court) the Preliminary Declaration of Disclosure (PDD) and the Final Declaration of Disclosure (FDD). The PDD is due some unspecified time after service of the Petition, and the FDD is due either before signing a marital settlement agreement or at least 45 days before trial. These Declarations are covered in *How to Do Your Own Divorce,* chapter 14. If what you are after is information, it is much easier to get it by discovery as described above rather than by trying to compel a declaration of disclosure—an involved procedure.

Do not agree without disclosure! You must *not* enter into a written marital settlement agreement (MSA) unless your spouse first serves you with both a Preliminary and Final Declaration of Disclosure, either before the MSA is signed or at the same time. Make serving both disclosures an explicit condition of any agreement. See chapter 5B for suggestions for how to get this accomplished.

D Motion to compel production of documents or things

When you make a request for production, if it is entirely ignored, you should file a motion to compel production. If the other side does not produce fully and properly or does not supply a signed verification (oath declaring the truth of the response), you should file a motion to compel. The harder decision is when your spouse provided you with some, but not all, of the documents you requested.

As you have to send a letter requesting more documents, your spouse might send you a further response before you make your motion. If your spouse provides more and more documents, at each step of the way you need to decide whether you now have enough documents or whether you need to continue pressing. Keep in mind that if only one month's bank statements is missing, it could be the one statement that has the information that is crucial for your case. On the other hand, people lose documents, and sometimes documents are missing simply because they are missing.

You don't want to appear unreasonable to the judge, so you are going to explain very clearly in your declaration supporting your discovery motion why you want the documents you requested.

Time limit for motion to compel production. If your spouse completely ignores the Request to Produce, you do not have a legal time limit to file a motion to compel. As a practical matter, you should proceed promptly and make your motion within a month or so. But if your spouse makes an evasive, inadequate or unverified response, you have only 45 days from the date you received the Response (or the latest supplemented Response) in which to file and serve a motion to force him/her to produce. If you want to serve your motion by mail, you must do so within 40 days from the date you were served with the Response. Do not miss this deadline! As soon as you receive the Response, calendar the deadline to serve and file the motion to compel. An appellate court in a non-divorce case held that if a party does not make the motion within 45 days, they can never make the motion and they cannot redo the initial request to produce and thereby restart the deadlines. On the other hand, in family law there is a fiduciary duty to provide information, so a different outcome might result. Don't take a chance. Do your motion well before the last moment.

Prerequisite to making motion to compel production. Before making the motion, you must write your spouse (or his/her attorney) a letter, keeping a copy, and explain why the response was inadequate and demand further response. You are not writing this letter only for the other side—you know a judge might see it, and you want the judge to see clearly why you need your documents. Therefore, you write your letter so that a stranger could understand exactly what you mean without having to refer to any other document. The letter should stand on its own. If the letter does not produce an adequate response, file a motion to compel production. Code of Civil Procedure section 2025 requires your motion to set forth "specific facts showing good cause justifying the discovery sought by the inspection demand." You need to be sure to say that this is an action for dissolution of marriage, and the other party has a fiduciary duty to provide you with information , then explain why each particular item should be produced.

Do your motion as described in chapter 12, filling out the forms as shown there, but with the modifications shown below. In these examples, we assume the moving party is Petitioner, but it could be the other way around.

MOTION TO COMPEL PRODUCTION OF DOCUMENTS

Notice of Motion:

In the caption, check the box for "Other," and type "Compel Production of Documents."

Application for Order and Supporting Declaration:

Item 9, Other relief: Type in "Order Respondent to produce Items x, y, and z, listed in the attached Declaration which is made part hereof within 15 days after the hearing."

Item 10, Facts: Prepare and attach a declaration like the one in Figure 18.1.

How to resist a Motion to Compel Production

In general, any document reasonably related to your divorce should be produced. Unreasonable refusal will ultimately make the judge angry and could cost you sanctions. However, there may be situations in which it is reasonable to resist production:

1. You don't have it, and you never had it, and you can't get it with a phone call.
2. The document has been destroyed for some legitimate reason. For example, you destroy copies of tax returns after 7 years, so you have to contact the IRS to get a copy (and you yourself prepared the return so can't get a copy from a tax preparer) and this will take time. The court will expect you to contact the IRS and get the copy.
3. The document never existed.
4. You have moved, and have many boxes of records which you can't check out in the time to respond. You've tried to find the requested document, but so far cannot. You need more time.

If any of these apply, explain it in your Responsive Declaration (chapter 14). You want to make it clear to the judge that the discovery request is unreasonable or that there is a reason why you can't comply. You can say the discovery motion is "harassment," but if the facts don't show that, merely flinging the accusation won't help. In every other regard, follow instructions in chapter 14 for responding to a motion.

Figure 18.1

DECLARATION RE MOTION TO COMPEL PRODUCTION

(page 1)

Marriage of YOUR LAST NAME & SPOUSE LAST NAME

Case No. [Your case number]

DECLARATION OF PETITIONER RE

MOTION TO COMPEL PRODUCTION OF DOCUMENTS

I, the undersigned, state:

I am the petitioner herein.

This is an action for dissolution of marriage, including issues of support, property and custody/visitation.

On or about [date], I caused a Request for Production of Documents to be served on respondent. Respondent failed to respond to the request (in whole OR in part and if it is in part:) and has failed to identify and/or produce the terms as set out below.

I am informed and believe that the items set forth below are relevant to the subject matter of this action and are reasonably calculated to lead to discovery of admissible evidence, and good cause exists for their production.

<u>ITEM 1:</u>

a. <u>Request:</u> [Set forth the request exactly as it appeared in your Request for Production. Example:] Federal income tax returns of the respondent for the years [year] through [year], including all attached schedules, W-2 forms, 1099 forms and K-1 forms and any an all amended returns and attachments, regardless of whether filed solely or jointly with another individual.

1

Declaration of Petitioner re Motion to Compel Production of Documents

Figure 18.2

DECLARATION RE MOTION TO COMPEL PRODUCTION

(page 2)

b. Response: [Set forth the response exactly as you received it. Example:] It is objected that the income tax returns for said years are privileged because they were filed jointly with my present spouse.

c. Argument and Factual Contentions: [Explain why the item should be produced. Example:] This action involves issues of child and spousal support, and the income tax returns are not privileged.

On or about [date], I wrote to Respondent['s attorney] and requested that he/she respond [further] to the request to produce; see copy of letter attached hereto and made part hereof. I received no further response as a result of that letter OR I received the following response to that letter:

Respondent's failure to respond, object to the request, or failure to comply with the request was without substantial justification.

I declare under penalty of perjury under the laws of the State of California that the foregoing is true and correct.

Executed on [date] at [City], California.

____
YOUR NAME, Petitioner

2

Declaration of Petitioner re Motion to Compel Production of Documents

E Compelling answers to written interrogatories

When you send written interrogatories (form or specially drafted), if they are entirely ignored, you need to file a motion to compel (below). If the other side made some sort of answers but there was no signed verification (oath declaring the truth of the answers), you should file a motion to compel. The harder decision is when your spouse provided you with vague, evasive or inadequate answers and objected to some of the questions.

Your declaration supporting your motion will explain why every single question is necessary to your case. Of course, if you are asking a very basic question like, "On what date do you contend that the parties separated?" this is clearly relevant information. On the other hand, if you are asking a detailed question about personal finances, you might want to explain the relevance in more detail. If your spouse wrote initial answers, then you sent a letter asking for more answers, then he/she sent you an additional response, every step will be set out in your motion. Your declaration also must set forth the efforts you made to reach an agreement regarding the need to answer the interrogatories.

Rule 335 says you're not supposed to attach anything to the discovery motion in order to incorporate it by reference, so you must rewrite each question that is in issue and each response you received, describe each effort to get a better response, and so on.

Deadline for filing a motion. If your spouse completely ignored your interrogatories, you do not have a deadline to make your motion. But if you received responses, your motion *must* be filed and served within 45 days of the service of the responses, or any supplemental responses, or on or before any specific later date to which the parties have agreed in writing (Code of Civil Procedure section 2030(l)).

Do your motion as described in chapter 12, filling out the forms as described there, but with the modifications shown below.

MOTION TO COMPEL ANSWERS TO INTERROGATORIES

Notice of Motion:

In the caption, check the box for "Other," and type "Compel answers to interrogatories."

Application for Order and Supporting Declaration:

Item 9, Other relief: Type "Respondent be ordered to submit verified responses to written interrogatories numbers x, y, and z within 15 days after the hearing on this motion."

Item 10, Facts: Prepare and attach a declaration like the one in Figure 18.3.

How to resist a motion to compel answers to written interrogatories

If your spouse has asked you reasonable questions that are clear enough that you can understand them, you should answer them as soon as you can, even after the motion is served on you. If you try to avoid answering reasonable questions, you might have to pay your spouse's fees incurred in forcing you to answer. If your spouse sent you extremely burdensome interrogatories that are obviously and solely for the purpose of harassment, you can legitimately object, but you have to explain why. The fact that your spouse knows the answer is not an objection; your spouse is entitled to know what you say about it.

If you feel that your spouse's questions infringe on your privacy in your life since you have separated, such as very personal questions about someone you are seeing, you may want to get advice about fighting this invasion of your privacy. However, if you are involved in a custody/visitation case, and this new person will be around your children, this could be a valid inquiry. If you refuse to answer the question, explain the privacy issue in your statement. The California State Constitution guarantees privacy as a right, so judges are sensitive to this issue. Your spouse will either accept your refusal or file a motion to compel an answer, in which case you file a Responsive Declaration setting forth your position. Usually, you can merely write a clear explanation as to each question you refuse to answer, but for a complex case legal advice might be necessary.

Responsive Declaration. As with all Responsive Declarations, you put X's in the boxes that correspond to your spouse's requests. Under Item 9 on the second page, explain why you should not have to answer the questions your spouse has written in the interrogatories. Begin by explaining why the whole group of interrogatories to which you object is improper and then go over every single interrogatory your spouse is insisting you should answer. Explain why that question is too vague, overly broad, asks for privileged information (such as communications with doctor, lawyer or psychotherapist), or invades your privacy (such as by asking for unnecessary information about a person you're seeing).

F Motions to enforce or stop a subpoena

Technically, when someone is served with a subpoena, the burden is on *them* to file a motion to quash it. However, people will sometime just ignore the subpoena. That puts the one who did the subpoena into the difficult position of having to file a motion against someone who is not a party to the action.

As with all discovery motions, it is a good idea to write a letter to the spouse and to the witness before you make the motion so the judge will know that you really had no choice but to take it to court.

MOTION TO ENFORCE A SUBPOENA

Notice of Motion:

In the caption, check the box for "Other," and type in "Compel compliance with subpoena."

Item 1, To: Put your spouse's name and the name of the witness.

Application for Order and Supporting Declaration:

Item 9, Other relief: Type in "That Witness (name) be directed to comply with the Subpoena, a copy of which is attached and made part hereof, including produce all requested records within 15 days after the hearing."

Item 10, Facts: Prepare and attach a declaration like the one in Figure 18.5.

How to stop or limit a subpoena

You could simply ignore a subpoena, in which case the issuing party would have to make the above motion to force you to comply, then you respond (chapter 14). However, if you ignore a subpoena to come to court without a good reason, the judge is going to be very unhappy. Better to file a motion to "quash" the subpoena. If you want protection from a subpoena, or if you want to protect a witness (such as a therapist or new mate), who was served with a subpoena, you can file a motion to "quash" or limit the subpoena. If it is "quashed," the subpoena is completely rejected by the court; otherwise, the judge might choose merely to limit its terms.

If a consumer subpoena was served improperly, you can move to quash it. For example, if there was no consumer or employee notice, then you could stop the production, or if the party was not served at

Figure 18.3

DECLARATION RE MOTION TO COMPEL ANSWERS TO INTERROGATORIES

(page 1)

Marriage of YOUR LAST NAME and SPOUSE LAST NAME

Case No. [Your case number]

DECLARATION OF PETITIONER RE
MOTION TO COMPEL ANSWERS TO WRITTEN INTERROGATORIES

I, the undersigned, state:

I am the petitioner herein.

This is an action for dissolution of marriage, including issues of support, property and custody/visitation.

On or about [date], I caused Written Interrogatories (first set, specially drafted) to be served on respondent. Respondent failed to respond to the interrogatories (in whole OR in part) and/or failed to provide a written verification under penalty of perjury, all as set out below.

I am informed and believe that the items set forth below are relevant to the subject matter of this action and are reasonably calculated to lead to discovery of admissible evidence.

[If some answers were served, give the following information for each item for which you need more information.]

<u>ITEM 1:</u>

a. <u>Question:</u> [Set forth the question exactly as it appeared in your Interrogatories. Example:] State your full name and address.

b. <u>Response:</u> [Set forth the response exactly as you received it. Example:] Joe Jones.

1

Declaration of Petitioner re Motion to Compel Answers to Written Interrogatories

Figure 18.4

DECLARATION RE MOTION TO COMPEL ANSWERS TO INTERROGATORIES

(page 2)

c. <u>Argument and Factual Contentions:</u> [Explain why the question should be answered. Example:] Respondent answered as to name but omitted the address. I believe respondent carries on a business at respondent's home, and this is why he/she does not want me to know the home address. Having a person's residence address is the basic beginning point for any civil discovery, and respondent is stonewalling this.

{After discussing each item, add:]

On or about [date], I wrote to respondent['s attorney] and requested that he/she respond [further] to the written interrogatories; see copy of letter attached hereto and made part hereof. I received no response to that letter OR I received the following response to that letter: (summarize response) and this response is still inadequate because

Respondent's failure to respond or object to the question was without substantial justification.

I declare under penalty of perjury under the Laws of the State of California that the foregoing is true and correct.

Executed on [date], at [City], California.

____
YOUR NAME, Petitioner

2

Declaration of Petitioner re Motion to Compel Answers to Written Interrogatories least five days before the witness was served, that is another ground for objection. However, moving to quash is a lot of work and if the records are relevant and the subpoena is reasonable, you would only delay the inevitable.

Object to production of privileged records. If your spouse tried to subpoena your counseling or medical records, unless you have yourself made an issue of your mental or physical condition, you can object to production of such records. The best way to object is to file a motion to quash the subpoena. You should also immediately contact your therapist or doctor and direct him/her not to produce the records without a court order.

MOTION TO QUASH SUBPOENA

Notice of Motion:

In the caption, check the box for "Other," and type in "Quash subpoena."

Application for Order and Supporting Declaration:

Item 9, Other relief: Type in "That the Subpoena, a copy of which is attached hereto and made part hereof, be quashed or limited as stated in the accompanying Declaration."

Item 10, Facts: Prepare and attach a declaration based on the one in Figure 18.7.

G Motions regarding depositions

If you served a person or institution with a subpoena, and he/she ignored it, or if someone came to a deposition and refused to answer or to produce documents under a subpoena, you can file a motion to compel them to abide by discovery rules. However, you must study Code of Civil Procedure section 2025 in detail and comply with it.

MOTION TO COMPEL DEPOSITION

Notice of Motion

In the caption, check the box for "Other," and type in "Compel deposition"

Application for Order and Supporting Declaration:

Item 9, Other relief: Type in "That Respondent be ordered to attend deposition within 15 days of the hearing and to testify."

Item 10, Facts: "On (date), Respondent was served with a Notice of Taking Deposition and a Subpoena to Deposition (copy attached and made part hereof as Exhibit A), directing Respondent to appear at a deposition on (date). On said date I was present at the address indicated in the Notice of Taking Deposition, and the court reporter was present, but Respondent did not appear. I phoned Respondent, and Respondent was at his/her office. He/she said he/she has no intention of appearing at a deposition. I have no way to obtain his/her testimony without the order of this court."

Figure 18.5
DECLARATION RE MOTION TO ENFORCE SUBPOENA
(page 1)

Marriage of YOUR LAST NAME and SPOUSE LAST NAME

Case No. [Your case number]

DECLARATION OF PETITIONER RE
MOTION TO ENFORCE SUBPOENA

I, the undersigned, state:

I am the petitioner herein.

This is an action for dissolution of marriage, including issues of support, property and custody/visitation.

On or about [date], I caused a Subpoena Duces Tecum re Deposition to be served on respondent's employer [company] Company. (A copy of the subpoena along with the proof of personal service is attached hereto and made part hereof.) Said employer failed to respond to the subpoena and has failed to produce the items as set out in the subpoena.

The items set forth in the subpoena are relevant to the subject matter of this action and are reasonably calculated to lead to discovery of admissible evidence, and good cause exists for their production. The subpoena requests payroll information regarding respondent. Respondent has failed and refused to produce any income information including income tax returns. Respondent did produce what purport to be copies of paystubs, but they are printouts from a computer, and I am afraid respondent printed them out at home. Therefore, I attempted to subpoena the wage information directly from respondent's employer, and now the employer has ignored the subpoena. The employer did not write or object. They just entirely ignored the subpoena.

1

Declaration of Petitioner re Motion to Enforce Subpoena

Figure 18.6

DECLARATION RE MOTION TO ENFORCE SUBPOENA

(page 2)

The employer's failure to respond, object to the request, or failure to comply with the request was without substantial justification.

I am requesting an order that [company] Company comply with the subpoena that was served on them, and that they produce the requested records within ten days after the hearing of this motion.

I declare under penalty of perjury under the Laws of the State of California that the foregoing is true and correct.

Executed on [date], at [City], California.

____
YOUR NAME, Petitioner

2

Declaration of Petitioner re Motion to Enforce Subpoena

Figure 18.7

DECLARATION RE MOTION TO QUASH SUBPOENA

(page 1)

Marriage of YOUR LAST NAME and SPOUSE LAST NAME

Case No. [Your case number]

DECLARATION OF RESPONDENT RE
MOTION TO QUASH SUBPOENA

I, the undersigned, state:

I am the petitioner herein.

This is an action for dissolution of marriage, including issues of support, property and custody/visitation.

On or about [date], Petitioner caused a Subpoena Duces Tecum re Deposition to be served on my friend [name], a friend of mine whom I have been dating since separation. (Copies of the subpoena and notice of taking deposition are attached hereto and made part hereof.) The subpoena and deposition are calculated to harass my friend and interfere with his/her privacy, not to produce discoverable information. For this reason, on or about [date], I wrote to petitioner['s attorney] and requested that he/she agree to cancel the subpoena; see copy of letter attached hereto and made part hereof. I received no response to that letter.

Petitioner has requested that my friend bring to the deposition all of his/her financial information and credit card statements as shown on the attached subpoena. My friend and I have completely separate finances, and my friend's information has no relevance to this divorce.

I request that unless petitioner can show good cause for taking my friend's deposition, the subpoena be entirely quashed as

1

Declaration of Petitioner re Motion to Quash Subpoena

Figure 18.8
DECLARATION RE MOTION TO QUASH SUBPOENA
(page 2)

it invades my privacy, my friend's privacy and is solely for the purpose of harassment. Alternatively, I request that the court quash each item requested in the subpoena for which petitioner does not show good cause for production, and that the court limit the scope of the deposition to only financial matters relevant to this case or contact my friend may have had with the children. However, my friend has had no contact with the children and has not even met them (as the deposition will confirm).

I declare under penalty of perjury under the Laws of the State of California that the foregoing is true and correct.

Executed on [date], at [City], California.

____
YOUR NAME, Respondent

2

Declaration of Petitioner re Motion to Quash Subpoena

How to resist a deposition

Any person served with a deposition notice—either a party or any witness—can file a motion to stop or limit the deposition.

To avoid producing documents, the person served with the subpoena or deposition notice must serve the other side with a written objection at least three calendar days before the deposition, specifying the error or irregularity (Code of Civil Procedure section 2025(g)). Any deposition taken after the service of a written objection shall not be used against the objecting party if the party did not attend the deposition and if the court determines that the objection was valid. In addition, a party can move for an order staying or preventing the taking of the deposition, and the deposition will be stayed (put off) until the motion can be heard and decided. This motion must be accompanied by a declaration showing that you tried to resolve the matter informally.

Additionally, before, during, or after a deposition, any party or deponent can move for a protective order (Code of Civil Procedure 2025(i)). The usual declaration regarding trying for informal resolution must be included. The court, for good cause shown, may make any order that justice requires to protect anyone from unwarranted annoyance, embarrassment, oppression, or undue burden and expense. There are many kinds of protective orders including, but not limited to, orders that:

(1) The deposition not be taken at all.
(2) The deposition be taken at a different time.
(3) The deposition be taken at a place other than that specified in the deposition notice.
(4) The deposition be taken only on certain specified terms and conditions.
(5) The testimony be recorded in a manner different from that specified in the deposition notice.
(6) Certain matters not be inquired into.
(7) The scope of the examination be limited to certain matters.
(8) All or certain of the writings or tangible things designated in the deposition notice not be produced, inspected, or copied.
(9) Designated persons, other than the parties to the action and their counsel, be excluded from attending the deposition.
(10) A trade secret or other confidential research, development, or commercial information not be disclosed, or disclosed only to specified persons or in a specified way.
(11) The deposition be sealed and thereafter opened only on order of the court.

If the motion for a protective order is denied in whole or in part, the court can order the deponent to provide or permit the discovery sought.

MOTION FOR PROTECTIVE ORDER

Notice of Motion

In the caption, check the box for "Other," and type in "Protective Order"

Application for Order and Supporting Declaration:

Item 9, Other relief: Type in the specific orders you want, such as: "The deposition not be taken," or "The deposition not be taken at [place], but instead at [place], which is within 75 miles of deponent's residence," or "The petitioner/respondent be prevented from inquiring into the following matters: deponent's personal relationship with [name] and anything about [name]'s finances," or "That [name] be excluded from attending the deposition."

Item 10, Facts: State the particular facts that justify your specific request, such as: "Deponent's deposition has already been taken and taking it again is only for the purpose of harassment," or "Deponent suffers from [ailment] and traveling more than 75 miles from home for the deposition is a hardship," or "[Name] had a personal relationship with deponent and has stalked, harassed and disturbed the peace of deponent, specifically [list incidents, giving dates, times and places, especially of any that resulted in complaints to police or arrests]. This person's presence at the deposition will be disruptive and, as no bailiff will be present, I fear for my physical and emotional safety if [name] attends the deposition." See Figure 18.7 for a declaration about inquiring into deponent's personal relationship with someone.

H Discovery cutoff date

Code of Civil Procedure 2024 requires discovery to be completed at least 30 days before the initial trial date, and discovery motions must be heard at least 15 days before. Discovery is considered completed on the day a response is due or on the day a deposition begins. Once you have a trial date set, you must be sure to get your discovery done well in advance of these deadlines. Even if your trial is postponed, this does not reopen discovery unless you obtain a court order to reopen it.

If you send out interrogatories (chapter 17B) to your spouse by mail, your spouse has 35 days to answer; if he/she does not answer or he/she gives incomplete or evasive answers, you need to file a Notice of Motion to compel, and your spouse is entitled to 26 days' mailed Notice of Motion plus time after the hearing to prepare answers. So you can see that this one part of discovery could easily require several months and, as you have to complete it by 30 days before trial, you must start almost a half-year before the trial to ensure that you can accomplish this one thing alone. Don't procrastinate.

Chapter 24 includes a motion to postpone both trial and the discovery cutoff.

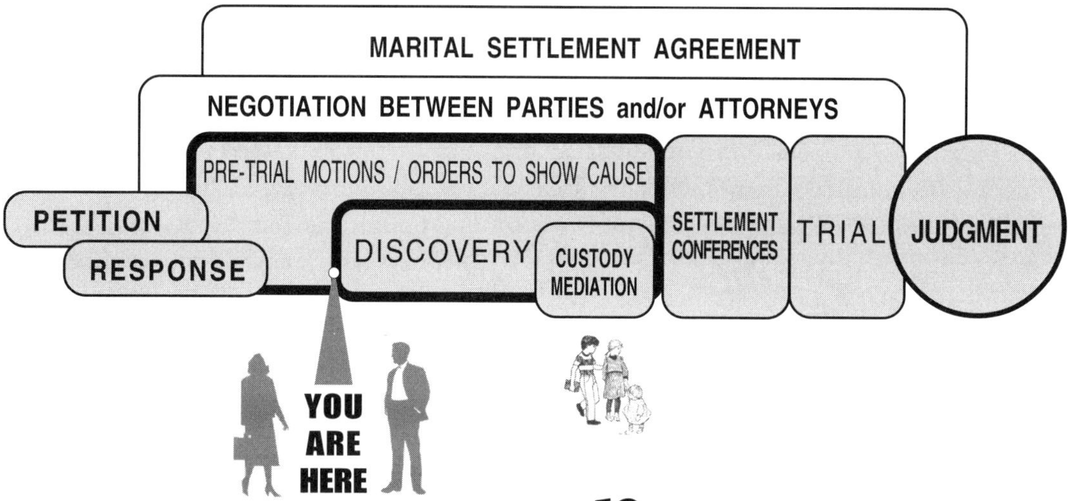

CHAPTER 19
VOCATIONAL (and other) EXAMINATIONS

A. General information
B. Vocational evaluation
C. Mental or physical examination
D. Drug/alcohol examination
E. Other examinations

A General information

The most common situation where an examination of a spouse might be ordered would be if you contend that your spouse could get a job or get a better job—in other words, could be making more money. To this end, the court could order a vocational evaluation. Less common is where you have a good reason for wanting a psychological or physical evaluation. In either case, the matter will have to be assigned to a qualified expert to do the examination.

Locating an expert. For any kind of exam, you are going to have to find a qualified expert. The best way would be to have a local Certified Family Law Specialist attorney (CFLS) refer you to someone. Call several attorneys and get as many names as they will give you. If you are representing yourself, you might find that many experts will not work with you. Period. They don't want the bother of working with emotional people who don't understand legal procedures. If you have limited resources, and if you are otherwise able to represent yourself, you might need an expert more than you need an attorney. But, in fact, you might find that you have to have both. The only way to find this out for certain is to spend some time searching in your area for an expert who will work with you.

Do it like this. Get all the names you can and call them all. Optionally, before you call, write each one a businesslike letter explaining that you are interested in hiring them to do an evaluation of a party to a divorce case in which you are representing yourself. If you can, give them some professional or business references. Then call around. Either way, when you write or call them, you want to sound clear headed and businesslike, as if you know what you are doing. If an evaluator says they only work for attorneys, ask if they can refer you to someone who might help you. If you know someone in a related profession, say a therapist or accountant, you could have them make the call and try to set something up for you.

Resisting requests for examination is discussed at the end of each section.

B Vocational evaluation

If you feel your spouse is not working at capacity, you can request a vocational examination. In no case can judges actually force a person to work, but if an examiner finds your spouse is qualified for a higher level of income or increased hours of work and that suitable jobs are available, the judge can "impute" income—that is, instead of using actual income to compute support, the judge uses a higher amount to approximate what your spouse *could* be earning. If the examiner recommends a course of education or training to prepare for higher income, the court could order it, then reevaluate support after the program is or should be completed.

A vocational evaluation should consist of interviews and possibly written tests to determine what abilities and experience your spouse has. The evaluator will write a report for the attorney and/or the court that should review your spouse's education, skills, work experience, interests and goals (or lack thereof). The evaluator should make a recommendation as to what employment and/or educational opportunities your spouse should pursue and indicate specifically how much money your spouse could make if he/she took various employment paths.

If your spouse will not voluntarily submit to a vocational evaluation, a motion can be made to compel him/her to submit to it. Generally, if a spouse is not employed full-time, or if there is some clear indication of not working up to full capacity, a vocational evaluation will be ordered. Of course, you will have to pay for the evaluation, which can range from $500 to $2,000, plus the cost of courtroom testimony later if there should be a trial or hearing on the issue.

First, locate a vocational evaluator. Before you can do anything else, you have to make an arrangement with a vocational evaluator who will agree to do the evaluation and report (see section A) Once you find someone to do the job, ask about fees and if a down payment is required.

No "hatchet" jobs. The judge will know which evaluators have good reputations and which ones will say almost anything for their fee. It is essential that you hire a neutral vocational examiner with a good reputation.

Send a request before making a motion. Write a letter to your spouse (or his/her attorney) and ask your spouse to submit voluntarily to a vocational evaluation (Figure 19.1). Provide the name, address and phone number of your chosen evaluator. Give your spouse a time limit to respond, such as ten days after the date of the letter, before you make your motion.

Give the evaluator your input. If your spouse agrees to do the evaluation, or if the court orders one, you should contact the evaluator right away and let him/her know your version of your spouse's education, work history and skills. If you have, for example, recent college transcripts—which you can obtain through discovery as discussed in chapter 17—you should give them to the vocational evaluator. You need some input into this process to ensure that your spouse does not tell the evaluator a lot of baloney that might be believed without your input. After the evaluator has talked to your spouse, you need to talk to the evaluator again as a reality check. When you are selecting the evaluator, explain at the very beginning that you want this kind of contact.

Figure 19.1
LETTER REQUESTING VOCATIONAL EVALUATION

Date

Spouse or his/her Attorney
Address
City, State, Zip

Re: Dissolution of Marriage

Dear [name]:

The purpose of this letter is to request that you [or, 'your client,' if your letter is addressed to an attorney] submit to a vocational evaluation by [name] who can be contacted at [phone]. His/her address is [address], California.

I have paid the fee for the vocational evaluation, so all that you need to do is contact him/her and make an appointment.

I expect that this can be done within the next two weeks. If, for some reason, you need additional time to make this appointment, please let me know the reason in writing. If I do not hear from you within two weeks, and an appointment is not made with the vocational examiner, I will be compelled to make a motion in this regard. I hope that will not be necessary.

Very truly yours,

YOUR NAME
Your Address
City, State, Zip
Your Phone

How to file a motion for vocational evaluation

Do your motion as described in chapter 12, filling out the forms as described there, but with the modifications shown below. Attach a copy of the letter you wrote asking your spouse to voluntarily submit to this evaluation as well as any written response he/she made.

MOTION TO COMPEL A VOCATIONAL EVALUATION

Notice of Motion:

In the caption, check the box for "Other," and type in "Vocational Evaluation."

Application for Order and Supporting Declaration:

Item 9, Other relief: Type in "Order Respondent to submit to vocational evaluation by (name) at (place), CA, and to cooperate with said vocational evaluator and to keep all appointments and provide all relevant information."

Item 10, Facts: "Respondent is not working (works only part-time) (employed beneath his/her capacity) and is capable of working (working full-time) (working at a higher-paying job) and earning significantly more. Respondent has (degrees, credentials, licenses) and has worked as (best job experiences). Income should be imputed to Respondent for support purposes. See attached letter to Respondent requesting voluntary vocational examination."

How to respond to a motion for vocational evaluation

Counter moves to a motion for vocational evaluation include:

- Get a suitable job at about your best level of pay.
- Keep records showing a diligent job search. Keep in mind that your spouse or his/her lawyer might contact the companies you said you contacted seeking work.
- Bring in medical records and possibly call a doctor as a witness (or get the doctor's declaration) to show you cannot work for medical reasons.
- Bring in a mental health practitioner (or declaration of one) to show your emotional problems disable you from working.
- Get your own vocational evaluation.

If you contend that physical or mental problems limit your ability to work, your spouse can subpoena your medical and mental/counseling records and take depositions of your doctors and counselors. Anything embarrassing that turns up can be used against you in the custody case even if discovered as part of vocational evaluation. Therefore, before you raise mental or physical problems, think about what is in your records that you might not want your spouse to read. You could call your doctor or therapist and ask his/her opinion on this. Keep in mind that for purposes of billing an insurance company, your therapist will have listed a diagnosis, so even if his/her notes aren't used against you, the diagnosis could be.

If you are ordered to see a vocational evaluator, you want to be viewed as cooperative. If you act hostile or resistant, this could be held against you in court. You might have been forced to do this evaluation, but you still need to show some semblance of cooperation. You want to win the vocational evaluator over to the position that you are working as hard as you can at the best job you can get and you are going to do this a lot better with honey than with vinegar.

C Mental or physical examination

Because mental examinations and physical examinations are subject to the same rules, they are discussed together. However, physical exams are quite rare, so we focus here on psychological evaluations. Similar considerations apply to both.

Do you really want an exam? A lot of people feel their ex needs his/her head examined, but actually getting it done can be a problem. Unless your spouse put mental or physical condition in issue by saying he/she can't work, the order is going to be mutual, meaning that if you get an order, you can be examined, too. Unfortunately, a lot of dubious mental health "experts" have attached themselves to family courts, making the outcome of any exam something of a gamble. A judge, not being a mental health expert, might direct specific questions to the expert. An ethical psychologist should not answer questions that are really moral or social judgments rather than something that can be based on psychological research. If there are no statistics, no data, no research, the psychologist's opinion is no better than yours or the judge's. It is unethical for mental health experts to give such opinions, but they do it all the time.

The judge can make his/her job easier by having the mental health person answer questions that should really be decided by the judge. The money for forensic (court) work is good, so many psychologists will answer questions they shouldn't for fear the judge will start using someone who will answer such questions. A psychologist might be asked, "Is the father's anger against the mother justified?" Any psychologist who tries to answer that is unquestionably outside his/her area of expertise and is usurping the court's function. The same can even be said as to psychologists who make custody evaluations. Those recommendations are really moral-social-political-personal, and the decision should be made (not rubber-stamped) by the judge. You should be very careful before you open the Pandora's Box of mental evaluations. It could easily make things worse rather than better.

Records remain confidential. Counseling and medical records remain privileged and confidential unless the party raises the issue of his/her condition. Just asking for custody or visitation does not put one's physical or mental condition at issue, but if a party says he/she cannot work because of a medical condition, medical records can be opened. Similarly, if a party says an emotional condition limits ability to work, his/her records lose their privilege. Note that a party can only put his/her own condition at issue. One cannot open up the other party's mental health records by accusing the other of being too emotionally unstable to care for children. However, if your spouse has a history of mental hospitalization and refuses to permit records to be examined, in a custody case a psychological evaluation might be appropriate. Even so, medical/counseling records remain confidential unless the party signs a release. If anyone from Family Court services, the judge, an expert—anyone at all—asks *you* to sign a form giving them the right to review your medical or counseling records, you have the legal right to say no.

First, locate an evaluator. Before you can do anything else, you have to make an arrangement with an expert who will agree to do the evaluation and report for you. How you do this is described in section A, above. Once you find someone who will do the job, ask about their fees and if a down payment is required. You can't proceed until you have lined up your evaluator.

Experts must be qualified. Subsection (b) of section 2032 of the Code of Civil Procedure provides that a mental evaluation can be performed only by a licensed clinical psychologist who holds a Ph.D. in psychology and has had at least five years of postgraduate experience in the diagnosis of emotional and mental disorders. More important, you want someone who will be fair to both mothers and fathers and not deal with you in stereotypes. Try to ensure that someone qualified is handling your case. Unfortunately, some psychologists who cannot maintain a private practice have gone into court work, so there can be a problem.

Send a request before making a motion. Write a letter (Figure 19.2) to your spouse (or his/her attorney), and ask your spouse to submit voluntarily to mental (or physical) examination. Provide the name, address and phone number of your chosen evaluator. Give your spouse a time limit to respond, such as ten days after the date of the letter, before you will make the motion. In practice, if a mental exam is really appropriate, it probably won't be done by agreement. Nonetheless, you should try.

Motion for psychological evaluation. Subsection (d) of Section 2032 provides that anyone who wants to get a mental examination must file a motion to get the court's permission for the exam. The law also says, "The motion for the examination shall specify the time, place, manner, conditions, scope, and nature of the examination, as well as the identity and the specialty, if any, of the person or persons who will perform the examination." You must also attach a declaration showing that you tried to get a voluntary agreement for the exam. Section 2032 has detailed provisions that are usually followed in, say, an injury lawsuit, but things are often more informal in family court.

Good cause must be shown. Section 2032 indicates that the court shall grant a motion for a physical or mental examination only for "good cause shown." Most judges think the mere fact that there is a divorce with a custody battle is good cause for ordering a psychological evaluation. This is highly debatable and to assume it would leave you open to attack. It would be best if your motion explains why in your particular case there is some indication of a need for the evaluation. You at least want to say that your spouse is acting erratic, or depressed, or suicidal or whatever, and that this emotional condition is interfering with his/her ability to care for the children.

The code also provides that the order granting a physical or mental examination shall specify the person or persons who may perform the examination, and the time, place, manner, diagnostic tests and procedures, conditions, scope, and nature of the examination. Most people making a motion for psychological evaluation have no idea what tests will be done. In fact, it would be most unusual to include this in your motion, but it is required under the law and some day this law might be applied.

Do your motion as described in chapter 12, filling out the forms as described there, but with the modifications shown below. In these examples, we assume the moving party is Petitioner, but it could be the other way around.

MOTION TO COMPEL A PSYCHOLOGICAL EVALUATION

Notice of Motion:

In the caption, check the box for "Other," and type in "Psychological Evaluation."

Application for Order and Supporting Declaration:

Item 9, Other relief: Type in "That Respondent be directed to submit to psychological evaluation by Dr. (name) who is a Ph.D. psychologist with 5 or more years of experience after being licensed as a psychologist, and that Respondent cooperate with said psychologist and keep all appointments and provide all relevant information."

Item 10, Facts: "There are issues of child custody and visitation in this case. Respondent has been acting erratic, and his/her actions are detrimental to the children. These actions include: (describe). Respondent has in the past made suicide attempts/threats. Respondent has been an inpatient/outpatient in a mental facility (list dates). Respondent is taking (drug such as lithium or Prozac or other psychotropic drug) for (emotional condition necessitating the drug, such as depression). Respondent has violent

Figure 19.2
LETTER REQUESTING PSYCHIATRIC EVALUATION

Date

Spouse or his/her Attorney
Address
City, State, Zip

Re: Dissolution of Marriage

Dear [name]:

The purpose of this letter is to request that you [or, 'your client,' if your letter is addressed to an attorney] submit to a psychological evaluation regarding parenting abilities by [name], Ph.D., who can be contacted at [phone]. His/her address is:

[address]

I am sure you are aware that in conflicted cases with custody/visitation issues, it is not unusual for the court to order a psychological evaluation. This seems particularly relevant in view of the fact that in the past you

attempted suicide
threatened suicide
were admitted to a mental health facility as an inpatient
have been in a drug/alcohol detox facility as an inpatient.

I hope you will understand that my concern is only that we both do the best for our children.

I will pay the fee for the psychological evaluation. All you need to do is contact the office, make an appointment, and let me know the appointment has been made.

I expect that the appointment can be made within the next ten days. If, for some reason, you need additional time to make this appointment, please let me know the reason in writing. If I do not hear from you within ten days, and an appointment is not made with the psychologist within that time, I will be compelled to make a motion in this regard. I hope this will not be necessary.

Very truly yours,

YOUR NAME
Your Address
City, State, Zip
Your Phone

rages which are not controlled by medication, and they seem to be getting worse lately." Detail the time, place, scope and nature of the examination, as well as the identity of the person who will conduct the evaluation.

How to resist a request for mental or physical evaluation

Code of Civil Procedure section 2032 governs mental evaluations. It is widely treated as if it does not apply to divorces, but it does. If you want to resist a psychological evaluation, you should at least insist that the basic requirements of the Code of Civil Procedure be applied. Even if you don't want to avoid the exam altogether, you may want to use the code section to ensure that the exam you are ordered to undergo will at least make some sense.

You can object if the motion is too informal. In custody cases, psychological evaluations are sometimes ordered without a specific motion. Family Court Services might try to force one on you, or perhaps the court will order it after someone makes an oral request. Code of Civil Procedure section 2032(d) requires a motion to obtain an order for an exam. Some judges are in the habit of ordering exams under Evidence Code 730 even with no motion at all being made. You can and should object if this happens. You need at least to say *on the record*—that is, in the courtroom with the court reporter writing or the videotape running—"Your Honor, I object." That's minimum. Even better to add, "No good cause has been shown for such an examination." And better yet to state, "Code of Civil Procedure section 2032(d) requires a noticed motion before any such examination can be ordered." Unfortunately, objecting to the judge who made the order is swimming upstream, but get it on the record anyway.

Good cause should be required. Regardless of whether it is your spouse, the judge, or Family Court Services that wants the exam, good cause should be required. Having to submit to a mental exam ordered by the government is intrusive. Merely entering into a divorce with custody issues should not by itself be considered good cause to order a mental evaluation. You can say that too, as part of your objection.

What tests should be specified in the order? Judges virtually never specify what tests should be used. That makes sense from their point of view, as virtually no tests have anything to do with custody or ability to parent, and certainly not with the parent-child relationship. The most commonly used test is the MMPI2 test, and there is *no* evidence that it is of any use at all in a custody case. It is merely convenient and, because it is computer-scored, it appears to be objective. But if you study these tests, you will find that a great deal of personal judgment is involved. The judges think they are receiving Scientific Truth and tend to over-rely on the psychological reports. If you want to resist such a test, you should object and insist that the order specify the tests. At the hearing on the issue, you could bring an expert Ph.D. psychologist to say these tests have nothing to do with custody. At present there is major overreliance on these tests. The overreliance amounts often to an abdication of judicial responsibility which is virtually handed over to the so-called expert psychologist.

What to do after such tests are ordered? If the psychological evaluation was crammed down your throat suddenly at court by a verbal request from your opponent or by the court itself, you can attempt to file a motion asking the court to rescind its order. This might not be successful, but it will help you to "make a record." If you end up getting crucified by the psychological examiner, this motion could at least lay the legal basis for appeal or later objection. Also, even if it is lost, you hope it will begin to make your judge think about the fact that possibly these tests are not God's Truth.

If you end up having to be examined, it is very important that you cooperate with the examiner. You want the examiner to make a recommendation in your favor, right? Be even-tempered, respectful and thoughtful. Stay calm and open. Because psychological evaluations are highly subjective, charming the examiner is very important. Even if you did not want the exam, it will not help to let the psychologist know how much you resent being there. Show your best side. If this person is examining your spouse as well, you need to bring objective documentation that will support any concerns you have, such as a copy of court records showing that your spouse has a drunk driving or spousal abuse conviction, or the kids never do their homework when they spend the night at your spouse's house, or your spouse always brings the kids to school late. Don't just say, "My ex is an alcoholic and was convicted of drunk driving." Bring copies of documents or declarations of others. Even if the examiner does not ask for them, offer them.

D Drug/alcohol examination

Blood and urine tests will determine what substances (drugs, alcohol, etc.) the parent has taken during the past four to eight hours. Obviously, this is useful only where someone is so deeply sunk into addiction or alcoholism that they don't ever go without for any period of time, or where you get a surprise order from the court that the person must go straight from court to the testing center. However, we now have a hair test available, too. Hair is like a diary, recording all the substances that have been taken for the last couple of months. Shaving one's head won't avoid the test as hair can be taken from wherever. The hair test is a good tool for finding the truth.

Parents should stop using drugs and alcohol. In the past blood and urine tests would not reveal the use of marijuana, but it can now be proved by means of hair tests. So, we are now seeing cases where a parent is limited to supervised visitation because a hair test revealed marijuana use. You can't prove you only use it when your children are not present. If you are in a custody or visitation case, you would be foolish not to give up all alcohol and drugs, even marijuana. This is very practical advice, and has nothing whatever to do with morality or social values.

To obtain a drug/alcohol exam, you need more than an accusation. Drug and alcohol testing is ordered regularly in family court. However, a party will probably not be ordered to submit to testing just on the basis of an accusation by a spouse. Some independent evidence of substance abuse is usually required; for example, a recent conviction for drunk driving or a drug- or alcohol-related crime, or the declaration of an independent witness. If a parent just quietly drinks into oblivion nightly, or smokes marijuana in private, getting a test could be difficult. However, when testing is ordered, it is sometimes ordered for both parents, even though there is only proof that one parent might have a problem.

Before you ask for the exam, you should know the name and address of the facility that will do the tests as well as the cost. Contact a family law specialist or Family Court Services or look in the phone book for a local facility that does the test you want. Contact them and find out what tests they do and what they charge. Ask what procedures the facility uses, particularly if a urine test is ordered. Unsupervised test takers might bring clean urine with them or otherwise trick a urine test. To avoid this, you would prefer a facility that watches the whole process. If you really want this test to get done, you should deposit the fee for your spouse with the facility in advance (as your spouse will claim he/she doesn't have money for the test). This should be explained in your motion, and the name, address and phone number of the facility should be in your motion.

Motion needs to specify times and conditions. Your motion needs to state something very specific for when the test must be taken and which test, for example, within twenty four hours after the hearing, your spouse must go to the named facility and submit to the hair test. Without a time limit, the order is nothing.

You may want a random blood or urine test as well as a hair test. Your spouse might admit to having used drugs but claim that he/she has now given them up, or he/she might have an excuse for certain substances showing up in the blood, such as claiming he/she took certain types of cough syrups or asthma inhalers, etc. Even with a hair test, your spouse could claim they have recently reformed, gone sober, attend AA, and so on. This is why you want an order that permits you to call for a blood or urine test on a random basis, to occur within 4 hours of asking for the test or the opening of the test facility (if you make your request on, say, a weekend when they're closed) whichever comes first. This will not clarify the marijuana situation, but it may eliminate other claims of new good behavior.

Do your motion as described in chapter 12, filling out the forms as described there, but with the modifications shown below.

MOTION TO COMPEL A DRUG OR ALCOHOL EXAM

Notice of Motion:

In the caption, check the box for "Other," and type in "Drug/alcohol test of Respondent."

Application for Order and Supporting Declaration:

Item 9, Other relief: Type in "Order Respondent to submit to drug/alcohol hair test at (name and address of facility that will do the testing) within 24 hours after hearing and thereafter to submit to random urine or blood drug/alcohol testing up to once every 2 weeks upon demand by Petitioner; results go to Family Court Services and Petitioner."

Item 10, Facts: "In (month, year) Respondent was convicted of drunk driving; in (month, year) Respondent was convicted of possession of drugs and is still on probation. I know Respondent's symptoms when using drugs/alcohol, and I believe Respondent is using again. Respondent takes our child in the car, and this endangers our child."

Protecting child when parent flunks might be difficult. If testing shows that there was drug or alcohol abuse, parents will typically have excuses for why they have such a residue, perhaps claiming that they used a decongestant with pseudoephedrine in it, such as Sudafed. So even flunking the test may not guarantee that visitation will become supervised or cut off. People who have substance problems are used to making excuses and may be very good at it. The judge may or may not see through the excuse.

Enforcement. There may be serious enforcement problems even with an order for drug/alcohol testing. The court may simply order the parent not to use drugs or alcohol before or during visitation, and if the parent breaks this order and shows up drunk to take the child, you may have to call the police to avoid sending your child in a car with someone who is under the influence. If you simply withhold the child and do not call the police, your spouse may accuse you of refusing to permit visitation and could charge you with contempt of court, which is punishable by jail. If you call the police, and your spouse turns out not to have been under the influence, you may find yourself accused of unfairly attacking your spouse by making false accusations, and you may be accused of stressing out the child by exposing him/her to the police. So enforcing an order can be quite problematic. But you will never forgive yourself if you don't try and something happens to your child.

How to resist a motion for drug/alcohol exam

The best way to resist an examination is to point out to the judge that there is absolutely nothing objective in your background to suggest that you have any drug/alcohol problem—you have never been arrested for driving under the influence, you never lost a job due to drugs/alcohol, etc. Also, it will make a difference to the judge if you simply look like a decent, healthy person, not one whose health may have been damaged by substances. You might even have a job that already does random drug/alcohol testing, and adding another for the court does not make sense.

E Other examinations

The court can, upon motion and a showing of good cause, order whatever tests it feels are necessary, such as ordering a party accused of forging documents to submit handwriting exemplars to an expert. Such orders are rare, but the court has the power to order whatever tests the judge feels are necessary based on the facts and issues in your case.

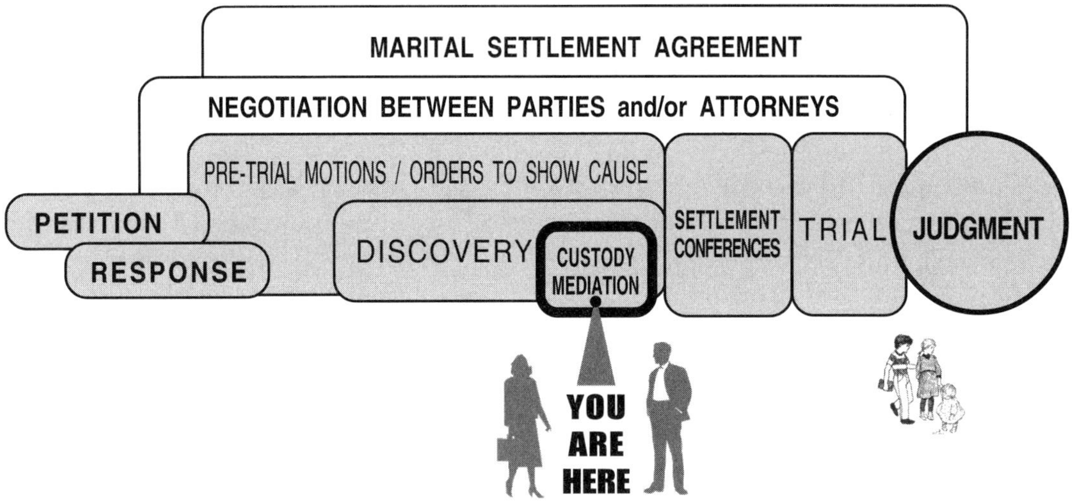

CHAPTER 20
PARENTING PROGRAMS AND MANDATORY MEDIATION

A. Parenting programs
B. Mandatory mediation
C. Motion to require participation
D. If your spouse ignores the order to participate
E. Custody/visitation issues can proceed separately

A Parenting programs

Many counties have found it very effective to hold classes for divorcing parents to give them some insights into what is important to children, how to parent after a divorce, and how the court deals with disagreements over parenting. If you have children, and if your county has such a program, both parents will be required to attend. From long experience, judges understand how important it is for parents to agree how to share parenting rather than fight over it, keeping the children's interests above their own. If your county has a parenting program, you will probably be given information about it when you file your first divorce papers. Check your local rules or ask at the clerk's office.

B Mandatory mediation

Before the court can make orders regarding custody or visitation, state law requires the parents to attempt mediation. It is required; you have to do it. If an emergency situation exists, the court might make a temporary order before you have attended mediation, but mediation must be attempted very shortly thereafter. If your spouse won't cooperate, use an OSC and get an order requiring it.

You can select your own private, non-court mediator and attend as often and as long as you like, or you could be assigned to a county-appointed mediator at Family Court Services where you typically attend very few sessions. Costs and rules vary, so check your local rules of court. If you have tried private mediation and failed, the court will likely want you to try the court-appointed mediator, too.

Mediation is sitting down with a neutral person who is expert at helping parents reach agreement about custody and visitation—in other words, how they will be parents to their children after divorce. You will not be allowed to take your custody/visitation issues to court without first trying mediation.

Take it from us, based on a lot of experience: if you can get a reasonable agreement, it is always better to resolve parenting issues yourselves, rather than letting a judge impose a decision. People who agree are far more likely to follow the terms than people who are told what to do. By failing to agree, you give the power to decide one of the most important and intimate issues in your lives to a judge—a busy, preoccupied stranger who doesn't know about you, your children or your life. Many judges just want to get the case out of their court as quickly as possible. Judges do not like to decide your parenting for you, but if they have to do it, the chances are good that you are not going to like the result. Far better if you and your children's other parent can keep control of your own lives by working it out yourselves. In most cases, mediation can work if you give it a chance. On the other hand, you should not make concessions that jeopardize the physical or emotional health of your children just for the hope of peace and quiet.

Mediation is not arbitration. Don't confuse mediation with arbitration. Arbitration takes place in a more informal environment than court with relaxed rules, but an arbitrator is just like a judge—a stranger who makes a final decision for you. You are still giving control to a third person. In mediation the neutral third person helps the parties communicate, balances the power, suggests alternatives, and in other ways helps you reach your own agreement.

Confidential counties and reporting counties. The law leaves it up to each county to decide whether or not the mediation is confidential. In counties which do not have confidential mediation, if parents fail to agree, the mediator will make a report or recommendation to the judge, so those counties are called "reporting" or "recommending" counties. In a reporting county, you need to keep in mind that anything you say in mediation might be reported to the judge. In all counties the mediator *must* report child abuse or molestation; even confidentiality rules do not stop that. Phone the court's Family Court Services or read your local rules of court to find out whether your county is confidential or reporting. If you are in a reporting county, you must approach mediation with the same seriousness as you would have for a court appearance.

The judges hire and supervise Family Court Services, so they tend to have great faith in them; in fact, there is an unfortunate tendency to rubber-stamp their recommendations. In many ways, what goes on in little rooms at Family Court Services will have more effect on your life than what goes on in the courtroom. Obviously, you want the mediator's recommendation to be favorable. You could attend private mediation first to try to reach an agreement in a confidential manner; in that case the law says that the mediation is confidential. Then, if that fails, you would go into the court's process in which mediation may be confidential or non-confidential, depending on the county.

Who else attends mediation? Different county rules vary from saying that nobody but mother and father can attend mediation to saying that lawyers must attend the first session and requiring children's attendance. In some counties like Santa Clara, mediators virtually never speak to children, and in other counties mediators routinely involve more family members. Before you go to mediation, you must find out what happens in your county so you bring the right people.

Mediation when there has been domestic violence. When there has been domestic violence, you are entitled to bring a support person to mediation (although they cannot participate), or you can ask to be seen separately from your spouse. However, as much as possible, you want to be present, otherwise you won't know what your spouse is saying. Ask the mediator if they can guarantee your safety. Usually, mediation will not work where one person is abusive or very controlling. If your spouse has abused you, and you are used to giving in to their dominance, you must be very, very careful not to repeat this harmful pattern in mediation. Do not agree to an order that you cannot live with or that is unsafe for your children. You do not have to make an agreement. You can go to court.

When do you mediate? In the best counties, mediation occurs even before the hearing of your emergency OSC. That way the parties get a chance to settle by agreement and, if the county is a reporting county, by the time the case first gets to court, someone will have seen the father and mother and will be able to make a report to the judge. In other counties there may be a backlog, and mediation can be more than a month away. In this case, temporary orders could issue before the mediation takes place.

C Motion to require participation

Urgent cases. If you are in an emergency situation which requires immediate child custody/visitation orders, as soon as you get into the court process the judge is going to make an order for mediation. Your local rules may even require certain language to be in your OSC, so you need to check them. You don't want your emergency OSC rejected because it failed to mention the need to contact Family Court Services.

Non-emergency situations. If you are dissatisfied with current parenting arrangements and can't get your spouse to do mediation on it, you can file a motion to compel mediation. Do your motion as described in chapter 12, filling out the forms as described there, but with the modifications shown below. In the facts, we write as if the moving party is Petitioner, but it could be the other way around.

MOTION TO COMPEL MEDIATION

Notice of Motion:

In the caption, check the box for "Other," and type in "Compel mediation."

Application and Declaration:

Item 9, Other relief: Type in "Order Respondent to attend mediation with Family Court Services and proceed to FCS immediately after the hearing to arrange a mutually convenient date for mediation which shall occur as soon as possible."

Item 10, Facts: Type in something like, "Respondent and I do not agree on custody and visitation of our children. I have asked Respondent to attend mediation on this issue, but he/she refuses. It is in the best interests of the children that Respondent be ordered to attend mediation with Family Court Services."

D If your spouse ignores the order to participate

Sometimes a parent who is under a court order to mediate will delay, miss appointments, or just flatly refuse to participate. If it looks like this might happen to you, you must keep a journal listing every communication and event with the date and time of each and good notes on the details of what happened. You will use these notes in making a follow-up OSC or motion.

First, write your spouse and tell him/her that it is necessary to comply with the order or you will go back to court for a stronger order or contempt of court. Date it and keep a copy.

If you want to continue to press for mediation (and fill the record with indications of your spouse's bad conduct), you have three choices:

1. An OSC to find your spouse in contempt for violating the order to attend mediation,
2. A motion to prohibit all visitation until your spouse completes mediation, or
3. An OSC to the same end.

Any one of these would be a real attention grabber, but the goal is to get your spouse's cooperation, not to interfere with visitation. Using children as a pawn is harmful to them and can poison the relationship between the parents forever. For this reason, you should try the contempt OSC first. Do *not* use the other options unless there is other evidence that sole custody and restricted visitation might be appropriate. You don't want the judge to think you are the kind of parent who would lightly use the child-parent relationship for your own ends.

1. OSC for contempt

This is dramatic and does not threaten or impair your children's relationship with their other parent. Your spouse must have been present in court when the order for mediation was stated or must have been served with a written copy of the order, and he/she must have had a reasonable time to comply with the order. If the order to mediate had no deadline, unless your spouse made a flat statement of, "I won't go to mediation," then a month without compliance could be considered noncompliance, especially if you can show letters and a log of calls attempting to get mediation going.

For contempt, you use a special form, Order to Show Cause and Affidavit for Contempt (FL-410), which is found on the companion CD in the forms folder. If you install FormZ, it will be installed for use with that program. This form is easy to use and even comes with its own instructions, which you should print out and read. For this particular contempt, you will use item 8c and possibly 8d to describe the order and the violation of that order. Otherwise, follow the OSC instructions in chapter 13.

2. Motion for sole custody and restricted visitation

Do your motion as described in chapter 12, filling out the forms as described there, but with the modifications shown below. In the facts, we write as if the moving party is Petitioner, but it could be the other way around.

Notice of Motion:

In the caption, check the boxes for custody and visitation.

Application and Declaration:

Item 1, Child custody: Check this box, type in each child's name, and under "b. Request custody to," type in "sole legal and physical custody to Petitioner."

Item 2, Child visitation: Check boxes 2 and (b). At b, type in "See space below item 2c." and in the space below item 2c, type in "Respondent shall have no visitation until after Respondent attends mediation."

Item 10, Facts: Attach a copy of the earlier order and any letters to your spouse demanding compliance. Type in something like "On (date) Respondent was ordered to participate in custody mediation. He/she has not done so (or done so inadequately) as detailed in the attached declaration. The children are in my custody, and have had the following visitation with Respondent: [once a month, or alternate weekends or whatever]. It is in their best interest that they be in my custody and not have visitation with Respondent until mediation is completed. The children are ages x and y."

3. OSC for sole custody and restricted visitation

Do your OSC as described in chapter 13, filling out the forms as described there, but with these modifications. Use the regular OSC form (FL-300). Request custody be awarded solely to you and that visitation be on terms you specify in the OSC, or that there be no visitation until after mediation and further court order, and ask that this happen immediately and stay in effect until your spouse participates.

Order to Show Cause:

In the caption, check the boxes for custody and visitation. At 2(c), type, "Phone Family Court Services at (phone) and immediately schedule mandatory mediation."

Application and Declaration:

Item 1, Child custody: Check this box, type in each child's name, and under "b. Request custody to," type in "sole legal and physical custody to Petitioner."

Item 2, Child visitation: Check boxes 2 and (b). At b, type in "None until after Respondent attends mediation."

Item 10, Facts: Attach a copy of the earlier order and any letters to your spouse demanding compliance. Type in something like "On (date) Respondent was ordered to participate in custody mediation. He/she has not done so (or done so inadequately) as detailed in the attached declaration. The children are in my custody, and have had the following visitation with Respondent: [once a month, or alternate weekends or whatever]. It is in their best interest that they be in my custody and not have visitation with Respondent until mediation is completed. The children are ages x and y."

E Custody/visitation issues can proceed separately

State law provides that custody/visitation issues have "preference" on the court's calendar, as children need to know what is happening to them and where they will live. Your court will honor this law (except in Santa Clara County), so that these issues might go to trial earlier than and separate from all other issues. Often, these issues will be split off from the other issues in your case when you are referred to mediation. The process with Family Court Services could then take on a life of its own, with Family Court Services referring you on to the next step in the custody/visitation process. This eventually results in a written recommendation to the court as to your custody/visitation situation. Once that report is received, and discovery (if any) is completed, the custody/visitation issues can proceed to trial. The timing is not related to the trial and resolution of other issues.

If your county doesn't have an automatic splitting of these issues, and you want the custody/visitation issues to get decided early while you don't mind the money issues waiting until later, you can file a Request for Separate Trial. Use the forms in chapter 21 to accomplish this "bifurcation" of issues.

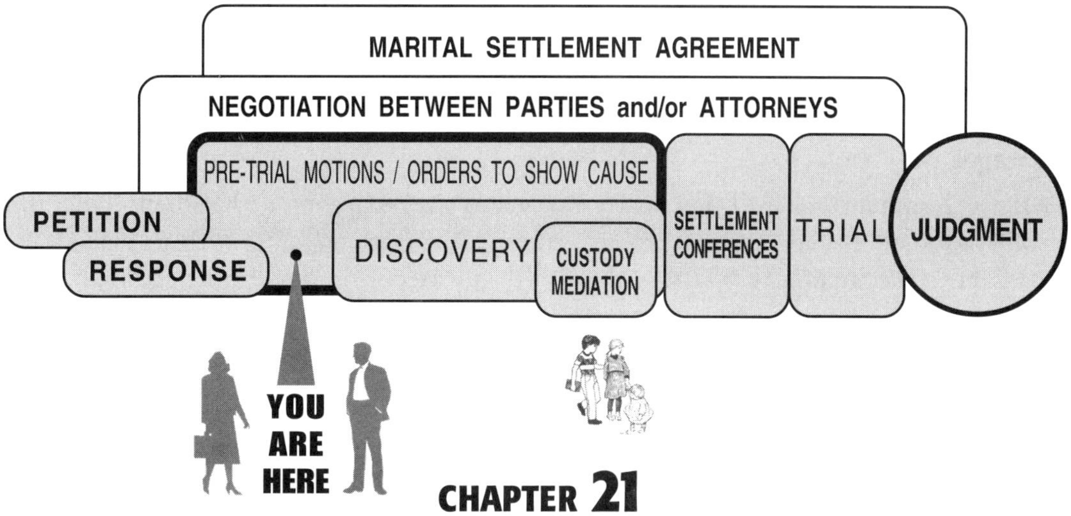

CHAPTER 21
STATUS-ONLY JUDGMENT
Divorce now, resolve other issues later

A Pros, cons and preconditions for status-only divorce

"Bifurcation" is the legal term for splitting off certain issues to be resolved separately. In a divorce case, by splitting (bifurcating) the dissolution from all the other issues, you can get divorced when the six-month waiting period is over, then continue working toward a resolution of other matters, in or out of court. In short, you can ask to be divorced right away and deal with everything else later.

Six-month waiting period applies. You can make a status-only motion at any time, but the marriage can't be dissolved until six months have passed from the date the Petition was served.

Is it worth it? Just because you can do something doesn't make it a good idea. Having the marriage dissolved has a host of preconditions and consequences that you should be aware of before you decide.

Retirement funds. If your spouse's name is on an IRA, 401(k), or pension fund of some value, you definitely should talk to a family law specialist attorney before asking for or consenting to a status-only divorce. You could lose valuable rights or suffer tax consequences if you neglect to do this.

Advantages

Emotional freedom. If you're asking for the divorce, you understand this one.

Legal freedom. You're more clearly on your own. You can get married again.

Message: it's really over. Getting the marriage dissolved can change your spouse's expectations or secret hopes; your spouse might resist the process less if you are no longer legally married.

Tax filing status. The lower your income, the less important this is. Taxes are higher if you are a married person filing separately. If you have custody of a child, no problem; you can file as head of household. If not, and your income is good, you would rather be divorced by December 31—which is when your tax status is determined—so you can file as single. This is only possible if the Petition in your case was served on or before June 30. If this is your motive, and if your Petition was served before June 30, work with a tax accountant to see how much a status-only judgment is worth.

Disadvantages

Possible loss of health insurance. If either party is covered by the other's group health insurance through work, it will be lost once a judgment of divorce is entered. However, under COBRA (a federal law), the one who lost coverage can buy it for 36 months after the divorce, assuming that he/she applies within a month of Judgment. This coverage is more expensive than regular coverage, so it would usually be cheaper to postpone the beginning of the COBRA 36-month period. After the 36 months, if a spouse has serious medical conditions, he/she might be unable to obtain health insurance.

PX privileges. If you are married to a serviceman on active duty for 20 years during the marriage, you are eligible for military PX privileges and other benefits. You wouldn't want to dissolve the marriage, say, after 19 years and 6 months. You would wait the other 6 months. If you are approaching this 20-year anniversary, check with the military about your possible benefits. The judge will listen to these practical considerations in determining the date of dissolution of marriage.

Social Security. If you are married for 10 years (being legally separated is okay), you are eligible for derivative social security benefits. Your derivative benefits would be half the amount of your spouse's, and this would not decrease your spouse's benefits. You can choose either the derivative benefits or your own benefits, whichever are greater. You would not want the marriage dissolved after, say, 9 years and 6 months. You would wait until you passed the 10-year mark.

Possible loss of pension benefits. A status-only dissolution might cause you to lose valuable pension rights. For example, your spouse might have life insurance through work that provides a lump-sum payment for a surviving spouse if he/she dies. But, if you are divorced, you are no longer the "surviving spouse." You become the surviving *former* spouse unless you get a special order declaring that you should be treated as a "surviving spouse" after the divorce. It would take an insurance or family law specialist to advise you about this.

Conditions the judge can impose on your judgment

Under Family Code 2337, the court can choose to impose various conditions when granting a status-only judgment:

(1) You could be ordered to assume responsibility for any taxes or penalties payable by the other party if the status-only divorce results in a tax liability that would not otherwise occur. This takes some unusual circumstances, so shouldn't cause a problem.

(2) If the early divorce means you can no longer keep your children or your spouse covered under your health insurance, the court could order you to obtain comparable insurance or to pay medical expenses until such time as a divorce would ordinarily be entered.

(3) You could be asked to indemnify your spouse for loss of survivor's benefits and losses due to certain pension plan options.

(4) Under some pension plans, a divorced employee spouse can cash-in the account without the signature of the ex. An order could be made to prevent this.

(5) If the early granting of the dissolution means that your spouse just misses the 10-year deadline for some social security benefits, you could be ordered to pay for the loss.

(6) Any other condition the court determines is just and equitable.

(7) If there are IRA's, 401k's, or a retirement plan, the spouse who wants to prevent the status-only dissolution can demand that you formally join the plan in the case and that certain orders be entered regarding them. If granted, the marriage can't be dissolved until those things are accomplished.

If the other party requests any of the protections listed in the code, they will probably be granted, but if the motion goes through with no opposition, these protections might not be included in the court's order. There is no way to know for sure ahead of time. If you need to be sure in advance, you'll need a final MSA, or get your spouse to join in a stipulated order on the motion for status-only divorce. On the other hand, if you've got a little time to spare, give it a try and if it doesn't work out, just drop it.

Must complete declarations of disclosure

Because a status-only judgment affects property rights—yes, even if you don't have any property—the Disclosure requirements are in effect. No judgment can be entered without each party having done both the Preliminary and Final Declarations of Disclosure (with current Income and Expense Declarations). This is a deal-breaker. The least you can get away with would be:

- The parties exchange a preliminary disclosure and Income and Expense Declarations,
- Both parties stipulate to waive the final disclosure only for the purpose of obtaining a Status-Only Judgment of Dissolution, as we illustrate in Figure 21.1.

The preliminary disclosures must be exchanged, and proofs of service filed with the court, before the date of your stipulation or, if no stipulation, before the hearing on your motion. See Book 1, *How to Do Your Own Divorce,* chapter 14, about declarations of disclosure.

B Stipulation for status-only judgment

If you and your spouse have both filed proofs of service of the Preliminary Declaration of Disclosure, and if you can agree, it is very easy to get a status-only judgment of dissolution. You can file a stipulation instead of a motion, or *after* the motion is filed if you reach agreement later. Simply prepare and sign the stipulation (Figure 21.1) and submit it to the court along with the following:

- A status-only judgment. Get the Judgment form from Book 1, *How to Do Your Own Divorce.* In the caption, check "Dissolution" and "Status only." Check boxes 4 and 4(a)(1) and 4(g). What you enter for the date at item 4(a)(1) depends on what county you are in. See the text note on the first page of *How to Do Your Own Divorce,* chapter 18 for what to enter here.
- A Notice of Entry of Judgment (*How to Do Your Own Divorce,* chapter 20) checked at item 2, and two stamped envelopes, one addressed to each party (or attorney of record).

C Motion for status-only judgment

Do your Notice of Motion exactly as described in chapter 12 and attach the Application for Separate Trial (Figure 21.3) along with a supporting Declaration (Figure 21.4).

Alternate valuation date. Rule of Court 5.126 requires you to state in your declaration the date property will be valued, so you need to think what difference this might make and pick a reasonable date. Property is typically valued at the time of trial, so you can choose "time of trial on the matter," but you can also request a different date for some or all assets, like date of separation, or some other date that makes some sense given your situation. Whatever you pick, you must give reasons supporting the date selected. Also state if the date applies to some or all assets, and if only some, identify each asset affected.

Figure 21.1
STIPULATION FOR STATUS-ONLY JUDGMENT
(page 1)

YOUR NAME
Your Address
City, State, Zip
Your Phone

Petitioner in propria persona

SUPERIOR COURT OF CALIFORNIA, COUNTY OF [County]

In re Marriage of)	No.: [Your case number]
Petitioner: YOUR NAME)	STIPULATION AND ORDER RE ENTRY OF STATUS-ONLY JUDGMENT OF DISSOLUTION OF MARRIAGE
Respondent: SPOUSE NAME)	

IT IS HEREBY STIPULATED by and between the parties hereto on this __ day of ___________, 20__, that each will comply with all terms and conditions of the following agreement:

The matter is bifurcated so that a Status-Only Judgment of Dissolution of Marriage may immediately be entered. Said Judgment shall immediately dissolve the marriage and shall retain jurisdiction over all other issues.

For only the purpose of entry of the Status-Only Judgment, the parties waive Final Declarations of Disclosure. (1) We are the parties in the above-listed action. (2) We have complied with Family Code section 2104 and our Preliminary Declarations of Disclosure have been completed and exchanged. (3) We have completed and exchanged a current Income & Expense Declaration that includes all material facts and information regarding our earnings, accumulations, and expenses. (4) We have fully complied with Family Code section 2102 and have fully augmented the Preliminary Declarations of Disclosure, including disclosure of all material facts and information regarding the characterization of all assets and liabilities, the valuation of all

1

Stipulation for Status-Only Judgment

Figure 21.2

STIPULATION FOR STATUS-ONLY JUDGMENT

(page 2)

assets and liabilities, the valuation of all be community property or in which it is contended the community has an interest, and the amounts of all obligations that are contended to be community obligations or for which it is contended the community has liability. (5) This waiver is knowingly, intelligently, and voluntarily entered into by each of us. (6) This waiver does not limit the legal disclosure obligations of each of us, but rather is a statement under penalty of perjury that those obligations have been fulfilled. Each of us further understands that noncompliance with those obligations will result in the court setting aside the judgment.

______________________________	______________________________
YOUR NAME, Petitioner in pro per	SPOUSE NAME, Respondent in pro per

The above agreement of the parties and their counsel having been duly considered by the Court, and good cause appearing therefore,

IT IS ORDERED that the above agreement is approved, and each party is ordered fully to comply with all terms and conditions thereof to be performed on his or her own part

Dated:

____
Judge of the Superior Court

(NOTE: SIGNATURE OF PARTY WITHOUT ATTORNEY MUST BE NOTARIZED.)

2

Stipulation for Status-Only Judgment

Figure 21.3
APPLICATION FOR SEPARATE TRIAL
Form FL-315

FL-315

PETITIONER: PETITIONER'S NAME RESPONDENT: RESPONDENT'S NAME OTHER:	CASE NUMBER: Your case number

APPLICATION FOR SEPARATE TRIAL

Attachment to [ ] **Order to Show Cause (form FL-300)** [X] **Notice of Motion (form FL-301)**

I, *(name)*: YOUR NAME , request that the court sever (bifurcate) and grant an early and separate trial on the following issue or issues:

1. a. [X] Dissolution of the status of the marriage (Fam. Code, § 2337).
   I will serve with this application my preliminary *Declaration of Disclosure* and completed *Schedule of Assets and Debts* unless they have been previously served or the parties have stipulated in writing to defer service.
   b. [ ] I request the following conditions be made:
      (1) [ ] That I indemnify and hold the other party harmless from "taxes, reassessments, interest, and penalties" payable in the event that a dissolution prior to the property division results in taxes that would not have been payable if the parties were still married at the time of the division.
      (2) [ ] That I maintain health and medical insurance for the other party and minor children as long as possible, and then must obtain comparable coverage or pay any expenses that would have been covered by insurance.
      (3) [ ] That I hold the other party harmless re probate homestead.
      (4) [ ] That I hold the other party harmless re probate family allowance.
      (5) [ ] That I hold the other party harmless re pension benefits, elections, or survivors' benefits.
      (6) [ ] That I join the pension plan and, if the other party has a private plan covered by ERISA, will cause a Qualified Domestic Relations Order (QDRO) to be served on the plan.
      (7) [ ] That I hold the other party harmless re social security benefits.
      (8) [ ] Any other condition that the court determines is just and equitable.
2. [ ] Permanent custody and visitation of the children of the marriage.
3. [ ] Date of separation of the parties.
4. [X] Alternate valuation date for property.
5. [ ] Validity of marital settlement agreement entered into prior to or during the marriage.
6. [ ] Other *(specify)*:
7. a. [X] I request that the court conduct this separate trial on the hearing date.
   or
   b. [ ] I will, at the hearing, ask the court to set a date for this separate trial.
8. The reasons in support of this request are *(specify)*:
   [ ] Points and authorities attached. [X] Supporting declarations attached.

   If you can fit your declaration in this space, put it here.

I declare under penalty of perjury under the laws of the State of California that the foregoing is true and correct.

Date: Date signed

YOUR NAME
(TYPE OR PRINT NAME)

▶ ______________________
(SIGNATURE OF DECLARANT)

Page 1 of 1

Form Adopted for Mandatory Use
Judicial Council of California
FL-315 [Rev. January 1, 2003]

APPLICATION FOR SEPARATE TRIAL
(Family Law)

Family Code, § 2337
www.courtinfo.ca.gov

Deadlines. If a date was set for trial, hearing on this motion must be set not less than 60 days before the date first set for trial. While most motions require 21 days' notice, this one has to be served at least 30 days before the hearing. If you serve it by mail, do it 35 days before the hearing. If your spouse files papers opposing the motion, and you want to reply, you must do it in writing within 5 days after your spouse's response. To reply to your spouse's response, use the Declaration form (Figure 12.4).

The status-only judgment. This should be prepared before the hearing along with a Notice of Entry of Judgment (where you check box 2) and two stamped envelopes addressed to yourself and the other side (see Book 1, *How to Do Your Own Divorce,* chapters 18 and 21). In the Judgment, check the box in the caption, "Status Only," complete items 2 and 3 and check 4g.

If your motion is granted, the party requesting the divorce will be sworn as a witness and testify that he/she is the petitioner (or respondent), that petitioner (or respondent) lived in California for six months and the county for three months immediately before the Petition was filed, that the facts in the Petition or Response are true, and that irreconcilable differences exist in the marriage. The judge will grant the divorce and sign your status-only judgment. However, if the judge imposes protective conditions (described above), you will have to prepare a Judgment that includes these as Further Orders under item 4(o) (see Book 1, chapter 18) and get the Judgment signed as described in chapters 16 and 26.

Have Judgment signed promptly. If you will need to obtain insurance coverage under the federal act COBRA, regarding health insurance after divorce (see above, section A, and *How to Do Your Own Divorce,* chapter 5.2), you must make sure the Judgment is promptly signed so you can apply for coverage within the short deadlines provided by that law.

D How to resist a motion for status-only judgment

To oppose a motion for status-only dissolution, you file an objection (Figure 21.5). However, you can't do this unless you have a good reason. The fact that you don't want the divorce will not prevent it from happening. Only legal or practical matters will work. For example, the fact that one spouse will lose his/her health insurance coverage upon divorce would carry weight with the court.

If your grounds for objecting are frivolous, just trying to get in your spouse's way, the judge might be irritated with you for refusing to cooperate for no good reason, especially if your case has been pending more than six months. A judge can award sanctions against you for opposing a Request for Separate Trial without good reason. So, unless you have a valid reason to prevent the divorce, just let it go. However, if, for example, either you or your spouse has significant retirement assets, you need protection. In this particular example, aside from objecting to the motion, you should also get advice from a specialist attorney immediately upon receiving news of the motion.

Know your rights. Be sure to study the protections listed in Family Code Section 2337, discussed at the end of section A, above. You can request any of the protections stated in it and, especially if your spouse has no attorney, he/she may not succeed in fulfilling the various conditions, so the dissolution may be delayed even though the motion is granted. In this manner, you can oppose the request for immediate divorce, and protect yourself at the same time, by insisting on complicated conditions such as the ones regarding pension rights.

Deadlines. You must serve any objections within twenty days after receiving notice.

Figure 21.4

DECLARATION IN SUPPORT OF REQUEST FOR SEPARATE TRIAL

Marriage of YOUR LAST NAME & SPOUSE LAST NAME

Case No. [Your case number]

DECLARATION OF PETITIONER

The undersigned states:

I am petitioner herein.

The Petition for dissolution of marriage was filed on [date] and Respondent was served with the Petition and Summons on [date].

(Choose A or B or make up C)

(A) Since that time Respondent has not cooperated in discovery, and this has delayed the progress of this case. In order to be ready for trial of all issues in this case, I will need to obtain an appraisal of the following asset(s): [List assets to be appraised such as house, pension, business.] Until I have full discovery and adequate documentation about said assets, I am unable to obtain an appraisal.

(B) Since that time Respondent and I have attempted to negotiate a complete settlement of all issues in this case, but we have not reached an agreement, and I do not know when we will do so.

It is my desire to be divorced immediately, and I am requesting that the court order a separate trial so that the status of the marriage may be dissolved before the other issues are resolved. I request that the court retain jurisdiction over all other issues and establish the valuation date for property as (give date).

Executed at [City], California, on [date].

I declare under penalty of perjury under the laws of the State of California that the foregoing is true and correct.

____

YOUR NAME, Petitioner

1

Stipulation for Status-Only Judgment

Figure 21.5
OBJECTION TO REQUEST FOR SEPARATE TRIAL
(page 1)

YOUR NAME
Your Address
City, State, Zip
Your Phone

Petitioner in propria persona

SUPERIOR COURT OF CALIFORNIA, COUNTY OF [County]

In re Marriage of	)	No.: [Your case number]
	)	
Petitioner: YOUR NAME	)	OBJECTION TO REQUEST
	)	FOR SEPARATE TRIAL
Respondent: SPOUSE NAME	)	(BIFURCATION)
______________________	)	

I, the undersigned, state:

I am the Respondent herein. I object to the court granting the Petitioner's request for separate trial and early dissolution of the marriage unless the court orders that before such change of status occurs Petitioner must comply with all the terms and conditions of Family Code section 2337. I have the following retirement or pension plan(s):

No Qualified Domestic Relations Order has been prepared.

I will be greatly disadvantaged by the early dissolution of the marriage as I suffer from the following medical problem(s):

These are covered by Petitioner's health insurance which is available at low or nominal cost. I believe I will be uninsurable or unable to obtain health insurance at reasonable cost, and I request that Petitioner be ordered not only to cooperate so that

1

Objection to Request for Separate Trial (Bifurcation)

Figure 21.6

OBJECTION TO REQUEST FOR SEPARATE TRIAL

(page 2)

I am covered by COBRA but also that Petitioner pay my post-COBRA health insurance for the number of months between the Status-Only Judgment dissolving our marriage and the Judgment resolving the other issues in the case.

Further, we have not exchanged (Preliminary or) Final Declarations of Disclosure. I am not willing to waive those, even for purposes of entering a Status-Only Judgment, and without those, the marriage cannot be dissolved. I request that any order for dissolution of the marriage not be effective until at least twenty days after I receive Petitioner's Final Declaration of Disclosure so that, if appropriate, I can call any objections arising from that information, once it is received, to the court's attention.

I declare under penalty of perjury under the Laws of the State of California that the foregoing is true and correct.
Executed on [date], at [City], California.

____
YOUR NAME, Petitioner

2

Objection to Request for Separate Trial (Bifurcation)

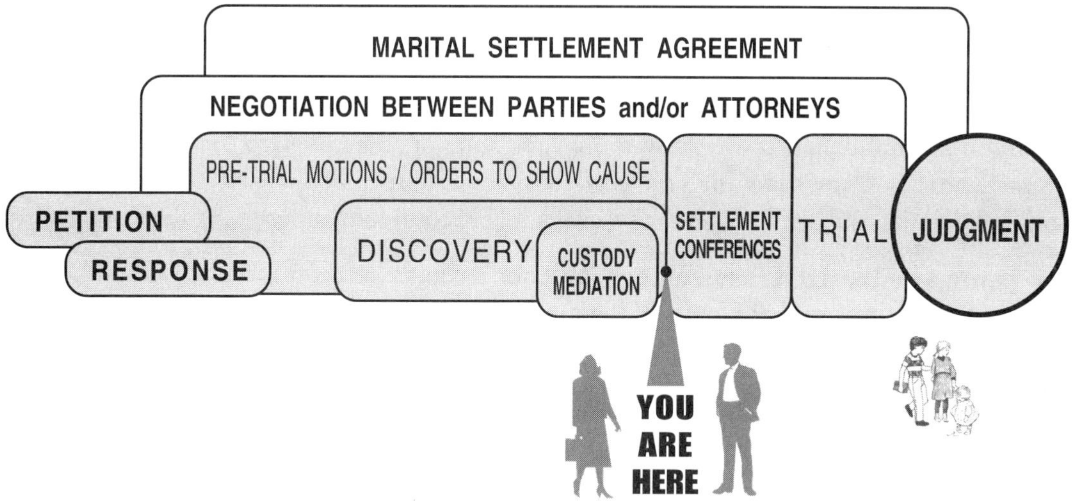

CHAPTER 22
AT-ISSUE MEMORANDUM –push the case toward trial

A. Setting a trial date brings your case to a close
B. How to do an At-Issue Memorandum
C. Responding to an At-Issue Memorandum
D. What to do when you get a trial date
E. Start planning for the Settlement Conference

A Setting a trial date brings your case to a close

Assuming your side of the case is in order, setting the case for trial is a good way to put pressure on cases that are dragging because, once a trial date is set, the other side must enter into an agreement or go to trial. To do this, you file a document telling he court that a Response has been filed, you have not settled, and you now want to set a trial date to finish the case. There is no state form for this and every county is a little different; some have local forms, some don't. The document you file might be called an At-Issue Memorandum, Memorandum to Set, Request for Status/Trial Setting Conference, or Request for Trial Setting. In this book, we use "At-Issue Memorandum" for all of them. Check your local rules.

Here's how it works. Filing an At-Issue Memo will cause the clerk to set a date for trial and, before trial, most counties will also schedule a Settlement Conference (except in Santa Clara County where you will be shunted off to an Early Disposition Conference after which you will get a case management conference, after which you can finally get a trial date). At the Settlement Conference, the judge will probably try to talk (or pressure) the parties into a settlement or at least a partial settlement. This is discussed in the next chapter.

Things can happen very rapidly after you file an At-Issue Memorandum, so don't file one until you've read chapters 23 and 25, and have done everything discussed there. Wait until you are *really* ready, before you crank it all into action.

Get help? After reading this chapter, you will understand how many things you have to get just right according to local rules and how, if something goes wrong or you miss something, you could undermine your case or lose outright. If you can afford it, this would be a very good time to get advice and coaching from a local family law specialist attorney—someone who knows your county and who is willing to do this kind of service for you. If you decide to get help, start looking right away, before you set these wheels in motion, because once things start to happen, it might be too late to arrange an appointment.

Preparation = confidence. If you are well prepared and not afraid to go to trial, you won't cave in to accept less than is fair. Okay, sometimes it's worth it to buy some peace, but even that decision should be based on reason rather than fear. If you can't get reasonably confident about going forward, get help.

One way to avoid a trial is to ask for one. Of course you are reluctant to undertake a big step like going to trial—who wouldn't be? However, if you request a trial, you'll have legal mechanisms pressing both parties to settle and the judge's assistance as well. Maybe. Some judges, anyway. Only about 5% of all cases actually end up in trial.

You *must* study local rules. Asking for a trial date and actually going to trial are fairly technical procedures that are different in every county, so you need to read and comply with local rules. Even if you are not the one asking for the trial date, if you are served with an At-Issue Memo, you should read the local rule and possibly reply if the other side has not complied. For example, let's say the local rule says that the statement in the At-Issue Memorandum about length of the trial will be taken as true if unopposed. If you have a different idea about the length of trial, you need to file an opposition.

If your spouse did not file a Response. If no Response was ever filed with the court, the case is not at issue and you do not use the At-Issue Memorandum. Instead you will take Respondent's default and finish the case on your own, as described in *How to Do Your Own Divorce,* chapter 17.

Reasons not to file an At-Issue Memorandum yet

Discovery cutoff. All discovery *must* be completed at least 30 days before the first date set for trial and discovery motions must be heard at least 15 days ahead (Code of Civil Procedure section 2024). You can't assume the other side will cooperate, which means motions to compel discovery might be required. You need to allow up to six months before trial for discovery and you do not want the pressure of a trial date looming ahead. If you are not finished with discovery, do *not* file an At-Issue Memorandum.

Appraisals and other preparation. In addition to discovery being near completion and having your case well organized and prepared, you want all major assets (such as a home, business, or stock options) to be appraised before you file your At-Issue Memorandum. If you file too early, you could find yourself at trial unprepared on some important issue and it will be too late to do anything about it. For example, getting appraisals and financial documents can sometimes be difficult and might require motions. Don't rush into a trial before you are really prepared.

B How to do an At-Issue Memorandum

To set a trial, you have to use a local form, different in every county. We'll call it "At-Issue Memorandum," but other counties have other names for it. Some counties don't have a form, so you have to type one. Check your local rules or talk to the court clerk and find out if they have a form to set trials, and where you can get a copy. Then review it and the local rules to see what you must put in the form.

Find out when trials are being set

Before you fill out the form, you want to find out approximately when cases are being set for your kind of trial so you know how to plan your calendar. Call the court clerk and ask, "If an At-Issue Memorandum is filed today, approximately when would the trial date be set?" The clerk might ask how long you expect the trial to last, because they have scheduling problems and need to know. They might use terms like "short cause" and "long cause." See chapter 11, section B, on calendaring.

Even when the question is correctly asked and you tell them everything they want to know, some clerks cannot or will not give you an answer. If the clerk can't help you, ask politely if they can refer you to someone who can help. Be politely persistent, go in personally and ask for help, but never, never, never piss off a clerk, even if they deserve it. Never. If all else fails, keep reading, we'll get to it.

Get a form or a format

If there is a local form for the At-Issue Memorandum, use it. There may be other documents that must accompany the form, and those will be specified in local rules. If your county does not have a local At-Issue Memorandum form, ask at the county law library, or check with a local family law attorney to get a sample of the format they like in your county, then type it up. It is expected that if you have to type an At-Issue Memorandum from scratch, you will need to include the information contained in our sample local form (Figure 22.1) which meets all the requirements of California Rule of Court 209.

What goes in the At-Issue Memo

How long your case will take to complete at trial. The court wants you to estimate (guess) not only how long your case will take to put on, but how long the other side might take. Without trial experience, this will be extremely difficult, particularly as it depends in part on how fast judges push trials in your county. Some proceed in a rather leisurely fashion while, in other courts, getting a full half-day of court time is a major achievement. You'll either have to consult a local family law specialist attorney to find out what is an appropriate estimate for your case or just make your own best guess and hope for the best.

Dates you are unavailable for trial. Consider yourself unavailable if you have future obligations that you really can't get out of (or really, really, really don't want to), such as prepaid vacations and required business travel. Attorneys consider anything that occupies their own schedule to be "unavailable," and anything in the schedule of a pro per to be nothing. For an attorney to be unavailable, they should be on prepaid vacation, or in another trial or major court proceeding. Trial should take precedence over other things like motions and depositions.

Assuming the clerk gave you a time period for trial settings, you should start listing your unavailable dates a month before the first likely trial date, and over a six- or seven-month period of time. You can't be too careful. If they can't or won't give you an estimate, list dates you will not be available starting one month after the date of your At-Issue Memorandum and continuing for the next year (which presumably won't be too burdensome as most people don't have their time calendared out for the next year).

Got kids? San Francisco wants you to assure them that all custody and visitation issues have been resolved or that the court has excused compliance with this provision. An excuse would presumably exist where custody/visitation issues are undergoing lengthy evaluation and financial issues are relatively simple. If you want to set a trial in San Francisco and custody/visitation is not resolved, you should do all you can to resolve custody/visitation by pushing all appointments for you and your spouse to happen as rapidly as possible. All counties are supposed to give custody issues trial preference, but San Francisco is the only county that has formally created a local rule to accomplish this.

A Pretrial Statement might be required with the At-Issue Memo

Here's something to watch out for. In some counties, a detailed pretrial statement and/or a request for admissions must accompany the At-Issue Memorandum. Your local rules will explain in detail what is

Figure 22.1

AT-ISSUE MEMORANDUM –SANTA CLARA COUNTY

(page 1)

ATTACHMENT L

ATTORNEY OR PARTY WITHOUT ATTORNEY (NAME AND ADDRESS) TELEPHONE NUMBER:	FOR COURT USE ONLY
YOUR NAME Your address City, State, Zip ATTORNEY FOR (Name): Petitioner / Respondent in pro per	
SUPERIOR COURT OF CALIFORNIA, COUNTY OF SANTA CLARA STREET ADDRESS: 170 Park Center Plaza MAILING ADDRESS: same CITY AND ZIP CODE: San Jose, CA 95113 BRANCH NAME: Family Law Division	
PLAINTIFF: PETITIONER'S NAME DEFENDANT: RESPONDENT'S NAME	
AT-ISSUE MEMORANDUM Nature of Case ☐ Personal Injury, Property Damage or Wrongful Death, involving Motor Vehicle ☐ All other Personal Injury, etc. ☒ Family Law ☐ Eminent Domain ☐ Other civil: ______	CASE NUMBER: Your case number

1. Jury trial requested: (Yes/No) NO
2. Time estimated for trial: 1/2 days.
3. Case entitled to preference (Yes/No) Yes under code section: short-cause trial
   IF SHORT CAUSE MEMO IS FILED, THE MATTER WILL PROCEED TO TRIAL WITHIN 30-90 DAYS, SPECIFY ANY CONFLICT DURING THAT TIME PERIOD, WITH REASON

   List every date on which you are not available for trial. Do not list things you can change, such as optional medical appointments that are months away.

4. Are you claiming an exemption to Arbitration? X Yes ___No; If yes, state why? Family law case
5. Does the amount in controversy exceed $50,000 as to any Plaintiff: X Yes ___No.
6. Do you object to the matter being ordered to Arbitration? ___Yes ___No.
7. Are you willing to stipulate to Arbitration, regardless of the amount in controversy? ___Yes X No
8. If Personal Injury:
   a. Nature and extent of injuries: ______
   b. Total medical expenses to date: ______
   c. Future medical expenses: ______
   d. Loss of earnings to date: ______
   e. Future loss of earnings: ______
   f. Other special or general damages: ______
9. Other:
   a. Nature of damages: ______
   b. Amount of damages: ______
   c. Relief sought: ______
10. Indicate party being represented:

Plaintiff: YOUR NAME — Defe...
Attorney: In pro per — Atto...
Firm: — Firm
Address: Your address — Add...
City, State, Zip
Telephone: Your phone number — Tele...

**For additional parties, use reverse side.

Rev. January 1, 2001 — AT-ISSUE MEM...

(page 2)

I hereby represent to the court that all essential parties have been served with process or have appeared herein and that this case is at issue as to all such parties; that no amended or supplemental complaint or cross-complaint or other affirmative pleading remains unanswered; that to my knowledge no other parties will be served with a summons prior to the time of the trial, and I know of no further pleading to be filed.

Date: Date of signature ______

Attorney(s) for Petitioner in pro per

Any party no in agreement with the information or estimates given in an At-Issue Memorandum shall within ten days after service thereof serve and file a memorandum in his behalf.

NOTICE RE FAMILY LAW CASES

Pursuant to Rule 3.6.A(4)a of the local rules of this Court, the party filing an At-Issue Memorandum shall also file a proof of service that a Statement of Position on all disputed issues has been simultaneously served on the opposing party or counsel.

THIS AT-ISSUE MEMORANDUM WILL NOT BE ACCEPTED FOR FILING UNLESS THE DECLARATION SET FORTH BELOW HAS BEEN SIGNED

I declare under penalty of perjury that Statement of Position has been served on the opposing party of counsel.

DATED AT City or place signed California, this day day of month, 20 03 .

______

PROOF OF SERVICE BY MAIL (C.C.P. 1013a)

I served the At-Issue Memorandum by depositing a copy(ies) thereof (enclosed in a sealed envelope(s), postage prepaid) in the

Note that Santa Clara rules require you to also serve a Statement of Position on all disputed issues.

wanted. Basically, what the court wants in the pretrial statement is a summary of your case and, possibly, some documents such as the Income and Expense Statement. Take a look at the Settlement Conference Statement in the next chapter. Some counties even want it on colored paper—for example, San Diego and San Mateo want it to be blue. Go figure. In Santa Clara County you serve, but do not file, a Statement of Position letter, stating your position on all disputed issues, and file a Proof of Service that this was done. San Francisco Rule 11.36 is an entire page of fine print listing just what the court wants. San Mateo County, also a full page, requires a pretrial statement with the At-Issue Memorandum in short-cause cases but later for long-cause cases. You *must* check your own local rules as soon as you begin considering an At-Issue Memorandum or as soon as you receive one from the other side. You don't want to be caught off guard.

Filing and serving

Just as with any motion, you make copies of your At-Issue Memo and any accompanying attachments. Prepare a Proof of Service by Mail if there is none built into the local form. Attach the original Proof of Service to the original At-Issue Memo, then make your copies, have your server mail the document, and have your server sign the original Proof of Service. Then file the package with the court. The court will send you a notice of your next court date which could be a case management conference, settlement conference or trial date.

Some counties do not follow this procedure but have you file a Request to Set for Trial (Figure 22.2). Once that is filed, if you have a long-cause case, in Los Angeles, for example, you are then subject to detailed orders which are in Los Angeles County Local Rule 14.6(b)(2); the court will set the matter for settlement conference and trial. Los Angeles Rule 14.6(b) calls for the court to order counsel to comply with requirements as to Mandatory Settlement Conference Briefs, Income and Expense Declarations, Exhibit and Witness Lists, Property Declarations, etc.

C Responding to an At-Issue Memorandum

If your case is ready

Even if you don't mind the case being set for trial, you might want to file a reply At-Issue Memorandum to inform the court of dates on which you are unavailable for trial. You don't want the trial to be set on a date when you are in Europe on a prepaid vacation. In counties that require some sort of pretrial statement (see above), you can take this opportunity to put your own case in front of the judge. Who knows, you might be assigned to a reader.

You have ten days to respond. Use the same At-Issue form that you received, but type "Counter" as the first word of its name (e.g., Counter Request for Trial Setting) and use that same name on the proof of service. Type it right on the form in the title of the document and in the footer, too. California Rule of Court 209(d) requires this document to be served on your spouse (or his/her attorney if there is one) within 10 days after the At-Issue Memorandum was served on you. Remember, if you serve your Counter At-Issue by mail, you must mail it 5 days before the 10 days expire. If you received any other documents along with the At-Issue Memorandum, you *must* respond to those, too. Be sure to check your local rules for applicable deadlines on those documents.

Warning: In some counties, if you do not promptly reply to the pretrial statement (or whatever they're called in your county), this can be conclusively interpreted as an admission to all of your spouse's positions! Be careful that you don't find yourself in this position. In some counties, you must respond or

Figure 22.2
REQUEST TO SET FOR TRIAL

YOUR NAME
Your Address
City, State, Zip
Your Phone

Petitioner in propria persona

SUPERIOR COURT OF CALIFORNIA, COUNTY OF [County]

In re Marriage of	)	No.: [Your case number]
	)	
Petitioner: YOUR NAME	)	REQUEST TO SET FOR TRIAL
Respondent: SPOUSE NAME	)	
________________________	)	

REQUEST IS HEREBY MADE that this matter be set for trial.

This is an action for dissolution of marriage.

The names, telephone numbers and addresses of parties in pro per and counsel of record are:

YOUR NAME	SPOUSE NAME (OR THEIR ATTORNEY)
Your Address	Address
City, State, Zip	City, State, Zip
Your Phone	Phone

Petitioner estimates that this matter will require EITHER one half day or less for trial and is a short-cause matter OR [number] days for trial and is a long-cause matter.

Dated: [Date]

____
YOUR NAME, Petitioner

1

Request to Set for Trial

you lose, but this depends on your local rules.

If your case is not ready

Sometimes a party who holds all the family financial information or all the information on some other crucial issue will try to rush you into trial so they will have an unfair advantage. If you have been making diligent efforts to prepare and you are being rushed into trial before you are ready, you should file a motion to strike your spouse's At-Issue Memorandum. This is different from a motion to continue the trial date (chapter 24). You use the motion to strike to *stop* a trial date from being set. You use a motion to continue if the trial date has *already* been set.

Judges get tired of parties asking for delays—it makes it harder for them to manage court work—but if your spouse is rushing you into trial, you are forced to ask for one anyway. You need to make it clear that you have been diligent but your spouse is rushing the case too fast. File a declaration listing everything you have done to get ready. If, in fact, you have not been preparing diligently, you are probably not going to be granted a continuance so you had better scramble as fast as possible to catch up.

You should check with the clerk to find out approximately when they are setting trials like yours. If similar cases are being set a year away, you might decide not to file a motion to strike the At-Issue Memorandum now, but try to prepare your case fast enough to be ready by the expected trial date. However, if trials are being set only a month or two away, and your case is not prepared, you need to move immediately to strike the At-Issue Memorandum. If motions are being set to occur in say, five weeks, and your trial is set to occur in four weeks, you may need to include in your motion a request for an order shortening time so your motion will be heard before the trial.

Do your motion exactly as described in chapter 12, filling out the forms as described there, but with the modifications shown below.

MOTION TO COMPEL STRIKE AT-ISSUE MEMO

Notice of Motion:

In the caption, check the box for "Other," and type in, "Strike At-Issue Memo."

Application for Order and Supporting Declaration:

Item 9, Other relief: Type in, "Strike the At-Issue Memorandum filed herein on (date) and not set the case for trial."

Item 10, Facts: Prepare and attach a declaration like the one in Figure 22.3.

Item 12. Order shortening time: Check this if you want an OST (see chapter 11B) and enter the number of days you must serve papers before the hearing—5 days is typical, or 2 days in an emergency. You must state facts at item 10 to justify this request.

While you are waiting for the hearing on your motion to strike, you must do everything you can to get the case ready for trial because you might lose the motion and the case could be set for trial over your objections. Chapters 8 and 17 discuss the things you can do to gather up information. Get as much as you can as rapidly as possible.

Warning. Many local rules have specific requirements for Counter At-Issue Memorandum and/or motions to strike. These are aimed at parties and attorneys who try to delay things because they didn't bother to do their preparation. Read your local rules carefully and follow all requirements exactly.

Figure 22.3
DECLARATION IN SUPPORT OF MOTION TO STRIKE AT-ISSUE MEMORANDUM

Note: Pleadings should be double-spaced. This illustration was altered to save space for this display.

Marriage of YOUR LAST NAME & SPOUSE LAST NAME

Case No. [Your case number]

DECLARATION IN SUPPORT OF MOTION TO

STRIKE AT-ISSUE MEMORANDUM

The undersigned states:

I am petitioner herein.

This action began when I filed the Petition on [date]. It was served on Respondent on [date]. The Response was filed on [date]. On [date] Respondent filed an At-Issue Memorandum. No trial date has been set.

This case is not ready for trial and cannot be ready for trial on the date set because of the following. The At-Issue Memorandum was filed prematurely. The parties have not exchanged (Preliminary and) Final Declarations of Disclosure.

[Sample: I have been unable to afford an attorney in this matter, and Respondent has blocked every effort I have made to obtain discovery in this matter. For example, he/she refused to provide me with a copy of his/her income tax return for the year(s) [year(s)] in spite of my written request.

If there are other things that have prevented you from preparing for trial, such as illness or work or problems with the children, state those facts.]

If this matter is set for trial, my rights will be severely prejudiced as I do not have access to the information necessary to document Respondent's income and our community property.

I am requesting that this court strike the At-Issue Memorandum and not place the case on the trial calendar until discovery can be completed and until complete and documented Declarations of Disclosure have been exchanged.

Executed at [place], California, on [date].

I declare under penalty of perjury under the laws of the State of California that the foregoing is true and correct.

____
YOUR NAME, Petitioner

1

Declaration in Support of Motion to Strike At-Issue Memorandum

D What to do when you get a trial date

Be sure you know all deadlines and procedures. When you receive your settlement conference date or trial date, deadlines start running on your case. They won't be written on documents or forms, so they can easily pass by unknown and unnoticed. In some counties, for example, if you do not do certain things, such as disclose in writing the name and address of every one of your expert witnesses by a certain date, you will lose your right to use them. And many counties require pretrial statements to be filed and served by a certain date. If you fail to study your local rules diligently, you could lose important rights without even knowing it.

Because of the importance of these deadlines and the ease with which they can be overlooked, once you know a court date is being set, this would be a very good time to meet with a specialist attorney in your county to discuss deadlines and what you must do to protect your rights and get your case going. As discussed in section A, it would be best find a local State Bar Certified Family Law Specialist attorney (CFLS), but certainly consult only an attorney who practices primarily family law in your county. If you decide to do this, hurry! You haven't a moment to lose.

Calendar your discovery cutoff. All discovery must be completed by at least 30 days before trial, and discovery motions must be heard at least 15 days before trial (chapter 17). Now that you have a trial date, you are under considerable pressure to complete any discovery that is still unfinished.

Final Declarations of Disclosure must be served at least 45 days before trial, or 50 days before if you mail them (see Book 1, chapter 14). As soon as you have your trial date, calendar this deadline and put a note 20 days before the deadline that you should prepare the documents. Don't just calendar the final deadline. Calendar enough time ahead get the task done on time.

Pretrial settlement statement reminder

Read your local rules very carefully to see if a pretrial settlement statement (or whatever it might be called in your county) is required with or after the At-Issue Memorandum. If it is, go back and read about pretrial statements in section B and read the next chapter about Settlement Statements, which are similar. Failure to do a good job on this can be disastrous. If you think you will need the help of an attorney, don't wait until it's too late.

E Start planning for the Settlement Conference

Long ago (chapter 6), you made a plan for your case. You are still working on it and it has been reflected in all the documents you have done. Your settlement offers reflected it. Any documents you were required to file with your At-Issue Memo reflected it. Now you are getting ready to do a settlement conference statement and/or trial brief which will continue to pound away at the same issues, evolving as some issues settle and others may have developed more clearly. Go on to the next chapter.

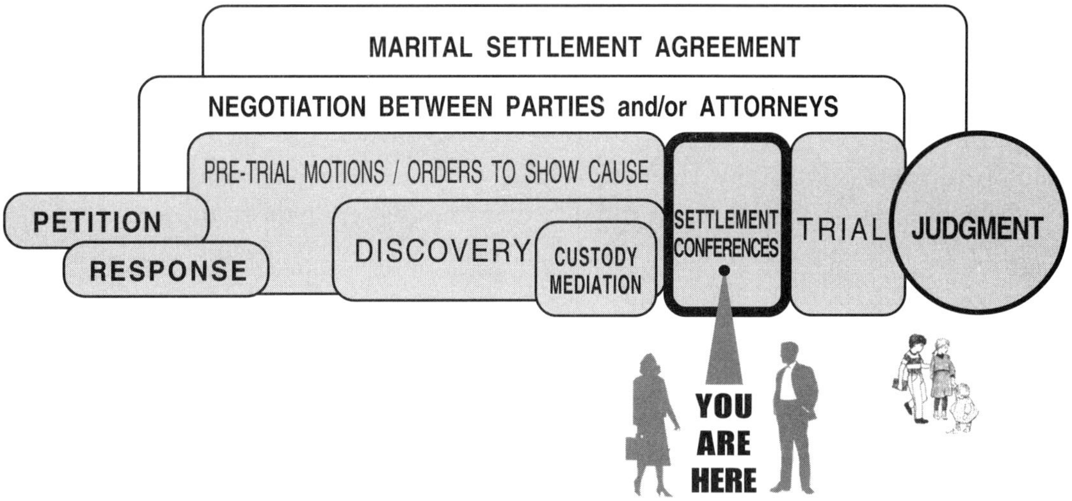

CHAPTER 23
SETTLEMENT CONFERENCES –judge helps you settle

A. What is a settlement conference?
B. Planning for the conference
C. The settlement conference statement
D. How to do a settlement conference
E. If you reach an agreement
F. After the conference

A What is a settlement conference?

All large counties and many small ones require parties to attend a settlement conference before a case can go to trial. Fortunately, neither party has to ask for it, which could be taken as a sign of weakness; rather, it is automatically set by the court as a result of filing an At-Issue Memorandum (or whatever your county calls it; see chapter 22).

A settlement conference is an informal meeting between the judge and the parties (or lawyers, if there are lawyers) for both sides to explore the possibilities for settlement. Judges don't want trials—they want you to agree. This is not because they are lazy, but because they know they will never understand your life and family as well as you do; that it will be far better for any children if you can agree; and better for both of you in the long run. They also know that trials are terribly expensive, both for you and for the county. Nonetheless, it takes two to agree, so if your spouse is not cooperative, you have no choice but to prepare for trial and actually have one if necessary.

Every judge will have his/her own style. Some don't give it much effort, but other judges play an active role in working out a settlement. They might, for example, tell the parties what decision is likely given the stated facts. Once you know what a judge is likely to do, you might as well accept the inevitable unless you can round up other evidence than you presented at the conference. Sometimes a judge will shuttle between lawyers and the parties, or perhaps talk separately to each party and point out in private the problems with his or her position. Of course, when you represent yourself, you *are* the lawyer, so you'll be in on all discussions.

Do it again. If the judge feels you made good progress toward an agreement but there wasn't enough time to finish, he/she might insist on another conference or even a series of settlement conferences. This could result in your trial date being postponed, even indefinitely, if the judge feels it will be worthwhile. Ironically, if one has counsel, going through a series of settlement conferences can cost more than a short trial. Nonetheless, in the settlement process you need to stay positive and try in good faith to settle.

Do it formally. At the end of any settlement conference, if anything important was agreed, you want to pin it down formally—either in writing and signed by the judge or on the record in the presence of a court reporter. This avoids any backsliding that might occur.

B Planning for the conference

You will use your Settlement Conference Statement (below) as your outline for the settlement conference itself. This is a continuation of the plan you made and followed from the beginning (chapter 6). By the time you show up, you should be completely familiar with all the facts, issues, and prior orders. In particular, you should know what you want and be prepared to make decisions.

There are two basic—and opposite—approaches to the settlement conference, so you need to think out in advance which one you want to use:

1. Begin with issues on which you are most likely to get agreement.
2. Begin with the toughest issue or the one with the greatest dollar value.

The point of the first approach, beginning with the easiest issue, is to get some momentum going in which you and your spouse are saying "yes." You want to begin a pattern of yes, yes, yes that will carry into the more difficult issues. When you reach difficult and emotion-packed issues, stop and formalize (put in writing) the matters you have agreed on before you go on, otherwise when everyone gets upset, you might blow away the agreements you thought you had.

The second approach, beginning with the toughest or biggest issue, can also be a good idea. If you can settle one or two big issues, you might find that all the rest fall almost automatically into place. If you could agree, for example, about the house and support, the rest of the items are small enough that neither of you might care to fight over them. Use the first approach if you have a very difficult, conflicted case in which agreeing on anything at all, no matter how small, would be a new approach and set a new tone of cooperation. Use the second approach if things have gone fairly well, and your ex seems pretty reasonable.

As you go through your settlement conference and are, hopefully, agreeing on issues, use your Settlement Conference Statement as a checklist to make sure that nothing falls through the cracks. You don't, for example, want to overlook health insurance when doing support. Your Settlement Conference Statement will focus you on your strategic issues but also serve as an exhaustive checklist.

C The settlement conference statement

You can turn this burden into a powerful weapon if you do it well. Many counties require you to prepare a detailed Settlement Conference Statement (sometimes called a Pretrial Statement) which must be served and filed a certain number of days before the conference (check local rules). Local rules can change any time, so you *must* make sure you have the latest version and you *must* read them very carefully.

Calendar deadlines and tasks. In reading the local rules, pay special attention to all deadlines. Every time a local rule says something like, "Ten days before the settlement conference, each party must file and serve a settlement conference statement," you enter a whole series of dates on your case calendar, like this: 10 days before the settlement conference, write "deadline for serving SC statement;" 15 days before settlement conference, write "deadline for mailing statement;" 30 days before settlement conference, write "begin writing SC statement." Find every deadline your local rules contain and calendar deadlines for serving by mail (which is easier), personal service (if it is too late to mail), filing with the court, and preparing the statement. Then look at your calendar, and do the tasks as early as you can. You are reducing the task from something impossibly huge like "Do Settlement Conference Statement and go to Settlement Conference" to something manageable, like "Start outline of statement on Wednesday."

1. How to do it

Your Settlement Conference Statement will be considered in detail by the judge and will also be used at trial. Many attorneys do this important document carelessly, but you won't, because you have been thinking about the facts in your case since chapter 6.

A different kind of fact. The purpose of the Statement is to summarize your entire case *at trial* in one document. It is based on *facts*, but presenting facts at trial is *very* different from the way it is done in a motion or OSC hearing. Instead of facts = documents + declarations, the rule now is that facts = documents + testimony. The testimony will be your own and that of whatever witnesses you can bring to court voluntarily or by subpoena. Each fact is a stone that you use to build your monumental statement. This is a very important opportunity to get the strength of your facts and your analysis of those facts in front of a judge. You are going to prepare an outstanding statement. Lawyers will come to you for advice.

Each county has its own requirements that will usually be clearly (if not exhaustively) defined in local rules, but here are is a general format with comments for you to consider for your own statement. Type up a caption like the one in Figure 22.2, except that the title of the document is "SETTLEMENT CONFERENCE STATEMENT," or whatever they call it in your county. Then do it like this:

I. INTRODUCTION

A. SUMMARY. The first paragraph should give the judge a summary of your basic perspective on the case, based on facts *(documents + witness testimony)* that you can prove. Be objective; do *not* be accusatory or critical. For example, "I am Petitioner, a woman who by mutual agreement did not work throughout a 30 year marriage, but rather stayed home and raised our three children. Now, Respondent doesn't want to pay reasonable spousal support and has abused me through misuse of the legal process." Or, "Respondent is the high income-earner in a short marriage of 3.2 years and Petitioner, who could be working at [or toward] a better wage, thinks she should be supported for over twice the length of the marriage." The idea is to let the judge know the gist of the case in one or two sentences. The introduction also needs to convey your view of the case in a way that has dramatic impact yet is based on facts you can prove. You don't want to be so plainly factual that you omit your point of view. Put your slant on things but be at least somewhat objective. Judges don't want emotionally loaded words and raw accusations. Seek balance. Avoid phrases that attribute to the other party desires, thoughts, or ideas. Instead, indicate how you feel about what the other side has said or done, or how that impacts you.

B. BACKGROUND and CHRONOLOGY. If your case is relatively simple, you don't need much more than dates of marriage and separation, children's birth dates, date the Petition was filed (and served if there was a delay between filing and serving), and what both parties do for a living or are capable of doing, including experience, education, training and past employment. If your case is complicated, go through all the major facts and arrange them in chronological order. Put the date on the far left and then in one very short sentence the event. If the case is very complicated, on the right you may also want to list a document that supports your position. This is an anchor the judge can use to keep from getting lost in a whirl of dates and facts. This is a convenient way for the judge to take in information.

Next, you deal with every single issue that has not already been decided. Organize it under categories like the ones suggested below. Put them in order of what's most important to you and, of course, omit any categories that are not in dispute.

II. CHILD CUSTODY and VISITATION

You need to explain your case to the judge in the same manner as discussed above: Introduction, chronology (if complicated at all), then discussion of the separate issues. If these issues were separated onto another track (as happens in some counties) and decided, and if they are relevant to any presently pending issues, give a thumbnail outline of any custody/visitation order, but make it clear that these issues are not presently pending for trial. In discussing child custody, always, always focus on the child's needs, not on your own. The standard followed by all judges is "best interest of the child." This means you have no interest. The parent's anguished cry of "I need more time with my child" will not move a judge. You need to explain why your child needs you and will benefit from more time with you.

III. CHILD and SPOUSAL SUPPORT

You need (1) a current Income and Expense Declaration of your own, with (2) your four most recent pay stubs, and (3) a computerized support printout. You get the printout by buying Nolo's CalSupport software, or call Divorce Helpline, or contact your local Family Court Facilitator, or a local divorce specialist attorney.

As to child support, if the judge accepts the data and options used in your computer calculation, the support reported will be ordered. Explain how you calculated the percentage of timeshare and how you arrived at the input data on the computerized support printout. As to spousal support, this is resolved on a case-by-case basis, not by any guideline amount. Family Code section 4320 contains a list of "factors" which the court *must* consider in setting spousal support. Discuss each of these factors (see *How to Do Your Own Divorce,* chapter 5). Tell the court why it should set a certain amount of support, whether it should be stepped up or down over time, and what should be the duration of spousal support. Finally, for any kind of support situation, discuss health insurance, life insurance, and any other types of benefits you want addressed. All temporary orders for insurance will be lost if not repeated in the Judgment.

IV. SEPARATE PROPERTY

Separate property is anything you had before marriage, earned after separation, or which you received as a gift or inheritance. Also, rent, interest or dividends received from separate property is separate. Sometimes you can retain separate property even if you added your spouse's name to the title. List every piece of separate property, and explain where it came from and why it is separate.

V. COMMUNITY PROPERTY

Under this heading, list A, B, C, etc. to address each significant item (or group of items) of community property, beginning with the most valuable and going down to the least. Don't list every single piece of furniture, but group smaller items into categories like "Tools," or "Furnishings," or, if you think it will help, you can attach documents or a separate list or set of lists of where each item is referred to as an "exhibit." Each item on your attached list should be clearly labeled as Exhibit A, B, C, etc. and identified in words—"copy of deed to family home," or "household furnishings." Use the Schedule of Assets and Debts form as a guide. Bring it with you.

VI. RESTRAINING ORDERS

Make sure you request the continuation of any existing orders that you want to keep effective over the next three years. Explain briefly the nature of your ex's conduct that required the initial protection. Don't assume that just because the court granted an initial restraining order, the judge will automatically repeat it now. Make your case. If your ex has violated orders, explain that. If you need more specific orders to try to control the conduct, explain that and state just what orders you want.

VII. ATTORNEY FEES and COSTS

There are two types of fee orders the court could make: (1) based on "need and ability," and (2) based on misconduct. Judges are much more inclined to make need-and-ability orders and less likely to sort things out enough to punish someone.

- The first type of order is based on each spouse's need for fees and respective ability to pay—basically an income test. However, keep in mind that even if one spouse earns much more than the other, after payment/receipt of support and taxes, the parties may be pretty much in an equal position. When judges make need-and-ability orders for fees, they sometimes take the approach that if one has, for example, 60% of the combined net spendable family income, that one should pay 60% of the total attorney fees. Therefore, that spouse will be ordered to pay only a part of the other's fees and costs on a need-and-ability basis.
- The second type of order is based on the other party's misconduct, which would have to be explained in detail. Additionally, judges want to know how much it cost you to fight the misconduct. For example, you might have paid $5,000 in attorney fees no matter what, but your total fees were $10,000, and you feel the extra $5,000 was caused by your ex's misconduct. You need to explain this in detail to the judge, not just accuse your ex in vague terms.

If your issues include support or attorney fees, you *must* attach a completed Income and Expense Declaration with any attachments required by local rule, such as pay stubs. It also is useful to attach a Schedule of Assets and Debts although you may not want to include account numbers in the copy filed with the court.

* * * *

The judge wants an overview, not 50 pages of homework. A judge once asked a lawyer why he wrote such a long brief, and the lawyer said, "I didn't have time to do a short one." Take the time to do a short one. Take out every word that is not absolutely necessary to the basic understanding of your case.

Include all claims. Include *all* claims that you are making, including even the ones that you expect to give up in the course of negotiations. The Settlement Conference Statement is not a settlement offer. It is a list of every single claim that you can reasonably assert at trial. If you leave out a claim, you lose it.

Attach appraisals and exams. If the division of property is an issue, and if there is no agreement on values, then any property of significant value should be appraised, or you should explain in your statement why you did not do this (for example, the other side would not cooperate and you didn't have time before trial to file a motion). You need to appraise everything from furniture to businesses to residences. Most counties require that appraisals and reports such as those of vocational examiners be attached to the Settlement Conference Statement. Failure to do so can result in the judge refusing to hear your evidence.

People often think they have an agreement on the value of property, but it isn't written. Then, when they come to the settlement conference, they find out that their spouse doesn't acknowledge the agreement. This can happen in any case where there is no written, signed agreement on values. Due to the high cost of appraisals, you might want to negotiate an agreement on the value of all or some of your property, assuming you can research its likely fair market value. An oral agreement is not enough; you need written agreements on values, signed by parties and counsel, or you need appraisals.

Trial of minor issues might not be allowed. The court may not permit you to go to trial about minor matters such as the family pet, or furniture, furnishings, appliances, etc. (These may not be minor to you emotionally, but the judge will regard them as such.) If minor matters are not agreed on by the end of the settlement conference, the court can send those issues to arbitration. The arbitrator will charge more than $200 per hour, and this could buy a lot of furniture. It makes sense to agree on these issues. On the other hand, you should not give all the furniture to your spouse just because your spouse will not agree to a fair division. It takes two to agree. You can't do it alone.

2. Serve the Settlement Conference Statement

You must serve the Settlement Conference Statement on your ex, or on his/her attorney if there is one. Check local rules to determine the deadlines. Attach the original proof of service to your original Statement and file it by the deadline.

Deadlines. It is very, very important to serve and file your Settlement Conference Statement on time, as established by local rule in each county. If you do not do so and you do not reach an agreement with your spouse, the judge can penalize you with a fine, refuse to let you go to trial as scheduled, or find that you have admitted matters that you did not want to admit. The importance of prompt service and filing of this statement cannot be overemphasized.

3. Prepare a proposed agreement?

You should prepare a proposed agreement to take to the Conference because you want it to be easy to settle; you want the other side to just "sign here" and it'll all be over. Bring many copies, double-spaced, so everyone can use it as an aid and to make the settlement discussion concrete and "doable." If it works, sometimes you can just write changes on that document, sign it, and get court approval. The judge could even have you go into court, testify to the jurisdictional facts of your case, and maybe sign the Judgment right there. As an alternative, you could bring a complete agreement on all issues and another agreement for things you can probably agree on, but reserving jurisdiction on difficult issues that you will need the court to decide. If you have your unrepresented spouse write any changes, this makes it harder to claim later that he/she didn't read it. Bring an extra clean copy to finalize neatly and sign.

D How to do a settlement conference

Be prepared to spend an entire half-day, or even a full day at the conference. Unless you already have an all-purpose judge, you might be assigned to a judge pro-tempore, who is almost always referred to as a "judge pro-tem," meaning a deputized lawyer serving as a temporary judge.

You will use the settlement conference as a good opportunity to settle your case according to the plan you've been working on since the beginning (chapter 6). If your settlement conference is in front of the judge who will hear the trial, then, even if you don't settle you can use this as an opportunity to make a good impression. You want to come across as very reasonable and ready to compromise, but also as firm and ready to fight if the other side won't follow law and reason.

Most conferences in judge's chambers. If the parties have lawyers, initially only the lawyers go talk to the judge. If a party does not have a lawyer, that party will talk to the judge. The parties do have to be present, but if there are one or two lawyers in the case, the judge will try to avoid the wear and tear of having direct contact with parties and will try to settle the case with lawyers only, if that will work. The conference usually occurs "in chambers"—the judge's personal office—rather than in the courtroom, but it can also be in a courtroom or a conference room in the courthouse.

How to present your case. The judge reviews the Settlement Conference Statements of both parties, then the parties (or their lawyers) and the judge discuss issues. Each party indicates that at trial, he/she would present certain evidence and there could be a debate as to how the law should be applied. For example, if there is an argument about support, your spouse could tell the judge about evidence that you have additional income and you could explain why you never had it or don't have it now that you're divorcing. The judge then lets the parties know how he/she would decide if the matter were to go to trial on the evidence just indicated. If the judge does this, there is not much point in going to trial unless you can get more evidence. Different judges tend to respond to cases in pretty much the same way, so even if you get a different judge, you would probably get the same result.

If you are not represented, you will present your own case. You should have your Settlement Conference Statement in your hand, and use it as an outline to present your case to the judge. Normally, it is best to begin with the biggest issue in the case and work down, just like we told you to do your statement. Be prepared to discuss the facts and law applying to your case. Basic divorce laws are discussed in Book 1, *How to Do Your Own Divorce,* Part One.

In your Settlement Conference Statement, you listed all the issues in your divorce and, if you knew of legal arguments about any of them, you discussed them there. If legal arguments arise at the Settlement Conference, you follow up what was said in your statement. If the legal issue is a complete surprise, you can (1) listen carefully to the judge or judge pro-tem and go with his/her opinion if it seems to make sense, (2) call an attorney who has previously been lined up to be available to give you legal advice on the spot, or (3) ask for a continuance to get more information and legal advice on the subject.

Possible penalty for not taking judge's advice. If there's no agreement, the judge might write his/her recommendations on a paper which will be placed in a sealed envelope and not viewed until after decision. Even if this trick is not used, whether the parties were reasonable in their positions will show in their Settlement Conference Statements. After trial, if it appears that one of the parties was unreasonable in not settling along lines suggested by the judge, that is, if one party did not achieve anything by insisting on a trial, then the trial judge can award attorney fees or sanctions due to that party's unreasonableness. For example, let's say that at the settlement conference the judge tells the parties that a certain amount of spousal support should be paid, but the husband refuses to agree. If the case goes to trial and the trial judge decides on a similar amount for spousal support, then that judge will probably make the husband pay the wife's attorney fees or part of them because of his unreasonable refusal to settle.

You need to give very serious consideration to the recommendation of the judge at the settlement conference. If he/she tells you something you don't like, don't ignore it; consider it very seriously, or you could end up paying if the judge was right.

E If you reach an agreement

If you reach an agreement at your settlement conference and you want to make sure it is binding and neither of you can back out, there are two ways to do this. You can ask to have the agreement recited on the record (a court reporter takes down every word), or ask to have it written down and signed by the judge after the parties have signed it.

If there appears to be an agreement, but you aren't sure it is what you really want, it is okay to ask for a brief recess so you can take a few minutes to think things over. It is also okay to say that you want to give it careful consideration and decide in a few days. On the other hand, if the other side is willing to agree and you delay your decision, they might change their mind later. A settlement conference requires a clear mind. You shouldn't let yourself get rushed into something you don't agree with because time runs out, but if you've reached a settlement you want, you should use this opportunity to make it final.

Judgment now? If you have a complete agreement on all issues, the judge may want to go on the record, detail the agreement, take testimony on the jurisdictional facts, and render a Judgment. To be prepared for this, bring with you a copy of chapter 20.3 of *How to Do Your Own Divorce,* so you will know what to say.

Pretrial orders? If the judge wants to do a judgment on the record, be sure to bring up the question of pretrial orders, if you had any and still want them to continue. Any orders made by the court before trial—whether as the result of an OSC, motion, or agreement (stipulation)—will cease to be effective if they are not restated in the Judgment (with the possible exception of domestic violence orders).

Prepare and present the Judgment. Once you leave court, one of the parties will have to prepare a Judgment exactly along the lines spoken by the judge, then present it for signature along with a Notice of Entry of Judgment and envelopes. Read about doing the Judgment in chapter 26.

Partial agreement. If you reach an agreement on some but not all issues, then you should ask to recite whatever agreement you reached in open court, or the judge will sign a written summary of your agreement. By getting it pinned down on the record, you will go to trial later only on issues that have not been resolved. Even if one party wants to insist on a "package deal" with all issues settling or none of them, the judge will usually resist going to trial on issues where there is no disagreement just because there is disagreement on other issues. But sometimes the judge will let someone demand a "package deal," so you will proceed to trial on all issues unless you have a complete agreement.

F After the conference

If you do not settle your case at the conference, you now have to study the local rules carefully to see what they want you to do before trial.

Many counties have a procedure with a deadline for giving the other side information about any expert witnesses you intend to use at trial. Some counties also require you to exchange information for nonexpert witnesses, so you have to list everyone you might even *possibly* call to testify.

Most counties require exchange of documents that will be used at trial. These deadlines are absolutely crucial to your case. If you miss a deadline, you could find yourself at trial with the judge prohibiting you from using witnesses or documents that were not listed, which, simply put, means you would lose.

So, the moral of this story is one you've heard before: study local rules and follow them!

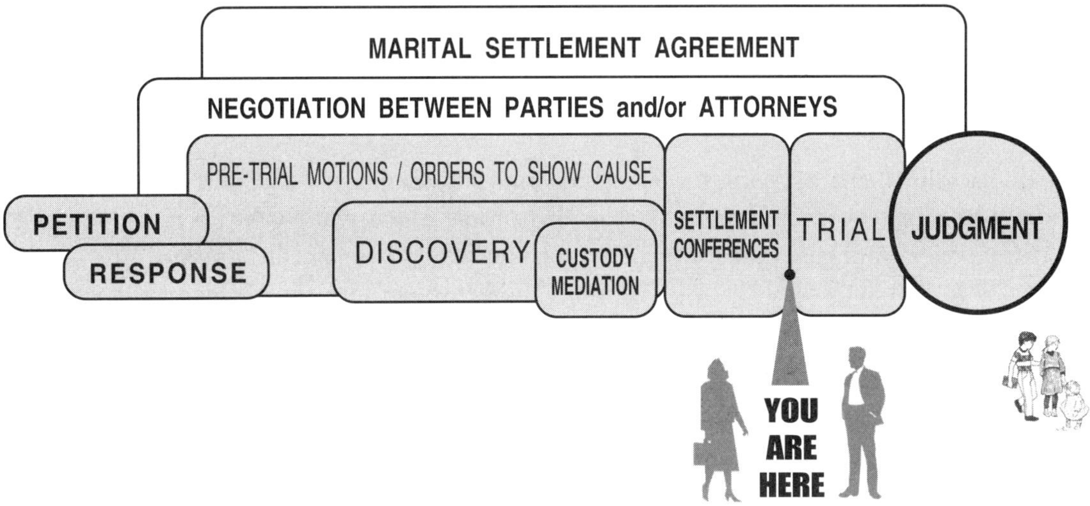

CHAPTER 24
MOTION TO POSTPONE THE TRIAL

A. Reasons to get your case postponed
B. Try to arrange an agreed continuance
C. Motion to continue trial and extend discovery

A Reasons to get your case postponed

In order to continue a trial, you must show "good cause," but with or without good cause, continuances are disfavored (California Rules of Court 375), so you will be swimming upstream if you try to have your trial continued. You will need to show the court a very good reason why you cannot proceed at the time scheduled.

Good reasons for a continuance

• **Unavailability of an essential witness.** If you have a crucial witness who cannot be available at the time of trial, this is a good reason to continue it. However, the mere fact that a witness says he/she is busy on the date of trial does not make him/her legally unavailable. If you could have subpoenaed the witness and neglected to do so, this would undermine your motion. On the other hand, if the witness was outside the United States at the time you received your trial date and has not yet returned, this would be a good reason to obtain a continuance.

• **Trial set too early.** If your opponent asked too early for the matter to be set on the trial calendar and you are within 45 days of trial, but declarations of disclosure have not yet been completed, the trial would need to be continued. If you had plenty of time to prepare, but you were just too upset to do it, this is not a reason that is likely to inspire a judge to continue your case. You must show that you have tried diligently and it was the other side that did things like delaying discovery, then a court might continue your trial.

• **Time to get an attorney.** Judges definitely prefer people to be represented. Keep notes of your efforts to get an attorney and be prepared to tell the judge who you called, date and time, and what they said. If the judge sees that you are really trying to get any good lawyer or a particular lawyer, this could help you get your continuance. On the other hand, if issues of domestic violence are involved and safety is an issue, the judge may want to hear that matter right away, with or without you being represented. The judge will not be happy to see you show up the next time without an attorney, so don't use this excuse unless you plan to follow through. Of course, you could ask for a continuance to *consult* an attorney, in which case show up later with proof that you did that and are now ready to proceed.

- **Prepaid vacations.** Often, people have prepaid vacations, then later get a court date that falls during their vacation. Most courts are sympathetic to this problem and won't want to make you lose your money. However, if your case puts forth the notion that you are financially strapped, the court could disapprove of your taking a very expensive vacation and deny your motion or remember it when you cry poverty at trial.

- **Family emergencies.** If you, your children, or a close relative are terribly ill, or there is a death in your family, you might get a continuance. However, as to the death, many judges seem not to understand how long it takes people to recover, so they might expect you back in action a week or two later.

- **Miscellaneous possibilities.** You had to move, or you have had serious health problems, or it is the busy season in your business and you have been required to work very long hours.

Reasons that might not fly

Sometimes you really want a continuance because you didn't prepare for the trial, but you can't use this as an excuse. Even if you try to conceal your true motive, the judge might figure it out and deny your continuance, especially if you float some lame excuses like:

- Didn't do the work on time.
- Upset, couldn't get started. However, if you were under a doctor's care or hospitalized for, say, depression, that might work.
- Don't want to be divorced.

Prove it if you can. If you have documentation to back up your reason—other than your own statement—attach it to your motion or take it to the appearance. For example, if you have a prepaid vacation, you need to attach copies of tickets or a statement to show the dates, payment, and the fact that it is not refundable. If you are required by your job to travel on the date of the hearing, you should get a letter from your employer and attach it.

The judge will also want to know how much time you need for a continuance—a week? Two? A month? More? Be prepared to say how much time you need and to justify why you are asking for a particular amount of time.

When making a motion, you need to present specific facts, not just make general assertions. For example, if you weren't able to prepare for the trial because your spouse stonewalled you and refused to give you information, you need to present facts to show the judge just how long it took to get essential information and how flimsy your spouse's excuses were. You should put all this into your declaration and attach letters and documents, perhaps a log of phone calls, to support your facts. Merely stating it as a conclusion is not sufficient.

Warning! Prepare as if your request will be denied

It is *always* possible that a judge will deny your request for a continuance, no matter how good your reasons. If you have the bad luck to make your motion when the court is on a campaign to clear up its calendar by being tough on continuances, your motion could be denied even though it otherwise would have been granted. It is absolutely imperative that while you make your motion to continue and wait for your hearing, you still prepare for trial on the assumption that your motion might be denied. You need to

(1) move to continue the trial and (2) serve subpoenas and prepare vigorously for trial in case you lose the motion. How to prepare for trial is discussed in the next chapter.

Reasons for continuing a hearing on OSC or motion

When it comes to a hearing on an OSC or motion, you can often get away with showing up at the hearing and making a verbal request to continue. Those hearings are different from a trial in that you get shorter notice, so it could be reasonable not to do a written motion. However, if you had notice of a hearing on a motion to take place many weeks in the future, it would be expected that you would file a written motion to continue. If the judge feels you waited too long to make your motion, you will be less likely to get your continuance. Reasons for continuing a hearing of an OSC or motion would be the same as those discussed above for continuing a trial.

B Try to arrange an agreed continuance

If both you and your spouse (or his/her attorney) agree to continue your hearing, settlement conference or trial to another date, the court will almost always permit it. However, judges sometimes take a harder line on trial and settlement conference dates. If both sides want to continue a trial, but the judge doesn't want to, the judge might take the case off-calendar entirely. Then you will have to file papers again (chapter 22) to get another trial date.

First call the clerk

You want your spouse to agree to a specific future date to which the matter will be continued, so first you have to find out what dates are available for the kind of appearance you want to reschedule. Phone or go down and talk to the court clerk to ask what length of continuance is possible and the shortest continuance you can get without specially going to court and getting the judge's permission. Now you are in a position to discuss a specific date with your spouse. Do it immediately, or the clerk's calendar might change.

Contact the other side

Phone your spouse (or his/her attorney if he/she has one) and explain why you think a later date would be more appropriate. Tell them the available dates you got from the clerk and agree on a specific date, or a range of agreeable dates, if possible. If your spouse has an attorney, you have to be careful not to let him/her pump you for information or get you to make statements that can be used against you later. Keep the discussion focused on the issue of the continuance. If your spouse has no attorney, you need to avoid getting into a screaming match. If that develops, politely say good-bye and switch to fax, email or mail.

You can also agree that the other side will arrange the continuance. If that happens, fax or email them a confirmation with dates that are acceptable to you. Find out if they will arrange the continuance by phone or in person at court on the day of the hearing. If it is done in court, it would be a good idea for you to be there to make sure the next date which is chosen is one that works for you. If they do it by phone, you should call the clerk to make sure it was done as agreed.

If the other side agrees

If you get your spouse (or his/her attorney) to agree to continue the appearance, be sure to ask for a fax or email confirmation of the agreement, with a letter to the same effect sent by mail. If they won't do this, send him/her a fax (or email if you know they regularly check email) confirming the agreement and ask him/her to reply if your communication does not state the arrangement correctly. Also mail the message and keep a copy.

Next you get the court to accept the agreed continuance. How you do this can vary in different counties. Phone the clerk, and ask if dates can be continued by phone. If so, get their okay for the date, and write a letter to the court clerk with a copy to your spouse confirming that the date is continued, stating the new time and date. If the clerk says that cases can only be continued by the judge, then you have to go to court on the date of the hearing. If you have an agreement with your spouse, the judge will probably go along, but always be prepared to go forward just in case the judge refuses.

Stipulated orders. In some cases, you will need to get an order in addition to the continuance. If you appear in court at the time set for the appearance, you can make your request orally; otherwise you will need to prepare a stipulated order (chapter 5), signed by the other side, that continues the hearing to another date and, if necessary, makes additional orders, such as:

- If there are restraining orders against your spouse, you need the judge to order them to stay in effect until the date of the next hearing.
- If it is a trial that is being postponed and you need the discovery date to be extended, you will need an order extending the cutoff date for discovery.

If the other side does not agree

If the other side refuses your request to continue, fax or courier them a letter that restates your request, with reasons, and state your understanding that they refused. Keep a copy and the receipt from the courier if you used one. This is so they can't later deny you made the request. If the first time you ask for a continuance is orally in court, sometimes the opposing party or opposing counsel will act as if this is a very inconvenient surprise. But if you have your confirming letter or fax, they probably won't try to pull this. If they do act surprised and inconvenienced, you can show your letter to the judge.

Trials. If your spouse does not want to continue a trial, you need to file a Notice of Motion to continue the trial, as shown below.

Hearings. If the other side does not agree to a continuance and you have time to file a motion, do it, probably with an order shortening time. Otherwise, you need to go to court at the appointed time. The best thing is to do both. When your case is called, you stand up and say "Present, Your Honor. I will be asking for a continuance." When the judge asks why, you need to be ready with two or three concise but convincing sentences that will make the judge think your request is reasonable. If you have any documentation to back up your statement, offer it. You must be ready to proceed as best you can in case the judge does not grant your continuance.

C Motion to continue trial and extend discovery

A motion to continue a trial should be made in writing as early as possible, just as soon as you know you'll need the continuance. If the judge feels you waited too long, that could work against you, especially if the other side has already got witnesses lined up and subpoenaed. The judge doesn't like to see the other side spend attorney fees, time and effort preparing for a trial that doesn't occur, so you might be asked to pay their fees if you have been slow. Don't delay.

Timing of motion. To be of maximum benefit, your motion to continue will have to be heard not only before the trial date, but also before the Settlement Conference Statement is due. If you prepare your motion to continue, and the court clerk cannot give you an early enough date (the latest possible date being the last day before the trial or hearing), you should immediately consult a family law specialist attorney to try to obtain the continuance for you.

Extending time for discovery

Discovery is automatically cut off 30 days before the date for your trial. Even if the judge orders your trial postponed, this does not mean that discovery is reopened. If the reason you need to continue the trial is that you are lacking essential information, in your motion you must also ask to reopen discovery. Explain why you have failed to obtain the information in a timely manner and convince the judge to give you more time. This is not easy. The judge is more likely to grant your motion if your spouse resisted discovery and yet asked the court for an early trial date than if you just were so upset that you couldn't do the work. All facts that support your need for a continuance, and your claim that you have diligently prepared your case, must be presented in your continuance motion. Judges don't like continuances. A lot of people ask for continuances just because they didn't do what they were supposed to do on time. You need to convince the judge that is not the situation in your case.

How to state your case

Whenever you do a motion, it is a good idea to orient the judge to the whole case. State when the Petition was filed, the length of the marriage, number of minor children, and give the judge a general idea of the major issues, what's at stake. Then explain the facts that support your motion, such as how you sent your spouse requests to produce and he/she refused or failed to produce, so you have had to begin sending out subpoenas for records, but there hasn't been enough time to complete discovery. The best thing is to attach copies of request letters and documents such as your request to produce and your spouse's evasive responses. Then you also summarize them at the hearing.

Do the motion

You need to find out from the court clerk when and in what department (courtroom) motions regarding trial dates are heard. Such calendar-related motions are often heard separately from other motions.

Do your motion exactly as described in chapter 12, filling out the forms as described there, but with the modifications shown below.

MOTION TO CONTINUE SETTLEMENT CONFERENCE, TRIAL, DISCOVERY CUTOFF

Notice of Motion:

In the caption, check the box for "Other," and type in "Continue Settlement Conference, Trial, discovery cutoff."

Application and Declaration:

Item 9, Other relief: Type in "Continue trial and settlement conference dates and reopen discovery."

Item 10, Facts: State facts that justify your request for continuance. Prepare and attach a declaration like the one in Figure 24.1.

Figure 24.1

DECLARATION RE MOTION TO CONTINUE SETTLEMENT CONFERENCE AND REOPEN DISCOVERY

Note: Pleadings should be double-spaced. This illustration was altered to save room.

Marriage of YOUR LAST NAME & SPOUSE LAST NAME

Case No. [Your case number]

DECLARATION IN SUPPORT OF MOTION TO CONTINUE SETTLEMENT CONFERENCE AND TRIAL DATES AND TO REOPEN DISCOVERY

The undersigned states:

I am petitioner herein.

This action began when I filed the Petition on [date]. It was served on Respondent on [date]. The Response was filed on [date]. On [date] Respondent filed an At-Issue Memorandum, and trial has been set to occur on [date], with mandatory settlement conference on [date].

This case is not ready for trial and cannot be ready for trial on the date set because of the following: [the following are example reasons]

[The At-Issue Memorandum was filed prematurely. The parties have not exchanged the Preliminary Declaration of Disclosure nor the Final Declaration of Disclosure.]

[I have been unable to afford an attorney, and Respondent has blocked every effort I have made to obtain discovery in this matter. For example, he/she refused to provide me with a copy of his/her income tax return for the years [state which years] in spite of my written request.]

[If there is anything else that has prevented you from preparing for trial, such as illness or work or problems with the children, state those facts here.]

If this matter is not continued, my rights will be severely prejudiced as I do not have access to the information necessary to document Respondent's income and our community property.

I request that this court continue the settlement conference and trial dates or remove the case from the trial calendar until discovery can be completed and until complete and documented Declarations of Disclosure have been exchanged, and that the court order that discovery be reopened.

Executed at [City], California, on [date].

I declare under penalty of perjury under the laws of the State of California that the foregoing is true and correct.

____
YOUR NAME, Petitioner

1

Declaration in Support of Motion to Continue Settlement Conference

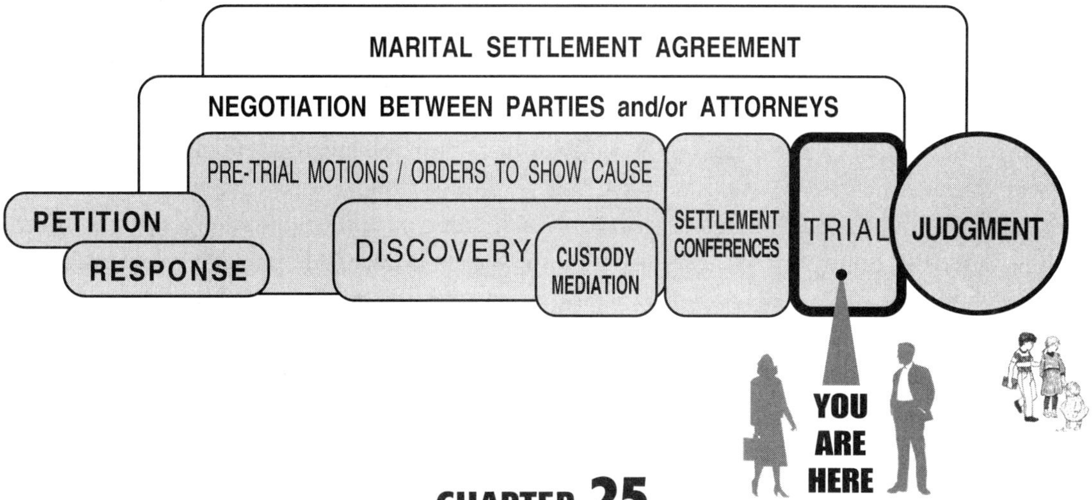

CHAPTER 25
GOING TO TRIAL

A. Preparing for trial
B. How to conduct a trial
C. How to be a good witness
D. Pretrial orders lost if not restated
E. At trial's end

A Preparing for trial

Subpoena witnesses. Will you need to subpoena witnesses or records to your trial? You will have to do this far in advance, at least 30 days. See chapter 15, section B.

Visit the court. Well before your trial, you should visit a courtroom to watch some trials, get familiar with how things work at your courthouse, how witnesses are examined, and how judges conduct trials, especially with unrepresented people. The trick is to figure out which court to watch. Counties differ as to how they assign judges to cases for trials. Some counties assign each case to one "all-purpose" judge who hears everything from first to last. Other counties have you show up at a "master calendar" department where cases are assigned to whichever courtrooms are available, if any. Ask the clerks to find out how things are done in your county and which judges hear family law cases. If your case might go to one of several family law judges, you have to pick one to watch or spend the time to watch them all.

Judges hear more OSCs than trials, so to see a trial you will ask a clerk what days and times the judge you want to watch has trials. So many trials settle at the last minute that often when trials are scheduled, the judge is not doing a trial but is in chambers doing something else like reviewing new OSCs. It can be difficult to find your judge actually doing a trial. Assuming you locate your judge in trial, see how much time is allowed for trials. Listen carefully to anything the judge tells the people who are in trial about how he/she likes the evidence to be presented.

Make a trial outline. Use your settlement conference or pretrial statement to organize your case and the documents in it. If you didn't prepare one, study chapter 23, section C now and prepare at least the outline of a Settlement Conference Statement. Use the headings as your trial outline. Go over each heading and make a list of documents and verbal testimony you will present for each fact involved in each issue that has not settled. Unlike pretrial hearings, every witness must be present in court to testify. As you proceed through trial, check off each document and each item of testimony as it comes out. No matter what interruptions or digressions come up, always come back to your trial outline and pick up where you left off. This is how you make sure you don't forget something important.

Organize documents and witnesses. So far, you have probably been organizing your case chronologically in various file folders, such as court papers, correspondence, discovery, and other. Now, to prepare for trial, create a witness-based organization by making one file folder for each witness. Start with yourself—your most important witness—then do the others. Make a file for each witness for the other side. Many counties require parties to give each other witness lists before trial and perhaps even require offers of proof for each witness. You should study your spouse's Settlement Conference Statement very carefully to see if it refers to any witnesses and consider anyone you know who might be able to testify for your spouse about each issue in your case.

Each of your witness folders will contain a list of questions you are going to ask this witness and your own folder will have a list of facts you want to testify about. For the other side's witnesses, you can probably anticipate most of what they will say and plan questions you will ask when it's your turn to cross-examine. You should have your questions typed and double-spaced so you can add to your list of questions when you take notes as they testify.

Documents. In addition to your questions, you will also organize the documents you are going to use. Each witness' file will have whatever documents you expect that witness to testify about, if any. Every time you are going to introduce a document or other piece of evidence, you underline that moment in your questions (or your script if it is your own testimony). When you come to the underlined place, you will be able to locate the document easily, as you will have the exhibits under your typed questions in the order in which they are referred to. You should have an original plus two copies of every document, or three if a child has an attorney. Keep all documents in their files and bring them to court.

Think about each witness; why are they being called; what they might say. If you can anticipate some legal issue that could come up when a particular witness testifies (such as an objection about hearsay), if you have any legal authority—say, that a lawyer-coach might have given you (copies of statutes, cases, etc.)—put that into the witness' file. If you obtained documents from a witness, make two or three copies and put them in the witness' file, original on top, where you can easily find them when the time comes to introduce them at trial.

Put the folders for your own witnesses in the order in which you expect to call them. You can't be certain of the exact order in which witnesses will be called if there are more than a few. Even your own witnesses can be late, busy or unavailable, so you might have to change the order in which you planned to present them. However, you'll have each witness' information in a separate folder, so you just grab the folder of whatever witness comes up.

When you use this method of organization, you reduce your job from the impossibly huge task of "go to trial" to the more manageable task of "create a folder for each witness and put them in order." This way, when you actually get to trial, all you have to do is go through the folders and do what's called for in each one. This will reduce your anxiety and improve your presentation.

Make a Trial Folder. Let it have a distinctive but unassuming cover. No one will know that this is your master plan. It should contain:

- Your trial outline (see above).
- Your and your opponent's trial briefs, if any.
- Preliminary matters that you want to take up at the very beginning. For example, a request to exclude witnesses (see below).

- Anything else that needs to be addressed at the beginning. For example, you might have an expert witness who is available only at a certain time, and you want permission to call that expert early and out of order, maybe in the middle of your spouse's case.
- A list of issues. This is a recapitulation of the major and minor headings in your Settlement Conference Statement that have not been settled.
- Your opening statement to the court about what you will prove in your case (section B, below). As there is no jury, the judges prefer that such statements be kept quite short.
- Your closing statement (section B, below).

This folder is your master guide at trial. All you have to do is make your opening statement, go through the witnesses' folders, examining your witnesses and cross-examining the other side's witnesses, then you make your closing statement and you're done. If you stay businesslike and only appropriately emotional (enough so the judge will know you really care and not so much that the judge thinks you're nuts), you can do it.

Link trial outline and witness folders. Look at your trial outline, and review all the witness folders. Make sure that at least one witness (possibly more than one) will testify on every single fact involved in each issue. This is the purpose of your outline—to make sure that you have facts in evidence to support every issue. Making a good trial outline of issues and linking them to everything in the witness files should keep you from letting anything drop through the cracks.

Lists of evidence. Prepare a list of all documents or other items you plan to introduce. On the left, write the name or other identification of each document, photo or thing. On the right, make two columns: "Identification" and "In evidence." At trial, when a document is first introduced, it will be given a letter or number (marked for identification) by the clerk, and you enter it in the "Identification" column. After the item has been identified and testified to by a witness, you ask to have it admitted into evidence. If it is admitted, you check the "In evidence" column. Now, make a similar form, in blank, to fill in at trial to keep track of all evidence presented by the other side. This way, you can easily keep track of all documents in the case and know at a glance whether or not each one has been admitted into evidence by the judge.

How to prepare witnesses. Make copies of section C, how to be a good witness, and give one to each witness. Be sure to tell them not to bring it into the courtroom. Before trial, you need to meet personally with each witness and discuss the questions you plan to ask and listen to the answers they give. It is very common for two people to remember one event quite differently, or your witness might have forgotten the event, which possibly was not as important to them as it is to you. Going over their testimony can help them remember. You want this refreshing of their recollection to occur when you talk informally, not in a courtroom. If you are going to show the witness any document in court, show them a copy in advance. You must be honorable and correct in what you say in conversations with witnesses because the other side is likely to inquire about this in court. When they cross-examine your witness and ask if you told them what to say and how to say it, you want the witness to be able to answer truthfully "No, he/she just helped me refresh my memory of these facts."

Assistants and support persons. You can bring a support person to sit with you at trial to help you emotionally and legally. Emotionally, his/her job is to help you stay calm and confident and to remember to keep your voice from being shrill or becoming angry. Legally, he/she can help keep track of papers, but this means he/she would have to have been involved in helping you prepare your case, or at least study your trial folders with you in order to be familiar with their contents. Then, if you can't see a paper that is right in front of you, but you're too distracted to see it, your support person could hand it to you. If you have a person who is supportive of you but very angry with your spouse, don't use him/her as a support person in court. Get someone who can stay calm and objective.

Exclusion of witnesses. If you want to make sure your spouse's witnesses won't sit there and watch each other and lie accordingly, put a note in your Trial Folder to ask the judge to exclude all witnesses from the courtroom. This must be raised right at the beginning, before the trial actually begins. If you have a support person to assist you at trial and give you moral support, but they will also be called as a witness, then you either give up the idea of excluding all witnesses or find another support person.

B How to conduct a trial

The trial is the time to present your witnesses, including your own testimony, and present documents that will be identified and verified by those witnesses.

No jury. In a divorce trial there is no jury. The judge makes all decisions.

Should you accept a judge pro-tem? When your case is called for trial, you might be asked if you will accept a judge pro-tempore, or "judge pro-tem." Lawyers never say "yes" to that question without knowing who the specific judge pro-tem is and being sure that he/she is a fair-minded person. As a nonlawyer, it will be difficult for you to know this, which is one of the benefits of having a lawyer. If you do not have a lawyer, you have to make the decision blindly whether to accept or reject the judge pro-tem. Rejecting a judge pro-tem could result in delay of your trial. If you know and like your judge, you can refuse the judge pro-tem. If you dislike your judge, you can take your chances with a judge pro-tem. If you don't know the pro-tem and are neutral towards your judge and you want to stall, refuse the judge pro-tem. If you want to hurry up and get to trial, accept the judge pro-tem.

If no courtroom is available. At the time and date set for trial, it sometimes happens that there is no courtroom available for the case, so it might be necessary to wait anywhere from an hour to several days, weeks or even months for a courtroom. You need to be prepared to begin immediately, but you also need to be prepared for the possibility that your case will be continued. This is why you have had all your subpoenaed witnesses sign the agreement to appear on phone notice (Figure 15.4). When trial of your case actually begins, you, or preferably a support person, will phone the witnesses and tell them to come to court. You must have arranged this with them beforehand, and you must be very sure they will come promptly and that they know that the judge might issue a bench warrant for them if they don't show up.

Call the day before. On the day before trial, you can phone the clerk in the courtroom to which your case is assigned, or the master calendar clerk, and ask whether cases set for trial are actually getting courtrooms on the next day. They might sigh and say, "Nothing is getting out." That means that there are a lot of cases showing up ready for trial, but all courtrooms are full and everything is getting postponed by the court. Or they may indicate that they are not sure. Of course, you can never rely on a clerk telling you that there will not be a courtroom, but it is some indication. If you are almost 100% sure that your case will *not* go to trial, you should put your witnesses on phone-call standby. If you are almost 100% sure your case will go to trial, confirm with all your witnesses by phone the time they should come to the courthouse. Do this even if you aren't quite sure. You can let them know how likely it is that they will end up testifying on this date.

Bring your checkbook. You might need to write a check on the spot to the court reporter for a transcript or to the clerk. If your trial lasts more than a half day, the court clerk can ask you to pay for the use of the courtroom. These fees are about $200 for a half day and $400 for a full day. If you think this might happen and you can't afford the fee for daily use of the courtroom, you should file a fee waiver form in advance (see *How to Do Your Own Divorce,* chapter 7 and that book's companion CD for forms). You will find that this waiver is only available to people who are *very* poor.

The trial begins

Who testifies at trial. In most divorce cases, only the husband and wife testify, although you are entitled to present any witnesses who have relevant information. If custody/visitation is an issue, the court's evaluator can testify and either party can present an opposing expert or other witnesses. If the value of property is an issue, experts such as real estate appraisers, actuaries for pensions, and business appraisers for businesses can testify regarding values. Anyone with relevant information, including a child, may testify, but a judge can refuse to permit a child to be involved.

Petitioner goes first. First the petitioner presents his/her case. The judge can decide to take witnesses in a different order, but is not likely to do so unless there are unusual circumstances, such as an out-of-town expert who needs to be called early or late. After each witness finishes his/her testimony, the other party or lawyer will be allowed to question or "cross-examine" that witness, then back to the first side for any necessary clarification of new points raised. Once all of petitioner's evidence has been presented, the respondent will be permitted to present all of his/her witnesses, followed by cross-examination by petitioner or petitioner's attorney. After that, the petitioner can present rebuttal evidence, if any, to try to counter whatever respondent presented, then the respondent can present rebuttal evidence. However, it is not proper on rebuttal to repeat what you already presented or go into any new matters that were not presented in the other party's case. The purpose of rebuttal is to respond to evidence the other just raised.

Anatomy of a trial

- **Opening statements.** This is a brief statement of the facts you are going to prove. Do not argue. Just state the facts in a very brief, objective but compelling story of your case.
- **Petitioner's case.** Petitioner presents witnesses, including him/her self. After each witness testifies, Respondent gets to cross-examine (ask questions), but only on subjects testified to by the witness on direct examination. After cross, Petitioner can ask questions on new subjects raised on cross-examination. Petitioner rests, case over.
- **Respondent's case.** Respondent presents witnesses, Petitioner cross-examines, Respondent can do recross if there's anything new raised on cross.
- **Rebuttal.** Petitioner puts on witnesses or introduces evidence to oppose new points made by Respondent that were not addressed by petitioner's original evidence. Respondent can cross-examine. It is not proper to repeat what you already presented or go into any new matters that were not presented in the other party's case.
- **Closing statements (argument).** Each party gets a chance to sum up their case and argue their point of view based on all evidence and law. This is the time to discuss the facts you've proved and how the law applies to them. You cannot argue facts on which no evidence was introduced and admitted.

Opening statements. When the judge indicates that you can start your case, ask if you can present an opening statement. If the judge has read your Settlement Conference Statement, he/she will probably not want one. If the judge tells you to go ahead, you should very briefly explain the basic issues that the judge will be asked to decide in your case and what you intend to prove about each one.

Your testimony. Each case is different, so we can't tell you what to say at trial, but it is very important for you to prepare ahead of time a clear, typed outline of what you want to say and take it with you to use as a checklist when you testify. Nervous people often talk too fast. Do not do that, as it will undermine your presentation. If what you are saying is important, you need to say it as if it is important—slowly and with emphasis. If the court reporter or judge repeatedly tells you to slow down, that's a pretty good clue that you should take a deep breath and slow down.

Issues with partial agreement. Sometimes parties agree on some of the facts in an issue, such as the value of the home, and only disagree, for example, as to whether it should be sold or one party be allowed to continue living in it. If this kind of situation arises, when the matter first comes up, you should stand up and state to the judge what facts both parties agree on and get the other side to state out loud that he/she agrees, too. Also state what the issues are that remain to be decided. Then you proceed to present evidence on matters on which there is no agreement.

Objection, sustained, overruled. In trial, someone might ask a question that is legally objectionable, not proper. When that occurs, it is appropriate to say, "I object." However, the person who is objecting is supposed to state the legal basis of the objection, such as, "I object, hearsay" or "I object, irrelevant." The judge might ask the party who objects to say why he/she thinks the question is improper, then the other side can say why it is proper. When an objection is made, the witness should not answer the question but should wait until the judge indicates whether or not the question is proper. After every objection, the judge should say that the objection is either "sustained" or "overruled." "Sustained" means that the objection is good and the witness should not answer. "Overruled" means the objection is not good and the witness should answer the question. After all this, the witness might be confused. At any time, if the witness is confused or doesn't understand the question, the witness should simply say, "I don't understand the question," or "Could you please repeat the question?" You can ask the court reporter to "read back the question." That way, if it was a good question that withstood an objection, you don't have to think it up all over again. Sometimes a judge will not rule out loud on an objection. If you want a clear record, you have to say, very politely, "Your Honor, for the record, I'd appreciate a ruling on my objection."

If an objection is sustained, you must either drop it or try to rephrase it to avoid the objection. For example, if the objection is that the question was compound, you could try to break it down into smaller parts. Or if the objection was "assumes a fact not in evidence," you can try to ask foundation questions about facts that were not earlier in evidence, then ask your question based on those facts.

No hearsay allowed (if there's an objection to it). Generally, a witness cannot talk about anything he/she did not personally see or hear. Among other things, this means they usually can't say what someone else said. It also means that you can't present a letter or declaration at the trial in place of live testimony. You can present a bill to show the amount of the bill, but you can't present letters. The difference is that the bill is not asserting a "fact." The bill itself is the fact. The letter that states facts is hearsay. Not even a notarized statement under penalty of perjury will be allowed if your spouse objects. If the other party tries to submit letters or declarations or even police/hospital reports, you need to object that these are hearsay. However, there are many exceptions to the hearsay rule, and the judge might accept certain types of hearsay such as a confession or admission against the declarant's interest.

Two common examples of hearsay are medical reports and police reports. If you want to introduce into evidence medical matters or facts that occurred when the police were called, you must have the doctor or law-enforcement person present in court to testify. What they wrote down at some other time is hearsay and such an objection will be sustained. You need the actual, live witness present in court, not just the report, record, letter, or notarized statement.

Entering a document into evidence. You can't simply bring letters or declarations from other people. If you want the court to know what someone has to say, you must bring that person to the trial. Hearsay is when the document is offered to prove the truth of the facts stated in the letter. But if the letter is not offered to show that what it says is true but only to explain the state of mind of, say, the person who received the letter, then it is not hearsay. You can overcome the hearsay objection by saying "I'm not offering it for the truth of the matter asserted," but then the writing must be relevant to something else, like a party's state of mind.

How to introduce a document into evidence. When you want to have the judge consider a writing, you must introduce it into evidence. You do that when you are testifying or one of your witnesses is testifying. You say, "I'd like to have a document marked for identification." Then you hand copies to the attorney for your spouse and the attorney for the child, if the child has an attorney. You give the original to the court clerk, keeping a copy for yourself. The clerk will mark the original "Exhibit X," whatever is next in order. Now go to the **evidence list** we told you to make in section A and note that this document is now Exhibit X. After a document is marked for identification, you have testimony about it. Ask your witness, "Can you tell me what Exhibit X is?" and have them describe what it is, where it comes from and what it says. If you are the witness, just explain it to the judge, such as "This is a copy of my spouse's checking account on the date of separation." Then you say, "I'd like to move Exhibit X into evidence." If the other party objects, you both tell the judge your positions and the judge decides. Some judges are lax and will simply listen and not state a ruling. If you need the evidence, you must push the judge for a ruling. When a document is admitted into evidence, go to your evidence list and put a check in the "In Evidence" column.

When you are done. At the end of your case, be sure to say, "I'd like to have admitted into evidence any of my exhibits that have not yet been admitted." Generally this will cause the judge to check with the clerk as to whether everything is in evidence (the judge isn't supposed to look at it if it is not in evidence). Any objections the other side has to your evidence will be discussed and the judge will decide what goes into evidence and what does not. If the judge fails to rule on any piece of evidence, you must ask whether it is in evidence or not so you end up with a clear record.

Closing statements. When both sides have finished their cases, ask if the judge will permit a closing argument. The judge will probably have most of the points in mind so will want only brief argument, if any, particularly if they are experienced in family law. On the other hand, if you had evidence whose relevance is not easily apparent, you might want to comment on what it shows. Don't let yourself be pressured to talk too fast and skip over things if you think the judge didn't pick them up the first time around.

Restatement of existing orders. If you have existing orders from an OSC or motion, they will be lost when the Judgment is entered (section D). If you want any of them to continue, you *must* ask the judge to do so at the end of your case.

C How to be a good witness

Ensure the truth is clearly told. When you testify in court, of course you will tell the truth in simple, clear terms. Don't memorize your testimony or it will seem artificial, but do think carefully ahead of time about what you are going to say so you don't stumble and seem vague or uncertain. Do not ramble around, but stick very closely to the exact question asked or the point being made.

The dual role of lawyer and party is difficult. You're trying to represent aggressively but this might be contrary to the image of yourself as a parent that you are trying to project. You might want to say to the judge, "Your Honor, while I'm the petitioner/respondent in this lawsuit, I would like the court to take notice that I am also my own attorney, due to financial necessity. As my own attorney, I am attempting to represent myself as an attorney would represent me, which may reflect more aggressive behavior than I would normally show in day-to-day circumstances. I trust the court will understand that my behavior here is different from my behavior with my children."

It is difficult for anyone to handle highly emotional issues and remain calm. In representing yourself you need to avoid becoming angry, excited, frightened, or intimidated. You need to stay calm. Get plenty of sleep the night before court and be sure to eat breakfast and lunch on court days. Even if you don't feel like eating, just regard the food as medicine and take it. You won't run well on empty. Tell yourself over and over how calm you are going to be. If you are in court and you find yourself responding emotionally, you need to take a deep breath. Sometimes your mind can start racing, spewing out ideas, questions, fears, all at once. That's a good time to take a deep breath and tell yourself to be calm. Just focus on what is going on. At times like this, you'll be glad if you have a good support person at the table with you.

How to answer questions. Answer questions very directly and very simply. Answer only the question asked and do not expand. The best answer starts with a "yes" or a "no" (if the question can be answered "yes" or "no"), and then has one to three sentences of explanation. For example, "Yes, we have three children." "Yes, we put a down payment on the home. My parents loaned $20,000 just to me and that entire amount was used for the down payment."

Listen to the question. Listen carefully to the question that is asked and answer only what is asked. This is particularly true when it is the judge who asks the question. Don't ramble. You can explain your answer, but answer only the specific question asked.

Do not worry about looking stupid. Do not worry about whether you look stupid, or good or bad. Just tell the truth; always tell the truth. Do not try to answer when you are not sure; just say, "I'm not sure." For example, if an attorney says to you in an indignant and shocked manner, "Didn't you read that before you signed it?" If you did not read it before signing it, just say "no." Do not let the attorney's manner bully you into an incorrect answer. Do not let your fear of looking stupid push you into making up answers.

No guesses. Do not guess. If your answer is an estimate or only an approximation, say so. It is okay to say you are making an estimate, but you should not just guess at an answer.

It is okay not to remember. If you do not remember something, say, "I don't remember." This is *very* important. If you are asked about doing something and you do not specifically remember what you did, say so. You can offer to testify as to your usual practices and tell the court this is what you are doing: "I don't remember what I did on February 27, but usually I go straight home from work, arriving about 6 p.m."

It is okay to talk to people about your case. If you are asked who you discussed your case with, be honest and tell the court who you talked to. On the other hand, discussions with an attorney are privileged and confidential, so while you can say you talked to an attorney, you should *never* reveal what was said by you or by the attorney.

State only what you personally saw or heard. In court if you are asked if you "know" something, this usually means you are being asked whether you personally saw or heard something. If your answer is based solely on what someone told you, say so. In everyday life people feel they "know" things that others have told them, but in court this is not acceptable.

Be careful of questions with "all" or "none." In court, if a question has the word "all" or "none," you need to understand that this does not mean "almost all" or "hardly any." "All" means absolutely every single one with no exceptions, and "none" means not even one. Be very careful about such questions. When asked "Is that all?" you may want to say "That is all that I can think of right now." Do not say "That's all he said," or "Nothing else occurred." You might remember more later.

Do not guess about lawyer's motives. Do not try to guess why you are being asked each question. Just focus on giving truthful answers. This is the best way to respond to tricky questions—with truth.

Miscellaneous guidelines

- Do not put your hand over your mouth while you testify.
- Do not chew gum.
- Do not allow yourself to get angry while on the stand, no matter how insulting the questions may be. Some lawyers purposely make witnesses angry because then they cannot think as well and are likely to make mistakes. This is especially important—and difficult—for people representing themselves, because the whole subject is so emotional and the court experience is overwhelming. This is one good reason for having a support person with you at the trial—a friendly face to look at and give you confidence or to give you a look that says, "Cool it."
- Do not memorize your testimony. You should have a checklist with you so you present your testimony in an orderly fashion and don't leave anything out. Under it, you will have an original plus two copies of every document you need, in the order in which you need them.
- Do not argue with the other party.
- Address all your remarks to the judge, not to your spouse or spouse's attorney. The only time you will talk to your spouse is when you cross-examine him/her.
- Never discuss the case in any way in courthouse hallways, rest rooms or elevators. That nice lady near you may be your spouse's lawyer's secretary or investigator.
- Be very careful not to allow your opponent to peek at your papers. Be aware of this when you stand in an elevator, talk to your opponent while holding a file, sit in the audience waiting for your case to be called, sit at the table in the courtroom, wherever. If you have notes or papers, unless you are reviewing them or presenting your case to the court, turn the papers over so they can't be seen. Don't leave them facing up on the counsel table or anywhere else that is not private.

How to dress for court. Make sure your clothing is neat, clean, and does not make much of a fashion statement. Dress as you would for an important business appointment or for church, unless you are being asked to pay support, in which case you will want to dress down a little. Do not wear anything sexy. A woman in court should keep makeup to a minimum and never wear anything tight or low-cut. You need to wear quiet colors, specifically not red, and solid colors are better than strong patterns.

Don't bicker at trial. Never argue with your spouse in front of the judge. Arguing will only make both of you look bad. Address all of your comments to the judge, not to your spouse, unless it is your turn to question your spouse on the stand.

Don't forget issues. Use your Settlement Conference Statement to make sure that none of your issues is overlooked. Put every issue in your Trial Outline and check each one off as it is covered to your satisfaction. You need to be sure to present evidence, consisting at least of your own verbal testimony, on every single one of your issues.

D Pretrial orders lost if not restated

Any orders made by the court before trial—whether as the result of an OSC, motion, or agreement (stipulation)—will expire when your Judgment is entered (with the possible exception of a domestic violence order). If you want any of those orders to continue, you *must* request that they be made a part of the Judgment. For example, if there was previously an order that your spouse pay for health insurance for you and the children, if you do not restate that order in the Judgment, it is lost. If a party failed to make payments under a temporary order and accrued an arrearage, the arrearage would still be due, but it is best to specify the amount of arrearages in the Judgment.

E At trial's end

The judge might verbally announce the decision at the end of the trial, or the judge can "take the matter under submission." When the judge takes the matter under submission, this means the judge is going to think about the decision for awhile and maybe do some legal research on the issues, then he/she will issue a written decision later. The judge is required to decide the case within 90 days after the end of the trial.

Make sure the verbal decision is complete. If the judge states the decision immediately in court, have pen and paper in hand and write down in detail everything that is said. Use your Trial Outline as a checklist to be sure the judge has covered every single thing that is important to you. If something was not clearly decided, respectfully request the judge to give you a decision on that issue. Once the judge steps down or calls the next matter, you've lost your chance so, if necessary, ask the judge to give you a minute to look at your notes and don't be afraid to ask for clarification or a repeat of some point.

Restatement of existing orders. If you asked the judge to continue any existing orders, make sure they are included in the verbal decision. If not, you have to remind the judge to cover them.

DV restraining orders. If you obtained domestic violence restraining orders before the Judgment, examine the DV-130 order form at item 4 to see when they expire. If you need to have them extended, you can ask to have similar orders included in your Judgment.

Transcript? If you missed some detail of the decision, go up to the court reporter, ask for his/her card and say you need a transcript (or videotape if trial was filmed) of the decision. If your opponent is the type who argues over everything, you will undoubtedly have a struggle about the wording of the Judgment, so order a transcript of the judgment now. Don't order a transcript of the full trial. Tell the reporter you only need a "partial" transcript, only the judge's order. You'll have to pay, of course. The reporter will tell you how much.

Never leave without the reporter's business card. This is important, because the reporter, no one else, keeps the official transcript. If you need one later, you must be able to find this person without having to conduct a search. Get the business card.

Take your things. Don't get flustered and forget to take your papers and things with you when you leave the courtroom. There are probably a lot of things in your file that the other side would love to get a look at.

Go on to chapter 26 and learn how to get your judgment.

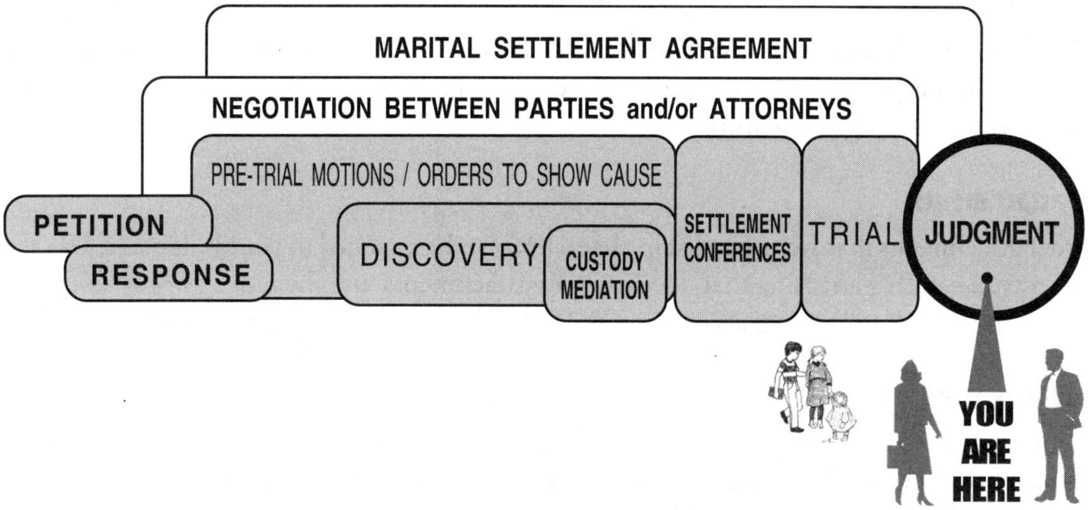

CHAPTER 26
GETTING YOUR JUDGMENT

A. How to get your Judgment
B. How to serve your Judgment

This is the end of the long road you have traveled. Your Judgment will resolve all property, support and child-related issues and, if necessary, include protective orders to keep the peace. Unless there is a timely appeal (or someone lied on their disclosure forms), the orders are final. However, orders on custody, visitation and support can be modified later if circumstances change in a legally significant way.

A How to get your Judgment

Who prepares the Judgment? If the judge doesn't do it, one of the parties has to. In some counties, local rules resolve who does it, so look there. Our suggestion is that if you want the Judgment, *you* prepare it, and do it as soon after trial as possible, preferably starting that same day.

Written decisions. At the end of your trial, the judge will either announce a decision verbally from the bench or send a written decision later. If the judge does not also send a signed order, you need to make one based exactly on the judge's decision. Only orders go into a Judgment, not the judge's findings or reasoning. For example, on the issue of spousal support a judge could discuss the parties' ages, health, education, job histories, incomes and expenses, length of the marriage, etc. None of that goes in the Judgment. What goes in the Judgment is what the parties get or must do, such as, "As and for spousal support, X shall pay to Y $_____ per month on the first day of each month, beginning on (date) and continuing until death of either party, remarriage of the payee or further order of the court," and so on.

Verbal decisions. If the judge announces the decision verbally, wait for a chance to go up to the court reporter and order a transcript of the decision. Tell the reporter you only want a "partial transcript" that includes the judge's orders, not the entire trial. You will probably have to give a down payment right there, so have your checkbook ready. Ask when the transcript will be ready and whether it can be mailed or if you should pick it up. If the latter, ask where you go to get it and when. Make sure you get the reporter's business card. While some court reporters are very good at promptly preparing transcripts, others are not and will require nagging. Immediately after this, sit down and go over the notes you took on the decision. Clean them up and add as much detail as you can. When you get home, start drafting your Judgment. Don't wait, even if you intend to use a transcript to make sure of the exact words. You can check the transcript later to be sure you got it exactly right. Now you are ready to take your Judgment back to court for the Judge's signature.

Order attachments

The order attachments that were detailed in chapter 16 can be attached to your Judgment. Use as many of them as you can. For anything that doesn't fit the attachments, use the judge's words as a guide and look at the useful Judgment language in chapter 18, Book 1, *How to Do Your Own Divorce.*

Approval by your spouse

Some counties require you to get your spouse (or spouse's attorney of record) to sign off on the Judgment, stating that it correctly reflects the judge's orders. Check local rules. Signing the Judgment is not an indication that the other side agrees with the decision, just as you don't necessarily agree with everything, even though you prepared the Judgment—it just means the Judgment correctly states what the judge ordered. If your local rules require the other side's approval, put the language below at the end of all orders, immediately above the Judge's signature line, which you might have to move to the end of your Further Orders.

I approve the above Judgment as to form and content:

Dated: ______________________________

Spouse Name

Your spouse must sign before you present the Judgment for the judge's signature. If your spouse is not represented, some counties will want his/her signature to be notarized. If you have trouble getting your spouse to sign, follow the same procedures discussed in chapter 16.

Notice of Entry of Judgment

Even after it is signed, the Judgment does not take effect until it is entered by the clerk. The clerk then mails notice that this has been done to both sides. To this end, when you present your Judgment for signature, you must also include the Notice of Entry of Judgment and two stamped envelopes addressed to you and the other side, as described in Book 1, *How to Do Your Own Divorce,* chapter 21.

B How to serve your Judgment

If your spouse attended the trial in person, you indicate this on the face of the Judgment and you don't need to serve him/her with a copy the Judgment. However, if your spouse did *not* attend the trial, you *must* have a copy of the Judgment served *personally* on him/her after it has been signed by the judge and entered by the clerk. Personal service and the Proof of Personal Service are discussed in Book 1, *How to Do Your Own Divorce,* chapters 12 and 13, and also see chapter 18.5.

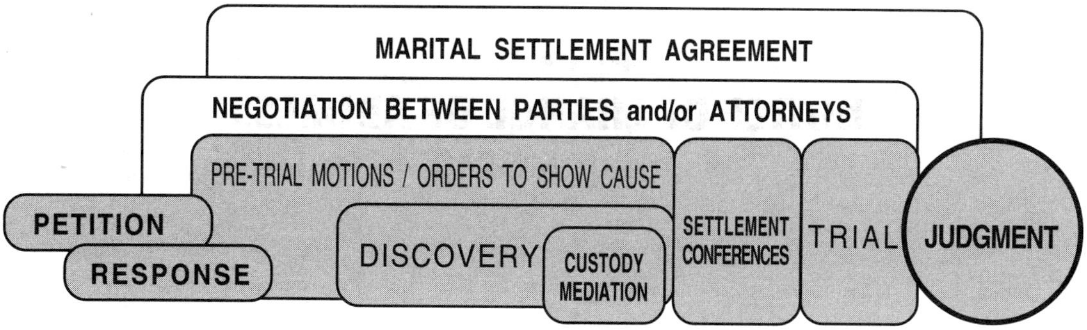

CHAPTER 27
AFTER THE JUDGMENT

A. You *must* keep your address current
B. Keep track of payor's or recipient's income
C. Always make changes official
D. Modify orders if circumstances change
E. Enforce your judgment
F. Restoring your former name
G. Moving away with the kids

Now that you have your Judgment, your case might be completely finished. However, there is still important ongoing business that you have to know about—such as keeping your address current in court records—and the possibility of a variety of post-judgment activities that might come up; for example, if one party or the other wants to modify part of the Judgment, or if the Judgment needs to be enforced.

Some things that come up after Judgment are easy and you can handle them with no further discussion; other things will require some assistance. Here is a discussion of many of the things that can come up and what you can do about them.

A You *must* keep your address current

The address that is recorded in your court file is what *must* be used to serve notice on you. For example, as long as a child of the marriage is a minor, or spousal support is being paid, your Judgment can be modified. If you move and do not correctly change your address in the court file, documents will be served by mail at your old address and you might lose a motion without ever knowing about it, or you might find out too late—and there is nothing you can do because it is *your* responsibility to keep your address current in the court file. So whenever you move, use the Notice of Change of Address form (Figure 27.1) to keep the court and your ex-spouse updated as to your address. This form can be found on the companion CD in the back of this book. Fill it out, make three copies, have a friend serve a copy on the other side by mail, complete a Proof of Service by Mail, then file the original and the proof of service with the clerk of the court.

If you move frequently, consider using a permanent address for court business. You could rent a post office box, but then you must *never* fail to check it almost daily. You could also use the address of a friend or relative, but this too must be 100% reliable. Someone there would have to contact you instantly if legal papers arrive. You can lose important rights if you fail to keep the court informed of your address.

Figure 27.1

NOTICE OF CHANGE OF ADDRESS

Form MC-040

MC-040

ATTORNEY OR PARTY WITHOUT ATTORNEY *(Name, state bar number, and address):*

YOUR NAME
Your address
City, State, Zip

TELEPHONE NO. *(Optional):* Your phone FAX NO. *(Optional):* Your fax
E-MAIL ADDRESS *(Optional):* Your emal
ATTORNEY FOR *(Name):* Petitioner / Respondent in pro per

FOR COURT USE ONLY

SUPERIOR COURT OF CALIFORNIA, COUNTY OF YOUR COUNTY
STREET ADDRESS: Street address
MAILING ADDRESS: PO Box, if any
CITY AND ZIP CODE: City, State, Zip
BRANCH NAME: Branch name, if any

PETITIONER/PLAINTIFF: PETITIONER'S NAME
RESPONDENT/DEFENDANT: RESPONDENT'S NAME
OTHER PARENT:

NOTICE OF CHANGE OF ADDRESS AND TELEPHONE NUMBER

CASE NUMBER: Your case number

PLEASE TAKE NOTICE that as of the date of this document, the ☐ Attorney for ☒ Petitioner ☐ Respondent ☐ Other Parent has changed his or her address for service of notices and documents.

The new address of *(name)*: YOUR NAME

is now: Your new address

Enter your current phone number.

The telephone number is: (_____) _____ - ______

ANY AND ALL NOTICES AND DOCUMENTS regarding this action should now be sent to the above address.

Date: Date signed

YOUR NAME
(TYPE OR PRINT NAME)

▶
(SIGNATURE)

Page 1 of 2

Form Approved for Optional Use
Judicial Council of California
MC-040 [New January 1, 2002]

NOTICE OF CHANGE OF ADDRESS AND TELEPHONE NUMBER

B Keep track of payor's or recipient's income

If you have an order for child support, or an order for spousal support that has not effectively limited the court's power to modify either the amount or duration, then a change in either party's income could be the basis for modification of the support order. Either party has the right to serve on the other a demand for a completed Income and Expense Declaration together with copies of the last federal income tax return. If you check and find out that there has been a significant increase in the payor's or recipient's income, you might decide to go back to court to request a modification of the support order.

No matter how sweetly you present it, a demand for income and expense information is not going to make the recipient feel warm and fuzzy. If things are going smoothly and you are getting paid regularly, you might not want to disturb the status-quo, even if it might gain you a few dollars. On the other hand, if you are fairly sure your ex-spouse has experienced a significant increase in income and you have nothing much to lose in the way of good relations, you might as well do it.

Use form FL-396, Request for Production of an Income and Expense Declaration After Judgment, which is found on the companion CD in the back of this book. Fill it out as shown in Figure 27.2. The back is filled out much like the Proof of Service by Mail form, Figure 13.3 in Book 1, *How to Do Your Own Divorce*. Serve it together with blank copies of the Income and Expense Declaration, also found in Book 1 and on the companion CD that comes with it. Serve papers either personally or by certified mail, return receipt requested, as described in chapter 12 of Book 1, *How to Do Your Own Divorce*.

C Always make changes official

People often work out different arrangements but don't make the small effort it takes to change their court order. They might drift into new and different visitation schedules or adjust the amount of money paid for support. Everything is calm and cool with the parties, but the old court order just keeps running along unchanged. Let's say the payor's income goes down, so the recipient feels comfortable taking a little less. Meanwhile, the original order keeps running and the unpaid amount accumulates. If the order is not modified, there will be no defense to a future action to collect unpaid support. Or, if Dad is ordered to have visitation every other weekend, but increases later to three days a week, the order should be modified while everyone is happy, because if a problem comes up, Mom can insist at any time on a return to the schedule that was ordered. It is fairly easy to change orders by agreement of the parties—you just have to prepare, sign and file a stipulated order. Use the example Stipulation in Figure 5.1 or, if the change is only for child support, you can use the form Stipulation to Establish or Modify Child Support, found in Book 1, *How to Do Your Own Divorce,* Figure 18.4. Unrepresented parties had better sign before a notary. After both parties sign, simply file it with the court clerk.

D Modify orders if circumstances change

Orders regarding children—support, custody, visitation—can be changed if circumstances change in a legally significant way. Spousal support orders, too, are subject to change if circumstances change, unless the order effectively restricted the power of the court to modify spousal support in the future.

Modification of orders is a big subject but not that hard to do. If you want to modify a *support* order, get Nolo's CD, *How to Modify Support Orders,* which comes complete with forms, advice, and step-by-step instructions for $24.95. Order information can be found in the front or back of this book.

If you want to modify custody or visitation or some other part of the Judgment, you'll need to file a motion following the general forms and instructions presented in chapter 12 of this book. Depending on the subject, you might want to get some help to do this.

E Enforce your judgment

In some cases, enforcement will be the most important aspect of your divorce. You have gone through all the work of getting your Judgment, so now, if your ex-spouse does not comply with every order, you need to enforce it. In most cases, if you make an effort to enforce your order, you can probably get compliance. The main thing is to not be passive or let yourself get worn down, but be firm and insist that your spouse obey the Judgment from the moment it is entered.

Below are some typical methods for enforcing a judgment that are available to you. Many are focused on support orders—the most common enforcement problem—but any kind of court order can be enforced with some of these methods. Some are possible for you to do without further instruction, but for others, you will need help.

1. **County Agencies.** The government is interested in enforcing support orders. Each county has a Family Court Facilitator and a Department of Child Support Services. They are more focused on child support, but will probably help you if you have spousal support that is part of the same order with child support; go see them and ask. The services are free and they can do certain things a private attorney can't, such as revoke licenses, intercept taxes, get copies of income tax returns, seize your ex's income tax refund, and so on.

2. **Abstract of Support Judgment.** This is a one-page statement you can record where your ex-spouse owns real property. Then if your ex-spouse tries to sell or refinance the property, they will first have to make sure that all support payments are brought current.

3. **Motion to Set Arrears and Enforce Support.** If your ex-spouse pays support on an irregular basis, and you would like to obtain a writ of execution or other enforcement, you can use a motion to set arrears, and you can also ask for other relief such as an order that your ex-spouse keep you informed of the name and address of his/her employer and inform you in writing of any job changes (hiring or firing) within five days of each such change.

4. **Writ of execution.** A writ of execution is a court order that the Sheriff seize an asset, for example, a bank account, and turn it over to you. If your ex-spouse owes you a set amount of money which is specified in the judgment or order, or if you have obtained an order establishing the arrearage, you can obtain a writ of execution and take his/her wages or bank account.

5. **OSC re Contempt.** This is a very dramatic way to get someone's attention. An Order to Show Cause (OSC) re Contempt directs a party to come to court and explain why they should not be held in contempt of court. If a person is found guilty of contempt, he/she can be sent to jail for five days for each count of contempt, although usually a lighter sentence is imposed, at least the first time. An OSC re contempt is used when a person has engaged in deliberate disobedience of a court order. For contempt, you use a special form, Order to Show Cause and Affidavit for Contempt (FL-410), which is found on the companion CD in the forms folder. If you install FormZ, it will be installed for use with that program. This form is easy to use and even comes with its own instructions, which you should print out and read. You will use item 8c and possibly 8d to describe the order and the violation of that order. Otherwise, follow the OSC instructions in chapter 13.

6. Police and District Attorney may help. In California, it is a felony for a parent to hide the child from the other parent with the intent of preventing court-ordered contact with the parent. In fact, even in the absence of an order, it is usually illegal for one parent to hide the child from the other. If this happens to you, contact the police.

7. Orders to ensure health insurance benefits. Sometimes your ex-spouse provides health insurance coverage for the children, but when you take a child to the doctor, you must pay first, then the insurer sends a reimbursement check to your ex-spouse. By use of a qualified medical child support order you can avoid this problem.

F Restoring your former name after divorce

The law is gender neutral, so technically speaking, either the husband or wife can restore a former name at the time of a divorce, but it is quite rare for the husband to do this. If, in your case, the husband had a former name and wants it restored, simply reverse gender in the rest of this discussion.

Restoration of former name is typically done at the time of Judgment, but it is possible to do it after the Judgment, too. If the wife did not request her former name (which can be either a maiden name or a former married name) at the time of the divorce, she can request it later. There is no time limit for doing this. Requesting restoration of a former name is a very simple process in which she fills out a simple form (FL-395 on the companion CD), gets the judge to sign it, and files it with the court clerk.

A husband cannot request restoration of the wife's former name; only she can make this request. The ex-wife who wants a former name restored does not have to give her ex-husband notice of this request, as he has no right to object. On the other hand, if he pays support, after her name is changed, he needs to know the name she uses so he can make out the check correctly.

Before going to court to change your name, you should be sure you want to do this. Changing your name with the court is the easy part. Changing all your other documents such as driver's license, social security card, passport, etc. is the difficult part. Before you do the legal paperwork, be sure you are willing to go through the bureaucratic hassle to make all these changes. Do not change your name just because you are angry. Women sometimes ask for their maiden name to be restored because they are angry with their ex, but they do not want to jump through all the hoops to change their documents. In fact, they sometimes keep right on using their married name. If you are not really going to resume using your former name and you are not going to change your documents, do not have your name changed.

G Moving away with the kids

We left the most difficult issue for last. Sometimes, one party wants to move away with the children to a different city or state or country. This can be a huge stress on the existing parenting relationship and is a common cause of post-Judgment litigation. It is a very knotty problem that takes a lot of discussion. If this comes up for you, you should get some advice from Divorce Helpline or a local family law attorney who does a lot of mediation. You want to learn how the law applies to your situation, and you are looking for alternatives, options, and practical solutions—ways to negotiate and settle this difficult issue. It is far, far better for everyone if you work hard to settle this issue without having to fight it out in court.

Figure 27.2

REQUEST FOR PRODUCTION OF INCOME AND EXPENSE DECLARATION AFTER JUDGMENT

Form FL-396

FL-396

ATTORNEY OR PARTY WITHOUT ATTORNEY *(Name and Address)*: YOUR NAME, Your address, City, State, Zip — TELEPHONE NO.: Your phone	FOR COURT USE ONLY
ATTORNEY FOR *(Name)*: Petitioner / Respondent in pro per	
SUPERIOR COURT OF CALIFORNIA, COUNTY OF YOUR COUNTY STREET ADDRESS: Street address MAILING ADDRESS: PO Box if any CITY AND ZIP CODE: City, State, Zip BRANCH NAME: Branch name, if any	
PETITIONER/PLAINTIFF: PETITIONER'S NAME RESPONDENT/DEFENDANT: RESPONDENT'S NAME	
REQUEST FOR PRODUCTION OF AN INCOME AND EXPENSE DECLARATION AFTER JUDGMENT	CASE NUMBER: Your case number

(NOTE: This request must be served on the petitioner or respondent and not on an attorney who was or is representing that party.)

To *(name)*: SPOUSE NAME

1\. a. As permitted by Family Code section 3664(a), declarant requires that you complete and return the attached *Income and Expense Declaration* (form FL-150) within 30 days after the date this request is served on you. Family Code section 3665(a) requires you to attach copies of your most recent state and federal income tax returns (whether individual or joint) to the completed *Income and Expense Declaration* (form FL-150).

b. The completed *Income and Expense Declaration* (form FL-150) should be mailed to the following person at the following address *(specify)*:

Your Name
Your address
City, State, Zip

2\. You may consult an attorney about completion of the *Income and Expense Declaration* (form FL-150) or you may proceed without an attorney. The information provided will be used to determine whether to ask for a modification of child, spousal, or family support at this time.

3\. If you wish to do so, you may serve a request for a completed *Income and Expense Declaration* (form FL-150) on me. Each of us may use this procedure once a year after judgment even though no legal matter is pending.

Date: Date signed

YOUR NAME ▶ ______________________

(TYPE OR PRINT NAME) (SIGNATURE OF DECLARANT)

WARNING: If a court later finds that the information provided in response to this request is incomplete or inaccurate or missing the prior year's tax returns, or that you did not submit the information in good faith, the court may order you to pay all costs necessary for me to get complete and accurate information. In addition you could be found to be in contempt and receive other penalties.

Page 1 of 2

Form Adopted for Mandatory Use
Judicial Council of California
FL-396 [Rev. January 1, 2003]

REQUEST FOR PRODUCTION OF AN INCOME AND EXPENSE DECLARATION AFTER JUDGMENT

Family Code, §§ 3664, 3665, 3668
www.courtinfo.ca.gov

Blank Forms

All Judicial Council forms are also on the companion CD and can be filled out on your PC. The typed pleadings are on the CD in word processor files that can be edited to fit your case.

Forms & Typed Pleadings on CD

All Judicial Council forms and all typed pleadings used in this book can be found on the companion CD in formats that can be used on your PC or Mac.

Order of Forms in Book

Chapter	Form number	
7	MC-050	Substitution of Attorney
12	FL-310	Application for Order and Supporting Declaration
12	FL-311	Child Custody and Visitation Attachment
12	MC-030	Declaration
12	FL-301	Notice of Motion
13	FL-300	Order to Show Cause
13	FL-305	Temporary Orders
13	FL-306	Application and Order for Reissuance of OSC
14	FL-320	Responsive Declaration to OSC or Notice of Motion
15	982(a)(15)	Civil Subpoena for Personal Appearance
15	982(a)(15.1)	Civil Subpoena (Duces Tecum)
16	FL-340	Findings and Order After Hearing
16	FL-341	Child Custody and Visitation Order Attachment
16	FL-341(A)	Supervised Visitation Order Attachment
16	FL-342	Child Support Information and Order Attachment
16	FL-342(A)	Non-Guideline Child Support Findings Attachment
16	FL-343	Spousal or Family Support Order Attachment
16	FL-344	Property Order Attachment
17	FL-145	Form Interrogatories
17	982(a)(15.2)	Deposition Subpoena for Production of Business Records
17	982(a)(15.5)	Notice to Consumer or Employee
17	982(a)(15.3)	Deposition Subpoena for Personal Appearance
17	982(a)(15.4)	Deposition Subpoena (Duces Tecum)
21	FL-315	Application for Separate Trial
27	FL-396	Request for Production of Income and Expense Declaration
27	FL-395	Ex Parte Application for Restoration of Former Name

ATTORNEY OR PARTY WITHOUT ATTORNEY *(Name and Address)*: TELEPHONE NO.:	*FOR COURT USE ONLY*
ATTORNEY FOR *(Name)*:	
NAME OF COURT: STREET ADDRESS: MAILING ADDRESS: CITY AND ZIP CODE: BRANCH NAME:	
CASE NAME:	
SUBSTITUTION OF ATTORNEY—CIVIL **(Without Court Order)**	CASE NUMBER:

THE COURT AND ALL PARTIES ARE NOTIFIED THAT *(name)*: makes the following substitution:

1. **Former legal representative** ☐ Party represented self ☐ Attorney *(name)*:
2. **New legal representative** ☐ Party is representing self* ☐ Attorney
   a. Name: b. State Bar No. *(if applicable)*:
   c. Address *(number, street, city, ZIP, and law firm name, if applicable)*:

   d. Telephone No. *(include area code)*:
3. The party making this substitution is a ☐ plaintiff ☐ defendant ☐ petitioner ☐ respondent ☐ other *(specify)*:

***NOTICE TO PARTIES APPLYING TO REPRESENT THEMSELVES**

- **Guardian**
- **Conservator**
- **Trustee**
- **Personal representative**
- **Probate fiduciary**
- **Corporation**
- **Guardian ad litem**
- **Unincorporated association**

If you are applying as one of the parties on this list, you may NOT act as your own attorney in most cases. Use this form to substitute one attorney for another attorney. SEEK LEGAL ADVICE BEFORE APPLYING TO REPRESENT YOURSELF.

NOTICE TO PARTIES WITHOUT ATTORNEYS

A party representing himself or herself may wish to seek legal assistance. Failure to take timely and appropriate action in this case may result in serious legal consequences.

4. I consent to this substitution.
   Date:

   .... ▶ ______________________________
   (TYPE OR PRINT NAME) (SIGNATURE OF PARTY)

5. ☐ I consent to this substitution.
   Date:

   .... ▶ ______________________________
   (TYPE OR PRINT NAME) (SIGNATURE OF FORMER ATTORNEY)

6. ☐ I accept this substitution.
   Date:

   .... ▶ ______________________________
   (TYPE OR PRINT NAME) (SIGNATURE OF NEW ATTORNEY)

(See reverse for proof of service by mail)

CASE NAME:	CASE NUMBER:

PROOF OF SERVICE BY MAIL
Substitution of Attorney – Civil

Instructions: *After having all parties served by mail with the Substitution of Attorney–Civil, have the person who mailed the document complete this Proof of Service by Mail. An unsigned copy of the Proof of Service by Mail should be completed and served with the document. Give the Substitution of Attorney–Civil and the completed Proof of Service by Mail to the clerk for filing. If you are representing yourself, someone else must mail these papers and sign the Proof of Service by Mail.*

1. I am over the age of 18 and **not a party to this cause**. I am a resident of or employed in the county where the mailing occurred. My residence or business address is *(specify)*:

2. I served the Substitution of Attorney–Civil by enclosing a true copy in a sealed envelope addressed to each person whose name and address is shown below and depositing the envelope in the United States mail with the postage fully prepaid.

   (1) Date of mailing: (2) Place of mailing *(city and state)*:

3. I declare under penalty of perjury under the laws of the State of California that the foregoing is true and correct.

Date:

. . . . ▶ ______________________________

(TYPE OR PRINT NAME) (SIGNATURE)

NAME AND ADDRESS OF EACH PERSON TO WHOM NOTICE WAS MAILED

4. a. Name of person served:
   b. Address *(number, street, city, and ZIP)*:

   c. Name of person served:
   d. Address *(number, street, city, and ZIP)*:

   e. Name of person served:
   f. Address *(number, street, city, and ZIP)*:

   g. Name of person served:
   h. Address *(number, street, city, and ZIP)*:

   i. Name of person served:
   j. Address *(number, street, city, and ZIP)*:

☐ List of names and addresses continued in attachment.

PETITIONER/PLAINTIFF: RESPONDENT/DEFENDANT:	CASE NUMBER:

(THIS IS NOT AN ORDER)

☐ **Petitioner** ☐ **Respondent** ☐ **Claimant** **requests the following orders be made:**

1. ☐ CHILD CUSTODY ☐ **To be ordered pending the hearing**
   a. Child *(name and age)*
   b. Request custody to *(name)*
   c. ☐ Modify existing order
      (1) filed on *(date)*:
      (2) ordering *(specify)*:

2. ☐ CHILD VISITATION ☐ **To be ordered pending the hearing**
   a. ☐ Reasonable
   b. ☐ Other *(specify)*:
   c. ☐ Petitioner ☐ Respondent shall not remove the minor child or children of the parties
      (1) ☐ from the State of California (2) ☐ other *(specify)*:
   d. ☐ Modify existing order
      (1) filed on *(date)*:
      (2) ordering *(specify)*:

3. ☐ CHILD SUPPORT *(A* Wage and Earnings Assignment Order *will be issued.)*
   a. Child (name and age)
   b. Monthly amount (if not by guideline) $
   c. ☐ Modify existing order
      (1) filed on *(date)*:
      (2) ordering *(specify)*:

4. ☐ SPOUSAL SUPPORT *(A* Wage and Earnings Assignment Order *will be issued.)*
   a. ☐ Amount requested *(monthly)*: $
   b. ☐ Terminate existing order
      (1) filed on *(date)*:
      (2) ordering *(specify)*:
   c. ☐ Modify existing order
      (1) filed on *(date)*:
      (2) ordering *(specify)*:

5. ☐ ATTORNEY FEES AND COSTS a. ☐ Fees: $ b. ☐ Costs: $

6. ☐ PROPERTY RESTRAINT ☐ **To be ordered pending the hearing**
   a. The ☐ petitioner ☐ respondent ☐ claimant are restrained from transferring, encumbering, hypothecating, concealing, or in any way disposing of any property, real or personal, whether community, quasi-community, or separate, except in the usual course of business or for the necessities of life.
      ☐ and applicant will be notified at least five business days before any proposed extraordinary expenditures and an accounting of such will be made to the court.
   b. ☐ Both parties are restrained and enjoined from cashing, borrowing against, canceling, transferring, disposing of, or changing the beneficiaries of any insurance or other coverage including life, health, automobile, and disability held for the benefit of the parties or their minor children.
   c. ☐ Neither party shall incur any debts or liabilities for which the other may be held responsible, other than in the ordinary course of business or for the necessities of life.

NOTE: TO OBTAIN DOMESTIC VIOLENCE RESTRAINING ORDERS, YOU MUST USE THE FORMS *REQUEST FOR ORDER (DOMESTIC VIOLENCE PREVENTION)* (FORM DV-100) AND *TEMPORARY RESTRAINING ORDER (DOMESTIC VIOLENCE PREVENTION)* (FORM DV-110).

Form Adopted for Mandatory Use
Judicial Council of California
FL-310 [Rev. January 1, 2003]

APPLICATION FOR ORDER AND SUPPORTING DECLARATION

Family Code, §§ 2045, 6224, 6226, 6320–6326, 6380–6383
www.courtinfo.ca.gov

PETITIONER/PLAINTIFF:	CASE NUMBER:
RESPONDENT/DEFENDANT:	

7. ☐ PROPERTY CONTROL ☐ **To be ordered pending the hearing**

a. ☐ Petitioner ☐ Respondent are given the exclusive temporary use, possession, and control of the following property we own or are buying *(specify)*:

b. ☐ Petitioner ☐ Respondent are ordered to make the following payments on liens and encumbrances coming due while the order is in effect:

Debt | Amount of payment | Pay to

8. ☐ **I request** that time for service of the Order to Show Cause and accompanying papers be shortened so that they may be served no less than *(specify number)*: days before the time set for the hearing. I need to have the order shortening time because of the facts specified in the attached declaration.

9. ☐ OTHER RELIEF *(specify)*:

10. ☐ FACTS IN SUPPORT of relief requested and change of circumstances for any modification are *(specify)*:

☐ contained in the attached declaration.

I declare under penalty of perjury under the laws of the State of California that the foregoing is true and correct.

Date:

(TYPE OR PRINT NAME) ▶ (SIGNATURE OF APPLICANT)

PETITIONER:	CASE NUMBER:
RESPONDENT:	

CHILD CUSTODY AND VISITATION APPLICATION ATTACHMENT

☐ to Petition or Application for Order ☐ To be ordered now and effective until the hearing.

1. ☐ **CUSTODY**

I request custody orders as follows:

Child's name	Birth date	Legal custody to *(Person who makes decisions about health, education, etc.)*	Physical custody to *(Person who the child lives with.)*

2. ☐ **VISITATION**

I request visitation orders as follows:

a. ☐ Reasonable right of visitation to the party without physical custody. *(Not appropriate in cases involving domestic violence.)*
b. ☐ See the attached ___________ page document dated: ______________.
c. ☐ The parties will go to mediation at:
d. ☐ No visitation.
e. ☐ Visitation for ☐ Father ☐ Mother will be:

(i) ☐ **WEEKENDS** *(starting)*:
(The 1st weekend of the month is the 1st weekend with a Saturday.)
☐ 1st ☐ 2nd ☐ 3rd ☐ 4th ☐ 5th weekend of the month

from ____________________ at ___________ ☐ a.m. ☐ p.m.
(day of week) *(time)*

to ____________________ at ___________ ☐ a.m. ☐ p.m.
(day of week) *(time)*

☐ The parents to alternate the 5th weekends, with the ☐ Father ☐ Mother having the first 5th weekend.
☐ Father to have 5th weekends in ☐ odd ☐ even months.
☐ Mother to have 5th weekends in ☐ odd ☐ even months.

(ii) ☐ **ALTERNATE WEEKENDS** *(specify starting date)*: ________________
☐ Father ☐ Mother to have the children with him/her *(specify days and times)*:

from ____________________ at ___________ ☐ a.m. ☐ p.m.
(day of week) *(time)*

to ____________________ at ___________ ☐ a.m. ☐ p.m.
(day of week) *(time)*

(iii) ☐ **WEEKDAYS** *(starting)*:
☐ Father ☐ Mother to have the children with him/her *(specify days and times)*:

from ____________________ at ___________ ☐ a.m. ☐ p.m.
(day of week) *(time)*

to ____________________ at ___________ ☐ a.m. ☐ p.m.
(day of week) *(time)*

(iv) ☐ **OTHER** *(specify days and times as well as any additional restrictions)*: ☐ See Attachment 2e.

PETITIONER:	CASE NUMBER:
RESPONDENT:	

CHILD CUSTODY AND VISITATION APPLICATION ATTACHMENT

3. ☐ **SUPERVISED VISITATION**

I request that *(name):* have supervised visitation with the minor children according to the schedule marked above and that the visits be supervised by *(name):* , who is a

☐ professional ☐ nonprofessional supervisor. The supervisor's phone number is *(specify):*

I request that the costs for supervision be paid as follows: Mother: _______ %, Father: _______ %

4. ☐ **TRANSPORTATION FOR VISITATION AND PLACE OF EXCHANGE**
   a. ☐ Transportation *to* the visits will be provided by *(name):*
   b. ☐ Transportation *from* the visits will be provided by *(name):*
   c. ☐ Drop-off/Pickup of the children will be at *(specify address):*
   d. ☐ The children will only be driven by a licensed and insured driver. The car or truck must have legal child restraint devices.
   e. ☐ During the exchanges, the parent driving the children will wait in the car and the other parent will wait in their home while the children go to the home.
   f. ☐ Other *(specify):*

5. ☐ **TRAVEL WITH CHILDREN** ☐ Father ☐ Mother ☐ Other *(name):*

must have written permission from the other parent or a court order to take the children outside of
   a. ☐ the State of California
   b. ☐ the following counties *(specify):*
   c. ☐ other places *(specify):*

6. ☐ **CHILD ABDUCTION PREVENTION ORDERS**

There is a risk that one of the parents will take the children out of California without the other parent's permission. I request the orders set out on form FL-312.

7. ☐ **CHILDREN'S HOLIDAY SCHEDULE**

I request the holiday and visitation schedule set out on attached ☐ form FL-341(C) ☐ Other.

8. ☐ **ADDITIONAL CUSTODY PROVISIONS**

I request the additional orders regarding custody set out on attached ☐ form FL-341(D) ☐ Other.

9. ☐ **JOINT LEGAL CUSTODY PROVISIONS**

I am requesting joint legal custody and want the following additional orders set out on attached ☐ form FL-341(E) ☐ Other.

10. ☐ **OTHER**

I request the following additional orders *(specify):*

ATTORNEY OR PARTY WITHOUT ATTORNEY *(Name and Address)*:	TELEPHONE NO.:	***FOR COURT USE ONLY***
ATTORNEY FOR *(Name)*:		
NAME OF COURT: STREET ADDRESS: MAILING ADDRESS: CITY AND ZIP CODE: BRANCH NAME:		
PLAINTIFF/PETITIONER: DEFENDANT/RESPONDENT:		
DECLARATION		CASE NUMBER:

I declare under penalty of perjury under the laws of the State of California that the foregoing is true and correct.

Date:

. . . . ▶ ______________________________

(TYPE OR PRINT NAME) (SIGNATURE OF DECLARANT)

☐ Petitioner/Plaintiff ☐ Respondent/Defendant ☐ Attorney

☐ Other *(specify)*:

(See reverse for a form to be used if this declaration will be attached to another court form before filing)

PLAINTIFF/PETITIONER: DEFENDANT/RESPONDENT:	CASE NUMBER:

This form must be attached to another form or court paper before it can be filed in court.

I declare under penalty of perjury under the laws of the State of California that the foregoing is true and correct.

Date:

(TYPE OR PRINT NAME)

(SIGNATURE OF DECLARANT)

☐ Petitioner/Plaintiff ☐ Respondent/Defendant ☐ Attorney
☐ Other *(Specify)*:

(See reverse for a form to be used if this declaration is not to be attached to another court paper before filing)

Form Approved by the
Judicial Council of California
MC-031 [New January 1, 1987]

ATTACHED DECLARATION

ATTORNEY OR PARTY WITHOUT ATTORNEY *(Name, state bar number, and address):*	*FOR COURT USE ONLY*
TELEPHONE NO.: FAX NO.:	
ATTORNEY FOR *(Name):*	
SUPERIOR COURT OF CALIFORNIA, COUNTY OF	
STREET ADDRESS:	
MAILING ADDRESS:	
CITY AND ZIP CODE:	
BRANCH NAME:	
PETITIONER/PLAINTIFF:	
RESPONDENT/DEFENDANT:	
NOTICE OF MOTION ☐ **MODIFICATION** ☐ **Child Custody** ☐ **Visitation** ☐ **Injunctive Order** ☐ **Child Support** ☐ **Spousal Support** ☐ **Other *(specify):*** ☐ **Attorney Fees and Costs**	CASE NUMBER:

1. TO *(name):*
2. A hearing on this motion for the relief requested in the attached application will be held as follows:

a. Date:	Time:	☐ Dept.:	☐ Rm.:

   b. Address of court ☐ same as noted above ☐ other *(specify):*

3. Supporting attachments:
   a. Completed *Application for Order and Supporting Declaration* (form FL-310) and a **blank** *Responsive Declaration* (form FL-320)
   b. ☐ Completed *Income and Expense Declaration* (form FL-150) and a **blank** *Income and Expense Declaration*
   c. ☐ Completed *Financial Statement (Simplified)* (form FL-155) and a **blank** *Financial Statement (Simplified)*
   d. ☐ Completed *Property Declaration* (form FL-160) and a **blank** *Property Declaration*
   e. ☐ Points and authorities
   f. ☐ Other *(specify):*

Date:

(TYPE OR PRINT NAME) ▶ (SIGNATURE)

ORDER

4. ☐ Time for ☐ service ☐ hearing is shortened. Service must be on or before *(date)*:
5. Any responsive declaration must be served on or before *(date):*
6. *If child custody or visitation is an issue in this proceeding, Family Code section 3170 requires mediation before or concurrently with the hearing listed above.* The parties are ordered to attend orientation and mandatory custody services as follows:

Date:

JUDICIAL OFFICER

NOTICE: If you have children from this relationship, the court is required to order payment of child support based on the income of both parents. The amount of child support can be large. It normally continues until the child is 18. You should supply the court with information about your finances. Otherwise, the child support order will be based on the information supplied by the other parent.
You do not have to pay any fee to file responsive declarations in response to this *Notice of Motion* (including a completed *Income and Expense Declaration* (form FL-150) or *Financial Statement (Simplified)* (form FL-155) that will show your finances). In the absence of an order shortening time, the original of the responsive declaration must be filed with the court and a copy served on the other party at least ten calendar days before the hearing date.

PETITIONER/PLAINTIFF:	CASE NUMBER:
RESPONDENT/DEFENDANT:	

7. PROOF OF SERVICE BY MAIL

a. I am at least age 18, **not a party to this action,** and am a resident or employed in the county where the mailing took place. My residence or business address is:

b. I served copies of the following documents by enclosing them in a sealed envelope with postage fully prepaid, depositing them in the United States mail as follows:

(1) Papers served:

(a) *Notice of Motion* and a completed *Application for Order and Supporting Declaration* (form FL-310) **and** a blank *Responsive Declaration* (form FL-320)

(b) ☐ Completed *Income and Expense Declaration* (form FL-150) **and** a blank *Income and Expense Declaration*

(c) ☐ Completed *Financial Statement (Simplified)* (form FL-155) **and** a blank *Financial Statement (Simplified)*

(d) ☐ Completed *Property Declaration* (form FL-160) **and** a blank *Property Declaration*

(e) ☐ Points and authorities

(f) Other *(specify):*

(2) Manner of service:

(a) Date of deposit:

(b) Place of deposit *(city and state):*

(c) Addressed as follows:

c. I declare under penalty of perjury under the laws of the State of California that the foregoing is true and correct.

Date:

________________________________ ▶ ________________________________

(TYPE OR PRINT NAME) (SIGNATURE OF DECLARANT)

ATTORNEY OR PARTY WITHOUT ATTORNEY *(Name, state bar number, and address):*

FOR COURT USE ONLY

TELEPHONE NO. *(Optional):* FAX NO. *(Optional):*
EMAIL ADDRESS *(Optional):*
ATTORNEY FOR *(Name):*

SUPERIOR COURT OF CALIFORNIA, COUNTY OF
STREET ADDRESS:
MAILING ADDRESS:
CITY AND ZIP CODE:
BRANCH NAME:

PETITIONER:

RESPONDENT:

ORDER TO SHOW CAUSE FOR ☐ **MODIFICATION**
☐ **Child Custody** ☐ **Visitation** ☐ **Injunctive Order**
☐ **Child Support** ☐ **Spousal Support** ☐ **Other *(specify):***
☐ **Attorney Fees and Costs**

CASE NUMBER:

1. TO *(name):*
2. YOU ARE ORDERED TO APPEAR IN THIS COURT AS FOLLOWS TO GIVE ANY LEGAL REASON WHY THE RELIEF SOUGHT IN THE ATTACHED APPLICATION SHOULD NOT BE GRANTED. **If child custody or visitation is an issue in this proceeding, Family Code section 3170 requires mediation before or concurrently with the hearing listed below.**

a. Date: Time: ☐ Dept.: ☐ Room:

b. The address of the court is ☐ same as noted above ☐ other *(specify):*

c. ☐ The parties are ordered to attend custody mediation services as follows:

3. THE COURT FURTHER ORDERS that a completed *Application for Order and Supporting Declaration* (form FL-310), a **blank** *Responsive Declaration* (form FL-320), and the following documents be served with this order:
   a. (1) ☐ Completed *Income and Expense Declaration* (form FL-150) and a **blank** *Income and Expense Declaration*
   (2) ☐ Completed *Financial Statement (Simplified)* (form FL-155) and a **blank** *Financial Statement (Simplified)*
   (3) ☐ Completed *Property Declaration* (form FL-160) and a **blank** *Property Declaration*
   (4) ☐ Points and authorities
   (5) ☐ Other *(specify):*

   b. ☐ Time for ☐ service ☐ hearing is shortened. Service must be on or before *(date):*
   Any responsive declaration must be served on or before *(date):*
   c. ☐ You are ordered to comply with the temporary orders attached.
   d. ☐ Other *(specify):*

Date:

JUDICIAL OFFICER

NOTICE: If you have children from this relationship, the court is required to order payment of child support based on the incomes of both parents. The amount of child support can be large. It normally continues until the child is 18. You should supply the court with information about your finances. Otherwise, the child support order will be based on the information supplied by the other parent.
You do not have to pay any fee to file declarations in response to this order to show cause (including a completed *Income and Expense Declaration* (form FL-150) or *Financial Statement (Simplified)* (form FL-155) that will show your finances). In the absence of an order shortening time, the original of the responsive declaration must be filed with the court and a copy served on the other party at least ten calender days before the hearing date.

Form Adopted for Mandatory Use
Judicial Council of California
FL-300 [Rev. January 1, 2003]

ORDER TO SHOW CAUSE

Family Code, §§ 215, 270 et seq., 3000 et seq., 3500 et seq., 4300
www.courtinfo.ca.gov

PETITIONER/PLAINTIFF:	CASE NUMBER:
RESPONDENT/DEFENDANT:	

TEMPORARY ORDERS
(Attachment to Order to Show Cause)

NOTE: TO OBTAIN DOMESTIC VIOLENCE RESTRAINING ORDERS, YOU MUST USE FORMS *REQUEST FOR ORDER (DOMESTIC VIOLENCE PREVENTION)* (FORM DV-100) AND *TEMPORARY RESTRAINING ORDER (DOMESTIC VIOLENCE PREVENTION)* (FORM DV-110).

1. ☐ PROPERTY RESTRAINT
   a. ☐ Petitioner ☐ Respondent is restrained from transferring, encumbering, hypothecating, concealing, or in any way disposing of any property, real or personal, whether community, quasi-community, or separate, except in the usual course of business or for the necessities of life.
      ☐ The other party is to be notified of any proposed extraordinary expenditures and an accounting of such is to be made to the court.
   b. ☐ Both parties are restrained and enjoined from cashing, borrowing against, canceling, transferring, disposing of, or changing the beneficiaries of any insurance or other coverage including life, health, automobile, and disability held for the benefit of the parties or their minor child or children.
   c. ☐ Neither party may incur any debts or liabilities for which the other may be held responsible, other than in the ordinary course of business or for the necessities of life.
2. ☐ PROPERTY CONTROL
   a. ☐ Petitioner ☐ Respondent is given the exclusive temporary use, possession, and control of the following property the parties own or are buying *(specify):*

   b. ☐ Petitioner ☐ Respondent is ordered to make the following payments on liens and encumbrances coming due while the order is in effect:

Debt	Amount of payment	Pay to

3. ☐ MINOR CHILDREN
   a. ☐ Petitioner ☐ Respondent will have the temporary physical custody, care, and control of the minor children of the parties, ☐ subject to the other party's rights of visitation as follows:

   b. ☐ Petitioner ☐ Respondent must not remove the minor child or children of the parties
      (1) ☐ from the State of California.
      (2) ☐ from the following counties *(specify):*
      (3) ☐ other *(specify):*
4. ☐ OTHER ORDERS *(specify):*

Date:

____
JUDGE OF THE SUPERIOR COURT

5. **The date of the court hearing is** *(insert date when known)*:

CLERK'S CERTIFICATE

I certify that the foregoing is a true and correct copy of the original on file in my office.

[SEAL]

Date: Clerk, by ____________________________, Deputy

FL-306/JV-251

ATTORNEY OR PARTY WITHOUT ATTORNEY *(Name and Address):* TELEPHONE NO.:	*FOR COURT USE ONLY*
ATTORNEY FOR *(Name):*	
SUPERIOR COURT OF CALIFORNIA, COUNTY OF STREET ADDRESS: MAILING ADDRESS: CITY AND ZIP CODE: BRANCH NAME:	
PETITIONER/PLAINTIFF: RESPONDENT/DEFENDANT: OTHER:	
APPLICATION AND ORDER FOR REISSUANCE OF ORDER TO SHOW CAUSE	CASE NUMBER(S):

1. Applicant is *(specify):*

2. Applicant requests the court to reissue the *Order to Show Cause* ☐ *and Temporary Restraining Order* originally issued as follows:
   a. Order to Show Cause was issued on *(date):*
   b. Order to Show Cause was last set for hearing on *(date):*
   c. Order to Show Cause has been reissued previously *(number of times):*

3. Applicant requests reissuance of the order because:
   a. ☐ Respondent/Defendant ☐ Petitioner/Plaintiff ☐ Other party could not be served as required before the hearing date.
   b. ☐ The hearing was continued because the parties were referred to court mediator or family court services.
   c. ☐ Other *(specify):*

I declare under penalty of perjury under the laws of the State of California that the foregoing is true and correct.

Date:

(TYPE OR PRINT NAME) (SIGNATURE)

ORDER

4. IT IS ORDERED that the *Order to Show Cause* issued as shown in item 2 above is reissued and reset for hearing in this court as follows:

Date:	time:	dept.:	room:
at the street address of the court shown above.			

   a. A copy of this order must be attached to documents that must be served on the ☐ Respondent/Defendant ☐ Petitioner/Plaintiff ☐ Other party as directed in the *Order to Show Cause*.
   b. All other orders contained in the *Order to Show Cause* and ☐ *Temporary Restraining Order* remain in full force and effect unless modified by this order. **THE *ORDER TO SHOW CAUSE* AND THIS ORDER EXPIRE ON THE DATE AND TIME OF THE HEARING SHOWN IN THE BOX ABOVE UNLESS EXTENDED BY THE COURT.**
   c. ☐ Other *(specify):*

Date:

JUDICIAL OFFICER

Form Adopted for Mandatory Use
Judicial Council of California
FL-306/JV-251 [Adopted January 1, 2003]

APPLICATION AND ORDER FOR REISSUANCE OF ORDER TO SHOW CAUSE
(Family Law—Governmental—Uniform Parentage—Custody and Support—Juvenile)

Code of Civil Procedure, § 527(d)
www.courtinfo.ca.gov

ATTORNEY OR PARTY WITHOUT ATTORNEY *(Name, state bar number, and address):* TELEPHONE NO.: FAX NO.: ATTORNEY FOR *(Name):*	*FOR COURT USE ONLY*
SUPERIOR COURT OF CALIFORNIA, COUNTY OF STREET ADDRESS: MAILING ADDRESS: CITY AND ZIP CODE: BRANCH NAME:	
PETITIONER/PLAINTIFF: RESPONDENT/DEFENDANT:	
RESPONSIVE DECLARATION TO ORDER TO SHOW CAUSE OR NOTICE OF MOTION	CASE NUMBER:
HEARING DATE: TIME: DEPARTMENT OR ROOM:	

1. ☐ CHILD CUSTODY
   a. ☐ I consent to the order requested.
   b. ☐ I do not consent to the order requested but I consent to the following order:

2. ☐ CHILD VISITATION
   a. ☐ I consent to the order requested.
   b. ☐ I do not consent to the order requested but I consent to the following order:

3. ☐ CHILD SUPPORT
   a. ☐ I consent to the order requested.
   b. ☐ I consent to guideline support.
   c. ☐ I do not consent to the order requested, but I consent to the following order:
      (1) ☐ Guideline
      (2) ☐ Other *(specify):*

4. ☐ SPOUSAL SUPPORT
   a. ☐ I consent to the order requested.
   b. ☐ I do not consent to the order requested.
   c. ☐ I consent to the following order:

5. ☐ ATTORNEY FEES AND COSTS
   a. ☐ I consent to the order requested.
   b. ☐ I do not consent to the order requested.
   c. ☐ I consent to the following order:

PETITIONER/PLAINTIFF:	CASE NUMBER:
RESPONDENT/DEFENDANT:	

6. ☐ PROPERTY RESTRAINT
   a. ☐ I consent to the order requested.
   b. ☐ I do not consent to the order requested.
   c. ☐ I consent to the following order:

7. ☐ PROPERTY CONTROL
   a. ☐ I consent to the order requested.
   b. ☐ I do not consent to the order requested.
   c. ☐ I consent to the following order:

8. ☐ OTHER RELIEF
   a. ☐ I consent to the order requested.
   b. ☐ I do not consent to the order requested.
   c. ☐ I consent to the following order:

9. ☐ SUPPORTING INFORMATION
   ☐ contained in the attached declaration.

NOTE: To respond to a request for domestic violence restraining orders requested in the *Request for Order (Domestic Violence Prevention)* (form DV-100) you must use the *Answer to Temporary Restraining Order (Domestic Violence Prevention)* (form DV-120).

I declare under penalty of perjury under the laws of the State of California that the foregoing is true and correct.

Date:

____________________________ ▶ ____________________________

(TYPE OR PRINT NAME) (SIGNATURE OF DECLARANT)

ATTORNEY OR PARTY WITHOUT ATTORNEY *(Name, state bar number, and address)*: TELEPHONE NO.: FAX NO.: ATTORNEY FOR *(Name)*:	*FOR COURT USE ONLY*
NAME OF COURT: STREET ADDRESS: MAILING ADDRESS: CITY AND ZIP CODE: BRANCH NAME:	
PLAINTIFF/ PETITIONER: DEFENDANT/ RESPONDENT:	
CIVIL SUBPOENA **For Personal Appearance at Trial or Hearing**	CASE NUMBER:

THE PEOPLE OF THE STATE OF CALIFORNIA, TO *(name, address, and telephone number of witness, if known)*:

1. **YOU ARE ORDERED TO APPEAR AS A WITNESS in this action at the date, time, and place shown in the box below UNLESS you make an agreement with the person named in item 2:**

a. Date:	Time:	☐ Dept.:	☐ Div.:	☐ Room:
b. Address:				

2. **IF YOU HAVE ANY QUESTIONS ABOUT THE TIME OR DATE FOR YOU TO APPEAR, OR IF YOU WANT TO BE CERTAIN THAT YOUR PRESENCE IS REQUIRED, CONTACT THE FOLLOWING PERSON BEFORE THE DATE ON WHICH YOU ARE TO APPEAR:**
   a. Name of subpoenaing party or attorney: b. Telephone number:

3. **Witness Fees:** You are entitled to witness fees and mileage actually traveled both ways, as provided by law, if you request them at the time of service. You may request them before your scheduled appearance from the person named in item 2.

DISOBEDIENCE OF THIS SUBPOENA MAY BE PUNISHED AS CONTEMPT BY THIS COURT. YOU WILL ALSO BE LIABLE FOR THE SUM OF FIVE HUNDRED DOLLARS AND ALL DAMAGES RESULTING FROM YOUR FAILURE TO OBEY.

Date issued:

. . . .
(TYPE OR PRINT NAME)

▶ ________________________________
(SIGNATURE OF PERSON ISSUING SUBPOENA)

____
(TITLE)

(Proof of service on reverse)

PLAINTIFF/PETITIONER:	CASE NUMBER:
DEFENDANT/RESPONDENT:	

PROOF OF SERVICE OF CIVIL SUBPOENA FOR PERSONAL APPEARANCE AT TRIAL OR HEARING

1. I served this *Civil Subpoena for Personal Appearance at Trial or Hearing* by personally delivering a copy to the person served as follows:

   a. Person served *(name)*:

   b. Address where served:

   c. Date of delivery:

   d. Time of delivery:

   e. Witness fees *(check one)*:
      (1) ☐ were offered or demanded and paid. Amount: . . . . . $ ______________
      (2) ☐ were not demanded or paid.

   f. Fee for service: . . . . $ ______________

2. I received this subpoena for service on *(date)*:

3. Person serving:
   a. ☐ Not a registered California process server.
   b. ☐ California sheriff or marshal.
   c. ☐ Registered California process server.
   d. ☐ Employee or independent contractor of a registered California process server.
   e. ☐ Exempt from registration under Business and Professions Code section 22350(b).
   f. ☐ Registered professional photocopier.
   g. ☐ Exempt from registration under Business and Professions Code section 22451.
   h. Name, address, telephone number, and, if applicable, county of registration and number:

I declare under penalty of perjury under the laws of the State of California that the foregoing is true and correct.

Date:

▶ ______________________________
(SIGNATURE)

(For California sheriff or marshal use only)
I certify that the foregoing is true and correct.

Date:

▶ ______________________________
(SIGNATURE)

ATTORNEY OR PARTY WITHOUT ATTORNEY *(Name, state bar number, and address)*: TELEPHONE NO.: FAX NO.: ATTORNEY FOR *(Name)*:	*FOR COURT USE ONLY*
NAME OF COURT: STREET ADDRESS: MAILING ADDRESS: CITY AND ZIP CODE: BRANCH NAME:	
PLAINTIFF/ PETITIONER: DEFENDANT/ RESPONDENT:	
CIVIL SUBPOENA (DUCES TECUM) for Personal Appearance and Production of Documents and Things at Trial or Hearing AND DECLARATION	CASE NUMBER:

THE PEOPLE OF THE STATE OF CALIFORNIA, TO *(name, address, and telephone number of witness, if known)*:

1. **YOU ARE ORDERED TO APPEAR AS A WITNESS in this action at the date, time, and place shown in the box below UNLESS your appearance is excused as indicated in box 3b below or you make an agreement with the person named in item 4 below.**

a. Date:	Time:	☐ Dept.:	☐ Div.:	☐ Room:
b. Address:				

2. **IF YOU HAVE BEEN SERVED WITH THIS SUBPOENA AS A CUSTODIAN OF CONSUMER OR EMPLOYEE RECORDS UNDER CODE OF CIVIL PROCEDURE SECTION 1985.3 OR 1985.6 AND A MOTION TO QUASH OR AN OBJECTION HAS BEEN SERVED ON YOU, A COURT ORDER OR AGREEMENT OF THE PARTIES, WITNESSES, *AND* CONSUMER OR EMPLOYEE AFFECTED MUST BE OBTAINED BEFORE YOU ARE REQUIRED TO PRODUCE CONSUMER OR EMPLOYEE RECORDS.**

3. YOU ARE *(item a or b must be checked)*:
   a. ☐ Ordered to appear in person and to produce the records described in the declaration on page two or the attached declaration or affidavit. The personal attendance of the custodian or other qualified witness and the production of the original records are required by this subpoena. The procedure authorized by Evidence Code sections 1560(b), 1561, and 1562 will not be deemed sufficient compliance with this subpoena.
   b. ☐ Not required to appear in person if you produce (i) the records described in the declaration on page two or the attached declaration or affidavit and (ii) a completed declaration of custodian of records in compliance with Evidence Code sections 1560, 1561, 1562, and 1271. (1) Place a copy of the records in an envelope (or other wrapper). Enclose the original declaration of the custodian with the records. Seal the envelope. (2) Attach a copy of this subpoena to the envelope or write on the envelope the case name and number; your name; and the date, time, and place from item 1 in the box above. (3) Place this first envelope in an outer envelope, seal it, and mail it to the clerk of the court at the address in item 1. (4) Mail a copy of your declaration to the attorney or party listed at the top of this form.

4. **IF YOU HAVE ANY QUESTIONS ABOUT THE TIME OR DATE YOU ARE TO APPEAR, OR IF YOU WANT TO BE CERTAIN THAT YOUR PRESENCE IS REQUIRED, CONTACT THE FOLLOWING PERSON BEFORE THE DATE ON WHICH YOU ARE TO APPEAR:**
   a. Name of subpoenaing party or attorney: b. Telephone number:

5. **Witness Fees:** You are entitled to witness fees and mileage actually traveled both ways, as provided by law, if you request them at the time of service. You may request them before your scheduled appearance from the person named in item 4.

DISOBEDIENCE OF THIS SUBPOENA MAY BE PUNISHED AS CONTEMPT BY THIS COURT. YOU WILL ALSO BE LIABLE FOR THE SUM OF FIVE HUNDRED DOLLARS AND ALL DAMAGES RESULTING FROM YOUR FAILURE TO OBEY.

Date issued:

. . . .
(TYPE OR PRINT NAME)

▶ ______________________________
(SIGNATURE OF PERSON ISSUING SUBPOENA)

____
(TITLE)

(Declaration in support of subpoena on reverse)

PLAINTIFF/PETITIONER:	CASE NUMBER:
DEFENDANT/RESPONDENT:	

The production of the documents or the other things sought by the subpoena on page one is supported by *(check one)*:

☐ the attached affidavit or declaration ☐ the following declaration:

DECLARATION IN SUPPORT OF CIVIL SUBPOENA (DUCES TECUM) FOR PERSONAL APPEARANCE AND PRODUCTION OF DOCUMENTS AND THINGS AT TRIAL OR HEARING

(Code Civ. Proc., §§ 1985, 1987.5)

1. I, the undersigned, declare I am the ☐ plaintiff ☐ defendant ☐ petitioner ☐ respondent
   ☐ attorney for *(specify)*: ☐ other *(specify)*:
   in the above-entitled action.

2. The witness has possession or control of the following documents or other things and shall produce them at the time and place specified in the *Civil Subpoena for Personal Appearance and Production of Documents and Things at Trial or Hearing* on page one of this form *(specify the exact documents or other things to be produced)*:

   ☐ Continued on Attachment 2.

3. Good cause exists for the production of the documents or other things described in paragraph 2 for the following reasons:

   ☐ Continued on Attachment 3.

4. These documents or other things described in paragraph 2 are material to the issues involved in this case for the following reasons:

   ☐ Continued on Attachment 4.

I declare under penalty of perjury under the laws of the State of California that the foregoing is true and correct.

Date:

. . . .
(TYPE OR PRINT NAME)

(SIGNATURE OF ☐ SUBPOENAING PARTY ☐ ATTORNEY FOR SUBPOENAING PARTY)

(Proof of service on page three)

PLAINTIFF/PETITIONER:	CASE NUMBER:
DEFENDANT/RESPONDENT:	

PROOF OF SERVICE OF CIVIL SUBPOENA (DUCES TECUM) FOR PERSONAL APPEARANCE AND PRODUCTION OF DOCUMENTS AND THINGS AT TRIAL OR HEARING AND DECLARATION

1. I served this *Civil Subpoena (Duces Tecum) for Personal Appearance and Production of Documents and Things at Trial or Hearing and Declaration* by personally delivering a copy to the person served as follows:
   a. Person served *(name)*:

   b. Address where served:

   c. Date of delivery:

   d. Time of delivery:

   e. Witness fees *(check one)*:
      (1) ☐ were offered or demanded and paid. Amount: . . . . . $ ____________
      (2) ☐ were not demanded or paid.

   f. Fee for service: . . . . $ ____________

2. I received this subpoena for service on *(date)*:

3. Person serving:
   a. ☐ Not a registered California process server.
   b. ☐ California sheriff or marshal.
   c. ☐ Registered California process server.
   d. ☐ Employee or independent contractor of a registered California process server.
   e. ☐ Exempt from registration under Business and Professions Code section 22350(b).
   f. ☐ Registered professional photocopier.
   g. ☐ Exempt from registration under Business and Professions Code section 22451.
   h. Name, address, telephone number, and, if applicable, county of registration and number:

I declare under penalty of perjury under the laws of the State of California that the foregoing is true and correct.

Date:

▶ ______________________________
(SIGNATURE)

(For California sheriff or marshal use only)
I certify that the foregoing is true and correct.

Date:

▶ ______________________________
(SIGNATURE)

FL-340

ATTORNEY OR PARTY WITHOUT ATTORNEY *(Name and Address)* TELEPHONE NO.:	FOR COURT USE ONLY
ATTORNEY FOR *(Name)*:	
SUPERIOR COURT OF CALIFORNIA, COUNTY OF STREET ADDRESS: MAILING ADDRESS: CITY AND ZIP CODE: BRANCH NAME:	
PETITIONER/PLAINTIFF: RESPONDENT/DEFENDANT: CLAIMANT:	
FINDINGS AND ORDER AFTER HEARING	CASE NUMBER:

1. This proceeding was heard
   on *(date)*: at *(time)*: in Dept.: Room:
   by Judge *(name)*: ☐ Temporary Judge

   ☐ Petitioner/plaintiff present ☐ Attorney present *(name)*:
   ☐ Respondent/defendant present ☐ Attorney present *(name)*:
   ☐ Claimant present ☐ Attorney present *(name)*:
   On the order to show cause or motion filed *(date)*: by *(name)*:

2. **THE COURT ORDERS**
3. Custody and visitation: ☐ As attached ☐ Not applicable
4. Child support: ☐ As attached ☐ Not applicable
5. Spousal-Family support: ☐ As attached ☐ Not applicable
6. Property orders: ☐ As attached ☐ Not applicable
7. Other orders: ☐ As attached ☐ Not applicable
8. ☐ Attorney fees *(specify amount)*: $
   Payable to *(name and address)*:

   Payable ☐ forthwith ☐ other *(specify)*:

9. All other issues are reserved until further order of court.

Date:

▶ ________________________________
JUDGE OF THE SUPERIOR COURT

Approved as conforming to court order.

▶ ________________________________
SIGNATURE OF ATTORNEY FOR ☐ PETITIONER / PLAINTIFF ☐ RESPONDENT / DEFENDANT

Form Adopted for Mandatory Use
Judicial Council of California
FL-340 [Rev. January 1, 2003]

FINDINGS AND ORDER AFTER HEARING
(Family Law—Custody and Support—Uniform Parentage)

www.courtinfo.ca.gov

PETITIONER / PLAINTIFF:	CASE NUMBER:
RESPONDENT / DEFENDANT:	

CHILD CUSTODY AND VISITATION ORDER ATTACHMENT

Attachment to ☐ **Findings and Order After Hearing** ☐ **Judgment** ☐ **Other**
☐ **Stipulation and Order for Custody and/or Visitation of Children**

1. ☐ **CUSTODY** Custody of the minor children of the parties is awarded as follows:

Child's name	Date of birth	Legal custody to *(Person who makes decisions about health, education, etc.)*	Physical custody to *(Person the child lives with.)*

2. ☐ **VISITATION**
   a. ☐ Reasonable right of visitation to the party without physical custody. *(Not appropriate in cases involving domestic violence.)*
   b. ☐ See the attached __________ page document dated: ____________.
   c. ☐ The parties will go to mediation at:
   d. ☐ No visitation.
   e. ☐ Visitation for ☐ Father ☐ Mother will be:

(i) ☐ **WEEKENDS** *(starting)*:
(The 1st weekend of the month is the 1st weekend with a Saturday.)
☐ 1st ☐ 2nd ☐ 3rd ☐ 4th ☐ 5th weekend of the month

from ____________________ at __________ ☐ a.m. ☐ p.m.
(day of week) *(time)*

to ____________________ at __________ ☐ a.m. ☐ p.m.
(day of week) *(time)*

☐ The parents will alternate the 5th weekends, with the ☐ Father ☐ Mother having the first 5th weekend.
☐ Father to have 5th weekends in ☐ odd ☐ even months.
☐ Mother to have 5th weekends in ☐ odd ☐ even months.

(ii) ☐ **ALTERNATE WEEKENDS** *(specify starting date)*: ______________
☐ Father ☐ Mother will have the children with him/her *(specify days and times)*.

from ____________________ at __________ ☐ a.m. ☐ p.m.
(day of week) *(time)*

to ____________________ at __________ ☐ a.m. ☐ p.m.
(day of week) *(time)*

(iii) ☐ **WEEKDAYS** *(starting)*:
☐ Father ☐ Mother will have the children with him/her *(specify days and times)*:

from ____________________ at __________ ☐ a.m. ☐ p.m.
(day of week) *(time)*

to ____________________ at __________ ☐ a.m. ☐ p.m.
(day of week) *(time)*

(iv) ☐ **OTHER** *(specify days and times as well as any additional restrictions)*: ☐ See Attachment 2e(iv).

PETITIONER / PLAINTIFF: RESPONDENT / DEFENDANT:	CASE NUMBER:

3. ☐ **SUPERVISED VISITATION**
until ☐ further order of the court ☐ other
☐ Father ☐ Mother will have supervised visitation with the minor children according to the schedule set forth on page 1. *(You must attach form FL-341(A).)*

4. ☐ **TRANSPORTATION FOR VISITATION**
   a. ☐ Transportation *to* the visits will be provided by ☐ Father ☐ Mother ☐ Other *(specify):*
   b. ☐ Transportation *from* the visits will be provided by ☐ Father ☐ Mother ☐ Other *(specify):*
   c. ☐ Drop-off/Pickup of the children will be at *(address):*
   d. ☐ The children will be driven only by a licensed and insured driver. The car or truck must have legal child restraint devices.
   e. ☐ During the exchanges, the parent driving the children will wait in the car and the other parent will wait in their home while the children go to the home.
   f. ☐ Other *(specify):*

5. ☐ **TRAVEL WITH CHILDREN** ☐ Father ☐ Mother ☐ Other *(name):*
must have written permission from the other parent or a court order to take the children outside of
   a. ☐ the State of California
   b. ☐ the following counties *(specify):*
   c. ☐ other places *(specify):*

6. ☐ **CHILD ABDUCTION PREVENTION**
There is a risk that one of the parents will take the children out of California without the other parent's permission. Form FL-341(B) is attached and must be obeyed.

7. ☐ **HOLIDAY SCHEDULE**
The children will spend holiday time as listed in attached ☐ form FL-341(C) ☐ Other.

8. ☐ **ADDITIONAL CUSTODY PROVISIONS**
The parents will follow the additional custody provisions as listed in attached ☐ form FL-341(D) ☐ Other.

9. ☐ **JOINT LEGAL CUSTODY**
The parents will share joint legal custody as listed in attached ☐ form FL-341(E) ☐ Other.

10. ☐ **OTHER** *(specify)*:

11. **JURISDICTION:** This court has jurisdiction to make child custody orders in this case under the Uniform Child Custody Jurisdiction and Enforcement Act (part 3 of the California Family Code commencing with section 3400).

12. **NOTICE AND OPPORTUNITY TO BE HEARD:** The responding party was given notice and an opportunity to be heard as provided by the laws of the State of California.

13. **COUNTRY OF HABITUAL RESIDENCE:** The country of habitual residence of the child or children in this case is
☐ the United States ☐ Other *(specify):*

14. **PENALTIES FOR VIOLATING THIS ORDER:** If you violate this order you may be subject to civil or criminal penalties, or both.

PETITIONER / PLAINTIFF: RESPONDENT / DEFENDANT:	CASE NUMBER:

SUPERVISED VISITATION ORDER
Attachment to *Child Custody and Visitation Order Attachment* (form FL-341)

1. Evidence has been presented in support of a request that the contact of ☐ Petitioner ☐ Respondent with the child(ren) be supervised based upon allegations of
   ☐ abduction of child(ren) ☐ physical abuse ☐ drug abuse ☐ neglect
   ☐ sexual abuse ☐ domestic violence ☐ alcohol abuse ☐ other *(specify):*

   ☐ Petitioner ☐ Respondent disputes these allegations and the court reserves the findings on these issues pending further investigation and hearing or trial.

2. The court finds, under Family Code section 3100, that the best interest of the child(ren) requires that visitation by ☐ Petitioner ☐ Respondent must, until further order of the court, be limited to contact supervised by the person(s) set forth in item 6 below pending further investigation and hearing or trial.

THE COURT MAKES THE FOLLOWING ORDERS

3. **CHILD(REN) TO BE SUPERVISED**

Child's name	Birth date	Age	Sex

4. **TYPE**
   a. ☐ Supervised visitation b. ☐ Supervised exchange only c. ☐ Therapeutic visitation

5. **SUPERVISED VISITATION PROVIDER**
   a. ☐ Professional (individual provider or supervised visitation center) b. ☐ Nonprofessional

6. **AUTHORIZED PROVIDER**

Name	Address	Telephone

   ☐ Any other mutually agreed-upon third party as arranged.

7. **DURATION AND FREQUENCY OF VISITS** *(see form FL-341 for specifics of visitation):*

8. **PAYMENT RESPONSIBILITY** Petitioner: ______% Respondent: ______%

9. ☐ Petitioner will contact professional provider or supervised visitation center no later than *(date):*
   ☐ Respondent will contact professional provider or supervised visitation center no later than *(date):*

10. **THE COURT FURTHER ORDERS**

Date:

JUDICIAL OFFICER

Form Adopted for Mandatory Use
Judicial Council of California
FL-341(A) [Rev. January 1, 2003]

Family Code, §§ 3100, 3031
www.courtinfo.ca.gov

PETITIONER / PLAINTIFF: RESPONDENT / DEFENDANT: OTHER PARENT:	CASE NUMBER:

CHILD SUPPORT INFORMATION AND ORDER ATTACHMENT

Attachment to ☐ **Findings and Order After Hearing** ☐ **Restraining Order After Hearing (CLETS)**
☐ **Judgment** ☐ **Other**

THE COURT USED THE FOLLOWING INFORMATION IN DETERMINING THE AMOUNT OF CHILD SUPPORT

1. ☐ A printout of a computer calculation and findings is attached and incorporated in this order for all required items not filled out below.

2. ☐ **INCOME**

   a. Each parent's monthly income is as follows:

	Gross monthly income	Net monthly income	Receiving TANF/CalWORKS
Mother:	$	$	☐
Father:	$	$	☐

   b. Imputation of Income. The court finds that the ☐ Mother ☐ Father has the capacity to earn: $ per: and has based the support order upon this imputed income.

3. ☐ **CHILDREN OF THIS RELATIONSHIP**

   a. Number of children who are the subjects of the support order *(specify)*:

   b. Approximate percentage of time spent with: Mother %
   Father %

4. ☐ **HARDSHIPS**

   Hardships for the following have been allowed in calculating child support:

	Mother	Father	Approximate ending time for the hardship
a. ☐ Other minor children:	$	$	
b. ☐ Extraordinary medical expenses:	$	$	
c. ☐ Catastrophic losses:	$	$	

THE COURT ORDERS

5. ☐ **LOW INCOME ADJUSTMENT**

   The court finds that the net income of the parent who will pay support is less than $1,000 per month. Based on the facts presented to the court, the principles provided in Family Code section 4053, and the impact of the contemplated adjustment on the respective net incomes of the mother and father, the court makes the following determination:

   a. ☐ There shall be no low income adjustment.

   b. ☐ There shall be a low income adjustment of: $ per month based upon *(specify)*:

6. ☐ **CHILD SUPPORT**

   a. **Base child support**

   ☐ Mother ☐ Father must pay child support beginning *(date)*:
   and continuing until further order of the court, or until the child marries, dies, is emancipated, reaches age 19, or reaches age 18 and is not a full-time high school student, whichever occurs first, as follows:

Child's name	Date of birth	Monthly amount	Payable to *(name)*

   Payable ☐ on the 1st of the month ☐ one-half on the 1st and one-half on the 15th of the month
   ☐ other *(specify)*:

   b. ☐ **Mandatory additional child support**

   (1) ☐ Child care costs related to employment or reasonably necessary job training.
   ☐ Mother must pay: % of total or ☐ $ per month child care costs.
   ☐ Father must pay: % of total or ☐ $ per month child care costs.
   ☐ Costs to be paid as follows *(specify)*:

THIS IS A COURT ORDER

PETITIONER / PLAINTIFF: RESPONDENT / DEFENDANT: OTHER PARENT:	CASE NUMBER:

THE COURT FURTHER ORDERS

6. b. **Mandatory additional child support *(continued)***

(2) ☐ Reasonable uninsured health care costs for the children

☐ Mother must pay: % of total or ☐ $ per month.

☐ Father must pay: % of total or ☐ $ per month.

☐ Costs to be paid as follows *(specify):*

c. ☐ **Additional child support**

(1) ☐ Costs related to the educational or other special needs of the children

☐ Mother must pay: % of total or ☐ $ per month.

☐ Father must pay: % of total or ☐ $ per month.

☐ Costs to be paid as follows *(specify):*

(2) ☐ Travel expenses for visitation

☐ Mother must pay: % of total or ☐ $ per month.

☐ Father must pay: % of total or ☐ $ per month.

☐ Costs to be paid as follows *(specify):*

Total child support per month: $

7. **HEALTH CARE EXPENSES**

a. Health insurance coverage for the minor children of the parties must be maintained by ☐ Mother ☐ Father, if available at no or reasonable cost through their respective places of employment or self-employment. Both parties are ordered to cooperate in the presentation, collection, and reimbursement of any health care claims.

b. ☐ Health insurance is not available to ☐ Mother ☐ Father at a reasonable cost at this time.

c. ☐ The party providing coverage must assign the right of reimbursement to the other party.

8. **EARNINGS ASSIGNMENT**

a. An *Order/Notice to Withhold Income for Child Support* (form FL-195) must issue. Note: The payor of child support is responsible for the payment of support directly to the recipient until support payments are deducted from the payor's wages, and for any support not paid by the assignment.

9. ☐ **NON-GUIDELINE ORDER**

This order does not meet the child support guideline set forth in Family Code section 4055. A *Non-Guideline Child Support Findings Attachment* (form FL-342(A)) is attached.

10. ☐ **EMPLOYMENT SEARCH ORDER (Fam. Code, § 4505)**

☐ Mother ☐ Father is ordered to seek employment with the following terms and conditions:

11. **OTHER ORDERS:**

12. **REQUIRED ATTACHMENTS**

A *Notice of Rights and Responsibilities — Health Care Costs and Reimbursement Procedures* and *Information Sheet on Changing a Child Support Order* (form FL-192) must be attached and is incorporated into this order.

13. **CHILD SUPPORT CASE REGISTRY FORM**

Both parties must complete and file with the court a *Child Support Case Registry Form* (form FL-191) within 10 days of the date of this order. Thereafter, the parties must notify the court of any change in the information submitted within 10 days of the change by filing an updated form.

NOTICE: Any party required to pay child support must pay interest on overdue amounts at the "legal" rate, which is currently 10 percent per year.

THIS IS A COURT ORDER

PETITIONER/PLAINTIFF:	CASE NUMBER:
RESPONDENT/DEFENDANT:	

NON-GUIDELINE CHILD SUPPORT FINDINGS ATTACHMENT

Attachment to ☐ Child Support Information and Order Attachment (form FL-342)
☐ Judgment (Family Law) (form FL-180) ☐ Other *(specify):*

The court makes the following findings required by Family Code sections 4056, 4057, and 4065:

1. **STIPULATION TO NON-GUIDELINE ORDER**
☐ The child support agreed to by the parties is ☐ below or ☐ above the statewide child support guidelines. The amount of support that would have been ordered under the guideline formula is: $ per month. The parties have been fully informed of their rights concerning child support. Neither party is acting out of duress or coercion. Neither party is receiving public assistance and no application for public assistance is pending. The needs of the children will be adequately met by this agreed-upon amount of child support. If the order is below the guideline, no change of circumstances will be required to modify this order. If the order is above the guideline, a change of circumstances will be required to modify this order.

OTHER REBUTTAL FACTORS

2. ☐ **Support calculation**
   a. The guideline amount of child support calculated is: $
   per month **payable** by ☐ mother ☐ father

   b. The court finds by a preponderance of the evidence that rebuttal factors exist. The rebuttal factors result in an ☐ increase ☐ decrease in child support. The revised amount of support is: $ per month.

   c. The court finds the child support amount revised by these factors to be in the best interest of the child and that application of the formula would be unjust or inappropriate in this case.
   These changes remain in effect ☐ until *(date):*
   ☐ until further order

   d. **The factors are:**
   (1) ☐ The sale of the family residence is deferred under Family Code section 3800, and the rental value of the family residence in which the children reside exceeds the mortgage payments, homeowners insurance, and property taxes by: $ per month. (Fam. Code, § 4057(b)(2).)

   (2) ☐ The parent paying support has extraordinarily high income, and the amount determined under the guideline would exceed the needs of the child. (Fam. Code, § 4057(b)(3).)

   (3) ☐ The ☐ mother ☐ father is not contributing to the needs of the children at a level commensurate with that party's custodial time. (Fam. Code, § 4057(b)(4).)

   (4) ☐ Special circumstances exist in this case. The special circumstances are:
   (i) ☐ The parents have different timesharing arrangements for different children. (Fam. Code, § 4057(b)(5)(A).)
   (ii) ☐ The parents have substantially equal custody of the children and one parent has a much lower or higher percentage of income used for housing than the other parent. (Fam. Code, § 4057(b)(5)(B).)
   (iii) ☐ The child has special medical or other needs that require support greater than the formula amount. These needs are (Fam. Code, § 4057(b)(5)(C)) *(specify):*

   (iv) ☐ Other (Fam. Code, § 4057(b)(5)) *(specify):*

Form Adopted for Mandatory Use
Judicial Council of California
FL-342(A) [Rev. January 1, 2003]

Family Code, § 4056
www.courtinfo.ca.gov

PETITIONER / PLAINTIFF:	CASE NUMBER:
RESPONDENT / DEFENDANT:	
OTHER PARENT:	

SPOUSAL OR FAMILY SUPPORT ORDER ATTACHMENT

Attachment to ☐ Findings and Order After Hearing or ☐ Judgment or ☐ Other

THE COURT FINDS

1. A printout of a computer calculation of the parties' financial circumstances is attached for all required items not filled out below.

2. **NET INCOME** *(Complete at least one):*
The parties' monthly income and deductions are as follows:

	Total gross monthly income	Total monthly deductions	Total hardship deductions	Net monthly disposable income
a. Petitioner: ☐ receiving TANF/CalWORKS				
b. Respondent: ☐ receiving TANF/CalWORKS				

3. **OTHER FACTORS REGARDING PERMANENT SPOUSAL SUPPORT:**
   a. ☐ The parties were married for ______ years _____ months.
   b. ☐ The Family Code § 4320 factors were considered, as listed in Attachment 3b.
   c. ☐ The marital standard of living was *(describe):*
   ☐ Continued in Attachment 3c.

   d. ☐ Other *(specify):*

THE COURT ORDERS

4. a. ☐ Petitioner ☐ Respondent must pay to ☐ Petitioner ☐ Respondent
as ☐ spousal support ☐ family support

$ per month, beginning *(date):* , payable until *(specify duration):*

☐ payable on the *(specify):* day of each month
☐ payable other *(specify):*

   b. Support must be paid by check, money order, or cash. The support payor's obligation to pay support will terminate on the death or remarriage of the support payee.
   c. An earnings assignment for the foregoing support must issue. Note: The payor of spousal/family support is responsible for the payment of support directly to the recipient until support payments are deducted from the payor's earnings and for any support not paid by the assignment.
   d. ☐ Service of the earnings assignment is stayed provided the payor is not more than days late in the payment of spousal/family support.

Form Approved for Optional Use
Judicial Council of California
FL-343 [Rev. January 1, 2003]

Family Code, §§ 150, 3651, 3653, 3654, 4320, 4330, 4337
www.courtinfo.ca.gov.

PETITIONER / PLAINTIFF: RESPONDENT / DEFENDANT: OTHER PARENT:	CASE NUMBER:

5. ☐ The parties must promptly inform each other of any change of employment, including the employer's name, address, and telephone number.

6. ☐ Notice: It is the goal of this State that each party must make reasonable good faith efforts to become self-supporting as provided for in Family Code section 4320. The failure to make reasonable good faith efforts may be one of the factors considered by the court as a basis for modifying or terminating support.

7. ☐ This order is for family support. Both parties must complete and file with the court a *Child Support Case Registry Form* (form FL-191) within 10 days of the date of this order. The parents must notify the court of any change of information submitted within 10 days of the change by filing an updated form. The *Notice of Rights and Responsibilities* and *Information Sheet on Changing a Child Support Order* (form FL-192) is attached.

8. ☐ Other *(specify)*:

NOTICE: Any party required to pay support must pay interest on overdue amounts at the "legal" rate, which is currently 10 percent.

THIS IS A COURT ORDER

PETITIONER : RESPONDENT:	CASE NUMBER:

PROPERTY ORDER ATTACHMENT TO FINDINGS AND ORDER AFTER HEARING

THE COURT ORDERS

1. ☐ **Property restraining orders**
   a. ☐ Petitioner ☐ Respondent ☐ Claimant is restrained from transferring, encumbering, hypothecating, concealing, or in any way disposing of any property, real or personal, whether community, quasi-community, or separate, except in the usual course of business or for the necessities of life.
   b. ☐ Petitioner ☐ Respondent must notify the other party of any proposed extraordinary expenses at least 5 business days before incurring such expenses, and make an accounting of such to the court.
   c. ☐ Petitioner ☐ Respondent is restrained from cashing, borrowing against, cancelling, transferring, disposing of, or changing the beneficiaries of any insurance or other coverage including life, health, automobile, and disability held for the benefit of the parties or their minor child or children.
   d. ☐ Petitioner ☐ Respondent must not incur any debts or liabilities for which the other may be held responsible, other than in the ordinary course of business or for the necessities of life.
2. ☐ **Possession of property**
   a. The exclusive use, possession, and control of the following property the parties own or are buying is given to:

Property	Given to

   b. ☐ As attached.
3. ☐ **Payment of debts**
   a. Payments on the following debts coming due while this order is in effect must be paid as follows:

Total debt	Amount of payments	Pay to	Paid by

   b. ☐ As attached.
4. ☐ These are temporary orders only. The court will make final orders at the time of judgment.
5. ☐ Other *(specify)*:

Form Adopted for Mandatory Use
Judicial Council of California
FL-344 [Rev. January 1, 2004]

Family Code, §§ 2045, 6324
www.courtinfo.ca.gov

ATTORNEY OR PARTY WITHOUT ATTORNEY *(Name and Address):* TELEPHONE NO.:

ATTORNEY FOR *(Name):*

SUPERIOR COURT OF CALIFORNIA, COUNTY OF

SHORT TITLE OF CASE:

FORM INTERROGATORIES—Family Law

Asking Party:

Answering Party:

Set No.:

CASE NUMBER:

Sec. 1. Instructions to Both Parties

These interrogatories are intended to provide for the exchange of relevant information without unreasonable expense to the answering party. They do not change existing law relating to interrogatories nor do they affect the answering party's right to assert any privilege or make any objection. **Privileges must be asserted.**

Sec. 2. Definitions

Words in **BOLDFACE CAPITALS** in these interrogatories are defined as follows:

(a) **PERSON** includes a natural person, partnership, any kind of business, legal, or public entity, and its agents or employees.

(b) **DOCUMENT** means all written, recorded, or graphic materials, however stored, produced, or reproduced.

(c) **ASSET or PROPERTY** includes any interest in real estate or personal property. It includes any interest in a pension, profit-sharing, or retirement plan.

(d) **DEBT** means any obligation including debts paid since the date of separation.

(e) **SUPPORT** means any benefit or economic contribution to the living expenses of another person, including gifts.

(f) If asked to **IDENTIFY A PERSON**, give the person's name, last known residence and business address, telephone numbers, and company affiliation at the date of the transaction referred to.

(g) If asked to **IDENTIFY A DOCUMENT**, attach a copy of the document unless you explain why not. If you do not attach the copy, describe the document, including its date and nature, and give the name, address, telephone number, and occupation of the person who has the document.

Sec. 3. Instructions to the Asking Party

Check the box next to each interrogatory you want the answering party to answer.

Sec. 4. Instructions to the Answering Party

You must answer these interrogatories under oath within 30 days, in accordance with Code of Civil Procedure section 2030.

You must furnish all information you have or can reasonably find out, including all information (not privileged) of your attorneys or under your control. If you don't know, say so.

If an interrogatory is answered by referring to a document, the document must be attached as an exhibit to the response and referred to in the response. If the document has more than one page, refer to the page and section where the answer can be found.

If a document to be attached to the response may also be attached to the *Schedule of Assets and Debts* (form FL-142), the document should be attached only to the response, and the form should refer to the response.

If an interrogatory cannot be answered completely, answer as much as you can, state the reason you cannot answer the rest, and state any information you have about the unanswered portion.

Sec. 5. Oath

Your answers to these interrogatories must be under oath, dated, and signed. Use the following form *at the end of your answers:*

"I declare under penalty of perjury under the laws of the State of California that the foregoing answers are true and correct."

______________ ______________________

(DATE) (SIGNATURE)

Form Approved for Optional Use
Judicial Council of California
FL-145 [Rev. January 1, 2003]

Code of Civil Procedure, §§ 2030(c), 2033.5
www.courtinfo.ca.gov

☐ 1. ***Personal History.*** State your full name, current residence address and work address, social security number, any other names you have used, and the dates between which you used each name.

☐ 2. ***Agreements.*** Are there any agreements between you and your spouse made before or during your marriage or after your separation that affect the disposition of **ASSETS, DEBTS,** or **SUPPORT** in this proceeding? If your answer is yes, for each agreement, state the date made and whether it was written or oral, and attach a copy of the agreement or describe its content.

☐ 3. ***Legal Actions.*** Are you a party or do you anticipate being a party to any legal or administrative proceeding other than this action? If your answer is yes, state your role and the name, jurisdiction, case number, and a brief description of each proceeding.

☐ 4. ***Persons Sharing Residence.*** State the name, age, and relationship to you of each **person** at your present address.

☐ 5. ***Support Provided Others.*** State the name, age, address, and relationship to you of each **PERSON** for whom you have provided **SUPPORT** during the past 12 months and the amount provided per month for each.

☐ 6. ***Support Received for Others.*** State the name, age, address, and relationship to you of each **PERSON** for whom you have received **SUPPORT** during the past twelve months and the amount received per month for each.

☐ 7. ***Current Income.*** List all income you received during the past 12 months, its source, the basis for its computation, and the total amount received from each. Attach your last three paycheck stubs.

☐ 8. ***Other Income.*** During the past three years have you received cash or other property from any source not identified in 7? If so, list the source, the date, and the nature and value of the property.

☐ 9. ***Tax Returns.*** Attach copies of all tax returns and schedules filed by or for you in any jurisdiction for the past three calendar years.

☐ 10. ***Schedule of Assets and Debts.*** Complete the *Schedule of Assets and Debts* (form FL-142) served with these interrogatories.

☐ 11. ***Separate Property Contentions.*** State the facts that support your contention that an asset or debt is separate property.

☐ 12. ***Property Valuations.*** Have you had written appraisals or offers to purchase during the past 12 months on any of the assets listed on your completed *Schedule of Assets and Debts*. If your answer is yes, **IDENTIFY THE DOCUMENT**.

☐ 13. ***Property Held by Others.*** Is there any **PROPERTY** held by any third party in which you have any interest or over which you have any control? If your answer is yes, indicate whether the property is shown on the *Schedule of Assets and Debts* completed by you. If it is not, describe and identify each such asset and state its present value and the basis for your valuation, and **IDENTIFY THE PERSON** holding the asset.

☐ 14. ***Retirement and Other Benefits.*** Do you have an interest in any disability, retirement, profit sharing, or deferred compensation plan? If your answer is yes, **IDENTIFY** each plan and provide the name, address, and telephone number of the administrator and custodian of records.

☐ 15. ***Claims of Reimbursement.*** Do you claim the legal right to be reimbursed for any expenditures of your separate or community property? If your answer is yes, state all supporting facts.

☐ 16. ***Credits.*** Do you claim reimbursement credits for payments of community debts since the date of separation? If your answer is yes, **IDENTIFY** the source of payment, the creditor, the date paid, and the amount paid. State whether you have added to the debt since the separation.

☐ 17. ***Insurance.*** **IDENTIFY** each health, life, automobile, and disability insurance policy or plan that you now own or that covers you, your children, or your assets. State the policy type, policy number, and name of company. **IDENTIFY** the agent and give the address.

☐ 18. ***Health.*** Is there any physical or emotional condition that limits your ability to work? If your answer is yes, state each fact on which you base your answer.

☐ 19. ***Children's Needs.*** Do you contend your children have any special needs? If so, identify the child with the need, the reason for the need, its cost, and its expected duration.

☐ 20. ***Attorney Fees.*** State the total amount of attorney fees and costs incurred by you in this proceeding, the amount paid, the source of money paid, and describe the billing arrangements.

☐ 21. ***Gifts.*** List any gifts you have made without the consent of your spouse in the past 24 months, their value, and the recipients.

ATTORNEY OR PARTY WITHOUT ATTORNEY *(Name, state bar number, and address)*:	*FOR COURT USE ONLY*
TELEPHONE NO.: FAX NO.: ATTORNEY FOR *(Name)*:	
NAME OF COURT: STREET ADDRESS: MAILING ADDRESS: CITY AND ZIP CODE: BRANCH NAME:	
PLAINTIFF/ PETITIONER: DEFENDANT/ RESPONDENT:	
DEPOSITION SUBPOENA **For Production of Business Records**	CASE NUMBER:

THE PEOPLE OF THE STATE OF CALIFORNIA, TO *(name, address, and telephone number of deponent, if known)*:

1. **YOU ARE ORDERED TO PRODUCE THE BUSINESS RECORDS described in item 3, as follows:**

To *(name of deposition officer)*:
On *(date)*: At *(time)*:
Location *(address)*:

Do not release the requested records to the deposition officer prior to the date and time stated above.

a. ☐ by delivering a true, legible, and durable **copy** of the business records described in item 3, enclosed in a sealed inner wrapper with the title and number of the action, name of witness, and date of subpoena clearly written on it. The inner wrapper shall then be enclosed in an outer envelope or wrapper, sealed, and mailed to the deposition officer at the address in item 1.

b. ☐ by delivering a true, legible, and durable **copy** of the business records described in item 3 to the deposition officer at the witness's address, on receipt of payment in cash or by check of the reasonable costs of preparing the copy, as determined under Evidence Code section 1563(b).

c. ☐ by making the **original** business records described in item 3 available for inspection at your business address by the attorney's representative and permitting **copying** at your business address under reasonable conditions during normal business hours.

2. *The records are to be produced by the date and time shown in item 1 (but not sooner than 20 days after the issuance of the deposition subpoena, or 15 days after service, whichever date is later). Reasonable costs of locating records, making them available or copying them, and postage, if any, are recoverable as set forth in Evidence Code section 1563(b). The records shall be accompanied by an affidavit of the custodian or other qualified witness pursuant to Evidence Code section 1561.*

3. **The records to be produced are described as follows:**

☐ Continued on Attachment 3.

4. **IF YOU HAVE BEEN SERVED WITH THIS SUBPOENA AS A CUSTODIAN OF CONSUMER OR EMPLOYEE RECORDS UNDER CODE OF CIVIL PROCEDURE SECTION 1985.3 OR 1985.6 AND A MOTION TO QUASH OR AN OBJECTION HAS BEEN SERVED ON YOU, A COURT ORDER OR AGREEMENT OF THE PARTIES, WITNESSES, *AND* CONSUMER OR EMPLOYEE AFFECTED MUST BE OBTAINED BEFORE YOU ARE REQUIRED TO PRODUCE CONSUMER OR EMPLOYEE RECORDS.**

DISOBEDIENCE OF THIS SUBPOENA MAY BE PUNISHED AS CONTEMPT BY THIS COURT. YOU WILL ALSO BE LIABLE FOR THE SUM OF FIVE HUNDRED DOLLARS AND ALL DAMAGES RESULTING FROM YOUR FAILURE TO OBEY.

Date issued:

. . . . ▶ ______________________________

(TYPE OR PRINT NAME) (SIGNATURE OF PERSON ISSUING SUBPOENA)

____

(TITLE)

(Proof of service on reverse)

PLAINTIFF/PETITIONER:	CASE NUMBER:
DEFENDANT/RESPONDENT:	

PROOF OF SERVICE OF DEPOSITION SUBPOENA FOR PRODUCTION OF BUSINESS RECORDS

1. I served this *Deposition Subpoena for Production of Business Records* by personally delivering a copy to the person served as follows:
   a. Person served *(name)*:

   b. Address where served:

   c. Date of delivery:

   d. Time of delivery:

   e. (1) ☐ Witness fees were paid.
   Amount: . . . . $ ____________
   (2) ☐ Copying fees were paid.
   Amount: . . . . $ ____________

   f. Fee for service: . . . . $ ____________

2. I received this subpoena for service on *(date)*:

3. Person serving:
   a. ☐ Not a registered California process server.
   b. ☐ California sheriff or marshal.
   c ☐ Registered California process server.
   d. ☐ Employee or independent contractor of a registered California process server.
   e. ☐ Exempt from registration under Business and Professions Code section 22350(b).
   f. ☐ Registered professional photocopier.
   g. ☐ Exempt from registration under Business and Professions Code section 22451.
   h. Name, address, telephone number, and, if applicable, county of registration and number:

I declare under penalty of perjury under the laws of the State of California that the foregoing is true and correct.

Date:

▶ ______________________________
(SIGNATURE)

(For California sheriff or marshal use only)
I certify that the foregoing is true and correct.

Date:

▶ ______________________________
(SIGNATURE)

ATTORNEY OR PARTY WITHOUT ATTORNEY *(Name, state bar number, and address)*:

TELEPHONE NO.: FAX NO.:

ATTORNEY FOR *(Name)*:

NAME OF COURT:
STREET ADDRESS:
MAILING ADDRESS:
CITY AND ZIP CODE:
BRANCH NAME:

PLAINTIFF/ PETITIONER:

DEFENDANT/ RESPONDENT:

CASE NUMBER:

NOTICE TO CONSUMER OR EMPLOYEE AND OBJECTION
(Code Civ. Proc., §§ 1985.3, 1985.6)

NOTICE TO CONSUMER OR EMPLOYEE

TO *(name)*:

1. PLEASE TAKE NOTICE THAT **REQUESTING PARTY *(name)*:** SEEKS YOUR RECORDS FOR EXAMINATION by the parties to this action on *(specify date)*:

   The records are described in the subpoena directed to **witness** *(specify name and address of person or entity from whom records are sought)*:

   A copy of the subpoena is attached.
2. IF YOU OBJECT to the production of these records, YOU MUST DO ONE OF THE FOLLOWING BEFORE THE DATE SPECIFIED IN ITEM a. OR b. BELOW:
   a. If you are a party to the above-entitled action, you must file a motion pursuant to Code of Civil Procedure section 1987.1 to quash or modify the subpoena and give notice of that motion to the **witness** and the **deposition officer** named in the subpoena at least five days before the date set for production of the records.
   b. If you are not a party to this action, you must serve on the **requesting party** and on the **witness**, before the date set for production of the records, a written objection that states the specific grounds on which production of such records should be prohibited. You may use the form below to object and state the grounds for your objection. You must complete the Proof of Service on the reverse side indicating whether you personally served or mailed the objection. The objection should **not** be filed with the court. **WARNING:** IF YOUR OBJECTION IS NOT RECEIVED BEFORE THE DATE SPECIFIED IN ITEM 1, YOUR RECORDS MAY BE PRODUCED AND MAY BE AVAILABLE TO ALL PARTIES.
3. YOU OR YOUR ATTORNEY MAY CONTACT THE UNDERSIGNED to determine whether an agreement can be reached in writing to cancel or limit the scope of the subpoena. If no such agreement is reached, and if you are not otherwise represented by an attorney in this action, YOU SHOULD CONSULT AN ATTORNEY TO ADVISE YOU OF YOUR RIGHTS OF PRIVACY.

Date:

. . . . ▶ ____________________

(TYPE OR PRINT NAME) (SIGNATURE OF ☐ REQUESTING PARTY ☐ ATTORNEY)

OBJECTION BY NON-PARTY TO PRODUCTION OF RECORDS

1. ☐ I object to the production of all of my records specified in the subpoena.
2. ☐ I object only to the production of the following specified records:

3. The specific grounds for my objection are as follows:

Date:

. . . . ▶ ____________________

(TYPE OR PRINT NAME) (SIGNATURE)

(Proof of service on reverse)

PLAINTIFF/PETITIONER: DEFENDANT/RESPONDENT:	CASE NUMBER:

PROOF OF SERVICE OF NOTICE TO CONSUMER OR EMPLOYEE AND OBJECTION

(Code Civ. Proc., §§ 1985.3, 1985.6)

☐ **Personal Service** ☐ **Mail**

1. At the time of service I was at least 18 years of age and **not a party to this legal action.**
2. I served a copy of the *Notice to Consumer or Employee and Objection* as follows *(check either a or b)*:
   a. ☐ **Personal service.** I personally delivered the *Notice to Consumer or Employee and Objection* as follows:
      (1) Name of person served: (3) Date served:
      (2) Address where served: (4) Time served:

   b. ☐ **Mail.** I deposited the *Notice to Consumer or Employee and Objection* in the United States mail, in a sealed envelope with postage fully prepaid. The envelope was addressed as follows:
      (1) Name of person served: (3) Date of mailing:
      (2) Address: (4) Place of mailing *(city and state)*:

      (5) I am a resident of or employed in the county where the *Notice to Consumer or Employee and Objection* was mailed.
   c. My residence or business address is *(specify)*:
   d. My phone number is *(specify)*:

I declare under penalty of perjury under the laws of the State of California that the foregoing is true and correct.

Date:

. . . . ▶ ______________________________

(TYPE OR PRINT NAME OF PERSON WHO SERVED) (SIGNATURE OF PERSON WHO SERVED)

PROOF OF SERVICE OF OBJECTION TO PRODUCTION OF RECORDS

(Code Civ. Proc., §§ 1985.3, 1985.6)

☐ **Personal Service** ☐ **Mail**

1. At the time of service I was at least 18 years of age and **not a party to this legal action.**
2. I served a copy of the *Objection to Production of Records* as follows *(complete either a or b)*:
   a. ON THE REQUESTING PARTY
      (1) ☐ **Personal service.** I personally delivered the *Objection to Production of Records* as follows:
         (i) Name of person served: (iii) Date served:
         (ii) Address where served: (iv) Time served:

      (2) ☐ **Mail.** I deposited the *Objection to Production of Records* in the United States mail, in a sealed envelope with postage fully prepaid. The envelope was addressed as follows:
         (i) Name of person served: (iii) Date of mailing:
         (ii) Address: (iv) Place of mailing *(city and state)*:

         (v) I am a resident of or employed in the county where the *Objection to Production of Records* was mailed.
   b. ON THE WITNESS
      (1) ☐ **Personal service.** I personally delivered the *Objection to Production of Records* as follows:
         (i) Name of person served: (iii) Date served:
         (ii) Address where served: (iv) Time served:

      (2) ☐ **Mail.** I deposited the *Objection to Production of Records* in the United States mail, in a sealed envelope with postage fully prepaid. The envelope was addressed as follows:
         (i) Name of person served: (iii) Date of mailing:
         (ii) Address: (iv) Place of mailing *(city and state)*:

         (v) I am a resident of or employed in the county where the *Objection to Production of Records* was mailed.
3. My residence or business address is *(specify)*:
4. My phone number is *(specify)*:

I declare under penalty of perjury under the laws of the State of California that the foregoing is true and correct.

Date:

. . . . ▶ ______________________________

(TYPE OR PRINT NAME OF PERSON WHO SERVED) (SIGNATURE OF PERSON WHO SERVED)

ATTORNEY OR PARTY WITHOUT ATTORNEY *(Name, state bar number, and address)*:	FOR COURT USE ONLY
TELEPHONE NO.: FAX NO.:	
ATTORNEY FOR *(Name)*:	
NAME OF COURT:	
STREET ADDRESS:	
MAILING ADDRESS:	
CITY AND ZIP CODE:	
BRANCH NAME:	
PLAINTIFF/ PETITIONER:	
DEFENDANT/ RESPONDENT:	
DEPOSITION SUBPOENA For Personal Appearance	CASE NUMBER:

THE PEOPLE OF THE STATE OF CALIFORNIA, TO *(name, address, and telephone number of deponent, if known)*:

1. **YOU ARE ORDERED TO APPEAR IN PERSON TO TESTIFY AS A WITNESS in this action at the following time and place:**

Date:	Time:	Address:

a. ☐ As a deponent who is not a natural person, you are ordered to designate one or more persons to testify on your behalf as to the matters described in item 2. (Code Civ. Proc., § 2025, subd. (d)(6).)

b. ☐ This deposition will be recorded stenographically ☐ through the instant visual display of testimony, and by ☐ audiotape ☐ videotape.

c. ☐ This videotape deposition is intended for possible use at trial under Code of Civil Procedure section 2025(u)(4).

2. ☐ If the witness is a representative of a business or other entity, the matters upon which the witness is to be examined are as follows:

3. *At the deposition, you will be asked questions under oath. Questions and answers are recorded stenographically at the deposition; later they are transcribed for possible use at trial. You may read the written record and change any incorrect answers before you sign the deposition. You are entitled to receive witness fees and mileage actually traveled both ways. The money must be paid, at the option of the party giving notice of the deposition, either with service of this subpoena or at the time of the deposition.*

DISOBEDIENCE OF THIS SUBPOENA MAY BE PUNISHED AS CONTEMPT BY THIS COURT. YOU WILL ALSO BE LIABLE FOR THE SUM OF FIVE HUNDRED DOLLARS AND ALL DAMAGES RESULTING FROM YOUR FAILURE TO OBEY.

Date issued:

(TYPE OR PRINT NAME) ▶ (SIGNATURE OF PERSON ISSUING SUBPOENA)

(TITLE)

(Proof of service on reverse)

PLAINTIFF/PETITIONER:	CASE NUMBER:
DEFENDANT/RESPONDENT:	

PROOF OF SERVICE OF DEPOSITION SUBPOENA FOR PERSONAL APPEARANCE

1. I served this *Deposition Subpoena for Personal Appearance* by personally delivering a copy to the person served as follows:
   a. Person served *(name)*:

   b. Address where served:

   c. Date of delivery:

   d. Time of delivery:

   e. Witness fees and mileage both ways *(check one)*:
      (1) ☐ were paid. Amount: . . . . $ ______________
      (2) ☐ were not paid.
      (3) ☐ were tendered to the witness's public entity employer as required by Government Code section 68097.2. The amount tendered was *(specify)*: . . . . $ ______________

   f. Fee for service: . . . . $ ______________

2. I received this subpoena for service on *(date)*:

3. Person serving:
   a. ☐ Not a registered California process server.
   b. ☐ California sheriff or marshal.
   c. ☐ Registered California process server.
   d. ☐ Employee or independent contractor of a registered California process server.
   e. ☐ Exempt from registration under Business and Professions Code section 22350(b).
   f. ☐ Registered professional photocopier.
   g. ☐ Exempt from registration under Business and Professions Code section 22451.
   h. Name, address, telephone number, and, if applicable, county of registration and number:

I declare under penalty of perjury under the laws of the State of California that the foregoing is true and correct.

Date:

▶ ______________________________
(SIGNATURE)

(For California sheriff or marshal use only)
I certify that the foregoing is true and correct.

Date:

▶ ______________________________
(SIGNATURE)

ATTORNEY OR PARTY WITHOUT ATTORNEY *(Name, state bar number, and address)*: TELEPHONE NO.: FAX NO.: ATTORNEY FOR *(Name)*:	*FOR COURT USE ONLY*
NAME OF COURT: STREET ADDRESS: MAILING ADDRESS: CITY AND ZIP CODE: BRANCH NAME:	
PLAINTIFF/ PETITIONER: DEFENDANT/ RESPONDENT:	
DEPOSITION SUBPOENA **For Personal Appearance and Production of Documents and Things**	CASE NUMBER:

THE PEOPLE OF THE STATE OF CALIFORNIA, TO *(name, address, and telephone number of deponent, if known)*:

1. **YOU ARE ORDERED TO APPEAR IN PERSON TO TESTIFY AS A WITNESS in this action at the following date, time, and place:**

Date:	Time:	Address:

   a. ☐ As a deponent who is not a natural person, you are ordered to designate one or more persons to testify on your behalf as to the matters described in item 4. (Code Civ. Proc., § 2025, subd. (d)(6).)
   b. You are ordered to produce the documents and things described in item 3.
   c. ☐ This deposition will be recorded stenographically ☐ through the instant visual display of testimony, and by ☐ audiotape ☐ videotape.
   d. ☐ This videotape deposition is intended for possible use at trial under Code of Civil Procedure section 2025(u)(4).
2. The personal attendance of the custodian or other qualified witness and the production of the original records are required by this subpoena. The procedure authorized by Evidence Code sections 1560(b), 1561, and 1562 will not be deemed sufficient compliance with this subpoena.
3. The documents and things to be produced and any testing or sampling being sought are described as follows:

   ☐ Continued on Attachment 3.
4. If the witness is a representative of a business or other entity, the matters upon which the witness is to be examined are described as follows:

   ☐ Continued on Attachment 4.
5. **IF YOU HAVE BEEN SERVED WITH THIS SUBPOENA AS A CUSTODIAN OF CONSUMER OR EMPLOYEE RECORDS UNDER CODE OF CIVIL PROCEDURE SECTION 1985.3 OR 1985.6 AND A MOTION TO QUASH OR AN OBJECTION HAS BEEN SERVED ON YOU, A COURT ORDER OR AGREEMENT OF THE PARTIES, WITNESSES, *AND* CONSUMER OR EMPLOYEE AFFECTED MUST BE OBTAINED BEFORE YOU ARE REQUIRED TO PRODUCE CONSUMER OR EMPLOYEE RECORDS.**
6. *At the deposition, you will be asked questions under oath. Questions and answers are recorded stenographically at the deposition; later they are transcribed for possible use at trial. You may read the written record and change any incorrect answers before you sign the deposition. You are entitled to receive witness fees and mileage actually traveled both ways. The money must be paid, at the option of the party giving notice of the deposition, either with service of this subpoena or at the time of the deposition.*

DISOBEDIENCE OF THIS SUBPOENA MAY BE PUNISHED AS CONTEMPT BY THIS COURT. YOU WILL ALSO BE LIABLE FOR THE SUM OF FIVE HUNDRED DOLLARS AND ALL DAMAGES RESULTING FROM YOUR FAILURE TO OBEY.

Date issued:

. . . .
(TYPE OR PRINT NAME)

▶ ______________________________
(SIGNATURE OF PERSON ISSUING SUBPOENA)

____
(TITLE)

(Proof of service on reverse)

PLAINTIFF/PETITIONER:	CASE NUMBER:
DEFENDANT/RESPONDENT:	

PROOF OF SERVICE OF DEPOSITION SUBPOENA FOR PERSONAL APPEARANCE AND PRODUCTION OF DOCUMENTS AND THINGS

1. I served this *Deposition Subpoena for Personal Appearance and Production of Documents and Things* by personally delivering a copy to the person served as follows:
   a. Person served *(name)*:

   b. Address where served:

   c. Date of delivery:

   d. Time of delivery:

   e. Witness fees and mileage both ways *(check one)*:
      (1) ☐ were paid. Amount: . . . . $ ______________
      (2) ☐ were not paid.
      (3) ☐ were tendered to the witness's public entity employer as required by Government Code section 68097.2. The amount tendered was *(specify)*: . . . . $ ______________

   f. Fee for service: . . . . $ ______________

2. I received this subpoena for service on *(date)*:

3. Person serving:
   a. ☐ Not a registered California process server.
   b. ☐ California sheriff or marshal.
   c. ☐ Registered California process server.
   d. ☐ Employee or independent contractor of a registered California process server.
   e. ☐ Exempt from registration under Business and Professions Code section 22350(b).
   f. ☐ Registered professional photocopier.
   g. ☐ Exempt from registration under Business and Professions Code section 22451.
   h. Name, address, telephone number, and, if applicable, county of registration and number:

I declare under penalty of perjury under the laws of the State of California that the foregoing is true and correct.

Date:

▶ ______________________________
(SIGNATURE)

(For California sheriff or marshal use only)
I certify that the foregoing is true and correct.

Date:

▶ ______________________________
(SIGNATURE)

PETITIONER: RESPONDENT: OTHER:	CASE NUMBER:

APPLICATION FOR SEPARATE TRIAL

Attachment to ☐ **Order to Show Cause (form FL-300)** ☐ **Notice of Motion (form FL-301)**

I, *(name):* , request that the court sever (bifurcate) and grant an early and separate trial on the following issue or issues:

1. a. ☐ Dissolution of the status of the marriage (Fam. Code, § 2337).
   I will serve with this application my preliminary *Declaration of Disclosure* and completed *Schedule of Assets and Debts* unless they have been previously served or the parties have stipulated in writing to defer service.
   b. ☐ I request the following conditions be made:
   (1) ☐ That I indemnify and hold the other party harmless from "taxes, reassessments, interest, and penalties" payable in the event that a dissolution prior to the property division results in taxes that would not have been payable if the parties were still married at the time of the division.
   (2) ☐ That I maintain health and medical insurance for the other party and minor children as long as possible, and then must obtain comparable coverage or pay any expenses that would have been covered by insurance.
   (3) ☐ That I hold the other party harmless re probate homestead.
   (4) ☐ That I hold the other party harmless re probate family allowance.
   (5) ☐ That I hold the other party harmless re pension benefits, elections, or survivors' benefits.
   (6) ☐ That I join the pension plan and, if the other party has a private plan covered by ERISA, will cause a Qualified Domestic Relations Order (QDRO) to be served on the plan.
   (7) ☐ That I hold the other party harmless re social security benefits.
   (8) ☐ Any other condition that the court determines is just and equitable.

2. ☐ Permanent custody and visitation of the children of the marriage.

3. ☐ Date of separation of the parties.

4. ☐ Alternate valuation date for property.

5. ☐ Validity of marital settlement agreement entered into prior to or during the marriage.

6. ☐ Other *(specify):*

7. a. ☐ I request that the court conduct this separate trial on the hearing date.
   or
   b. ☐ I will, at the hearing, ask the court to set a date for this separate trial.

8. The reasons in support of this request are *(specify):*
   ☐ Points and authorities attached. ☐ Supporting declarations attached.

I declare under penalty of perjury under the laws of the State of California that the foregoing is true and correct.

Date:

_______________________________ ▶ _______________________________
(TYPE OR PRINT NAME) (SIGNATURE OF DECLARANT)

Form Adopted for Mandatory Use
Judicial Council of California
FL-315 [Rev. January 1, 2003]

Family Code, § 2337
www.courtinfo.ca.gov

ATTORNEY OR PARTY WITHOUT ATTORNEY *(Name and Address):* TELEPHONE NO.:	*FOR COURT USE ONLY*
ATTORNEY FOR *(Name):*	
SUPERIOR COURT OF CALIFORNIA, COUNTY OF STREET ADDRESS: MAILING ADDRESS: CITY AND ZIP CODE: BRANCH NAME:	
PETITIONER/PLAINTIFF: RESPONDENT/DEFENDANT:	
REQUEST FOR PRODUCTION OF AN INCOME AND EXPENSE DECLARATION AFTER JUDGMENT	CASE NUMBER:

(NOTE: This request must be served on the petitioner or respondent and not on an attorney who was or is representing that party.)

To *(name):*

1. a. As permitted by Family Code section 3664(a), declarant requires that you complete and return the attached *Income and Expense Declaration* (form FL-150) within 30 days after the date this request is served on you. Family Code section 3665(a) requires you to attach copies of your most recent state and federal income tax returns (whether individual or joint) to the completed *Income and Expense Declaration* (form FL-150).

   b. The completed *Income and Expense Declaration* (form FL-150) should be mailed to the following person at the following address *(specify):*

2. You may consult an attorney about completion of the *Income and Expense Declaration* (form FL-150) or you may proceed without an attorney. The information provided will be used to determine whether to ask for a modification of child, spousal, or family support at this time.

3. If you wish to do so, you may serve a request for a completed *Income and Expense Declaration* (form FL-150) on me. Each of us may use this procedure once a year after judgment even though no legal matter is pending.

Date:

(TYPE OR PRINT NAME) (SIGNATURE OF DECLARANT)

WARNING: If a court later finds that the information provided in response to this request is incomplete or inaccurate or missing the prior year's tax returns, or that you did not submit the information in good faith, the court may order you to pay all costs necessary for me to get complete and accurate information. In addition you could be found to be in contempt and receive other penalties.

PETITIONER/PLAINTIFF:	CASE NUMBER:
RESPONDENT/DEFENDANT:	

PROOF OF SERVICE BY MAIL

REQUEST FOR PRODUCTION OF AN INCOME AND EXPENSE DECLARATION AFTER JUDGMENT

1. I am at least 18 years old and **not a party to this cause.** I am a resident of or employed in the county where the mailing took place, and my residence or business address is *(specify):*

2. I served a copy of the following documents:
   a. a completed *Request for Production of an Income and Expense Declaration After Judgment*, and
   b. a **blank** *Income and Expense Declaration* (a four-page form) (form FL-150).

3. I served a copy of the foregoing documents by mailing them in a sealed envelope with postage fully prepaid, certified mail, return receipt requested, as follows:
   a. ☐ I deposited the envelope with the United States Postal Service.
   b. ☐ I placed the envelope for collection and processing for mailing following this business's ordinary practice with which I am readily familiar. On the same day correspondence is placed for collection and mailing, it is deposited in the ordinary course of business with the United States Postal Service.

4. Manner of service
   a. Date of mailing:
   b. Place mailed from:
   c. Addressed as follows:
      Name:

      Street:

   City, state, and zip code:

I declare under penalty of perjury under the laws of the State of California that the foregoing is true and correct.

Date:

▶

(TYPE OR PRINT NAME) (SIGNATURE OF DECLARANT)

ATTORNEY OR PARTY WITHOUT ATTORNEY *(Name and Address):* TELEPHONE NO.:

FOR COURT USE ONLY

ATTORNEY FOR *(Name):*

SUPERIOR COURT OF CALIFORNIA, COUNTY OF

STREET ADDRESS:

MAILING ADDRESS:

CITY AND ZIP CODE:

BRANCH NAME:

MARRIAGE OF

PETITIONER:

RESPONDENT:

EX PARTE APPLICATION FOR RESTORATION OF FORMER NAME AFTER ENTRY OF JUDGMENT AND ORDER

CASE NUMBER:

APPLICATION

1. A judgment of dissolution or nullity was entered on *(date):*

2. Applicant now requests that his or her former name be restored. The applicant's former name is *(specify):*

Date:

(TYPE OR PRINT NAME) ▶ (SIGNATURE OF APPLICANT) (USE CURRENT NAME)

ORDER

3. IT IS ORDERED that applicant's former name is restored to *(specify):*

Date:

JUDICIAL OFFICER

[SEAL]

CLERK'S CERTIFICATE

I certify that the foregoing is a true and correct copy of the original on file in my office.

Date: Clerk, by ______________________, Deputy

Form Adopted for Mandatory Use
Judicial Council of California
FL-395 [Rev. January 1, 2003]

EX PARTE APPLICATION FOR RESTORATION OF FORMER NAME AFTER ENTRY OF JUDGMENT AND ORDER (Family Law)

Family Code, § 2080
www.courtinfo.ca.gov

A combined index covering Book 1 and Book 2 is available online at **www.nolodivorce.com/index.** Using your browser, you can print it or download it and use it on your computer. You will need Adobe Acrobat Reader which, if you don't already have it, comes with this book's companion CD.

Why isn't the index printed in the books? Good question.

First: Although new laws and forms typically take effect January 1 and July 1, we often get forms at the last minute, then have to process them for book and CD, then rush to press, which has a three to four week turnaround, then there are delays for shipping and distribution. So, in order to get the latest information on the street as fast as possible, we can't wait for a time-consuming index revision.

Second: These two books are not necessarily revised at the same time so, if we printed the index in each book, an index printed in one book could become out-of-sync with the index in the other book. An online index is more reliable once it is updated.

More useful products – order coupon

Free CD updates for 60 days

We guarantee that your Bonus CD is current or we will make it current for free if you include a copy of your sales receipt when you send us the registration.

Mail to Nolo Press Occidental, 501 Mission Street, Suite 2, Santa Cruz, CA 95060 Bk2– February 2004

Name: Mr., Mrs., Ms. ________________________________

Address ________________________________

Email address (for notice of CD updates) ________________________

City ____________________ State ________ Zip __________

Daytime phone ____________________ Fax ____________________

Date of purchase ________________ Vendor ____________________

☐ Proof of purchase enclosed

NOTE: If you purchased this book directly from **Nolo Press Occidental,** you are automatically registered and do not need to send in this coupon, but you **do** need to register if you purchased from **Nolo.com** or the **Berkeley** store.